FUNDAMENTALS OF PYTHON®: DATA STRUCTURES

KENNETH A. LAMBERT

Cengage Learning PTR

CENGAGE
Learning®

Professional • Technical • Reference

Australia • Brazil • Japan • Korea • Mexico • Singapore • Spain • United Kingdom • United States

CENGAGE
Learning·

Professional • Technical • Reference

**Fundamentals of Python®:
Data Structures
Kenneth A. Lambert**

**Publisher and General Manager,
Cengage Learning PTR:** Stacy L. Hiquet

Associate Director of Marketing:
Sarah Panella

Manager of Editorial Services:
Heather Talbot

Senior Marketing Manager:
Mark Hughes

Senior Acquisitions Editor: Mitzi Koontz

Project Editor/Copy Editor:
Gill Editorial Services

Technical Reviewer: Serge Palladino

Interior Layout Tech: MPS Limited

Cover Designer: Luke Fletcher

Indexer/Proofreader:
Kelly Talbot Editing Services

For product information and technology assistance, contact us at
Cengage Learning Customer & Sales Support, 1-800-354-9706.

For permission to use material from this text or product,
submit all requests online at **cengage.com/permissions**.

Further permissions questions can be emailed to
permissionrequest@cengage.com.

Python is a registered trademark of the Python Software Foundation. All other trademarks are the property of their respective owners.

All images © Cengage Learning unless otherwise noted.

Library of Congress Control Number: 2013932034

ISBN-13: 978-1-285-75200-6

ISBN-10: 1-285-75200-7

Cengage Learning PTR

20 Channel Center Street

Boston, MA 02210

USA

Cengage Learning is a leading provider of customized learning solutions with office locations around the globe, including Singapore, the United Kingdom, Australia, Mexico, Brazil, and Japan. Locate your local office at: **international.cengage.com/region**.

Cengage Learning products are represented in Canada by Nelson Education, Ltd.

For your lifelong learning solutions, visit **cengageptr.com**.

Visit our corporate website at **cengage.com**.

Printed in the United States of America
1 2 3 4 5 6 7 15 14 13

To my grandchildren, Lucy and Wyatt Redpath
and Lennox Barker.
Kenneth A. Lambert
Lexington, VA

Acknowledgments

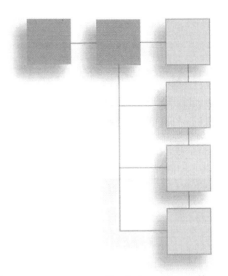

I would like to thank my friend, Martin Osborne, for many years of advice, friendly criticism, and encouragement on several of my book projects.

I would also like to thank my students in Computer Science 112 at Washington and Lee University for classroom testing this book over several semesters.

Finally, I would like to thank Serge Palladino, MQA tester, who helped to ensure that the content of all data and solution files used for this text were correct and accurate; Karen Gill, my project editor and copy editor; and Mitzi Koontz, senior acquisitions editor at Cengage Learning PTR.

About the Author

Kenneth A. Lambert is a professor of computer science and the chair of that department at Washington and Lee University. He has taught introductory programming courses for 29 years and has been an active researcher in computer science education. Lambert has authored or coauthored a total of 25 textbooks, including a series of introductory C++ textbooks with Douglas Nance and Thomas Naps, a series of introductory Java textbooks with Martin Osborne, and a series of introductory Python textbooks. His most recent textbook is *Easy GUI Programming in Python.*

Contents

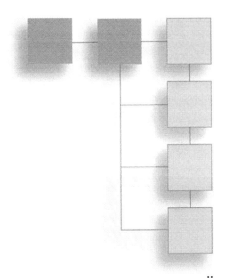

INTRODUCTION

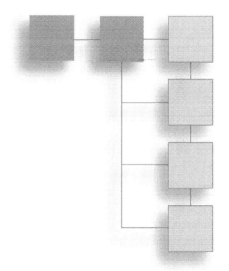

Welcome to *Fundamentals of Python: Data Structures*. This text is intended for a second semester course in programming and problem solving with data structures. It covers the material taught in a typical Computer Science 2 course (CS2) at the undergraduate level. Although this book uses the Python programming language, you need only have a basic knowledge of programming in a high-level programming language before beginning Chapter 1.

WHAT YOU'LL LEARN

The book covers four major aspects of computing:

- **Programming basics**—Data types, control structures, algorithm development, and program design with functions are basic ideas that you need to master to solve problems with computers. You'll review these core topics in the Python programming language and employ your understanding of them to solve a wide range of problems.

- **Object-Oriented Programming (OOP)**—Object-Oriented Programming is the dominant programming paradigm used to develop large software systems. You'll be introduced to the fundamental principles of OOP so that you can apply them successfully. Unlike other textbooks, this book helps you develop a professional-quality framework of collection classes to illustrate these principles.

- **Data structures**—Most useful programs rely on data structures to solve problems. At the most concrete level, data structures include arrays and various types of linked structures. You'll use these data structures to implement various types of collection structures, such as stacks, queues, lists, trees, bags, sets, dictionaries, and graphs. You'll also learn to use complexity analysis to evaluate the space/time trade-offs of different implementations of these collections.

■ **Software development life cycle**—Rather than isolate software development techniques in one or two chapters, this book deals with them throughout in the context of numerous case studies. Among other things, you'll learn that coding a program is often not the most difficult or challenging aspect of problem solving and software development.

WHY PYTHON?

Computer technology and applications have become increasingly more sophisticated over the past two decades, and so has the computer science curriculum, especially at the introductory level. Today's students learn a bit of programming and problem solving and are then expected to move quickly into topics like software development, complexity analysis, and data structures that, 20 years ago, were relegated to advanced courses. In addition, the ascent of object-oriented programming as the dominant paradigm has led instructors and textbook authors to bring powerful, industrial-strength programming languages such as C++ and Java into the introductory curriculum. As a result, instead of experiencing the rewards and excitement of solving problems with computers, beginning computer science students often become overwhelmed by the combined tasks of mastering advanced concepts as well as the syntax of a programming language.

This book uses the Python programming language as a way of making the second course in computer science more manageable and attractive for students and instructors alike. Python has the following pedagogical benefits:

■ Python has simple, conventional syntax. Python statements are very close to those of pseudocode algorithms, and Python expressions use the conventional notation found in algebra. Thus, you can spend less time dealing with the syntax of a programming language and more time learning to solve interesting problems.

■ Python has safe semantics. Any expression or statement whose meaning violates the definition of the language produces an error message.

■ Python scales well. It is easy for beginners to write simple programs in Python. Python also includes all the advanced features of a modern programming language, such as support for data structures and object-oriented software development, for use when they become necessary.

- Python is highly interactive. You can enter expressions and statements at an interpreter's prompts to try out experimental code and receive immediate feedback. You can also compose longer code segments and save them in script files to be loaded and run as modules or standalone applications.

- Python is general purpose. In today's context, this means that the language includes resources for contemporary applications, including media computing and web services.

- Python is free and is in widespread use in the industry. You can download Python to run on a variety of devices. There is a large Python user community, and expertise in Python programming has great resume value.

To summarize these benefits, Python is a comfortable and flexible vehicle for expressing ideas about computation, both for beginners and for experts. If you learn these ideas well in the first year, you should have no problems making a quick transition to other languages needed for courses later in the curriculum. Most importantly, you will spend less time staring at a computer screen and more time thinking about interesting problems to solve.

ORGANIZATION OF THIS BOOK

The approach in this book is easygoing, with each new concept introduced only when it is needed.

Chapter 1 provides a review of the features of Python programming that are needed to begin a second course in programming and problem solving in Python. The content of this chapter is organized so that you can skim it quickly if you have experience in Python programming, or you can dig a bit deeper to get up to speed in the language if you are new to Python.

The remainder of this book, in Chapters 2 through 12, covers the major topics in a typical CS2 course, especially the specification, implementation, and application of abstract data types, with the collection types as the primary vehicle and focus. Along the way, you will be thoroughly exposed to object-oriented programming techniques and the elements of good software design. Other important CS2 topics include recursive processing of data, search and sort algorithms, and the tools used in software development, such as complexity analysis and graphical notations (UML) to document designs.

Chapter 2 introduces the concept of an abstract data type (ADT) and provides an overview of various categories of collection ADTs.

Chapters 3 and 4 explore the data structures used to implement most collections and the tools for analyzing their performance trade-offs. Chapter 3 introduces complexity analysis with big-O notation. Enough material is presented to enable you to perform simple analyses of the running time and memory usage of algorithms and data structures, using search and sort algorithms as examples. Chapter 4 covers the details of processing arrays and linear linked structures, the concrete data structures used to implement most collections. You'll learn the underlying models of computer memory that support arrays and linked structures and the time/space trade-offs that they entail.

Chapters 5 and 6 shift the focus to the principles of object-oriented design. These principles are used to organize a professional-quality framework of collection classes that will be covered in detail in later chapters.

Chapter 5 is concerned with the critical difference between interface and implementation. A single interface and several implementations of a bag collection are developed as a first example. Emphasis is placed on the inclusion of conventional methods in an interface, to allow different types of collections to collaborate in applications. For example, one such method creates an iterator, which allows you to traverse any collection with a simple loop. Other topics covered in this chapter include polymorphism and information hiding, which directly stem from the difference between interface and implementation.

Chapter 6 shows how class hierarchies can reduce the amount of redundant code in an object-oriented software system. The related concepts of inheritance, dynamic binding of method calls, and abstract classes are introduced here and used throughout the remaining chapters.

Armed with these concepts and principles, you'll then be ready to consider the other major collection ADTs, which form the subject of Chapters 7 through 12.

Chapters 7 through 9 present the linear collections, stacks, queues, and lists. Each collection is viewed first from the perspective of its users, who are aware only of an interface and a set of performance characteristics possessed by a chosen implementation. The use of each collection is illustrated with one or more applications, and then several implementations are developed and their performance trade-offs are analyzed.

Chapters 10 through 12 present advanced data structures and algorithms as a transition to later courses in computer science. Chapter 10 discusses various tree structures, including binary search trees, heaps, and expression trees. Chapter 11 examines the implementation of the unordered collections, bags, sets, and dictionaries, using hashing strategies. Chapter 12 introduces graphs and graph-processing algorithms.

As mentioned earlier, this book is unique in presenting a professional-quality framework of collection types. Instead of encountering a series of apparently unrelated collections, you will explore the place of each collection in an integrated whole. This approach allows you to see what the collection types have in common as well as what makes each one unique. At the same time, you will be exposed to a realistic use of inheritance and class hierarchies, topics in object-oriented software design that are difficult to motivate and exemplify at this level of the curriculum.

SPECIAL FEATURES

This book explains and develops concepts carefully, using frequent examples and diagrams. New concepts are then applied in complete programs to show how they aid in solving problems. The chapters place an early and consistent emphasis on good writing habits and neat, readable documentation.

The book includes several other important features:

- **Case studies**—These present complete Python programs ranging from the simple to the substantial. To emphasize the importance and usefulness of the software development life cycle, case studies are discussed in the framework of a user request, followed by analysis, design, implementation, and suggestions for testing, with well-defined tasks performed at each stage. Some case studies are extended in end-of-chapter programming projects.

- **Chapter summaries**—Each chapter after the first one ends with a summary of the major concepts covered in the chapter.

- **Key terms**—When a new term is introduced in the text, it appears in italic.

- **Exercises**—Most major sections of each chapter after the first one end with exercise questions that reinforce the reading by asking basic questions about the material in the section. Each chapter after the second one ends with a set of review exercises.

- **Programming projects**—Each chapter ends with a set of programming projects of varying difficulty.

- **Appendix**—The appendix includes information on the collection framework used in the book.

WE APPRECIATE YOUR FEEDBACK

We have tried to produce a high-quality text, but should you encounter any errors, please report them to lambertk@wlu.edu. A listing of errata, should they be found, as well as other information about the book will be posted on the website http://home.wlu.edu/~lambertk/python/.

COMPANION WEBSITE DOWNLOADS

You may download the companion website files from www.cengageptr.com/downloads.

CHAPTER 1

BASIC PYTHON PROGRAMMING

This chapter gives a quick overview of Python programming. It is intended to bring those new to or rusty in Python up to speed, but it does not pretend to be a thorough introduction to computer science or the Python programming language. For a more detailed treatment of programming in Python, see my book *Fundamentals of Python: First Programs* (Course Technology/Cengage Learning, 2012). For documentation on the Python programming language, visit www.python.org.

If your computer already has Python, check the version number by running the `python` or `python3` command at a terminal prompt. (Linux and Mac users first open a terminal window, and Windows users first open a DOS window.) You are best off using the most current version of Python available. Check for that at www.python.org, and download and install the latest version if necessary. You will need Python 3.0 or higher to run the programs presented in this book.

BASIC PROGRAM ELEMENTS

Like all contemporary programming languages, Python has a vast array of features and constructs. However, Python is among the few languages whose basic program elements are quite simple. This section discusses the essentials to get you started in Python programming.

Programs and Modules

A Python program consists of one or more modules. A module is just a file of Python code, which can include statements, function definitions, and class definitions. A short Python program, also called a *script*, can be contained in one module. Longer, more complex programs typically include one main module and one or more supporting modules. The main module contains the starting point of program execution. Supporting modules contain function and class definitions.

An Example Python Program: Guessing a Number

Next you'll see a complete Python program that plays a game of guess the number with the user. The computer asks the user to enter the lower and upper bounds of a range of numbers. The computer then "thinks" of a random number in that range and repeatedly asks the user to guess this number until the user enters a correct guess. The computer gives a hint to the user after each guess and displays the total number of guesses at the end of the process. The program includes several of the types of Python statements to be discussed later in this chapter, such as input statements, output statements, assignment statements, loops, and conditional statements. The program also includes a single function definition.

Here is the code for the program, in the file numberguess.py:

```python
"""
Author: Ken Lambert
Plays a game of guess the number with the user.
"""

import random

def main():
    """Inputs the bounds of the range of numbers
    and lets the user guess the computer's number until
    the guess is correct."""
    smaller = int(input("Enter the smaller number: "))
    larger = int(input("Enter the larger number: "))
    myNumber = random.randint(smaller, larger)
    count = 0
    while True:
        count += 1
        userNumber = int(input("Enter your guess: "))
        if userNumber < myNumber:
            print("Too small")
        elif userNumber > myNumber:
            print("Too large")
        else:
            print("You've got it in", count, "tries!")
            break

if __name__ == "__main__":
    main()
```

Here is a trace of a user's interaction with the program:

```
Enter the smaller number: 1
Enter the larger number: 32
Enter your guess: 16
Too small
Enter your guess: 24
Too large
Enter your guess: 20
You've got it in 3 tries!
```

Editing, Compiling, and Running Python Programs

You can run complete Python programs, such as most of the examples presented in this book, by entering a command in a terminal window. For example, to run the program contained in the file numberguess.py, enter the following command in most terminal windows:

```
python3 numberguess.py
```

To create or edit a Python module, try using Python's IDLE (short for Integrated DeveLopment Environment). To start IDLE, enter the idle or idle3 command at a terminal prompt or launch its icon if it's available. You can also launch IDLE by double-clicking on a Python source code file (any file with a .py extension) or by right-clicking on the file and selecting Open or Edit with IDLE. Make sure that your system is set to open IDLE when files of this type are launched.

IDLE gives you a shell window for interactively running Python expressions and statements. Using IDLE, you can move back and forth between editor windows and the shell window to develop and run complete programs. IDLE also formats your code and color-codes it.

When you open an existing Python file with IDLE, the file appears in an editor window, and the shell pops up in a separate window. To run a program, move the cursor into the editor window and press the F5 (function-5) key. Python compiles the code in the editor window and runs it in the shell window.

When you run a program that includes several Python modules, the compiled code for every module except the main module is saved to a byte code file (a file with a .pyc extension). Python loads these files for subsequent runs of the program, if no changes to the corresponding .py files are made.

If a Python program appears to hang or not quit normally, you can exit by pressing Ctrl+C or closing the shell window.

Program Comments

A program comment is text ignored by the Python compiler but valuable to the reader as documentation. An end-of-line comment in Python begins with a # symbol and extends to the end of the current line. It is color-coded in red (although you can't tell that in this grayscale book). For example,

```
# This is an end-of-line comment.
```

A multiline comment is a string enclosed in triple single quotes or triple double quotes. Such comments are also called *docstrings*, to indicate that they can document major constructs within a program. The numberguess program shown earlier includes two doc-strings. The first one, at the top of the program file, serves as a comment for the entire numberguess module. The second one, just below the header of the main function, describes what this function does. As well shall see shortly, docstrings play a critical role in giving help to a programmer within the Python shell.

Lexical Elements

The lexical elements in a language are the types of words or symbols used to construct sentences. As in all high-level programming languages, some of Python's basic symbols are keywords, such as if, while, and def. Also included among lexical items are identifiers (names), literals (numbers, strings, and other built-in data structures), operators, and delimiters (quote marks, commas, parentheses, square brackets, and braces).

Spelling and Naming Conventions

Python keywords and names are case-sensitive. Thus, while is a keyword, whereas While is a programmer-defined name. Python keywords are spelled in lowercase letters and are color-coded in orange in an IDLE window.

All Python names are color-coded in black, except when they are introduced as function, class, or method names, in which case they appear in blue. A name can begin with a letter or an underscore ('_'), followed by any number of letters, underscores, or digits.

In this book, the names of modules, variables, functions, and methods are spelled in lowercase letters. With the exception of modules, when one of these names contains one or more embedded names, the embedded names are capitalized. The names of classes follow the same conventions but begin with a capital letter. When a variable names a constant, all the letters are uppercase, and an underscore separates any embedded names. Table 1.1 shows examples of these naming conventions.

Table 1.1 Examples of Python Naming Conventions

Type of Name	Examples
Variable	`salary, hoursWorked, isAbsent`
Constant	`ABSOLUTE_ZERO, INTEREST_RATE`
Function or method	`printResults, cubeRoot, isEmpty`
Class	`BankAccount, SortedSet`

© 2014 Cengage Learning®

Use names that describe their role in a program. In general, variable names should be nouns or adjectives (if they denote Boolean values), whereas function and method names should be verbs if they denote actions, or nouns or adjectives if they denote values returned.

Syntactic Elements

The syntactic elements in a language are the types of sentences (expressions, statements, definitions, and other constructs) composed from the lexical elements. Unlike most high-level languages, Python uses white space (spaces, tabs, or line breaks) to mark the syntax of many types of sentences. This means that indentation and line breaks are significant in Python code. A smart editor like Python's IDLE can help indent code correctly. The programmer need not worry about separating sentences with semicolons and marking blocks of sentences with braces. In this book, I use an indentation width of four spaces in all Python code.

Literals

Numbers (integers or floating-point numbers) are written as they are in other programming languages. The Boolean values `True` and `False` are keywords. Some data structures, such as strings, tuples, lists, and dictionaries, also have literals, as you will see shortly.

String Literals

You can enclose strings in single quotes, double quotes, or sets of three double quotes or three single quotes. The last notation is useful for a string containing multiple lines of text. Character values are single-character strings. The \ character is used to escape nongraphic characters such as the newline (\n) and the tab (\t), or the \ character itself. The next code segment, followed by the output, illustrates the possibilities.

```
print("Using double quotes")
print('Using single quotes')
print("Mentioning the word 'Python' by quoting it")
print("Embedding a\nline break with \\n")
print("""Embedding a
line break with triple quotes""")
```

Output:

```
Using double quotes
Using single quotes
Mentioning the word 'Python' by quoting it
Embedding a
line break with \n
Embedding a
line break with triple quotes
```

Operators and Expressions

Arithmetic expressions use the standard operators (+, -, *, /) and infix notation. The / operator produces a floating-point result with any numeric operands, whereas the // operator produces an integer quotient. The + operator means concatenation when used with collections, such as strings and lists. The ** operator is used for exponentiation.

The comparison operators <, <=, >, >=, ==, and != work with numbers and strings.

The == operator compares the internal contents of data structures, such as two lists, for structural equivalence, whereas the is operator compares two values for object identity. Comparisons return True or False.

The logical operators and, or, and not treat several values, such as 0, None, the empty string, and the empty list, as False. In contrast, most other Python values count as True.

The subscript operator, [], used with collection objects, will be examined shortly.

The selector operator, ., is used to refer to a named item in a module, class, or object.

The operators have the standard precedence (selector, function call, subscript, arithmetic, comparison, logical, assignment). Parentheses are used in the usual manner, to group subexpressions for earlier evaluation

The ** and = operators are right associative, whereas the others are left associative.

Function Calls

Functions are called in the usual manner, with the function's name followed by a parenthesized list of arguments. For example,

```
min(5, 2)    # Returns 2
```

Python includes a few standard functions, such as abs and round. Many other functions are available by import from modules, as you will see shortly.

The print Function

The standard output function print displays its arguments on the console. This function allows a variable number of arguments. Python automatically runs the str function on each argument to obtain its string representation and separates each string with a space before output. By default, print terminates its output with a newline.

The input Function

The standard input function input waits for the user to enter text at the keyboard. When the user presses the Enter key, the function returns a string containing the characters entered. This function takes an optional string as an argument and prints this string, without a line break, to prompt the user for the input.

Type Conversion Functions and Mixed-Mode Operations

You can use some data type names as type conversion functions. For example, when the user enters a number at the keyboard, the input function returns a string of digits, not a numeric value. The program must convert this string to an int or a float before numeric processing. The next code segment inputs the radius of a circle, converts this string to a float, and computes and outputs the circle's area:

```
radius = float(input("Radius: "))
print("The area is", 3.14 * radius ** 2)
```

Like most other languages, Python allows operands of different numeric types in arithmetic expressions. In those cases, the result type is the same type as the most general operand type. For example, the addition of an int and a float produces a float as the result.

Optional and Keyword Function Arguments

Functions may allow optional arguments, which can be named with keywords when the function is called. For example, the print function by default outputs a newline after its arguments are displayed. To prevent this from happening, you can give the optional argument end a value of the empty string, as follows:

```
print("The cursor will stay on this line, at the end", end = "")
```

Required arguments have no default values. Optional arguments have default values and can appear in any order when their keywords are used, as long as they come after the required arguments.

For example, the standard function round expects one required argument, a rounded number, and a second, optional argument, the number of figures of precision. When the second argument is omitted, the function returns the nearest whole number (an int). When the second argument is included, the function returns a float.

In general, the number of arguments passed to a function when it is called must be at least the same number as its required arguments.

Standard functions and Python's library functions check the types of their arguments when the function is called. Programmer-defined functions can receive arguments of any type, including functions and types themselves.

Variables and Assignment Statements

A Python variable is introduced with an assignment statement. For example

```
PI = 3.1416
```

sets PI to the value 3.1416. The syntax of a simple assignment statement is

```
<identifier> = <expression>
```

Several variables can be introduced in the same assignment statement, as follows:

```
minValue, maxValue = 1, 100
```

To swap the values of the variables a and b, you write

```
a, b = b, a
```

Assignment statements must appear on a single line of code, unless the line is broken after a comma, parenthesis, curly brace, or square bracket. When these options are unavailable, another means of breaking a line within a statement is to end it with the escape symbol \. You typically place this symbol before or after an operator in an expression. Here are some admittedly unrealistic examples:

```
minValue = min(100,
               200)

product = max(100, 200) \
          * 30
```

When you press Enter after a comma or the escape symbol, IDLE automatically indents the next line of code.

Python Data Typing

In Python, any variable can name a value of any type. Variables are not declared to have a type, as they are in many other languages; they are simply assigned a value.

Consequently, data type names almost never appear in Python programs. However, all values or objects have types. The types of operands in expressions are checked at run time, so type errors do not go undetected; however, the programmer does not have to worry about mentioning data types when writing code.

Import Statements

The `import` statement makes visible to a program the identifiers from another module. These identifiers might name objects, functions, or classes. There are several ways to express an `import` statement. The simplest is to import the module name, as in

```
import math
```

This makes any name defined in the math module available to the current module, by using the syntax `math.<name>`. Thus, `math.sqrt(2)` would return the square root of 2.

A second style of importing brings in a name itself, which you can use directly without the module name as a prefix:

```
from math import sqrt
print(sqrt(2))
```

You can import several individual names by listing them:

```
from math import pi, sqrt
print(sqrt(2) * pi)
```

You can import all names from a module using the `*` operator, but that is not considered good programming practice.

Getting Help on Program Components

Although the Python website at www.python.org has complete documentation for the Python language, help on most language components is also readily available within the Python shell. To access such help, just enter the function call `help(<component>)` at the shell prompt, where `<component>` is the name of a module, data type, function, or method. For example, `help(abs)` and `help (math.sqrt)` display documentation for the abs and math.sqrt functions, respectively. Calls of help(int) and help(math) show documentation for all the operations in the int type and math module, respectively.

Note that if a module is not the built-in module that Python loads when the shell starts, the programmer must first import that module before asking for help on it. For example, the following session with the shell displays the documentation for the numberguess program discussed earlier in this chapter:

```
>>> import numberguess
>>> help(numberguess)
Help on module numberguess:

NAME
    numberguess

DESCRIPTION
    Author: Ken Lambert
    Plays a game of guess the number with the user.

FUNCTIONS
    main()
        Inputs the bounds of the range of numbers,
        and lets the user guess the computer's number until
        the guess is correct.

FILE
    /Users/ken/Documents/CS2Python/Chapters/Chapter1/numberguess.py
```

Control Statements

Python includes the usual array of control statements for sequencing, conditional execution, and iteration. A sequence of statements is a set of statements written one after the other. Each statement in a sequence must begin in the same column. This section examines the control statements for conditional execution and iteration.

Conditional Statements

The structure of Python's conditional statements is similar to that of other languages. The keywords if, elif, and else are significant, as is the colon character and indentation.

The syntax of the one-way if statement is

```
if <Boolean expression>:
    <sequence of statements>
```

A Boolean expression is any Python value; as mentioned earlier, some of these count as False, and the others count as True. If the Boolean expression is True, the sequence of statements is run; otherwise, nothing happens. The sequence of (one or more) statements must be indented and aligned at least one space or tab (typically four spaces). The colon character is the only separator; if there is only one statement in the sequence, it may immediately follow the colon on the same line.

The syntax of the two-way `if` statement is

```
if <Boolean expression>:
    <sequence of statements>
else:
    <sequence of statements>
```

Note the indentation and the colon following the keyword `else`. Exactly one of these two sequences of statements will be run. The first sequence is run if the Boolean expression is `True`; the second sequence is run if the Boolean expression is `False`.

The syntax of the multiway `if` statement is

```
if <Boolean expression>:
    <sequence of statements>
elif <Boolean expression>:
    <sequence of statements>
...
else:
<sequence of statements>
```

A multiway `if` statement runs exactly one sequence of statements. The multiway `if` statement includes one or more alternative Boolean expressions, each of which follows the keyword `elif`. You can omit the trailing `else:` clause.

The next example outputs the appropriate answer to a question about the relative sizes of two numbers:

```
if x > y:
    print("x is greater than y")
elif x < y:
    print("x is less than y")
else:
    print("x is equal to y")
```

Using if __name__ == "__main__"

The `numberguess` program discussed earlier includes the definition of a `main` function and the following `if` statement:

```
if __name__ == "__main__":
    main()
```

The purpose of this `if` statement is to allow the programmer either to run the module as a standalone program or to import it from the shell or another module. Here is how this works. Every Python module includes a set of built-in module variables, to which the Python virtual machine automatically assigns values when the module is loaded. If the module is being loaded as a standalone program (either by running it from a terminal prompt or by loading it from an IDLE window), the module's __name__ variable is set to the string "__main__". Otherwise, this variable is set to the module's name—in this case, "numberguess". Either assignment is accomplished before any of the code within the module is loaded. Thus, when control reaches the `if` statement at the end of the module, the module's `main` function will be called only if the module has been launched as a standalone program.

The `if` __name__ == "__main__" idiom is useful when developing standalone program modules, because it allows the programmer to view help on the module just by importing it into the shell. Likewise, the programmer can use this idiom in supporting modules to run a test bed function during module development within IDLE.

Loop Statements

The structure of Python's `while` loop statement is similar to that of other languages. Here is the syntax:

```
while <Boolean expression>:
    <sequence of statements>
```

The next example computes and prints the product of the numbers from 1 to 10:

```
product = 1
value = 1
while value <= 10:
    product *= value
    value += 1
print(product)
```

Note the use of the extended assignment operator `*=`. The line of code in which this appears is equivalent to

```
product = product * value
```

Python includes a `for` loop statement for more concise iteration over a sequence of values. The syntax of this statement is

```
for <variable> in <iterable object>:
    <sequence of statements>
```

When this loop runs, it assigns to the loop variable each value contained in the iterable object and runs the sequence of statements in the context of each such assignment. Examples of iterable objects are strings and lists. The next code segment uses Python's range function, which returns an iterable sequence of integers, to compute the product shown earlier:

```
product = 1
for value in range(1, 11):
    product *= value
print(product)
```

Python programmers generally prefer a for loop to iterate over definite ranges or sequences of values. They use a while loop when the continuation condition is an arbitrary Boolean expression.

STRINGS AND THEIR OPERATIONS

As in other languages, a Python string is a compound object that includes other objects, namely, its characters. However, each character in a Python string is itself a single-character string and is written literally in a similar manner. Python's string type, named str, includes a large set of operations, some of which are introduced in this section.

Operators

When strings are compared with the comparison operators, the pairs of characters at each position in the two strings are compared, using ASCII ordering. Thus, "a" is less than "b", but "A" is less than "a".

The + operator builds and returns a new string that contains the characters of the two operands.

The subscript operator in its simplest form expects an integer in the range from 0 to the length of the string minus 1. The operator returns the character at that position in the string. Thus,

```
"greater"[0]   # Returns "g"
```

Although a string index cannot exceed its length minus 1, negative indexes are allowed. When an index is negative, Python adds this value to the string's length to locate the character to be returned. In these cases, the index provided cannot be less than the negation of the string's length.

Strings are immutable; that is, once you create them, you cannot modify their internal contents. Thus, you cannot use a subscript to replace the character at a given position in a string.

A variation of the subscript, called the *slice operator*, is what you use to obtain a substring of a string. The syntax of the slice is

```
<a string>[<lower>:<upper>]
```

The value of <lower>, if it is present, is an integer ranging from 0 to the length of the string minus 1. The value of <upper>, if it is present, is an integer ranging from 0 to the length of the string.

When you omit both values, the slice returns the entire string. When the first value is omitted, the slice returns a substring starting with the string's first character. When the second value is omitted, the slice returns a substring ending with the string's last character. Otherwise, the slice returns a substring starting with the character at the lower index and ending with the character at the upper index minus 1.

Here are some examples of the slice operator in action:

```
"greater"[:]      # Returns "greater"
"greater"[2:]     # Returns "eater"
"greater"[:2]     # Returns "gr"
"greater"[2:5]    # Returns "eat"
```

The reader is encouraged to experiment with the slice operator in the Python shell.

Formatting Strings for Output

Many data-processing applications require output that has a tabular format. In this format, numbers and other information are aligned in columns that can be either left justified or right justified. A column of data is left justified if its values are vertically aligned beginning with their leftmost characters. A column of data is right justified if its values are vertically aligned beginning with their rightmost characters. To maintain the margins between columns of data, left justification requires the addition of spaces to the right of the datum, whereas right justification requires adding spaces to the left of the datum. A column of data is centered if there is an equal number of spaces on either side of the data within that column.

The total number of data characters and additional spaces for a given datum in a formatted string is called its *field width*.

The print function automatically begins printing an output datum in the first available column. The next example, which displays the exponents 7 through 10 and the values of 10^7 through 10^{10}, shows the format of two columns produced by the print statement:

```
>>> for exponent in range(7, 11):
        print(exponent, 10 ** exponent)
7 10000000
8 100000000
9 1000000000
10 10000000000
>>>
```

Note that when the exponent reaches 10, the output of the second column shifts over by a space and looks ragged. The output would look neater if the left column were left-justified and the right column were right-justified. When you format floating-point numbers for output, you should specify the number of digits of precision to be displayed as well as the field width. This is especially important when displaying financial data in which exactly two digits of precision are required.

Python includes a general formatting mechanism that allows the programmer to specify field widths for different types of data. The next session shows how to right justify and left justify the string "four" within a field width of 6:

```
>>> "%6s" % "four"     # Right justify
'  four'
>>> "%-6s" % "four"    # Left justify
'four  '
```

The first line of code right justifies the string by padding it with two spaces to its left. The next line of code left justifies by placing two spaces to the string's right.

The simplest form of this operation is the following:

```
<format string> % <datum>
```

This version contains a format string, the format operator %, and a single data value to be formatted. The format string can contain string data and other information about the format of the datum. To format the string data value, you can use the notation %<field width>s in the format string. When the field width is positive, the datum is right justified; when the field width is negative, you get left justification. If the field width is less than or equal to the datum's print length in characters, no justification is added. The % operator works with this information to build and return a formatted string.

To format integers, the letter d is used instead of s. To format a sequence of data values, you construct a format string that includes a format code for each datum and place the data values in a tuple following the % operator. The form of the second version of this operation follows:

```
<format string> % (<datum-1>, …, <datum-n>)
```

Armed with the format operation, the powers of 10 loop can now display the numbers in nicely aligned columns. The first column is left justified in a field width of 3, and the second column is right justified in a field width of 12.

```
>>> for exponent in range(7, 11):
        print("%-3d%12d" % (exponent, 10 ** exponent))

7       10000000
8      100000000
9     1000000000
10   10000000000
```

The format information for a data value of type float has the form

```
%<field width>.<precision>f
```

where .<precision> is optional. The next session shows the output of a floating-point number without, and then with, a format string:

```
>>> salary = 100.00
>>> print("Your salary is $" + str(salary))
Your salary is $100.0
>>> print("Your salary is $%0.2f" % salary)
Your salary is $100.00
>>>
```

Here is another, minimal, example of the use of a format string, which says to use a field width of 6 and a precision of 3 to format the float value 3.14:

```
>>> "%6.3f" % 3.14
' 3.140'
```

Note that Python adds a digit of precision to the number's string and pads it with a space to the left to achieve the field width of 6. This width includes the place occupied by the decimal point.

Objects and Method Calls

In addition to standard operators and functions, Python includes a vast number of methods that operate on objects. A method is similar to a function, in that it expects arguments, performs a task, and returns a value. However, a method is always called on an associated object. The syntax of a method call is

```
<object>.<method name>(<list of arguments>)
```

Here are some examples of method calls on strings:

```
"greater".isupper()              # Returns False
"greater".upper()                # Returns "GREATER"
"greater".startswith("great")    # Returns True
```

If you try to run a method that an object does not recognize, Python raises an exception and halts the program. To discover the set of methods that an object recognizes, you run Python's dir function, in the Python shell, with the object's type as an argument. For example, dir(str) returns a list of the names of the methods recognized by string objects. Running help(str.upper) prints documentation on the use of the method str.upper.

Some method names, such as __add__ and __len__, are run when Python sees an object used with certain operators or functions. Thus, for example

```
len("greater")     # Is equivalent to "greater".__len__()
"great" + "er"     # Is equivalent to "great".__add__("er")
"e" in "great"     # Is equivalent to "great".__contains__("e")
```

The reader is encouraged to explore the str methods with the dir and help functions.

BUILT-IN PYTHON COLLECTIONS AND THEIR OPERATIONS

Modern programming languages include several types of collections, such as lists, that allow the programmer to organize and manipulate several data values at once. This section explores the built-in collections in Python; the rest of the book discusses how to add new types of collections to the language.

Lists

A list is a sequence of zero or more Python objects, commonly called *items*. A list has a literal representation, which uses square brackets to enclose items separated by commas. Here are some examples:

```
[]                         # An empty list
["greater"]                # A list of one string
["greater", "less"]        # A list of two strings
["greater", "less", 10]    # A list of two strings and an int
["greater", ["less", 10]]  # A list with a nested list
```

Like strings, lists can be sliced and concatenated with the standard operators. However, the results returned in this case are lists. Unlike strings, lists are mutable, meaning that you can replace, insert, or remove items contained in them. This fact has two consequences. First, the lists returned by the slice and concatenation operators are new lists, not pieces of the original list. Second, the list type includes several methods called mutators, whose purpose is to modify the structure of a list. You can enter dir(list) in a Python shell to view them.

The most commonly used list mutator methods are append, insert, pop, remove, and sort. Here are some examples of their use:

```
testList = []                 # testList is []
testList.append(34)           # testList is [34]
testList.append(22)           # testList is [34, 22]
testList.sort()               # testList is [22, 34]
testList.pop()                # Returns 22; testList is [34]
testList.insert(0, 22)        # testList is [22, 34]
testList.insert(1, 55)        # testList is [22, 55, 34]
testList.pop(1)               # Returns 55; testList is [22, 34]
testList.remove(22)           # testList is [34]
testList.remove(55)           # raises ValueError
```

The string methods split and join extract a list of words from a string and glue a list of words together to form a string, respectively:

```
"Python is cool".split()      # Returns ['Python', 'is', 'cool']
" ".join(["Python", "is", "cool"])    # Returns 'Python is cool'
```

You are encouraged to explore the list methods with the dir and help functions.

Tuples

A *tuple* is an immutable sequence of items. Tuple literals enclose items in parentheses, and a tuple must include at least two items. A tuple is essentially like a list without mutator methods. For the available tuple methods, run dir(tuple) in the Python shell.

Loops Over Sequences

The for loop is used to iterate over items in a sequence, such as a string, a list, or a tuple. For example, the following code segment prints the items in a list:

```
testList = [67, 100, 22]
for item in testList:
    print(item)
```

This is equivalent to but simpler than an index-based loop over the list:

```
testList = [67, 100, 22]
for index in range(len(testList)):
    print(testList[index])
```

Dictionaries

A dictionary contains zero or more entries. Each entry associates a unique key with a value. Keys are typically strings or integers, whereas values are any Python objects.

A dictionary literal encloses the key-value entries in a set of braces. Here are some examples:

```
{}                                  # An empty dictionary
{"name":"Ken"}                      # One entry
{"name":"Ken", "age":61}            # Two entries
{"hobbies":["reading", "running"]}  # One entry, value is a list
```

You use the subscript operator to access a value at a given key, add a value at a new key, and replace a value at a given key. The pop method removes the entry and returns the value for a given key. The keys method returns an iterable object over the keys, whereas the values method returns an iterable object over the values. The for loop iterates over a dictionary's keys.

The reader is encouraged to explore the dict methods with the dir and help functions and to experiment with dictionaries and their operations in a Python shell.

Searching for a Value

The programmer can search strings, lists, tuples, or dictionaries for a given value by running the in operator with the value and the collection. This operator returns True or False. The target value for a dictionary search should be a potential key.

When it is known that a given value is in a sequence (string, list, or tuple), the index method returns the position of the first such value.

For dictionaries, the methods get and pop can take two arguments: a key and a default value. A failed search returns the default value, whereas a successful search returns the value associated with the key.

Pattern Matching with Collections

Although the subscript can be used to access items within lists, tuples, and dictionaries, it is often more convenient to access several items at once by means of pattern matching. For example, the value returned by a color chooser dialog is a tuple that contains two items. The first item is a nested tuple of three numbers, and the second item is a string. Thus, the outer tuple has the form ((<r>, <g>, <b>), <string>). It's best for the three numbers to be assigned to three distinct variables and the string to a fourth variable, for further processing. Here is the code to accomplish this, using the subscript operator:

```
rgbTuple = colorTuple[0]
hexString = colorTuple[1]
r = rgbTuple[0]
g = rgbTuple[1]
b = rgbTuple[2]
```

A pattern match uses an assignment of a structure to another structure of exactly the same form. The target structure includes variables that will pick up the values at the corresponding positions in the source structure. You can then use the variables for further processing. Using pattern matching, you can accomplish this task in a single line of code, as follows:

```
((r, g, b), hexString) = rgbTuple
```

CREATING NEW FUNCTIONS

Although Python is an object-oriented language, it includes a number of built-in functions and allows the programmer to create new functions as well. These new functions can utilize recursion, and they can receive and return functions as data. Python thus allows the programmer to design solutions using a thoroughly functional style of programming. This section introduces some of these ideas.

Function Definitions

The syntax of a Python function definition is

```
def <function name>(<list of parameters>):
    <sequence of statements>
```

The rules and conventions for spelling function names and parameter names are the same as for variable names. The list of required parameters can be empty or can include names separated by commas. Again, unlike some other programming languages, no data types are associated with the parameter names or with the function name itself.

Here is a simple function to compute and return the square of a number:

```
def square(n):
    """Returns the square of n."""
    result = n ** 2
    return result
```

Note the use of the string with triple quotes beneath the function header. This is a docstring. This string behaves like a comment within the function but also will be displayed when the user enters `help(square)` at a Python shell prompt. Every function you define should include a docstring that states what the function does and gives information about any arguments or returned values.

Functions can introduce new variables, also called *temporary variables*. In the `square` function, `n` is a parameter and `result` is a temporary variable. A function's parameters and temporary variables exist only during the lifetime of a function call and are not visible to other functions or the surrounding program. Thus, several different functions may use the same parameters and variable names without conflicts.

When a function does not include a `return` statement, it automatically returns the value `None` after its last statement executes.

You can define functions in any order in a module, as long as no function is actually executed before its definition has been compiled. The next example shows an illegal function call at the beginning of a module:

```
first()                 # Raises a NameError (function undefined yet)
def first():
    second()                # Not an error, because not actually
    print("Calling first.")   # called until after second is defined
def second():
    print("Calling second.")
first()                 # Here is where the call should go
```

When Python runs the first line of code, function `first` has not yet been defined, so an exception is raised. Were you to place a comment symbol # at the beginning of this line and run the code again, the program would run to a normal termination. In this case, even though function `second` appears to be called before it is defined, it is not actually called until function `first` is called, by which time both functions have been defined.

You can specify parameters as optional, with default values, using the notation `<parameter name> = <default value>`. Required parameters (those without default values) must precede optional parameters in the parameter list.

Recursive Functions

A *recursive function* is a function that calls itself. To prevent a function from repeating itself indefinitely, it must contain at least one selection statement. This statement examines a condition called a *base case* to determine whether to stop or to continue with a recursive step.

Let's examine how to convert an iterative algorithm to a recursive function. Here is a definition of a function displayRange that prints the numbers from a lower bound to an upper bound:

```python
def displayRange(lower, upper):
    """Outputs the numbers from lower to upper."""
    while lower <= upper:
        print(lower)
        lower = lower + 1
```

How would you go about converting this function to a recursive one? First, you should note two important facts:

- The loop's body continues execution while lower <= upper.

- When the function executes, lower is incremented by 1 but upper never changes.

The equivalent recursive function performs similar primitive operations, but the loop is replaced with an if statement and the assignment statement is replaced with a recursive call of the function. Here is the code with these changes:

```python
def displayRange(lower, upper):
    """Outputs the numbers from lower to upper."""
    if lower <= upper:
        print(lower)
        displayRange(lower + 1, upper)
```

Although the syntax and design of the two functions are different, the same algorithmic process is executed. Each call of the recursive function visits the next number in the sequence, just as the loop does in the iterative version of the function.

Most recursive functions expect at least one argument. This data value tests for the base case that ends the recursive process. It is also modified in some way before each recursive step. The modification of the data value should produce a new data value that allows the function to reach the base case eventually. In the case of displayRange, the value of the argument lower is incremented before each recursive call so that it eventually exceeds the value of the argument upper.

The next example is a recursive function that builds and returns a value. Python's sum function expects a collection of numbers and returns their sum. This function should return the sum of the numbers from a lower bound through an upper bound. The recursive ourSum function returns 0 if lower exceeds upper (the base case). Otherwise, the function adds lower to the ourSum of lower+ 1 and upper and returns this result. Here is the code for this function:

```python
def ourSum(lower, upper):
    """Returns the sum of the numbers from lower thru upper."""
```

```
    if lower > upper:
        return 0
    else:
        return lower + ourSum(lower + 1, upper)
```

The recursive call of ourSum adds the numbers from lower + 1 through upper. The function then adds lower to this result and returns it.

To get a better understanding of how recursion works, it is helpful to trace its calls. You can do that for the recursive version of the ourSum function. You add an argument for a margin of indentation and print statements to trace the two arguments and the value returned on each call. The first statement on each call computes the indentation, which is then used in printing the two arguments. The value computed is also printed with this indentation just before each call returns. Here is the code, followed by a session showing its use:

```
def ourSum(lower, upper, margin = 0):
    """Returns the sum of the numbers from lower to upper,
    and outputs a trace of the arguments and return values
    on each call."""
    blanks = " " * margin
    print(blanks, lower, upper)
    if lower > upper:
        print(blanks, 0)
        return 0
    else:
        result = lower + ourSum(lower + 1, upper, margin + 4)
        print(blanks, result)
        return result
```

Usage:

```
>>> ourSum(1, 4)
 1 4
     2 4
         3 4
             4 4
                 5 4
                 0
             4
         7
     9
 10
 10
>>>
```

The displayed pairs of arguments are indented further to the right as the calls of ourSum proceed. Note that the value of lower increases by 1 on each call, whereas the value of upper stays the same. The final call of ourSum returns 0. As the recursion unwinds, each value returned is aligned with the arguments above it and increases by the current value of lower. This type of tracing can be a useful debugging tool for recursive functions.

Nested Function Definitions

Definitions of other functions may be nested within a function's sequence of statements. Consider the following two definitions of a recursive factorial function. The first definition uses a nested helper function to carry out the recursion with required parameters. The second definition gives the second parameter a default value to simplify the design.

```python
# First definition
def factorial(n):
    """Returns the factorial of n."""
    def recurse(n, product):
        if n == 1: return product
        else: return recurse(n - 1, n * product)
    recurse(n, 1)
```

```python
# Second definition
def factorial(n, product = 1):
    """Returns the factorial of n."""
    if n == 1: return product
    else: return factorial(n - 1, n * product)
```

Higher-Order Functions

Python functions are first-class data objects. This means you can assign them to variables, save them in data structures, pass them as arguments to other functions, and return them as the values of other functions. A *higher-order function* is a function that receives another function as an argument and applies it in some way. Python includes two built-in higher-order functions, map and filter, that are useful for processing iterable objects.

Suppose you want to convert a list of integers to another list of the string representations of those integers. You could use a loop to visit each integer, convert it to a string, and append it to a new list, as follows:

```python
newList = []
for number in oldList: newList.append(str(number))
```

Alternatively, you can use the `map` function. This function expects a function and an iterable object as arguments and returns another iterable object wherein the argument function is applied to each item contained in the iterable object. In short, `map` essentially transforms each item in an iterable object. Thus, the code

```
map(str, oldList)
```

creates the iterable object containing the strings, and the code

```
newList = list(map(str, oldList))
```

creates a new list from that object.

Suppose you want to drop all of the zero grades from a list of exam scores. The following loop would accomplish this:

```
newList = []
for number in oldList:
    if number > 0: newList.append(number)
```

Alternatively, you can use the `filter` function. This function expects a Boolean function and an iterable object as arguments. The `filter` function returns an iterable object in which each item is passed to the Boolean function. If this function returns `True`, the item is retained in the returned iterable object; otherwise, the item is dropped from it. In short, `filter` essentially keeps the items that pass a test in an iterable object. Thus, assuming the programmer has already defined the Boolean function `isPositive`, the code

```
filter(isPositive, oldList)
```

creates the iterable object containing the non-zero grades, and the code

```
newList = list(filter(isPositive, oldList))
```

creates a new list from that object.

Creating Anonymous Functions with lambda

Programmers can avoid defining one-time helper functions such as `isPositive` by creating an anonymous function to pass to `map` or `filter`, on the fly. They use a Python `lambda` form for this purpose. The syntax of `lambda` is

```
lambda <argument list> : <expression>
```

Note that the expression cannot include a sequence of statements, as in other Python functions. The code

```
newList = list(filter(lambda number: number > 0, oldList))
```

uses an anonymous Boolean function to drop the zero grades from the list of grades.

Another high-order function, functools.reduce, boils an iterable object's items down to a single value by applying a function of two arguments to each next item and the result of the previous application. Thus, the for loop to compute the product of a sequence of numbers shown earlier can be rewritten as

```
import functools
product = functools.reduce(lambda x, y: x * y, range(1, 11))
```

CATCHING EXCEPTIONS

When the Python virtual machine encounters a semantic error during program execution, it raises an exception and halts the program with an error message. Examples of semantic errors are undefined variable names, attempts to divide by 0, and list indices out of range. The signaling of such errors is a boon to the programmer, who can then correct them to produce a better program. However, some errors, such as bad digits in an input number, are users' mistakes. In these cases, the program should not allow the resulting exceptions to halt execution but should trap these and allow the user to recover gracefully.

Python includes a try-except statement that allows a program to trap or catch exceptions and perform the appropriate recovery operations. Here is the syntax of the simplest form of this statement:

```
try:
    <statements>
except <exception type>:
    <statements>
```

When you run this statement, the statements within the try clause are executed. If one of these statements raises an exception, control is immediately transferred to the except clause. If the type of exception raised matches the type in this clause, its statements are executed. Otherwise, control is transferred to the caller of the try-except statement and further up the chain of calls, until the exception is successfully handled or the program halts with an error message. If the statements in the try clause raise no exceptions, the except clause is skipped and control proceeds to the end of the try-except statement.

In general, you should try to include the exception type that matches the type of exception expected under the circumstances; if no such type exists, the more general Exception type will match any exception than happens to be raised.

The following demo program defines recursive function called safeIntegerInput. This function traps a ValueError exception that is raised if the user enters bad digits during input. The function forces the user to continue until a well-formed integer is entered, whereupon the integer is returned to the caller.

```
"""
Author: Ken Lambert
Demonstrates a function that traps number format errors during input.
"""

def safeIntegerInput(prompt):
    """Prompts the user for an integer and returns the
    integer if it is well-formed.   Otherwise, prints an
    error message and repeats this process."""
    inputString = input(prompt)
    try:
        number = int(inputString)
        return number
    except ValueError:
        print("Error in number format:", inputString)
        return safeIntegerInput(prompt)

if __name__ == "__main__":
    age = safeIntegerInput("Enter your age: ")
    print("Your age is", age)
```

Here is a trace of a session with this program:

```
Enter your age: abc
Error in number format: abc
Enter your age: 6i
Error in number format: 6i
Enter your age: 61
Your age is 61
```

FILES AND THEIR OPERATIONS

Python provides great support for managing and processing several types of files. This section examines some manipulations of text files and object files.

Text File Output

You can view the data in a text file as characters, words, numbers, or lines of text, depending on the text file's format and on the purposes for which the data are used. When the data are treated as integers or floating-point numbers, they must be separated by whitespace characters—spaces, tabs, and newlines. For example, a text file containing six floating-point numbers might look like

```
34.6 22.33 66.75
77.12 21.44 99.01
```

when examined with a text editor. Note that this format includes a space or a newline as a separator of items in the text.

All data output to or input from a text file must be strings. Thus, numbers must be converted to strings before output, and these strings must be converted back to numbers after input.

You can output data to a text file using a file object. Python's open function, which expects a file pathname and a mode string as arguments, opens a connection to the file on disk and returns a file object. The mode string is 'r' for input files and 'w' for output files. Thus, the following code opens a file object on a file named myfile.txt for output:

```
>>> f = open("myfile.txt", 'w')
```

If the file does not exist, it is created with the given pathname. If the file already exists, Python opens it. When data are written to the file and the file is closed, any data previously existing in the file are erased.

String data are written (or output) to a file using the method write with the file object. The write method expects a single string argument. If you want the output text to end with a newline, you must include the escape character \n in the string. The next statement writes two lines of text to the file:

```
>>> f.write("First line.\nSecond line.\n")
```

When all the outputs are finished, the file should be closed using the method close, as follows:

```
>>> f.close()
```

Failure to close an output file can result in data being lost.

Writing Numbers to a Text File

The file method write expects a string as an argument. Therefore, other types of data, such as integers or floating-point numbers, must first be converted to strings before being written to an output file. In Python, the values of most data types can be converted to strings by using the str function. The resulting strings are then written to a file with a space or a newline as a separator character.

The next code segment illustrates the output of integers to a text file. Five hundred random integers between 1 and 500 are generated and written to a text file named integers.txt. The newline character is the separator.

```
import random
f = open("integers.txt", 'w')
for count in range(500):
```

```
    number = random.randint(1, 500)
    f.write(str(number) + "\n")
f.close()
```

Reading Text from a Text File

You open a file for input in a manner similar to opening a file for output. The only thing that changes is the mode string, which, in the case of opening a file for input, is `'r'`. However, if the pathname is not accessible from the current working directory, Python raises an error. Here is the code for opening `myfile.txt` for input:

```
>>> f = open("myfile.txt", 'r')
```

There are several ways to read data from an input file. The simplest way is to use the file method `read` to input the entire contents of the file as a single string. If the file contains multiple lines of text, the newline characters will be embedded in this string. The next session with the shell shows how to use the method `read`:

```
>>> text = f.read()
>>> text
'First line.\nSecond line.\n'
>>> print(text)
First line.
Second line.
>>>
```

After input is finished, another call to `read` returns an empty string, to indicate that the end of the file has been reached. To repeat an input, you must reopen the file. It is not necessary to close the file.

Alternatively, an application might read and process the text one line at a time. A `for` loop accomplishes this nicely. The `for` loop views a file object as a sequence of lines of text. On each pass through the loop, the loop variable is bound to the next line of text in the sequence. Here is a session that reopens the example file and visits the lines of text in it:

```
>>> f = open("myfile.txt", 'r')
>>> for line in f:
        print(line)
First line.

Second line.

>>>
```

Note that `print` appears to output an extra newline. This is because each line of text input from the file retains its newline character.

In cases where you might want to read a specified number of lines from a file (say, the first line only), you can use the file method `readline`. The `readline` method consumes a line of input and returns this string, including the newline. If `readline` encounters the end of the file, it returns the empty string. The next code segment uses a `while True` loop to input all the lines of text with `readline`:

```
>>> f = open("myfile.txt", 'r')
>>> while True:
        line = f.readline()
        if line == "":
            break
        print(line)
```

First line.

Second line.

```
>>>
```

Reading Numbers from a File

All the `file` input operations return data to the program as strings. If these strings represent other types of data, such as integers or floating-point numbers, the programmer must convert them to the appropriate types before manipulating them further. In Python, the string representations of integers and floating-point numbers can be converted to the numbers themselves by using the functions `int` and `float`, respectively.

When reading data from a file, another important consideration is the format of the data items in the file. Earlier, you saw an example code segment that output integers separated by newlines to a text file. During input, these data can be read with a simple `for` loop. This loop accesses a line of text on each pass. To convert this line to the integer contained in it, the programmer runs the string method `strip` to remove the newline and then runs the `int` function to obtain the integer value.

The next code segment illustrates this technique. It opens the file of random integers written earlier, reads them, and prints their sum.

```
f = open("integers.txt", 'r')
sum = 0
for line in f:
    line = line.strip()
    number = int(line)
    sum += number
print("The sum is", sum)
```

Obtaining numbers from a text file in which they are separated by spaces is a bit trickier. One method proceeds by reading lines in a `for` loop, as before. But each line now can contain several integers separated by spaces. You can use the string method `split` to obtain a list of the strings representing these integers and then process each string in this list with another `for` loop.

The next code segment modifies the previous one to handle integers separated by spaces or newlines.

```
f = open("integers.txt", 'r')
sum = 0
for line in f:
    wordlist = line.split()
    for word in wordlist:
        number = int(word)
        sum += number
print("The sum is", sum)
```

Note that the line does not have to be stripped of the newline, because `split` takes care of that automatically.

Reading and Writing Objects with pickle

You can convert any object to text for storage, but the mapping of complex objects to text and back again can be tedious and cause maintenance headaches. Fortunately, Python includes a module that allows the programmer to save and load objects using a process called *pickling*. The term comes from the process of converting cucumbers to pickles for preservation in jars. However, in the case of computational objects, you can get the cucumbers back again. Any object can be pickled before you save it to a file, and then "unpickled" as you load it from a file into a program. Python takes care of all of the conversion details automatically.

You start by importing the `pickle` module. Files are opened for input and output using the `"rb"` and `"wb"` flags (for byte streams) and closed in the usual manner. To save an object, you use the function `pickle.dump`. Its first argument is the object to be "dumped," or saved to a file, and its second argument is the file object.

For example, you can use the `pickle` module to save the objects in a list named `lyst` to a file named `items.dat`. You do not need to know what types of objects are in the list or how many objects are there. Here is the code:

```
import pickle

lyst = [60, "A string object", 1977]
fileObj = open("items.dat", "wb")
```

```
for item in lyst:
    pickle.dump(item, fileObj)
fileObj.close()
```

In this example, you could have written the entire list to the file instead of each of its objects. However, you won't be able to do that with some types of collections discussed in this book, such as those based on linked structures. Therefore, you should adopt a policy of writing individual items in a collection to a file and re-creating the collection from file inputs.

You can load pickled objects into a program from a file using the function `pickle.load`. If the end of the file has been reached, this function raises an exception. This complicates the input process, because you have no apparent way to detect the end of the file before the exception is raised. However, Python's `try-except` statement comes to your rescue. This statement allows an exception to be caught and the program to recover.

You can now construct an input file loop that continues to load objects until the end of the file is encountered. When this happens, an `EOFError` is raised. The `except` clause then closes the file and breaks out of the loop. Here is the code to load objects from the file `items.dat` into a new list named `lyst`:

```
lyst = list()
fileObj = open("items.dat", "rb")
while True:
    try:
        item = pickle.load(fileObj)
        lyst.append(item)
    except EOFError:
        fileObj.close()
        break
print(lyst)
```

CREATING NEW CLASSES

A *class* describes the data and the methods pertaining to a set of objects. It provides a blueprint for creating objects and the code to execute when methods are called on them. All data types in Python are classes.

The syntax of a Python class definition is

```
def <class name>(<parent class name>):
    <class variable assignments>
    <instance method definitions>
```

Class names are capitalized by convention. The code for a class definition usually goes in a module whose filename is the name of that class in lowercase. Related classes may appear in the same module.

The *parent class* name is optional, in which case, it is assumed to be object. All Python classes belong to a hierarchy, with object at the root. Several methods, such as __str__ and __eq__, are defined in object and are automatically inherited by all subclasses.

Instance methods are run on objects of a class. They include code for accessing or modifying instance variables. An *instance variable* refers to storage held by an individual object.

Class variables refer to storage held in common by all objects of a class.

To illustrate these ideas, this section will now explore the code for the definition of a Counter class. A counter object, as the name implies, tracks an integer count. A counter's value is initially 0 and can be reset to 0 at any time. You can increment or decrement a counter, obtain its current integer value, obtain its string representation, or compare two counters for equality. Here is the code for the class:

```python
class Counter(object):
    """Models a counter."""

    # Class variable
    instances = 0

    # Constructor
    def __init__(self):
        """Sets up the counter."""
        Counter.instances += 1
        self.reset()

    # Mutator methods
    def reset(self):
        """Sets the counter to 0."""
        self._value = 0

    def increment(self, amount = 1):
        """Adds amount to the counter."""
        self._value += amount

    def decrement(self, amount = 1):
        """Subtracts amount from the counter."""
        self._value -= amount

    # Accessor methods
    def getValue(self):
```

```
            """Returns the counter's value."""
            return self._value

    def __str__(self):
        """Returns the string representation of the counter."""
        return str(self._value)

    def __eq__(self, other):
        """Returns True if self equals other
        or False otherwise."""
        if self is other: return True
        if type(self) != type(other): return False
        return self._value == other._value
```

Here is an interaction with some counter objects in the Python shell:

```
>>> from counter import Counter
>>> c1 = Counter()
>>> print(c1)
0
>>> c1.getValue()
0
>>> str(c1)
'0'
>>> c1.increment()
>>> print(c1)
1
>>> c1.increment(5)
>>> print(c1)
6
>>> c1.reset()
>>> print(c1)
0
>>> c2 = Counter()
>>> Counter.instances
2
>>> c1 == c1
True
>>> c1 == 0
False
>>> c1 == c2
True
>>> c2.increment()
>>> c1 == c2
False
>>>
```

And now for some brief observations:

The Counter class is a subclass of object.

The class variable instances tracks the number of counter objects created. Except where it is initially introduced by assignment, a class variable must have the class name as a prefix.

The syntax of an instance method definition is the same as that of a function definition; however, an extra parameter, named self, always appears at the beginning of the parameter list. In the context of a method definition, the name self refers to the object on which that method is run.

The instance method __init__, also called the constructor, is run automatically when an instance of Counter is created. This method initializes the instance variable and updates the class variable. Note that __init__ calls the instance method reset, using the syntax self.reset(), to initialize the single instance variable.

The other instance methods are of two types: mutators and accessors. A mutator modifies or changes the internal state of an object by modifying its instance variables. An accessor simply observes or uses the values of the object's instance variables without changing them.

On its first call, the instance method reset introduces the instance variable self._value. Thereafter, any other calls of this method change the value of this variable to 0.

An instance variable always has the prefix self. Unlike parameters or temporary variables, an instance variable is visible in any method within a class. In this book, instance variables within some classes are spelled with a single leading _ character. This convention helps the reader distinguish them from parameters and temporary variables and discourages the writer from accessing them outside of the class definition.

The increment and decrement methods use default arguments, which give the programmer the option of specifying the amounts or not.

The __str__ method in the Counter class overrides the same method in the object class. Python runs __str__ on an object when that object is passed as an argument to the str function. When a method is run on an object, Python looks for the method's code first in that object's own class. If the method is not found there, Python looks in its parent class, and so on. If the code for the method is not found (after looking in the object class), Python raises an exception.

When Python's print function receives an argument, the argument's __str__ method is automatically run to obtain its string representation for output. The programmer is encouraged to include an __str__ method for each programmer-defined class, to assist in debugging.

Python runs the __eq__ method when it sees the == operator. The default definition of this method, in the object class, runs the is operator, which compares the two operands for object identity. As you can see, you also want two distinct counter objects to be considered equal, as long as the two objects have the same value. Because the second operand of == can be any object, the __eq__ method asks if operands' types are the same before accessing their instance variables. Note that you can also access an instance variable using the dot notation on an object.

There are many more things that could be said about developing your own Python classes, but the rest of this book explores the topic quite thoroughly and deliberately.

Projects

1. Write a program that takes the radius of a sphere (a floating-point number) as input and outputs the sphere's diameter, circumference, surface area, and volume.

2. An employee's total weekly pay equals the hourly wage multiplied by the total number of regular hours plus any overtime pay. Overtime pay equals the total overtime hours multiplied by 1.5 times the hourly wage. Write a program that takes as inputs the hourly wage, total regular hours, and total overtime hours and displays an employee's total weekly pay.

3. A standard science experiment is to drop a ball and see how high it bounces. Once the "bounciness" of the ball has been determined, the ratio gives a bounciness index. For example, if a ball dropped from a height of 10 feet bounces 6 feet high, the index is 0.6 and the total distance traveled by the ball is 16 feet after one bounce. If the ball were to continue bouncing, the distance after two bounces would be 10 ft + 6 ft + 6 ft + 3.6 ft = 25.6 ft. Note that distance traveled for each successive bounce is the distance to the floor plus 0.6 of that distance as the ball comes back up. Write a program that lets the user enter the initial height of the ball and the number of times the ball is allowed to continue bouncing. Output should be the total distance traveled by the ball.

4. The German mathematician Gottfried Leibniz developed the following method to approximate the value of π:
   $$\pi/4 = 1 - 1/3 + 1/5 - 1/7 + \dots$$
   Write a program that allows the user to specify the number of iterations used in this approximation and displays the resulting value.

5. The TidBit Computer Store has a credit plan for computer purchases. There is a 10% down payment and an annual interest rate of 12%. Monthly payments are 5% of the listed purchase price minus the down payment. Write a program that takes the purchase price as input. The program should display a table, with appropriate headers, of a payment schedule for the lifetime of the loan. Each row of the table should contain the following items:

■ The month number (beginning with 1)

■ The current total balance owed

■ The interest owed for that month

■ The amount of principal owed for that month

■ The payment for that month

■ The balance remaining after payment

The amount of interest for a month is equal to balance * rate / 12. The amount of principal for a month is equal to the monthly payment minus the interest owed.

6. The Payroll Department keeps a list of employee information for each pay period in a text file. The format of each line of the file is

```
<last name> <hourly wage> <hours worked>
```

Write a program that inputs a filename from the user and prints a report to the terminal of the wages paid to the employees for the given period. The report should be in tabular format with the appropriate header. Each line should contain an employee's name, the hours worked, and the wages paid for that period.

7. Statisticians would like to have a set of functions to compute the *median* and *mode* of a list of numbers. The median is the number that would appear at the midpoint of a list if it were sorted. The mode is the number that appears most frequently in the list. Define these functions in a module named stats.py. Also include a function named mean, which computes the average of a set of numbers. Each function expects a list of numbers as an argument and returns a single number.

8. Write a program that allows the user to navigate through the lines of text in a file. The program prompts the user for a filename and inputs the lines of text into a list. The program then enters a loop in which it prints the number of lines in the file and prompts the user for a line number. Actual line numbers range from 1 to the number of lines in the file. If the input is 0, the program quits. Otherwise, the program prints the line associated with that number.

9. A simple software system for a library models a library as a collection of books and patrons. A patron can have at most three books out on loan at any given time. A book also has a list of patrons waiting to borrow it. Each book has a title, an author, a patron to whom it has been checked out, and a list of patrons waiting for that book to be returned. Each patron has a name and the number of books it has currently checked out. Develop the classes Book and Patron to model these objects. Think first of the interface or set of methods used with each class, and then choose appropriate data structures for the state of the objects. Also, write a short script to test these classes.

10. Develop a Library class that can manage the books and patrons from Project 9. This class should include methods for adding, removing, and finding books and patrons. There should also be methods for borrowing and returning a book. Write a script to test all these methods.

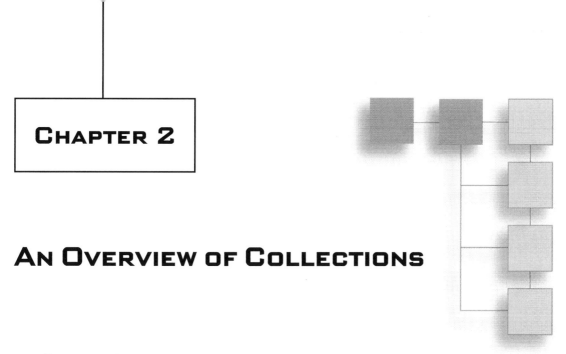

CHAPTER 2

AN OVERVIEW OF COLLECTIONS

A *collection*, as the name implies, is a group of zero or more items that can be treated as a conceptual unit. Nearly every nontrivial piece of software involves the use of collections. Although some of what you learn in computer science comes and goes with changes in technology, the basic principles of organizing collections endure. Although they may differ in structure and use, all collections have the same fundamental purpose: they help programmers effectively organize data in programs.

Collections can be viewed from two perspectives. Users or clients of collections are concerned with what they do in various applications. Developers or implementers of collections are concerned with how they can best perform as general-purpose resources.

This chapter gives an overview of different types of collections from the perspective of the users of those collections. It introduces the different types of collections, the commonly available operations on them, and the commonly used implementations.

COLLECTION TYPES

As you already know, Python includes several built-in collection types: the string, the list, the tuple, the set, and the dictionary. The string and the list are probably the most common and fundamental types of collections. Other important types of collections include stacks, queues, priority queues, binary search trees, heaps, graphs, bags, and various types of sorted collections.

Collections can be homogeneous, meaning that all items in the collection must be of the same type, or heterogeneous, meaning the items can be of different types. In many programming languages, collections are homogeneous, although most Python collections can contain multiple types of objects.

Collections are typically *dynamic* rather than *static*, meaning they can grow or shrink with the needs of a problem. Also, their contents can change throughout the course of a program. One exception to this rule is the *immutable collection*, such as Python's string or tuple. An immutable collection's items are added during its creation; after that, no items may be added, removed, or replaced.

Another important distinguishing characteristic of collections is the manner in which they are organized. This chapter now examines the organization used in several broad categories of collections: linear collections, hierarchical collections, graph collections, unordered collections, and sorted collections.

Linear Collections

The items in a *linear collection*, like people in a line, are ordered by position. Each item except the first has a unique predecessor, and each item except the last has a unique successor. As shown in Figure 2.1, D2's predecessor is D1, and D2's successor is D3.

Figure 2.1
A linear collection.
© 2014 Cengage Learning®

Everyday examples of linear collections are grocery lists, stacks of dinner plates, and a line of customers waiting at an ATM.

Hierarchical Collections

Data items in *hierarchical collections* are ordered in a structure resembling an upside-down tree. Each data item except the one at the top has just one predecessor, called its *parent*, but potentially many successors, called its *children*. As shown in Figure 2.2, D3's predecessor (parent) is D1, and D3's successors (children) are D4, D5, and D6.

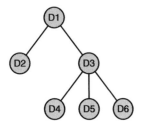

Figure 2.2
A hierarchical collection.
© 2014 Cengage Learning®

A file directory system, a company's organizational tree, and a book's table of contents are examples of hierarchical collections.

Graph Collections

A *graph collection*, also called a *graph*, is a collection in which each data item can have many predecessors and many successors. As shown in Figure 2.3, all elements connected to D3 are considered to be both its predecessors and its successors, and they are also called its *neighbors*.

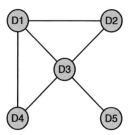

Figure 2.3
A graph collection.
© 2014 Cengage Learning®

Examples of graphs are maps of airline routes between cities and electrical wiring diagrams for buildings.

Unordered Collections

As the name implies, items in an *unordered collection* are not in any particular order, and it's not possible to meaningfully speak of an item's predecessor or successor. Figure 2.4 shows such a structure.

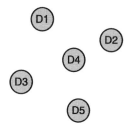

Figure 2.4
An unordered collection.
© 2014 Cengage Learning®

A bag of marbles is an example of an unordered collection. Although you can put marbles into a bag and take marbles out of a bag in any order you want, within the bag, the marbles are in no particular order.

Sorted Collections

A *sorted collection* imposes a *natural ordering* on its items. Examples are the entries in a phone book (the 20th century paper variety) and the entries on a class roster.

To impose a natural ordering, there must be some rule for comparing items, such that item$_i$ <= item$_{i+1}$, for the items visited in a sorted collection.

Although a sorted list is the most common example of a sorted collection, sorted collections need not be linear or ordered by position. From the client's perspective, sets, bags, and dictionaries may be sorted, even though their items are not accessible by position. A special type of hierarchical collection, known as a binary search tree, also imposes a natural ordering on its items.

A sorted collection allows the client to visit all of its items in sorted order. Some operations, such as searching, may be more efficient on a sorted collection than on its unsorted cousin.

A Taxonomy of Collection Types

With the major categories of collections in mind, you can now place the different commonly used types of collections in a taxonomy, as shown in Figure 2.5. This taxonomy will help you organize the Python classes that represent these types in later chapters of this book.

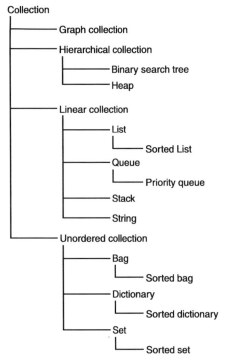

Collection
  Graph collection
  Hierarchical collection
    Binary search tree
    Heap
  Linear collection
    List
      Sorted List
    Queue
      Priority queue
    Stack
    String
  Unordered collection
    Bag
      Sorted bag
    Dictionary
      Sorted dictionary
    Set
      Sorted set

Figure 2.5

A taxonomy of collection types.

© 2014 Cengage Learning®

Note that a type name in this taxonomy does not imply a particular implementation of a collection; as you will see shortly, there may be more than one implementation of a particular type of collection. Also, some of the names, such as "Collection" and "Linear collection," specify a category of collection types rather than a particular collection type. These categories will be useful, however, for organizing features and behavior that particular types of collections have in common.

OPERATIONS ON COLLECTIONS

The manipulations that you can perform on a collection vary with the type of collection being used, but generally, the operations fall into several broad categories that are outlined in Table 2.1.

Table 2.1   Categories of Operations on Collections

Category of Operation	Description
Determine the size	Use Python's `len` function to obtain the number of items currently in the collection.
Test for item membership	Use Python's `in` operator to search for a given target item in the collection. Returns `True` if the item is found, or `False` otherwise.
Traverse the collection	Use Python's `for` loop to visit each item in the collection. The order in which the items are visited depends upon the type of collection.
Obtain a string representation	Use Python's `str` function to obtain the string representation of the collection.
Test for equality	Use Python's `==` operator to determine whether two collections are equal. Two collections are equal if they are of the same type and contain the same items. The order in which pairs of items are compared depends on the type of collection.
Concatenate two collections	Use Python's `+` operator to obtain a new collection of the same type as the operands, and containing the items in the two operands.
Convert to another type of collection	Create a new collection with the same items as a source collection. Cloning is a special case of type conversion, where the two collections are of the same type.
Insert an item	Add the item to the collection, possibly at a given position.
Remove an item	Remove the item from the collection, possibly at a given position.
Replace an item	Combine removal and insertion into one operation.
Access or retrieve an item	Obtain an item, possibly at a given position.

Note that several of these operations are associated with standard Python operators, functions, or control statements, such as in, +, len, str, and the for loop. You are already familiar with their use with Python strings and lists.

There is no single name for the insertion, removal, replacement, or access operations in Python. However, there are a few standard variations. For example, the method pop is used to remove items at given positions from a Python list or values at given keys from a Python dictionary. The method remove is used to remove given items from a Python set or a Python list. As new types of collections are developed that are not already supported in Python, every effort will be made to use standard operator, function, or method names for their operations.

One collection operation that you might not be familiar with is type conversion. You already know about type conversion from its use in the input of numbers. In that context, you convert a string of digits from the keyboard to an int or float by applying the int or float function to the input string. (See Chapter 1, "Basic Python Programming," for details.)

You can convert one type of collection to another type of collection in a similar manner. For example, you can convert a Python string to a Python list and a Python list to a Python tuple, as shown in the following session:

```
>>> message = "Hi there!"
>>> lyst = list(message)
>>> lyst
['H', 'i', ' ', 't', 'h', 'e', 'r', 'e', '!']
>>> toople = tuple(lyst)
>>> toople
('H', 'i', ' ', 't', 'h', 'e', 'r', 'e', '!')
>>>
```

The argument to the list or tuple function need not be another collection; it can be any *iterable object*. An iterable object allows the programmer to visit a sequence of items with a Python for loop. (That's right—that sounds like a collection: all collections are also iterable objects!) For example, you can create a list from a range, as follows:

```
>>> lyst = list(range(1, 11, 2))
>>> lyst
[1, 3, 5, 7, 9]
>>>
```

Other functions, such as the dict function for dictionaries, expect more specific types of iterable objects as arguments, such as a list of (key, value) tuples.

Generally, if the argument is omitted, a collection's type conversion function returns a new, empty collection of that type.

A special case of type conversion is cloning, which returns an exact copy of the argument to the conversion function. This should be the case when the argument's type is the same as the conversion function. For example, the next code segment makes a copy of a list and then compares the two lists using the is and == operators. Because the two lists are not the same object, is returns False. Because the two lists are distinct objects but are of the same type and have the same structure (each pair of elements is the same at each position in the two lists), == returns True.

```
>>> lyst1 = [2, 4, 8]
>>> lyst2 = list(lyst1)
>>> lyst1 is lyst2
False
>>> lyst1 == lyst2
True
>>>
```

Not only do the two lists in this example have the same structure, but they share the same items. That is, the list function makes a *shallow copy* of its argument list; these items are not themselves cloned before being added to the new list. This policy does not cause problems when the items are immutable (numbers, strings, or Python tuples). However, when collections share mutable items, side effects can occur. To prevent these from happening, the programmer can create a *deep copy* by writing a for loop over the source collection, which explicitly clones its items before adding them to the new collection.

The following chapters adopt the policy of providing a type conversion function for most collection types. This function takes an iterable object as an optional argument and performs a shallow copy of the items visited.

IMPLEMENTATIONS OF COLLECTIONS

Naturally, programmers who work with programs that include collections have a rather different perspective on those collections than the programmers who are responsible for implementing them in the first place.

Programmers who use collections need to know how to instantiate and use each type of collection. From their perspective, a collection is a means for storing and accessing data items in some predetermined manner, without concern for the details of the collection's implementation. In other words, from a user's perspective, a collection is an abstraction, and for this reason, in computer science, collections are also called *abstract data types* (ADTs). The user of an ADT is concerned only with learning its interface, or the set of operations that objects of that type recognize.

Developers of collections, on the other hand, are concerned with implementing a collection's behavior in the most efficient manner possible, with the goal of providing the best performance to users of the collections. Numerous implementations are usually possible. However, many of these take so much space or run so slowly that they can be dismissed as pointless. Those that remain tend to be based on several underlying approaches to organizing and accessing computer memory. Chapter 3, "Searching, Sorting, and Complexity Analysis" and 4, "Arrays and Linked Structures," explore these approaches in detail.

Some programming languages, like Python, provide only one implementation of each of the available collection types. Other languages, like Java, provide several. For example, Java's `java.util` package includes two implementations of lists, named `ArrayList` and `LinkedList`, and two implementations of sets and maps (like Python dictionaries), named `HashSet`, `TreeSet`, `HashMap`, and `TreeMap`. Java programmers use the same interfaces (set of operations) with each implementation but are free to choose among implementations with respect to their performance characteristics and other criteria.

One aim of this book is to give the Python programmer the same options as the Java programmer, as well as to introduce abstract collection types and their implementations that are not available in either language. For each category of collections (linear, hierarchical, graph, unordered, sorted), you'll see one or more abstract collection types and one or more implementations of each type.

The idea of abstraction is not unique to a discussion of collections. It is an important principle in many endeavors both in and out of computer science. For example, when studying the effect of gravity on a falling object, you might try to create an experimental situation in which you can ignore incidental details such as the color and taste of the object (for example, the sort of apple that hit Newton on the head). When studying mathematics, you wouldn't concern yourself with what numbers might be used to count fishhooks or arrowheads, but try to discover abstract and enduring principles of numbers. A house plan is an abstraction of the physical house that allows you to focus on structural elements without being overwhelmed by incidental details such as the color of the kitchen cabinets—details that are important to the overall look of the completed house, but not to the relationships among the house's main parts.

In computer science, abstraction is used for ignoring or hiding details that are, for the moment, nonessential. A software system is often built layer by layer, with each layer treated as an abstraction by the layers above that utilize it. Without abstraction, you would need to consider all aspects of a software system simultaneously, which is an impossible task. Of course, you must consider the details eventually, but you can do so in a small and manageable context.

In Python, functions and methods are the smallest units of abstraction, classes are the next in size, and modules are the largest. This text implements abstract collection types as classes or sets of related classes in modules. The general techniques for organizing these classes, which comprise object-oriented programming, are covered in Chapters 5, "Interfaces, Implementations, and Polymorphism," and 6, "Inheritance and Abstract Classes." A complete list of the collection classes covered in this book is given in the Appendix, "A Collection Framework for Python Programmers."

SUMMARY

- Collections are objects that hold zero or more other objects. A collection has operations for accessing its objects, inserting them, removing them, determining the collection's size, and traversing or visiting the collection's objects.

- The five main categories of collections are linear, hierarchical, graph, unordered, and sorted.

- Linear collections order their items by position, with each but the first having a unique predecessor and each but the last having a unique successor.

- With one exception, the items in a hierarchical collection have a unique predecessor and zero or more successors. A single item called the root has no predecessor.

- The items in a graph can have zero or more successors and zero or more predecessors.

- The items in an unordered collection are in no particular order.

- Collections are iterable—each item contained within a collection can be visited with a for loop.

- An abstract data type is a set of objects and operations on those objects. Collections are thus abstract data types.

- A data structure is an object that represents the data contained in a collection.

REVIEW QUESTIONS

1. Examples of linear collections are
   a. Sets and trees
   b. Lists and stacks

2. Examples of unordered collections are

   a. Queues and lists

   b. Sets and dictionaries

3. A hierarchical collection can represent a

   a. Line of customers at a bank

   b. File directory system

4. A graph collection can represent a

   a. Set of numbers

   b. Map of flight paths between cities

PROJECTS

1. Explore the interfaces of Python's built-in collection types `str`, `list`, `tuple`, `set`, and `dict` by using the `dir` and `help` functions at a shell prompt. The syntax for using these is `dir(<type name>)` and `help(<type name>)`.

2. For comparison with Python, browse Java's collection types, in the `java.util` package, at http://docs.oracle.com/javase/7/docs/api/.

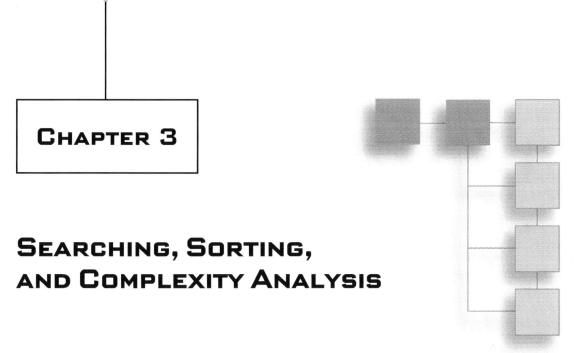

CHAPTER 3

SEARCHING, SORTING, AND COMPLEXITY ANALYSIS

Algorithms are one of the basic building blocks of computer programs. (The other, data structures, will be examined in Chapter 4, "Arrays and Linked Structures.") An algorithm describes a computational process that halts with a solution to a problem. There are many criteria for assessing the quality of an algorithm. The most essential criterion is correctness—namely, that the algorithm in fact solves the problem it's intended to solve. Readability and ease of maintenance are also important qualities. This chapter examines another important criterion of the quality of algorithms—run-time performance.

When an algorithmic process runs on a real computer with finite resources, economic thinking comes into play. Such a process consumes two resources: processing time and space or memory. When run with the same problems or data sets, a process that consumes less of these two resources is of higher quality than a process that consumes more, and so are the corresponding algorithms.

This chapter introduces tools for complexity analysis—for assessing the run-time performance or efficiency of algorithms. You apply these tools to search algorithms and sort algorithms, which typically do much of the work in computer applications. However, the analytical tools and techniques introduced in this chapter will be used throughout this book.

MEASURING THE EFFICIENCY OF ALGORITHMS

Some algorithms consume an amount of time or memory that is below a threshold of tolerance. For example, most users are happy with any algorithm that loads a file in less than one second. For such users, any algorithm that meets this requirement is as good as any other. Other algorithms take an amount of time that is ridiculously impractical (say, thousands of years) with large data sets. You can't use these algorithms and instead need to find others, if they exist, that perform better.

When choosing algorithms, you often have to settle for a space/time trade-off. An algorithm can be designed to gain faster run times at the cost of using extra space (memory) or the other way around. Some users might be willing to pay for more memory to get a faster algorithm, whereas others would rather settle for a slower algorithm that economizes on memory. Although memory is now quite inexpensive for desktop and laptop computers, the space/time trade-off continues to be relevant for miniature devices.

In any case, because efficiency is a desirable feature of algorithms, it is important to pay attention to the potential of some algorithms for poor performance. This section considers several ways to measure the efficiency of algorithms.

Measuring the Run Time of an Algorithm

One way to measure the time cost of an algorithm is to use the computer's clock to obtain an actual run time. This process, called *benchmarking* or *profiling*, starts by determining the time for several different data sets of the same size and then calculates the average time. Next, similar data are gathered for larger and larger data sets. After several such tests, enough data are available to predict how the algorithm will behave for a data set of any size.

Consider a simple, if unrealistic, example. The following program implements an algorithm that counts from 1 to a given number. Thus, the problem size is the number. You start with the number 10,000,000, time the algorithm, and output the running time to the terminal window. You then double the size of this number and repeat this process. After five such increases, there is a set of results from which you can generalize. Here is the code for the tester program:

```
"""
File: timing1.py
Prints the running times for problem sizes that double,
using a single loop.
"""

import time

problemSize = 10000000
print("%12s%16s" % ("Problem Size", "Seconds"))
for count in range(5):

    start = time.time()
    # The start of the algorithm
```

```
work = 1
for x in range(problemSize):
    work += 1
    work -= 1
# The end of the algorithm
elapsed = time.time() - start

print("%12d%16.3f" % (problemSize, elapsed))
problemSize *= 2
```

The tester program uses the time() function in the time module to track the running time. This function returns the number of seconds that have elapsed between the current time on the computer's clock and January 1, 1970 (also called *The Epoch*). Thus, the difference between the results of two calls of time.time() represents the elapsed time in seconds. Note also that the program does a constant amount of work, in the form of two extended assignment statements, on each pass through the loop. This work consumes enough time on each iteration so that the total running time is significant but has no other impact on the results. Figure 3.1 shows the output of the program.

Problem Size	Seconds
10000000	3.8
20000000	7.591
40000000	15.352
80000000	30.697
160000000	61.631

Figure 3.1

The output of the tester program.

© 2014 Cengage Learning®

A quick glance at the results reveals that the running time more or less doubles when the size of the problem doubles. Thus, you might predict that the running time for a problem of size 32,000,000 would be approximately 124 seconds.

As another example, consider the following change in the tester program's algorithm:

```
for j in range(problemSize):
    for k in range(problemSize):
        work += 1
        work -= 1
```

In this version, the extended assignments have been moved into a nested loop. This loop iterates through the size of the problem within another loop that also iterates through the size of the problem. This program was left running overnight. By morning it had processed only the first data set, 10,000,000. The program was then terminated and run again with a smaller problem size of 1000. Figure 3.2 shows the results.

Problem Size	Seconds
1000	0.387
2000	1.581
4000	6.463
8000	25.702
16000	102.666

Figure 3.2

The output of the second tester program.

© 2014 Cengage Learning®

Note that when the problem size doubles, the number of seconds of running time more or less quadruples. At this rate, it would take 175 days to process the largest number in the previous data set!

This method permits accurate predictions of the running times of many algorithms. However, there are two major problems with this technique:

■ Different hardware platforms have different processing speeds, so the running times of an algorithm differ from machine to machine. Also, the running time of a program varies with the type of operating system that lies between it and the hardware. Finally, different programming languages and compilers produce code whose performance varies. For example, an algorithm coded in C usually runs slightly faster than the same algorithm in Python byte code. Thus, predictions of performance generated from the results of timing on one hardware or software platform generally cannot be used to predict potential performance on other platforms.

■ It is impractical to determine the running time for some algorithms with very large data sets. For some algorithms, it doesn't matter how fast the compiled code or the hardware processor is. They are impractical to run with very large data sets on any computer.

Although timing algorithms may in some cases be a helpful form of testing, you also might want an estimate of the efficiency of an algorithm that is independent of a particular hardware or software platform. As you will learn in the next section, such an estimate tells you how well or how poorly the algorithm would perform on any platform.

Counting Instructions

Another technique used to estimate the efficiency of an algorithm is to count the instructions executed with different problem sizes. These counts provide a good predictor of the amount of abstract work an algorithm performs, no matter what platform the algorithm runs on. Keep in mind, however, that when you count instructions, you are counting the instructions in the high-level code in which the algorithm is written, not instructions in the executable machine language program.

When analyzing an algorithm in this way, you distinguish between two classes of instructions:

- Instructions that execute the same number of times regardless of the problem size
- Instructions whose execution count varies with the problem size

For now, you ignore instructions in the first class, because they do not figure significantly in this kind of analysis. The instructions in the second class normally are found in loops or recursive functions. In the case of loops, you also zero in on instructions performed in any nested loops or, more simply, just the number of iterations that a nested loop performs. For example, try wiring the previous program to track and display the number of iterations the inner loop executes with the different data sets:

```
"""
File: counting.py
Prints the number of iterations for problem sizes
that double, using a nested loop.
"""

problemSize = 1000
print("%12s%15s" % ("Problem Size", "Iterations"))
for count in range(5):
    number = 0

    # The start of the algorithm
    work = 1
    for j in range(problemSize):
        for k in range(problemSize):
            number += 1
            work += 1
            work -= 1
    # The end of the algorithm

    print("%12d%15d" % (problemSize, number))
    problemSize *= 2
```

As you can see from the results, the number of iterations is the square of the problem size (Figure 3.3).

Problem Size	Iterations
1000	1000000
2000	4000000
4000	16000000
8000	64000000
16000	256000000

Figure 3.3

The output of a tester program that counts iterations.

© 2014 Cengage Learning®

Here is a similar program that tracks the number of calls of a recursive Fibonacci function for several problem sizes. Note that the function now expects a second argument, which is a counter object. Each time the function is called at the top level, a new counter object (as defined in Chapter 1, "Basic Python Programming") is created and passed to it. On that call and each recursive call, the function's counter object is incremented.

```python
"""
File: countfib.py
Prints the number of calls of a recursive Fibonacci
function with problem sizes that double.
"""

from counter import Counter

def fib(n, counter):
    """Count the number of calls of the Fibonacci
    function."""
    counter.increment()
    if n < 3:
        return 1
    else:
        return fib(n - 1, counter) + fib(n - 2, counter)

problemSize = 2
print("%12s%15s" % ("Problem Size", "Calls"))
for count in range(5):
    counter = Counter()

    # The start of the algorithm
    fib(problemSize, counter)
    # The end of the algorithm

    print("%12d%15s" % (problemSize, counter))
    problemSize *= 2
```

The output of this program is shown in Figure 3.4.

Problem Size	Calls
2	1
4	5
8	41
16	1973
32	4356617

Figure 3.4

The output of a tester program that runs the Fibonacci function.

© 2014 Cengage Learning®

As the problem size doubles, the instruction count (number of recursive calls) grows slowly at first and then quite rapidly. At first, the instruction count is less than the square of the problem size. However, when the problem size reaches 16, the instruction count of 1973 is significantly larger than 256, or 16^2. You will determine the rate of growth of this algorithm more precisely later in this chapter.

The problem with tracking counts in this way is that, with some algorithms, the computer still cannot run fast enough to show the counts for very large problem sizes. Counting instructions is the right idea, but you need to turn to logic and mathematical reasoning for a complete method of analysis. The only tools you need for this type of analysis are paper and pencil.

Measuring the Memory Used by an Algorithm

A complete analysis of the resources used by an algorithm includes the amount of memory required. Once again, focus on rates of potential growth. Some algorithms require the same amount of memory to solve any problem. Other algorithms require more memory as the problem size gets larger. Later chapters consider several of these algorithms.

Exercises 3.1

1. Write a tester program that counts and displays the number of iterations of the following loop:

```
while problemSize > 0:
    problemSize = problemSize // 2
```

2. Run the program you created in Exercise 1 using problem sizes of 1,000, 2,000, 4,000, 10,000, and 100,000. As the problem size doubles or increases by a factor of 10, what happens to the number of iterations?

3. The difference between the results of two calls of the function `time.time()` is an elapsed time. Because the operating system might use the CPU for part of this time, the elapsed time might not reflect the actual time that a Python code segment uses the CPU. Browse the Python documentation for an alternative way of recording the processing time, and describe how this would be done.

COMPLEXITY ANALYSIS

In this section, you develop a method of determining the efficiency of algorithms that allows you to rate them independently of platform-dependent timings or impractical instruction counts. This method, called *complexity analysis*, entails reading the algorithm and using pencil and paper to work out some simple algebra.

Orders of Complexity

Consider the two counting loops discussed earlier. The first loop executes n times for a problem of size n. The second loop contains a nested loop that iterates n^2 times. The amount of work done by these two algorithms is similar for small values of n but is very different for large values of n. Figure 3.5 and Table 3.1 illustrate this divergence. Note that "work" in this case refers to the number of iterations of the most deeply nested loop.

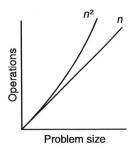

Figure 3.5

A graph of the amounts of work done in the tester programs.

© 2014 Cengage Learning®

Table 3.1   The Amounts of Work in the Tester Programs

Problem Size	Work of the First Algorithm	Work of the Second Algorithm
2	2	4
10	10	100
1,000	1,000	1,000,000

© 2014 Cengage Learning®

The performances of these algorithms differ by an *order of complexity*. The performance of the first algorithm is *linear* in that its work grows in direct proportion to the size of the problem (problem size of 10, work of 10; 20 and 20; and so on). The behavior of the second algorithm is *quadratic* in that its work grows as a function of the square of the problem size (problem size of 10, work of 100). As you can see from the graph and the table, algorithms with linear behavior do less work than algorithms with quadratic behavior for most problem sizes n. In fact, as the problem size gets larger, the performance of an algorithm with the higher order of complexity becomes worse more quickly.

Several other orders of complexity are commonly used in the analysis of algorithms. An algorithm has *constant* performance if it requires the same number of operations for any problem size. List indexing is a good example of a constant-time algorithm. This is clearly the best kind of performance to have.

Another order of complexity that is better than linear but worse than constant is called *logarithmic*. The amount of work of a logarithmic algorithm is proportional to the $\log_2$ of the problem size. Thus, when the problem doubles in size, the amount of work only increases by 1 (that is, just add 1).

The work of a *polynomial time algorithm* grows at a rate of n^k, where k is a constant greater than 1. Examples are n^2, n^3, and n^{10}.

Although n^3 is worse in some sense than n^2, they are both of the polynomial order and are better than the next higher order of complexity. An order of complexity that is worse than polynomial is called *exponential*. An example rate of growth of this order is 2^n. Exponential algorithms are impractical to run with large problem sizes. The most common orders of complexity used in the analysis of algorithms are summarized in Figure 3.6 and Table 3.2.

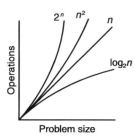

Figure 3.6

A graph of some sample orders of complexity.

© 2014 Cengage Learning®

Table 3.2   Some Sample Orders of Complexity

n	Logarithmic ($\log_2 n$)	Linear (n)	Quadratic (n^2)	Exponential (2^n)
100	7	100	10,000	Off the chart
1,000	10	1,000	1,000,000	Off the chart
1,000,000	20	1,000,000	1,000,000,000,000	Really off the chart

© 2014 Cengage Learning®

Big-O Notation

An algorithm rarely performs a number of operations exactly equal to n, n^2, or k^n. An algorithm usually performs other work in the body of a loop, above the loop, and below the loop. For example, you might more precisely say that an algorithm performs $2n + 3$ or $2n^2$ operations. In the case of a nested loop, the inner loop might execute one fewer pass after each pass through the outer loop, so that the total number of iterations might be more like ½ n^2 – ½ n, rather than n^2.

The amount of work in an algorithm typically is the sum of several terms in a polynomial. Whenever the amount of work is expressed as a polynomial, one term is *dominant*. As n becomes large, the dominant term becomes so large that you can ignore the amount of work represented by the other terms. Thus, for example, in the polynomial ½ n^2 – ½ n, you focus on the quadratic term, ½ n^2, in effect dropping the linear term, ½ n, from consideration. You can also drop the coefficient ½ because the ratio between ½ n^2 and n^2 does not change as n grows. For example, if you double the problem size, the run times of algorithms that are ½ n^2 and n^2 increase by a factor of 4. This type of analysis is sometimes called *asymptotic analysis* because the value of a polynomial asymptotically approaches or approximates the value of its largest term as n becomes very large.

One notation that computer scientists use to express the efficiency or computational complexity of an algorithm is called *big-O notation*. "O" stands for "on the order of," a reference to the order of complexity of the work of the algorithm. Thus, for example, the order of complexity of a linear-time algorithm is O(n). Big-O notation formalizes our discussion of orders of complexity.

The Role of the Constant of Proportionality

The *constant of proportionality* involves the terms and coefficients that are usually ignored during big-O analysis. However, when these items are large, they may affect the algorithm, particularly for small and medium-sized data sets. For example, no one can ignore the difference between n and $n/2$, when n is $1,000,000. In the example algorithms discussed thus far, the instructions that execute within a loop are part of the constant of proportionality, as are the instructions that initialize the variables before the loops are entered. When analyzing an algorithm, you must be careful to determine that any instructions do not hide a loop that depends on a variable problem size. If that is the case, then the analysis must move down into the nested loop, as you saw in the last example.

Now try to determine the constant of proportionality for the first algorithm discussed in this chapter. Here is the code:

```
work = 1
for x in range(problemSize):
    work += 1
    work -= 1
```

Note that, aside from the loop itself, there are three lines of code, each of them assignment statements. Each of these three statements runs in constant time. Also assume that on each iteration, the overhead of managing the loop, which is hidden in the loop header, runs an instruction that requires constant time. Thus, the amount of abstract work performed by this algorithm is $3n + 1$. Although this number is greater than just n, the running times for the two amounts of work, n and $3n + 1$, increase at the same rate.

Exercises 3.2

1. Assume that each of the following expressions indicates the number of operations performed by an algorithm for a problem size of n. Point out the dominant term of each algorithm and use big-O notation to classify it.

    a. $2^n - 4n^2 + 5n$

    b. $3n^2 + 6$

    c. $n^3 + n^2 - n$

2. For problem size n, algorithms A and B perform n^2 and $\frac{1}{2} n^2 + \frac{1}{2} n$ instructions, respectively. Which algorithm does more work? Are there particular problem sizes for which one algorithm performs significantly better than the other? Are there particular problem sizes for which both algorithms perform approximately the same amount of work?

3. At what point does an n^4 algorithm begin to perform better than a 2^n algorithm?

SEARCH ALGORITHMS

Now you'll see several algorithms that you can use for searching and sorting lists. You'll learn the design of an algorithm and then see its implementation as a Python function. Finally, you'll see an analysis of the algorithm's computational complexity. To keep things simple, each function processes a list of integers. Lists of different sizes can be passed as parameters to the functions. The functions are defined in a single module that is used in the case study later in this chapter.

Search for the Minimum

Python's min function returns the minimum or smallest item in a list. To study the complexity of this algorithm, you'll develop an alternative version that returns the *index* of the minimum item. The algorithm assumes that the list is not empty and that the items are in arbitrary order. The algorithm begins by treating the first position as that of the minimum item. It then searches to the right for an item that is smaller and, if it is found, resets the position of the minimum item to the current position. When the algorithm reaches the end of the list, it returns the position of the minimum item. Here is the code for the algorithm, in function indexOfMin:

```
def indexOfMin(lyst):
    """Returns the index of the minimum item."""
    minIndex = 0
    currentIndex = 1
    while currentIndex < len(lyst):
        if lyst[currentIndex] < lyst[minIndex]:
            minIndex = currentIndex
        currentIndex += 1
    return minIndex
```

As you can see, there are three instructions outside the loop that execute the same number of times regardless of the size of the list. Thus, you can discount them. Within the loop are three more instructions. Of these, the comparison in the if statement and the increment of currentIndex execute on each pass through the loop. There are no nested or hidden loops in these instructions. This algorithm must visit every item in the list to guarantee that it has located the position of the minimum item. Thus, the algorithm must make $n - 1$ comparisons for a list of size n. Therefore, the algorithm's complexity is $O(n)$.

Sequential Search of a List

Python's in operator is implemented as a method named __contains__ in the list class. This method searches for a particular item (called the *target item*) within a list of arbitrarily arranged items. In such a list, the only way to search for a target item is to begin with the item at the first position and compare it to the target. If the items are equal, the method returns True. Otherwise, the method moves on to the next position and compares its item with the target. If the method arrives at the last position and still cannot find the target, it returns False. This kind of search is called a *sequential search* or a *linear search*. A more useful sequential search function would return the index of a target if it's found, or –1 otherwise. Here is the Python code for a sequential search function:

```python
def sequentialSearch(target, lyst):
    """Returns the position of the target item if found,
    or -1 otherwise."""
    position = 0
    while position < len(lyst):
        if target == lyst[position]:
            return position
        position += 1
    return -1
```

The analysis of a sequential search is a bit different from the analysis of a search for a minimum, as you will see in the next subsection.

Best-Case, Worst-Case, and Average-Case Performance

The performance of some algorithms depends on the placement of the data that are processed. The sequential search algorithm does less work to find a target at the beginning of a list than at the end of the list. For such algorithms, you can determine the best-case performance, the worst-case performance, and the average performance. In general, it's suggested that you worry more about average- and worst-case performances than about best-case performances.

An analysis of a sequential search considers three cases:

1. In the worst case, the target item is at the end of the list or not in the list at all. Then the algorithm must visit every item and perform n iterations for a list of size n. Thus, the worst-case complexity of a sequential search is $O(n)$.

2. In the best case, the algorithm finds the target at the first position, after making one iteration, for an $O(1)$ complexity.

3. To determine the average case, you add the number of iterations required to find the target at each possible position and divide the sum by n. Thus, the algorithm performs $(n + n - 1 + n - 2 + \cdots + 1)/n$, or $(n + 1)/2$ iterations. For very large n, the constant factor of 2 is insignificant, so the average complexity is still $O(n)$.

Clearly, the best-case performance of a sequential search is rare compared to the average- and worst-case performances, which are essentially the same.

Binary Search of a Sorted List

A sequential search is necessary for data that are not arranged in any particular order. When searching sorted data, you can use a binary search.

To understand how a binary search works, think about what happens when you look up a person's number in a phone book (the hard-copy kind in use during the 20th century). The data in a phone book are already sorted, so you don't do a sequential search. Instead, you estimate the name's alphabetical position in the book and open the book as close to that position as possible. After you open the book, you determine if the target name lies, alphabetically, on an earlier page or a later page, and flip back or forward through the pages as necessary. You repeat this process until you find the name or conclude that it's not in the book.

Now consider an example of a binary search in Python. To begin, assume that the items in the list are sorted in ascending order (as they are in a phone book). The search algorithm goes directly to the middle position in the list and compares the item at that position to the target. If there is a match, the algorithm returns the position. Otherwise, if the target is less than the current item, the algorithm searches the portion of the list before the middle position. If the target is greater than the current item, the algorithm searches the portion of the list after the middle position. The search process stops when the target is found or the current beginning position is greater than the current ending position.

Here is the code for the binary search function:

```python
def binarySearch(target, sortedLyst):
    left = 0
    right = len(sortedLyst) - 1
    while left <= right:
        midpoint = (left + right) // 2
        if target == sortedLyst[midpoint]:
            return midpoint
        elif target < sortedLyst[midpoint]:
            right = midpoint - 1
        else:
            left = midpoint + 1
    return -1
```

There is just one loop with no nested or hidden loops. Once again, the worst case occurs when the target is not in the list. How many times does the loop run in the worst case? This is equal to the number of times the size of the list can be divided by 2 until the quotient is 1. For a list of size n, you essentially perform the reduction $n/2/2 \ldots /2$ until the result is 1. Let k be the number of times you divide n by 2. To solve for k, you have $n/2^k = 1$, and $n = 2^k$, and $k = \log_2 n$. Thus, the worst-case complexity of binary search is $O(\log_2 n)$.

Figure 3.7 shows the portions of the list being searched in a binary search with a list of 9 items and a target item, 10, that is not in the list. The items compared to the target are shaded. Note that none of the items in the left half of the original list are visited.

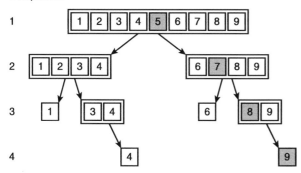

Comparison

Figure 3.7

The items of a list visited during a binary search for 10.

© 2014 Cengage Learning®

The binary search for the target item 10 requires four comparisons, whereas a sequential search would have required 10 comparisons. This algorithm actually appears to perform better as the problem size gets larger. Our list of nine items requires at most four comparisons, whereas a list of 1,000,000 items requires at most only 20 comparisons!

Binary search is certainly more efficient than sequential search. However, the kind of search algorithm you choose depends on the organization of the data in the list. There is an additional overall cost to a binary search, having to do with keeping the list in sorted order. In a moment, you'll examine some strategies for sorting a list and analyze their complexity. But first, you'll read a few words about comparing data items.

Comparing Data Items

Both the binary search and the search for the minimum assume that the items in the list are comparable with each other. In Python, this means that the items are of the same type and that they recognize the comparison operators ==, <, and >. Objects of several built-in Python types, such as numbers, strings, and lists, can be compared using these operators.

To allow algorithms to use the comparison operators ==, <, and > with a new class of objects, the programmer should define the __eq__, __lt__, and __gt__ methods in that class. The header of __lt__ is the following:

```
def __lt__(self, other):
```

This method returns True if self is less than other, or False otherwise. The criteria for comparing the objects depend on their internal structure and on the manner in which they should be ordered.

For example, SavingsAccount objects might include three data fields: for a name, a PIN, and a balance. If you assume that the accounts should be ordered alphabetically by name, then the following implementation of the __lt__ method is called for:

```
class SavingsAccount(object):
    """This class represents a savings account
    with the owner's name, PIN, and balance."""

    def __init__(self, name, pin, balance = 0.0):
        self._name = name
        self._pin = pin
        self._balance = balance

    def __lt__(self, other):
        return self._name < other._name

    # Other methods, including __eq__
```

Note that the __lt__ method calls the < operator with the _name fields of the two account objects. The names are strings, and the string type already includes an __lt__ method. Python automatically runs the __lt__ method when the < operator is applied, in the same way that it runs the __str__ method when the str function is called.

The next session shows a test of comparisons with several account objects:

```
>>> s1 = SavingsAccount("Ken", "1000", 0)
>>> s2 = SavingsAccount("Bill", "1001", 30)
>>> s1 < s2
False
>>> s2 < s1
True
>>> s1 > s2
True
>>> s2 > s1
False
>>> s2 == s1
False
>>> s3 = SavingsAccount("Ken", "1000", 0)
```

```
>>> s1 == s3
True
>>> s4 = s1
>>> s4 == s1
True
```

You can now place the accounts in a list and sort them by name.

Exercises 3.3

1. Suppose that a list contains the values 20, 44, 48, 55, 62, 66, 74, 88, 93, 99 at index positions 0 through 9. Trace the values of the variables `left`, `right`, and `midpoint` in a binary search of this list for the target value 90. Repeat for the target value 44.

2. The method that's usually used to look up an entry in a phone book is not exactly the same as a binary search because, when using a phone book, you don't always go to the midpoint of the sublist being searched. Instead, you estimate the position of the target based on the alphabetical position of the first letter of the person's last name. For example, when you are looking up a number for "Smith," you look toward the middle of the second half of the phone book first, instead of in the middle of the entire book. Suggest a modification of the binary search algorithm that emulates this strategy for a list of names. Is its computational complexity any better than that of the standard binary search?

BASIC SORT ALGORITHMS

Computer scientists have devised many ingenious strategies for sorting a list of items. Several of those are considered here. The algorithms examined in this section are easy to write but are inefficient; the algorithms discussed in the next section are harder to write but are more efficient. (This is a common trade-off.) Each of the Python sort functions that are developed operates on a list of integers and uses a `swap` function to exchange the positions of two items in the list. Here is the code for that function:

```
def swap(lyst, i, j):
    """Exchanges the items at positions i and j."""
    # You could say lyst[i], lyst[j] = lyst[j], lyst[i]
    # but the following code shows what is really going on
    temp = lyst[i]
    lyst[i] = lyst[j]
    lyst[j] = temp
```

Selection Sort

Perhaps the simplest strategy is to search the entire list for the position of the smallest item. If that position does not equal the first position, the algorithm swaps the items at those positions. The algorithm then returns to the second position and repeats this process, swapping the smallest item with the item at the second position, if necessary. When the algorithm reaches the last position in the overall process, the list is sorted. The algorithm is called *selection sort* because each pass through the main loop selects a single item to be moved. Figure 3.8 shows the states of a list of five items after each search and swap pass of a selection sort. The two items just swapped on each pass have asterisks next to them, and the sorted portion of the list is shaded.

UNSORTED LIST	AFTER 1st PASS	AFTER 2nd PASS	AFTER 3rd PASS	AFTER 4th PASS
5	1*	1	1	1
3	3	2*	2	2
1	5*	5	3*	3
2	2	3*	5*	4*
4	4	4	4	5*

Figure 3.8

A trace of data during a selection sort.

© 2014 Cengage Learning®

Here is the Python function for a selection sort:

```
def selectionSort(lyst):
    i = 0
    while i < len(lyst) - 1:              # Do n - 1 searches
        minIndex = i                      # for the smallest
        j = i + 1
        while j < len(lyst):              # Start a search
            if lyst[j] < lyst[minIndex]:
                minIndex = j
            j += 1
        if minIndex != i:                 # Exchange if needed
            swap(lyst, minIndex, i)
        i += 1
```

This function includes a nested loop. For a list of size *n*, the outer loop executes *n* – 1 times. On the first pass through the outer loop, the inner loop executes *n* – 1 times. On the second pass through the outer loop, the inner loop executes *n* – 2 times. On the last pass through the outer loop, the inner loop executes once. Thus, the total number of comparisons for a list of size n is the following:

$$(n - 1) + (n - 2) + \cdots + 1 =$$
$$n (n - 1) / 2 =$$
$$\tfrac{1}{2} n^2 - \tfrac{1}{2} n$$

For large n, you can pick the term with the largest degree and drop the coefficient, so selection sort is $O(n^2)$ in all cases. For large data sets, the cost of swapping items might also be significant. Because data items are swapped only in the outer loop, this additional cost for selection sort is linear in the worst and average cases.

Bubble Sort

Another sort algorithm that is relatively easy to conceive and code is called a bubble sort. Its strategy is to start at the beginning of the list and compare pairs of data items as it moves down to the end. Each time the items in the pair are out of order, the algorithm swaps them. This process has the effect of bubbling the largest items to the end of the list. The algorithm then repeats the process from the beginning of the list and goes to the next-to-last item, and so on, until it begins with the last item. At that point, the list is sorted.

Figure 3.9 shows a trace of the bubbling process through a list of five items. This process makes four passes through a nested loop to bubble the largest item down to the end of the list. Once again, the items just swapped are marked with asterisks, and the sorted portion is shaded.

UNSORTED LIST	AFTER 1st PASS	AFTER 2nd PASS	AFTER 3rd PASS	AFTER 4th PASS
5	4*	4	4	4
4	5*	2*	2	2
2	2	5*	1*	1
1	1	1	5*	3*
3	3	3	3	5*

Figure 3.9
A trace of data during a bubble sort.
© 2014 Cengage Learning®

Here is the Python function for a bubble sort:

```
def bubbleSort(lyst):
    n = len(lyst)
    while n > 1:                    # Do n - 1 bubbles
        i = 1                       # Start each bubble
```

```
    while i < n:
        if lyst[i] < lyst[i - 1]:    # Exchange if needed
            swap(lyst, i, i - 1)
        i += 1
    n -= 1
```

As with the selection sort, a bubble sort has a nested loop. The sorted portion of the list now grows from the end of the list up to the beginning, but the performance of the bubble sort is quite similar to the behavior of a selection sort: the inner loop executes $\frac{1}{2} n^2 - \frac{1}{2} n$ times for a list of size n. Thus, bubble sort is $O(n^2)$. Like selection sort, bubble sort won't perform any swaps if the list is already sorted. However, bubble sort's worst-case behavior for exchanges is greater than linear. The proof of this is left as an exercise for you.

You can make a minor adjustment to the bubble sort to improve its best-case performance to linear. If no swaps occur during a pass through the main loop, then the list is sorted. This can happen on any pass and in the best case will happen on the first pass. You can track the presence of swapping with a Boolean flag and return from the function when the inner loop does not set this flag. Here is the modified bubble sort function:

```
def bubbleSortWithTweak(lyst):
    n = len(lyst)
    while n > 1:
        swapped = False
        i = 1
        while i < n:
            if lyst[i] < lyst[i - 1]:    # Exchange if needed
                swap(lyst, i, i - 1)
                swapped = True
            i += 1
        if not swapped: return            # Return if no swaps
        n -= 1
```

Note that this modification only improves best-case behavior. On the average, the behavior of this version of bubble sort is still $O(n^2)$.

Insertion Sort

Our modified bubble sort performs better than a selection sort for lists that are already sorted. But our modified bubble sort can still perform poorly if many items are out of order in the list. Another algorithm, called an insertion sort, attempts to exploit the partial ordering of the list in a different way. The strategy is as follows:

■ On the ith pass through the list, where i ranges from 1 to $n - 1$, the ith item should be inserted into its proper place among the first i items in the list.

- After the *i*th pass, the first *i* items should be in sorted order.

- This process is analogous to the way in which many people organize playing cards in their hands. That is, if you hold the first $i - 1$ cards in order, you pick the *i*th card and compare it to these cards until its proper spot is found.

- As with our other sort algorithms, insertion sort consists of two loops. The outer loop traverses the positions from 1 to $n - 1$. For each position *i* in this loop, you save the item and start the inner loop at position $i - 1$. For each position *j* in this loop, you move the item to position $j + 1$ until you find the insertion point for the saved (*i*th) item.

Here is the code for the insertionSort function:

```
def insertionSort(lyst):
    i = 1
    while i < len(lyst):
        itemToInsert = lyst[i]
        j = i - 1
        while j >= 0:
            if itemToInsert < lyst[j]:
                lyst[j + 1] = lyst[j]
                j -= 1
            else:
                break
        lyst[j + 1] = itemToInsert
        i += 1
```

Figure 3.10 shows the states of a list of five items after each pass through the outer loop of an insertion sort. The item to be inserted on the next pass is marked with an arrow; after it is inserted, this item is marked with an asterisk.

UNSORTED LIST	AFTER 1st PASS	AFTER 2nd PASS	AFTER 3rd PASS	AFTER 4th PASS
2	2	1*	1	1
5←	5 (no insertion)	2	2	2
1	1←	5	4*	3*
4	4	4←	5	4
3	3	3	3←	5

Figure 3.10

A trace of data during bubble sort.

© 2014 Cengage Learning®

Once again, analysis focuses on the nested loop. The outer loop executes $n - 1$ times. In the worst case, when all the data are out of order, the inner loop iterates once on the first pass through the outer loop, twice on the second pass, and so on, for a total of $\frac{1}{2} n^2 - \frac{1}{2} n$ times. Thus, the worst-case behavior of insertion sort is $O(n^2)$.

The more items in the list that are in order, the better insertion sort gets until, in the best case of a sorted list, the sort's behavior is linear. In the average case, however, insertion sort is still quadratic.

Best-Case, Worst-Case, and Average-Case Performance Revisited

As mentioned earlier, for many algorithms, you cannot apply a single measure of complexity to all cases. Sometimes an algorithm's behavior improves or gets worse when it encounters a particular arrangement of data. For example, the bubble sort algorithm can terminate as soon as the list becomes sorted. If the input list is already sorted, the bubble sort requires approximately n comparisons. In many other cases, however, bubble sort requires approximately n^2 comparisons. Clearly, you may need a more detailed analysis to make programmers aware of these special cases.

As discussed earlier, thorough analysis of an algorithm's complexity divides its behavior into three types of cases:

- **Best case**—Under what circumstances does an algorithm do the least amount of work? What is the algorithm's complexity in this best case?

- **Worst case**—Under what circumstances does an algorithm do the most amount of work? What is the algorithm's complexity in this worst case?

- **Average case**—Under what circumstances does an algorithm do a typical amount of work? What is the algorithm's complexity in this typical case?

You'll now review three examples of this kind of analysis for a search for a minimum, sequential search, and bubble sort.

Because the search for a minimum algorithm must visit each number in the list, unless it is sorted, the algorithm is always linear. Therefore, its best-case, worst-case, and average-case performances are $O(n)$.

Sequential search is a bit different. The algorithm stops and returns a result as soon as it finds the target item. Clearly, in the best case, the target element is in the first position. In the worst case, the target is in the last position. Therefore, the algorithm's best-case performance is $O(1)$ and its worst-case performance is $O(n)$. To compute the average-case performance, you add all the comparisons that must be made to locate a target in each position and divide by n. This is $(1 + 2 + \cdots + n)/n$, or $n/2$. Therefore, by approximation, the average-case performance of sequential search is also $O(n)$.

The smarter version of bubble sort can terminate as soon as the list becomes sorted. In the best case, this happens when the input list is already sorted. Therefore, bubble sort's best-case performance is O(n). However, this case is rare (1 out of $n!$). In the worst case, even this version of bubble sort has to bubble each item down to its proper position in the list. The algorithm's worst-case performance is clearly O(n^2). Bubble sort's average-case performance is closer to O(n^2) than to O(n), although the demonstration of this fact is a bit more involved than it is for sequential search.

As you will see, there are algorithms whose best-case and average-case performances are similar but whose performance can degrade to a worst case. Whether you are choosing an algorithm or developing a new one, it is important to be aware of these distinctions.

Exercises 3.4

1. Which configuration of data in a list causes the smallest number of exchanges in a selection sort? Which configuration of data causes the largest number of exchanges?

2. Explain the role that the number of data exchanges plays in the analysis of selection sort and bubble sort. What role, if any, does the size of the data objects play?

3. Explain why the modified bubble sort still exhibits O(n^2) behavior on the average.

4. Explain why insertion sort works well on partially sorted lists.

FASTER SORTING

The three sort algorithms considered thus far have O(n^2) running times. There are several variations on these sort algorithms, some of which are marginally faster, but they, too, are O(n^2) in the worst and average cases. However, you can take advantage of some better algorithms that are O($n \log n$). The secret to these better algorithms is a divide-and-conquer strategy. That is, each algorithm finds a way of breaking the list into smaller sublists. These sublists are then sorted recursively. Ideally, if the number of these subdivisions is $\log(n)$ and the amount of work needed to rearrange the data on each subdivision is n, then the total complexity of such a sort algorithm is O($n \log n$). In Table 3.3, you can see that the growth rate of work of an O($n \log n$) algorithm is much slower than that of an O(n^2) algorithm.

Table 3.3 Comparing $n \log n$ and n^2

n	n log n	n²
512	4,608	262,144
1,024	10,240	1,048,576
2,048	22,458	4,194,304
8,192	106,496	67,108,864
16,384	229,376	268,435,456
32,768	491,520	1,073,741,824

© 2014 Cengage Learning®

This section examines two recursive sort algorithms that break the n^2 barrier—quicksort and merge sort.

Overview of Quicksort

Here is an outline of the strategy used in the *quicksort* algorithm:

1. Begin by selecting the item at the list's midpoint. This item is called the *pivot*. (Later, this chapter covers alternative ways to choose the pivot.)

2. Partition items in the list so that all items less than the pivot are moved to the left of the pivot, and the rest are moved to its right. The final position of the pivot itself varies, depending on the actual items involved. For instance, the pivot ends up being rightmost in the list if it is the largest item and leftmost if it is the smallest. But wherever the pivot ends up, that is its final position in the fully sorted list.

3. Divide and conquer. Reapply the process recursively to the sublists formed by splitting the list at the pivot. One sublist consists of all items to the left of the pivot (now the smaller ones), and the other sublist has all items to the right (now the larger ones).

4. The process terminates each time it encounters a sublist with fewer than two items.

Partitioning

From the programmer's perspective, the most complicated part of the algorithm is the operation of partitioning the items in a sublist. There are two principal ways of doing this. Informally, what follows is a description of the easier method as it applies to any sublist:

1. Swap the pivot with the last item in the sublist.

2. Establish a boundary between the items known to be less than the pivot and the rest of the items. Initially, this boundary is positioned immediately before the first item.

3. Starting with the first item in the sublist, scan across the sublist. Every time you encounter an item less than the pivot, swap it with the first item after the boundary and advance the boundary.

4. Finish by swapping the pivot with the first item after the boundary.

Figure 3.11 illustrates these steps as applied to the numbers 12 19 17 18 14 11 15 13 16. In Step 1, the pivot is established and swapped with the last item. In Step 2, the boundary is established before the first item. In Steps 3–6, the sublist is scanned for items less than the pivot, these are swapped with the first item after the boundary, and the boundary is advanced. Notice that items to the left of the boundary are less than the pivot at all times. Finally, in Step 7, the pivot is swapped with the first item after the boundary, and the sublist has been successfully partitioned.

Let the sublist consist of the numbers shown with a pivot of 14.		12	19	17	18	14	11	15	13	16
Swap the pivot with the last item.		12	19	17	18	16	11	15	13	14
Establish the boundary before the first item.	:	12	19	17	18	16	11	15	13	14
Scan for the first item less than the pivot.	:	12	19	17	18	16	11	15	13	14
Swap this item with the first item after the boundary. In this example, the item gets swapped with itself.	:	12	19	17	18	16	11	15	13	14
Advance the boundary.	12	:	19	17	18	16	11	15	13	14
Scan for the next item less than the pivot.	12	:	19	17	18	16	11	15	13	14
Swap this item with the first item after the boundary.	12	:	11	17	18	16	19	15	13	14
Advance the boundary.	12	11	:	17	18	16	19	15	13	14
Scan for the next item less than the pivot.	12	11	:	17	18	16	19	15	13	14
Swap this item with the first item after the boundary.	12	11	:	13	18	16	19	15	17	14
Advance the boundary.	12	11	13	:	18	16	19	15	17	14
Scan for the next item less than the pivot; however, there is not one.	12	11	13	:	18	16	19	15	17	14
Interchange the pivot with the first item after the boundary. At this point, all items less than the pivot are to the pivot's left and the rest are to its right.	12	11	13	:	14	16	19	15	17	18

Figure 3.11

Partitioning a sublist.

© 2014 Cengage Learning®

After you have portioned a sublist, reapply the process to its left and right sublists (12 11 13 and 16 19 15 17 18) and so on, until the sublists have lengths of at most one.

Complexity Analysis of Quicksort

Now you'll see an informal analysis of the quicksort's complexity. During the first partition operation, you scan all the items from the beginning of the list to its end. Thus, the amount of work during this operation is proportional to n, the list's length.

The amount of work after this partition is proportional to the left sublist's length plus the right sublist's length, which together yield $n - 1$. And when these sublists are divided, there are four pieces whose combined length is approximately n, so the combined work is proportional to n yet again. As the list is divided into more pieces, the total work remains proportional to n.

To complete the analysis, you need to determine how many times the lists are partitioned. Make the optimistic assumption that, each time, the dividing line between the new sublists turns out to be as close to the center of the current sublist as possible. In practice, this is not usually the case. You already know from the discussion of the binary search algorithm that when you divide a list in half repeatedly, you arrive at a single element in about $\log_2 n$ steps. Thus, the algorithm is $O(n \log n)$ in the best-case performance.

For the worst-case performance, consider the case of a list that is already sorted. If the pivot element chosen is the first element, then there are $n - 1$ elements to its right on the first partition, $n - 2$ elements to its right on the second partition, and so on, as shown in Figure 3.12.

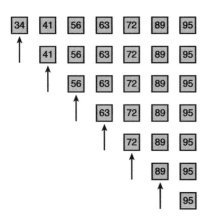

Figure 3.12
A worst-case scenario for quicksort (arrows indicate pivot elements).
© 2014 Cengage Learning®

Although no elements are exchanged, the total number of partitions is $n - 1$ and the total number of comparisons performed is $\frac{1}{2} n^2 - \frac{1}{2} n$, the same number as in selection sort and bubble sort. Thus, in the worst case, the quicksort algorithm is $O(n^2)$.

If you implement a quicksort as a recursive algorithm, your analysis must also consider memory usage for the call stack. Each recursive call requires a constant amount of memory for a stack frame, and there are two recursive calls after each partition. Thus, memory usage is O(log n) in the best case and O(n) in the worst case.

Although the worst-case performance of quicksort is rare, programmers certainly prefer to avoid it. Choosing the pivot at the first or last position is not a wise strategy. Other methods of choosing the pivot, such as selecting a random position or choosing the median of the first, middle, and last elements, can help to approximate O(n log n) performance in the average case.

Implementation of Quicksort

The quicksort algorithm is most easily coded using a recursive approach. The following script defines a top-level quicksort function for the client, a recursive quicksortHelper function to hide the extra arguments for the endpoints of a sublist, and a partition function. The script runs quicksort on a list of 20 randomly ordered integers.

```
def quicksort(lyst):
    quicksortHelper(lyst, 0, len(lyst) - 1)

def quicksortHelper(lyst, left, right):
    if left < right:
        pivotLocation = partition(lyst, left, right)
        quicksortHelper(lyst, left, pivotLocation - 1)
        quicksortHelper(lyst, pivotLocation + 1, right)

def partition(lyst, left, right):
    # Find the pivot and exchange it with the last item
    middle = (left + right) // 2
    pivot = lyst[middle]
    lyst[middle] = lyst[right]
    lyst[right] = pivot
    # Set boundary point to first position
    boundary = left
    # Move items less than pivot to the left
    for index in range(left, right):
        if lyst[index] < pivot:
            swap(lyst, index, boundary)
            boundary += 1
    # Exchange the pivot item and the boundary item
    swap (lyst, right, boundary)
    return boundary
```

```
# Earlier definition of the swap function goes here
import random

def main(size = 20, sort = quicksort):
    lyst = []
    for count in range(size):
        lyst.append(random.randint(1, size + 1))
    print(lyst)
    sort(lyst)
    print(lyst)

if __name__ == "__main__":
    main()
```

Merge Sort

Another algorithm called *merge sort* employs a recursive, divide-and-conquer strategy to break the $O(n^2)$ barrier. Here is an informal summary of the algorithm:

■ Compute the middle position of a list and recursively sort its left and right sublists (divide and conquer).

■ Merge the two sorted sublists back into a single sorted list.

■ Stop the process when sublists can no longer be subdivided.

Three Python functions collaborate in this top-level design strategy:

■ mergeSort—The function called by users.

■ mergeSortHelper—A helper function that hides the extra parameters required by recursive calls.

■ merge—A function that implements the merging process.

Implementing the Merging Process

The merging process uses an array of the same size as the list. (Chapter 4 explores arrays in detail.) This array is called the copyBuffer. To avoid the overhead of allocating and deallocating the copyBuffer each time merge is called, the buffer is allocated once in mergeSort and subsequently passed as an argument to mergeSortHelper and merge. Each time mergeSortHelper is called, it needs to know the bounds of the sublist with which it is working. These bounds are provided by two other parameters: low and high. Here is the code for mergeSort:

```
from arrays import Array
def mergeSort(lyst):
    # lyst          list being sorted
    # copyBuffer temporary space needed during merge
    copyBuffer = Array(len(lyst))
    mergeSortHelper(lyst, copyBuffer, 0, len(lyst) - 1)
```

After checking that it has been passed a sublist of at least two items, mergeSortHelper computes the midpoint of the sublist, recursively sorts the portions below and above the midpoint, and calls merge to merge the results. Here is the code for mergeSortHelper:

```
def mergeSortHelper(lyst, copyBuffer, low, high):
    # lyst          list being sorted
    # copyBuffer temp space needed during merge
    # low, high    bounds of sublist
    # middle        midpoint of sublist
    if low < high:
        middle = (low + high) // 2
        mergeSortHelper(lyst, copyBuffer, low, middle)
        mergeSortHelper(lyst, copyBuffer, middle + 1, high)
        merge(lyst, copyBuffer, low, middle, high)
```

Figure 3.13 shows the sublists generated during recursive calls to mergeSortHelper, starting from a list of eight items. Note that, in this example, the sublists are evenly subdivided at each level and there are 2^k sublists to be merged at level k. Had the length of the initial list not been a power of two, then an exactly even subdivision would not have been achieved at each level and the last level would not have contained a full complement of sublists. Figure 3.14 traces the process of merging the sublists generated in Figure 3.13.

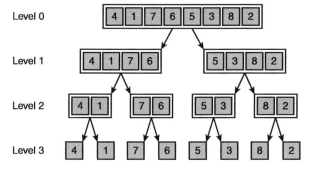

Figure 3.13
Sublists generated during calls of mergeSortHelper.
© 2014 Cengage Learning®

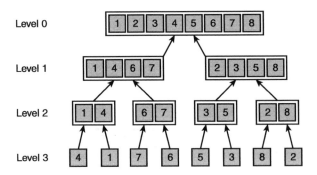

Figure 3.14

Merging the sublists generated during a merge sort.

© 2014 Cengage Learning®

Finally, here is the code for the merge function:

```
def merge(lyst, copyBuffer, low, middle, high):
    # lyst          list that is being sorted
    # copyBuffer    temp space needed during the merge process
    # low           beginning of first sorted sublist
    # middle        end of first sorted sublist
    # middle + 1    beginning of second sorted sublist
    # high          end of second sorted sublist

    # Initialize i1 and i2 to the first items in each sublist
    i1 = low
    i2 = middle + 1

    # Interleave items from the sublists into the
    # copyBuffer in such a way that order is maintained.
    for i in range(low, high + 1):
        if i1 > middle:
            copyBuffer[i] = lyst[i2]  # First sublist exhausted
            i2 += 1
        elif i2 > high:
            copyBuffer[i] = lyst[i1]  # Second sublist exhausted
            i1 += 1
        elif lyst[i1] < lyst[i2]:
            copyBuffer[i] = lyst[i1]  # Item in first sublist <
            i1 += 1
        else:
            copyBuffer[i] = lyst[i2]  # Item in second sublist <
            i2 += 1

    for i in range(low, high + 1):      # Copy sorted items back to
        lyst[i] = copyBuffer[i]         # proper position in lyst
```

The merge function combines two sorted sublists into a larger sorted sublist. The first sublist lies between low and middle and the second between middle + 1 and high. The process consists of three steps:

1. Set up index pointers to the first items in each sublist. These are at positions low and middle + 1.

2. Starting with the first item in each sublist, repeatedly compare items. Copy the smaller item from its sublist to the copy buffer and advance to the next item in the sublist. Repeat until all items have been copied from both sublists. If the end of one sublist is reached before the other's, finish by copying the remaining items from the other sublist.

3. Copy the portion of copyBuffer between low and high back to the corresponding positions in lyst.

Complexity Analysis for Merge Sort

The running time of the merge function is dominated by the two for statements, each of which loops (high - low + 1) times. Consequently, the function's running time is O(high - low), and all the merges at a single level take O(n) time. Because mergeSortHelper splits sublists as evenly as possible at each level, the number of levels is O(log n), and the maximum running time for this function is O(n log n) in all cases.

The merge sort has two space requirements that depend on the list's size. First, O(log n) space is required on the call stack to support recursive calls. Second, O(n) space is used by the copy buffer.

Exercises 3.5

1. Describe the strategy of quicksort and explain why it can reduce the time complexity of sorting from O(n^2) to O(n log n).

2. Why is quicksort not O(n log n) in all cases? Describe the worst-case situation for quicksort and give a list of 10 integers, 1–10, that would produce this behavior.

3. The partition operation in quicksort chooses the item at the midpoint as the pivot. Describe two other strategies for selecting a pivot value.

4. Sandra has a bright idea: When the length of a sublist in quicksort is less than a certain number—say, 30 elements—run an insertion sort to process that sublist. Explain why this is a bright idea.

5. Why is merge sort an O(n log n) algorithm in the worst case?

AN EXPONENTIAL ALGORITHM: RECURSIVE FIBONACCI

Earlier in this chapter, you ran the recursive Fibonacci function to obtain a count of the recursive calls with various problem sizes. You saw that the number of calls seemed to grow much faster than the square of the problem size. Here is the code for the function once again:

```
def fib(n):
    """The recursive Fibonacci function."""
    if n < 3:
        return 1
    else:
        return fib(n - 1) + fib(n - 2)
```

Another way to illustrate this rapid growth of work is to display a *call tree* for the function for a given problem size. Figure 3.15 shows the calls involved when you use the recursive function to compute the sixth Fibonacci number. To keep the diagram reasonably compact, you write (6) instead of fib(6).

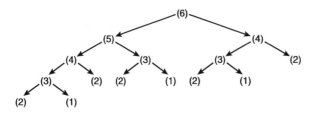

Figure 3.15

A call tree for fib(6).

© 2014 Cengage Learning®

Note that fib(4) requires only 4 recursive calls, which seems linear, but fib(6) requires 2 calls of fib(4), among a total of 14 recursive calls. Indeed, it gets much worse as the problem size grows, with possibly many repetitions of the same subtrees in the call tree.

Exactly how bad is this behavior, then? If the call tree were fully balanced, with the bottom two levels of calls completely filled in, a call with an argument of 6 would generate $2 + 4 + 8 + 16 = 30$ recursive calls. Note that the number of calls at each filled level is twice that of the level above it. Thus, the number of recursive calls generally is $2^{n+1} - 2$ in fully balanced call trees, where n is the argument at the top or the root of the call tree. This is clearly the behavior of an exponential, $O(k^n)$ algorithm. Although the bottom two levels of the call tree for recursive Fibonacci are not completely filled in, its call tree is close enough in shape to a fully balanced tree to rank recursive Fibonacci as an exponential algorithm. The constant k for recursive Fibonacci is approximately 1.63.

Exponential algorithms are generally impractical to run with any but very small problem sizes. Although recursive Fibonacci is elegant in its design, there is a less beautiful but much faster version that uses a loop to run in linear time. (See the next section.)

Alternatively, recursive functions that are called repeatedly with the same arguments, such as the Fibonacci function, can be made more efficient by a technique called *memoization*. According to this technique, the program maintains a table of the values for each argument used with the function. Before the function recursively computes a value for a given argument, it checks the table to see if that argument already has a value. If so, that value is simply returned. If not, the computation proceeds and the argument and value are added to the table afterward.

Computer scientists devote much effort to the development of fast algorithms. As a rule, any reduction in the order of magnitude of complexity, say, from $O(n^2)$ to $O(n)$, is preferable to a "tweak" of code that reduces the constant of proportionality.

Converting Fibonacci to a Linear Algorithm

Although the recursive Fibonacci function reflects the simplicity and elegance of the recursive definition of the Fibonacci sequence, the run-time performance of this function is unacceptable. A different algorithm improves on this performance by several orders of magnitude and, in fact, reduces the complexity to linear time. In this section, you develop this alternative algorithm and assess its performance.

Recall that the first two numbers in the Fibonacci sequence are 1s, and each number after that is the sum of the previous two numbers. Thus, the new algorithm starts a loop if n is at least the third Fibonacci number. This number will be at least the sum of the first two $(1 + 1 = 2)$. The loop computes this sum and then performs two replacements: the first number becomes the second one, and the second one becomes the sum just computed. The loop counts from 3 through n. The sum at the end of the loop is the nth Fibonacci number. Here is the pseudocode for this algorithm:

```
Set sum to 1
Set first to 1
Set second to 1
Set count to 3
While count <= N
    Set sum to first + second
    Set first to second
    Set second to sum
    Increment count
```

The Python function `fib` now uses a loop. You can test the function within the script used for the earlier version. Here is the code for the function, followed by the output of the script:

```
def fib(n, counter):
    """Count the number of iterations in the Fibonacci
    function."""
    sum = 1
    first = 1
    second = 1
    count = 3
    while count <= n:
        counter.increment()
        sum = first + second
        first = second
        second = sum
        count += 1
    return sum
```

```
Problem Size     Iterations
        2             0
        4             2
        8             6
       16            14
       32            30
```

As you can see, the performance of the new version of the function has improved to linear. Removing recursion by converting a recursive algorithm to one based on a loop can often, but not always, reduce its run-time complexity.

CASE STUDY: AN ALGORITHM PROFILER

Profiling is the process of measuring an algorithm's performance by counting instructions or timing execution. In this case study, you develop a program to profile sort algorithms.

Request

Write a program that allows a programmer to profile different sort algorithms.

Analysis

The profiler should allow a programmer to run a sort algorithm on a list of numbers. The profiler can track the algorithm's running time, the number of comparisons, and the number of exchanges. In addition, when the algorithm exchanges two values, the profiler can print a trace of the list. The programmer can provide his own list of numbers to the profiler or ask the profiler to generate a list of randomly ordered numbers of a given size. The programmer can also ask for a list of unique numbers or a list that contains duplicate values. For ease of use, the profiler allows the programmer to specify most of these features as options before the algorithm is run. The default behavior is to run the algorithm on a randomly ordered list of 10 unique numbers where the running time, comparisons, and exchanges are tracked.

The profiler is an instance of the class `Profiler`. The programmer profiles a sort function by running the profiler's `test` method with the function as the first argument and any of the options mentioned earlier. The next session shows several test runs of the profiler with the selection sort algorithm and different options:

```
>>> from profiler import Profiler
>>> from algorithms import selectionSort

>>> p = Profiler()

>>> p.test(selectionSort)        # Default behavior
Problem size: 10
Elapsed time: 0.0
Comparisons: 45
Exchanges:   7

>>> p.test(selectionSort, size = 5, trace = True)
[4, 2, 3, 5, 1]
[1, 2, 3, 5, 4]
Problem size: 5
Elapsed time: 0.117
Comparisons: 10
Exchanges:   2

>>> p.test(selectionSort, size = 100)
Problem size: 100
Elapsed time: 0.044
Comparisons: 4950
Exchanges:   97

>>> p.test(selectionSort, size = 1000)
Problem size: 1000
Elapsed time: 1.628
Comparisons: 499500
Exchanges:   995

>>> p.test(selectionSort, size = 10000,
           exch = False, comp = False)
Problem size: 10000
Elapsed time: 111.077
```

The programmer configures a sort algorithm to be profiled as follows:

1. Define a sort function and include a second parameter, a `Profiler` object, in the sort function's header.

2. In the sort algorithm's code, run the methods `comparison()` and `exchange()` with the `Profiler` object where relevant, to count comparisons and exchanges.

The interface for the `Profiler` class is listed in Table 3.4.

Table 3.4 The Interface for the Profiler Class

Profiler Method	What It Does
`p.test(function, lyst = None, size = 10, unique = True, comp = True, exch = True, trace = False)`	Runs `function` with the given settings and prints the results.
`p.comparison()`	Increments the number of comparisons if that option has been specified.
`p.exchange()`	Increments the number of exchanges if that option has been specified.
`p.__str__()`	Same as `str(p)`. Returns a string representation of the results, depending on the options.

© 2014 Cengage Learning®

Design

The programmer uses two modules:

■ `profiler`—This module defines the `Profiler` class.

■ `algorithms`—This module defines the sort functions, as configured for profiling.

The sort functions have the same design as those discussed earlier in this chapter, except that they receive a `Profiler` object as an additional parameter. The `Profiler` methods `comparison` and `exchange` are run with this object whenever a sort function performs a comparison or an exchange of data values, respectively. In fact, any list-processing algorithm can be added to this module and profiled just by including a `Profiler` parameter and running its two methods when comparisons or exchanges are made.

As shown in the earlier session, you import the `Profiler` class and the `algorithms` module into a Python shell and perform the testing at the shell prompt. The profiler's test method sets up the `Profiler` object, runs the function to be profiled, and prints the results.

Implementation (Coding)

Here is a partial implementation of the `algorithms` module. Most of the sort algorithms developed earlier in this chapter have been omitted. However, `selectionSort` is included to show how the statistics are updated.

```
"""
File: algorithms.py
Algorithms configured for profiling.
"""

def selectionSort(lyst, profiler):
    i = 0
    while i < len(lyst) - 1:
        minIndex = i
        j = i + 1
        while j < len(lyst):
            profiler.comparison()            # Count
            if lyst[j] < lyst[minIndex]:
                minIndex = j
            j += 1
        if minIndex != i:
            swap(lyst, minIndex, i, profiler)
        i += 1

def swap(lyst, i, j, profiler):
    """Exchanges the elements at positions i and j."""
    profiler.exchange()                      # Count
    temp = lyst[i]
    lyst[i] = lyst[j]
    lyst[j] = temp

# Testing code can go here, optionally
```

The `Profiler` class includes the four methods listed in the interface as well as some helper methods for managing the clock.

```
"""
File: profiler.py

Defines a class for profiling sort algorithms.
A Profiler object tracks the list, the number of comparisons
and exchanges, and the running time. The Profiler can also
print a trace and can create a list of unique or duplicate
numbers.
```

Example use:

```
from profiler import Profiler
from algorithms import selectionSort

p = Profiler()
p.test(selectionSort, size = 15, comp = True,
        exch = True, trace = True)
"""

import time
import random

class Profiler(object):

    def test(self, function, lyst = None, size = 10,
            unique = True, comp = True, exch = True,
            trace = False):
        """
        function: the algorithm being profiled
        target: the search target if profiling a search
        lyst: allows the caller to use her list
        size: the size of the list, 10 by default
        unique: if True, list contains unique integers
        comp: if True, count comparisons
        exch: if True, count exchanges
        trace: if True, print the list after each exchange

        Run the function with the given attributes and print
        its profile results.
        """
        self._comp = comp
        self._exch = exch
        self._trace = trace
        if lyst != None:
            self._lyst = lyst
        elif unique:
            self._lyst = range(1, size + 1)
            random.shuffle(self._lyst)
        else:
            self._lyst = []
            for count in range(size):
                self._lyst.append(random.randint(1, size))
        self._exchCount = 0
        self._cmpCount = 0
        self._startClock()
        function(self._lyst, self)
```

```
        self._stopClock()
        print(self)

    def exchange(self):
        """Counts exchanges if on."""
        if self._exch:
            self._exchCount += 1
        if self._trace:
            print(self._lyst)

    def comparison(self):
        """Counts comparisons if on."""
        if self._comp:
            self._cmpCount += 1

    def _startClock(self):
        """Record the starting time."""
        self._start = time.time()

    def _stopClock(self):
        """Stops the clock and computes the elapsed time
        in seconds, to the nearest millisecond."""
        self._elapsedTime = round(time.time() - self._start, 3)

    def __str__(self):
        """Returns the results as a string."""
        result = "Problem size: "
        result += str(len(self._lyst)) + "\n"
        result += "Elapsed time: "
        result += str(self._elapsedTime) + "\n"
        if self._comp:
            result += "Comparisons: "
            result += str(self._cmpCount) + "\n"
        if self._exch:
            result += "Exchanges:      "
            result += str(self._exchCount) + "\n"
        return result
```

SUMMARY

- Different algorithms for solving the same problem can be ranked according to the time and memory resources that they require. Generally, algorithms that require less running time and less memory are considered better than those that require more of these resources. However, there is often a trade-off between the two types of resources. Running time can occasionally be improved at the cost of using more memory, or memory usage can be improved at the cost of slower running times.

■ You can measure the running time of an algorithm empirically with the computer's clock. However, these times will vary with the hardware and the types of programming language used.

■ Counting instructions provide another empirical measurement of the amount of work that an algorithm does. Instruction counts can show increases or decreases in the rate of growth of an algorithm's work, independently of hardware and software platforms.

■ The rate of growth of an algorithm's work can be expressed as a function of the size of its problem instances. Complexity analysis examines the algorithm's code to derive these expressions. Such an expression enables the programmer to predict how well or poorly an algorithm will perform on any computer.

■ Big-O notation is a common way of expressing an algorithm's run-time behavior. This notation uses the form $O(f(n))$, where n is the size of the algorithm's problem and $f(n)$ is a function expressing the amount of work done to solve it.

■ Common expressions of run-time behavior are $O(\log_2 n)$ (logarithmic), $O(n)$ (linear), $O(n^2)$ (quadratic), and $O(k^n)$ (exponential).

■ An algorithm can have different best-case, worst-case, and average-case behaviors. For example, bubble sort and insertion sort are linear in the best case, but quadratic in the average and worst cases.

■ In general, it is better to try to reduce the order of an algorithm's complexity than it is to try to enhance performance by tweaking the code.

■ A binary search is substantially faster than a sequential search. However, the data in the search space for a binary search must be in sorted order.

■ The $n \log n$ sort algorithms use a recursive, divide-and-conquer strategy to break the n^2 barrier. Quicksort rearranges items around a pivot item and recursively sorts the sublists on either side of the pivot. Merge sort splits a list, recursively sorts each half, and merges the results.

■ Exponential algorithms are primarily of theoretical interest and are impractical to run with large problem sizes.

REVIEW QUESTIONS

1. Timing an algorithm with different problem sizes

   a. Can give you a general idea of the algorithm's run-time behavior

   b. Can give you an idea of the algorithm's run-time behavior on a particular hardware platform and a particular software platform

2. Counting instructions

   a. Provide the same data on different hardware and software platforms

   b. Can demonstrate the impracticality of exponential algorithms with large prob-
      lem sizes

3. The expressions $O(n)$, $O(n^2)$, and $O(k^n)$ are, respectively,

   a. Exponential, linear, and quadratic

   b. Linear, quadratic, and exponential

   c. Logarithmic, linear, and quadratic

4. A binary search assumes that the data are

   a. Arranged in no particular order

   b. Sorted

5. A selection sort makes at most

   a. n^2 exchanges of data items

   b. n exchanges of data items

6. The best-case behavior of insertion sort and modified bubble sort is

   a. Linear

   b. Quadratic

   c. Exponential

7. An example of an algorithm whose best-case, average-case, and worst-case
   behaviors are the same is

   a. Sequential search

   b. Selection sort

   c. Quicksort

8. Generally speaking, it is better to

   a. Tweak an algorithm to shave a few seconds of running time

   b. Choose an algorithm with the lowest order of computational complexity

9. The recursive Fibonacci function makes approximately

   a. n^2 recursive calls for problems of a large size n

   b. 2^n recursive calls for problems of a large size n

10. Each level in a completely filled binary call tree has

    a. Twice as many calls as the level above it

    b. The same number of calls as the level above it

PROJECTS

1. A sequential search of a sorted list can halt when the target is less than a given element in the list. Define a modified version of this algorithm and state the computational complexity, using big-O notation, of its best-, worst-, and average-case performances.

2. The list method reverse reverses the elements in the list. Define a function named reverse that reverses the elements in its list argument (without using the method reverse). Try to make this function as efficient as possible, and state its computational complexity using big-O notation.

3. Python's pow function returns the result of raising a number to a given power. Define a function expo that performs this task and state its computational complexity using big-O notation. The first argument of this function is the number, and the second argument is the exponent (nonnegative numbers only). You can use either a loop or a recursive function in your implementation.

4. An alternative strategy for the expo function uses the following recursive definition:

expo(number, exponent)

= 1, when exponent = 0

= number * expo(number, exponent – 1), when exponent is odd

= (expo(number, exponent / 2))^2, when exponent is even

Define a recursive function expo that uses this strategy, and state its computational complexity using big-O notation.

5. Python's list method sort includes the keyword argument reverse, whose default value is False. The programmer can override this value to sort a list in descending order. Modify the selectionSort function discussed in this chapter so that it allows the programmer to supply this additional argument to redirect the sort.

6. Modify the recursive Fibonacci function to employ the memoization technique discussed in this chapter. The function should expect a dictionary as an additional argument. The top-level call of the function receives an empty dictionary. The function's keys and values should be the arguments and values of the recursive

calls. Also, use the counter object discussed in this chapter to count the number of recursive calls.

7. Profile the performance of the memoized version of the Fibonacci function defined in Project 6. The function should count the number of recursive calls. State its computational complexity using big-O notation, and justify your answer.

8. The function makeRandomList creates and returns a list of numbers of a given size (its argument). The numbers in the list are unique and range from 1 through the size. They are placed in random order. Here is the code for the function:

```
def makeRandomList(size):
    lyst = []
    for count in range(size):
        while True:
            number = random.randint(1, size)
            if not number in lyst:
                lyst.append(number)
                break
    return lyst
```

You can assume that range, randint, and append are constant time functions. You can also assume that random.randint more rarely returns duplicate numbers as the range between its arguments increases. State the computational complexity of this function using big-O notation, and justify your answer.

9. Modify the quicksort function so that it calls insertion sort to sort any sublist whose size is less than 50 items. Compare the performance of this version with that of the original one, using data sets of 50, 500, and 5,000 items. Then adjust the threshold for using the insertion sort to determine an optimal setting.

10. A computer supports the calls of recursive functions using a structure known as the call stack. Generally speaking, the computer reserves a constant amount of memory for each call of a function. Thus, the memory used by a recursive function can be subjected to complexity analysis. State the computational complexity of the memory used by the recursive factorial and Fibonacci functions.

CHAPTER 4

ARRAYS AND LINKED STRUCTURES

The terms *data structure* and *concrete data type* refer to the internal representation of a collection's data. The two data structures most often used to implement collections in programming languages are *arrays* and *linked structures*. These two types of structures take different approaches to storing and accessing data in the computer's memory. These approaches in turn lead to different space/time trade-offs in the algorithms that manipulate the collections. This chapter examines the data organization and concrete details of processing that are particular to arrays and linked structures. Their use in implementing various types of collections is discussed in later chapters.

THE ARRAY DATA STRUCTURE

An array represents a sequence of items that can be accessed or replaced at given index positions. You are probably thinking that this description resembles that of a Python list. In fact, the data structure underlying a Python list is an array. Although Python programmers would typically use a list where you might use an array, the array rather than the list is the primary implementing structure in the collections of Python and many other programming languages. Therefore, you need to become familiar with the array way of thinking.

Some of what this chapter has to say about arrays also applies to Python lists, but arrays are much more restrictive. A programmer can access and replace an array's items at given positions, examine an array's length, and obtain its string representation—but that's all. The programmer cannot add or remove positions or make the length of the array larger or smaller. Typically, the length or capacity of an array is fixed when it is created.

Python's `array` module does include an `array` class, which behaves more like a list but is limited to storing numbers. For purposes of the discussion that follows, you will define a new class named `Array` that adheres to the restrictions mentioned earlier but can hold items of any type. Ironically, this `Array` class uses a Python list to hold its items. The class defines methods that allow clients to use the subscript operator `[]`, the `len` function, the `str` function, and the `for` loop with array objects. The `Array` methods needed for these operations are listed in Table 4.1. The variable `a` in the left column refers to an `Array` object.

Table 4.1   Array Operations and the Methods of the Array Class

User's Array Operation	Method in the Array Class
a = Array(10)	__init__(capacity, fillValue = None)
len(a)	__len__()
str(a)	__str__()
for item in a:	__iter__()
a[index]	__getitem__(index)
a[index] = newItem	__setitem__(index, newItem)

© 2014 Cengage Learning®

When Python encounters an operation in the left column of Table 4.1, it automatically calls the corresponding method in the right column with the `Array` object. For example, Python automatically calls the `Array` object's __iter__ method when the `Array` object is traversed in a `for` loop. Note that the programmer must specify the capacity or the physical size of an array when it is created. The default fill value, `None`, can be overridden to provide another fill value if desired.

Here is the code for the `Array` class (in `arrays.py`):

```
"""
File: arrays.py

An Array is like a list, but the client can use
only [], len, iter, and str.

To instantiate, use

<variable> = Array(<capacity>, <optional fill value>)

The fill value is None by default.
"""
```

```
class Array(object):
    """Represents an array."""

    def __init__(self, capacity, fillValue = None):
        """Capacity is the static size of the array.
        fillValue is placed at each position."""
        self._items = list()
        for count in range(capacity):
            self._items.append(fillValue)

    def __len__(self):
        """-> The capacity of the array."""
        return len(self._items)

    def __str__(self):
        """-> The string representation of the array."""
        return str(self._items)

    def __iter__(self):
        """Supports traversal with a for loop."""
        return iter(self._items)

    def __getitem__(self, index):
        """Subscript operator for access at index."""
        return self._items[index]

    def __setitem__(self, index, newItem):
        """Subscript operator for replacement at index."""
        self._items[index] = newItem
```

Here is a shell session that shows the use of an array:

```
>>> from arrays import Array
>>> a = Array(5)                    # Create an array with 5 positions
>>> len(a)                          # Show the number of positions
5
>>> print(a)                        # Show the contents
[None, None, None, None, None]
>>> for i in range(len(a)):         # Replace contents with 1..5
        a[i] = i + 1

>>> a[0]                            # Access the first item
1
>>> for item in a:                  # Traverse the array to print all
        print(item)

1
2
3
4
5
```

As you can see, an array is a very restricted version of a list.

Random Access and Contiguous Memory

The subscript, or index operation, makes it easy for the programmer to store or retrieve an item at a given position. The array index operation is also very fast. Array indexing is a *random access* operation. During random access, the computer obtains the location of the ith item by performing a constant number of steps. Thus, no matter how large the array, it takes the same amount of time to access the first item as it does to access the last item.

The computer supports random access for arrays by allocating a block of *contiguous memory* cells for the array's items. One such block is shown in Figure 4.1.

Block of contiguous memory for array

Machine address		Array index
10011101		0
10011110		1
10011111		2
10100000		3
10100001		4

Figure 4.1

A block of contiguous memory.

© 2014 Cengage Learning®

For simplicity, the figure assumes that each data item occupies a single memory cell, although this need not be the case. The machine addresses are 8-bit binary numbers.

Because the addresses of the items are in numerical sequence, the address of an array item can be computed by adding two values: the array's *base address* and the item's *offset*. The array's base address is the machine address of the first item. An item's offset is equal to its index, multiplied by a constant representing the number of memory cells (in Python, always 1) required by an array item. To summarize, the index operation in a Python array has two steps:

1. Fetch the base address of the array's memory block.
2. Return the result of adding the index to this address.

In this example, the base address of the array's memory block is 10011101_2, and each item requires a single cell of memory. Then the address of the data item at index position 2 is $2_{10} + 10011101_2$, or 10011111_2.

The important point to note about random access is that the computer does not have to search for a given cell in an array, in which it starts with the first cell and counts cells until the ith cell is reached. Random access in constant time is perhaps the most desirable feature of an array. However, this feature requires that the array be represented in a block of contiguous memory. As you will see shortly, this requirement entails some costs when you implement other operations on arrays.

Static Memory and Dynamic Memory

Arrays in older languages such as FORTRAN and Pascal were static data structures. The length or capacity of the array was determined at compile time, so the programmer needed to specify this size with a constant. Because the programmer couldn't change the length of an array at run time, he needed to predict how much array memory would be needed by all applications of the program. If the program always expected a known, fixed number of items in the array, there was no problem. But in the other cases, in which the number of data items varied, programmers had to ask for enough memory to cover the cases where the largest number of data items would be stored in an array. Obviously, this requirement resulted in programs that wasted memory for many applications. Worse still, when the number of data items exceeded the length of the array, the best a program could do was to return an error message.

Modern languages such as Java and C++ provide a remedy for these problems by allowing the programmer to create *dynamic arrays*. Like a static array, a dynamic array occupies a contiguous block of memory and supports random access. However, the length of a dynamic array need not be known until run time. Thus, the Java or C++ programmer can specify the length of a dynamic array during instantiation. The Python `Array` class behaves in a similar manner.

Fortunately, there is a way for the programmer to readjust the length of an array to an application's data requirements at run time. These adjustments can take three forms:

- Create an array with a reasonable default size at program start-up.
- When the array cannot hold more data, create a new, larger array and transfer the data items from the old array.
- When the array seems to be wasting memory (some data have been removed by the application), decrease its length in a similar manner.

Needless to say, these adjustments happen automatically with a Python list.

Physical Size and Logical Size

When working with an array, programmers must often distinguish between its length or physical size and its logical size. The *physical size* of an array is its total number of array cells, or the number used to specify its capacity when the array is created. The *logical size* of an array is the number of items in it that should be currently available to the application. When the array is always full, the programmer need not worry about this distinction. However, such cases are rare. Figure 4.2 shows three arrays with the same physical size, but different logical sizes. The cells currently occupied by data are shaded.

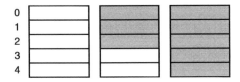

Figure 4.2

Arrays with different logical sizes.

© 2014 Cengage Learning®

As you can see, you can access cells in the first two arrays that contain *garbage*, or data not currently meaningful to the application. Thus, the programmer must take care to track both the physical size and the logical size of an array in most applications.

In general, the logical size and the physical size tell you several important things about the state of the array:

- If the logical size is 0, the array is empty. That is, the array contains no data items.

- Otherwise, at any given time, the index of the last item in the array is the logical size minus 1.

- If the logical size equals the physical size, there is no more room for data in the array.

Exercises 4.1

1. Explain how random access works and why it is so fast.

2. What are the differences between an array and a Python list?

3. Explain the difference between the physical size and the logical size of an array.

Operations on Arrays

You'll now learn the implementation of several operations on arrays. The array type does not already provide these operations; the programmer who uses the array must write them. In these examples, you can assume the following data settings:

```
DEFAULT_CAPACITY  = 5
logicalSize = 0
a = Array(DEFAULT_CAPACITY)
```

As you can see, the array has an initial logical size of 0 and a default physical size, or capacity, of 5. For each operation that uses this array, you'll read a description of the implementation strategy and an annotated Python code segment. Once again, these operations are used to define methods for collections that contain arrays.

Increasing the Size of an Array

When a new item is about to be inserted and the array's logical size equals its physical size, it is time to increase the size of the array. Python's list type performs this operation during a call of the method insert or append, when more memory for the array is needed. The resizing process consists of three steps:

1. Create a new, larger array.

2. Copy the data from the old array to the new array.

3. Reset the old array variable to the new array object.

Here is the code for this operation:

```
if logicalSize == len(a):
    temp = Array(len(a) + 1)      # Create a new array
    for i in range(logicalSize):  # Copy data from the old
        temp [i] = a[i]           # array to the new array
    a = temp                      # Reset the old array variable
                                  # to the new array
```

Note that the old array's memory is left out for the garbage collector. You also take the natural course of increasing the array's length by one cell to accommodate each new item. However, consider the performance implications of this decision. When the array is resized, the number of copy operations is linear. Thus, the overall time performance for adding n items to an array is $1 + 2 + 3 + \cdots + n$ or $n (n+1) / 2$ or $O(n^2)$.

You can achieve more reasonable time performance by doubling the size of the array each time you increase its size, as follows:

```
temp = Array(len(a) * 2)          # Create new array
```

The analysis of the time performance of this version is left as an exercise for you. The gain in time performance is, of course, achieved at the cost of wasting some memory. However, the overall space performance of this operation is linear because a temporary array is required no matter what your strategy is.

Decreasing the Size of an Array

When the logical size of an array shrinks, cells go to waste. When an item is about to be removed and the number of these unused cells reaches or exceeds a certain threshold, say, three-fourths of the physical size of the array, it is time to decrease the physical size. This operation occurs in Python's list type whenever the method pop results in memory wasted beyond a certain threshold. The process of decreasing the size of an array is the inverse of increasing it. Here are the steps:

1. Create a new, smaller array.

2. Copy the data from the old array to the new array.

3. Reset the old array variable to the new array object.

The code for this process kicks in when the logical size of the array is less than or equal to one-fourth of its physical size and its physical size is at least twice the default capacity that you have established for the array. The algorithm reduces the physical size of the array to one-half of its physical size, as long as that is not less than its default capacity. Here is the code:

```
if logicalSize <= len(a) // 4 and len(a) >= DEFAULT_CAPACITY * 2:
    temp = Array(len(a) // 2)        # Create new array
    for i in range(logicalSize):     # Copy data from old array
        temp [i] = a [i]             # to new array
    a = temp                         # Reset old array variable to
                                     # new array
```

Note that this strategy allows some memory to be wasted when shrinking the array. This strategy tends to decrease the likelihood of further resizings in either direction. The time/space analysis of the contraction operation is left as an exercise for you.

Inserting an Item into an Array That Grows

Inserting an item into an array differs from replacing an item in an array. In the case of a replacement, an item already exists at the given index position, and a simple assignment to that position suffices. Moreover, the logical size of the array does not change. In the case of an insertion, the programmer must do four things:

1. Check for available space before attempting an insertion and increase the physical size of the array, if necessary, as described earlier.

2. Shift the items from the logical end of the array to the target index position down by one. This process opens a hole for the new item at the target index.

3. Assign the new item to the target index position.

4. Increment the logical size by one.

Figure 4.3 shows these steps for the insertion of the item D5 at position 1 in an array of four items.

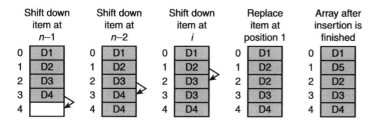

Figure 4.3

Inserting an item into an array.

© 2014 Cengage Learning®

As you can see, the order in which the items are shifted is critical. If you start at the target index and copy down from there, you lose two items. Thus, you must start at the logical end of the array and work back up to the target index, copying each item to the cell of its successor. Here is the Python code for the insertion operation:

```
# Increase physical size of array if necessary

# Shift items down by one position
for i in range(logicalSize, targetIndex, -1):
    a[i] = a[i - 1]

# Add new item and increment logical size
a[targetIndex] = newItem
logicalSize += 1
```

The time performance for shifting items during an insertion is linear on the average, so the insertion operation is linear.

Removing an Item from an Array

Removing an item from an array inverts the process of inserting an item into the array. Here are the steps in this process:

1. Shift the items from the one following the target index position to the logical end of the array up by one. This process closes the hole left by the removed item at the target index.

2. Decrement the logical size by one.

3. Check for wasted space and decrease the physical size of the array, if necessary.

Figure 4.4 shows these steps for the removal of an item at position 1 in an array of five items.

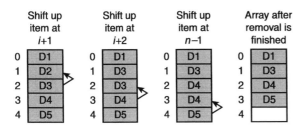

Figure 4.4

Removing an item from an array.

© 2014 Cengage Learning®

As with insertions, the order in which you shift items is critical. For a removal, you begin at the item following the target position and move toward the logical end of the array, copying each item to the cell of its predecessor. Here is the Python code for the removal operation:

```
# Shift items up by one position
for i in range(targetIndex, logicalSize - 1):
    a[i] = a[i + 1]
```

```
# Decrement logical size
logicalSize -= 1
```

```
# Decrease size of array if necessary
```

Once again, because the time performance for shifting items is linear on the average, the time performance for the removal operation is linear.

Complexity Trade-Off: Time, Space, and Arrays

The array structure presents an interesting trade-off between running-time performance and memory usage. Table 4.2 tallies the running times of each array operation as well as two additional ones: insertions and removals of items at the logical end of an array.

Table 4.2 The Running Times of Array Operations	
Operation	**Running Time**
Access at ith position	O(1), best and worst cases
Replacement at ith position	O(1), best and worst cases
Insert at logical end	O(1), average case
Remove from logical end	O(1), average case

Insert at *i*th position	O(*n*), average case
Remove from *i*th position	O(*n*), average case
Increase capacity	O(*n*), best and worst cases
Decrease capacity	O(*n*), best and worst cases

© 2014 Cengage Learning®

As you can see, an array provides fast access to any items already present and provides fast insertions and removals at the logical last position. Insertions and removals at arbitrary positions can be slower by an order of magnitude. Resizing also takes linear time, but doubling the size or cutting it in half can minimize the number of times that this must be done.

The insertion and removal operations are potentially O(*n*) in the use of memory, due to occasional resizing. Once again, if you use the techniques discussed earlier, this is only the worst-case performance. The average-case use of memory for these operations is O(1).

The only real memory cost of using an array is that some cells in an unfilled array go to waste. A useful concept for assessing an array's memory usage is its *load factor*. An array's load factor equals the number of items stored in the array divided by the array's capacity. For example, the load factor is 1 when an array is full, 0 when the array is empty, and 0.3 when an array of 10 cells has 3 of them occupied. You can keep the number of wasted cells to a minimum by resizing when the array's load factor drops below a certain threshold, say, 0.25.

Exercises 4.2

1. Explain why some items in an array might have to be shifted when a given item is inserted or removed.

2. When the programmer shifts array items during an insertion, which item is moved first: the one at the insertion point or the last item? Why?

3. State the run-time complexity for inserting an item when the insertion point is the logical size of the array.

4. An array currently contains 14 items, and its load factor is 0.70. What is its physical capacity?

Two-Dimensional Arrays (Grids)

The arrays studied so far can represent only simple sequences of items and are called *one-dimensional arrays*. For many applications, *two-dimensional arrays* or *grids* are more useful. A table of numbers, for instance, can be implemented as a two-dimensional array. Figure 4.5 shows a grid with four rows and five columns.

	Col 0	Col 1	Col 2	Col 3	Col 4
Row 0	0	1	2	3	4
Row 1	10	11	12	13	14
Row 2	20	21	22	23	24
Row 3	30	31	32	33	34

Figure 4.5

A two-dimensional array or grid with four rows and five columns.
© 2014 Cengage Learning®

Suppose this grid is named `table`. To access an item in `table`, you use two subscripts to specify its row and column positions, remembering that indexes start at 0:

```
x = table[2][3]   # Set x to 23, the value in (row 2, column 3)
```

In this section, you learn how to create and process simple two-dimensional arrays or grids. These grids are assumed to be rectangular and are of fixed dimensions.

Processing a Grid

In addition to the double subscript, a grid must recognize two methods that return the number of rows and the number of columns. For purposes of discussion, these methods are named `getHeight` and `getWidth`, respectively. The techniques for manipulating one-dimensional arrays are easily extended to grids. For instance, the following code segment computes the sum of all the numbers in the variable `table`. The outer loop iterates four times and moves down the rows. Each time through the outer loop, the inner loop iterates five times and moves across the columns in a different row.

```
sum = 0
for row in range(table.getHeight()):        # Go through rows
    for column in range(table.getWidth()):  # Go through columns
        sum += table[row][column]
```

Because the methods `getHeight` and `getWidth` are used instead of the numbers 4 and 5, this code will work for a grid of any dimensions.

Creating and Initializing a Grid

Let's assume that there exists a `Grid` class for two-dimensional arrays. To create a `Grid` object, you can run the `Grid` constructor with three arguments: its height, its width, and an initial fill value. The next session instantiates `Grid` with 4 rows, 5 columns, and a fill value of 0. Then it prints the resulting object:

```
>>> from grid import Grid
>>> table = Grid(4, 5, 0)
>>> print(table)
0 0 0 0 0
0 0 0 0 0
0 0 0 0 0
0 0 0 0 0
```

After a grid has been created, you can reset its cells to any values. The following code segment traverses the grid to reset its cells to the values shown in Figure 4.5:

```
# Go through rows
for row in range(table.getHeight()):
    # Go through columns
    for column in range(table.getWidth()):
        table[row][column] = int(str(row) + str(column))
```

Defining a Grid Class

A `Grid` class is similar to the `Array` class presented earlier. Users can run methods to determine the number of rows and columns and obtain a string representation. However, no iterator is provided. A grid is conveniently represented using an array of arrays. The length of the top-level array equals the number of rows in the grid. Each cell in the top-level array is also an array. The length of this array is the number of columns in the grid, and this array contains the data in a given row. The method __getitem__ is all that you need to support the client's use of the double subscript. Here is the code for the `Grid` class (in `grid.py`):

```
"""
Author: Ken Lambert
"""

from arrays import Array

class Grid(object):
    """Represents a two-dimensional array."""

    def __init__(self, rows, columns, fillValue = None):
        self._data = Array(rows)
        for row in range (rows):
            self._data[row] = Array(columns, fillValue)
```

```
def getHeight(self):
    """Returns the number of rows."""
    return len(self._data)

def getWidth(self):
    "Returns the number of columns."""
    return len(self._data[0])

def __getitem__(self, index):
    """Supports two-dimensional indexing
    with [row][column]."""
    return self._data[index]

def __str__(self):
    """Returns a string representation of the grid."""
    result = ""
    for row in range (self.getHeight()):
        for col in range (self.getWidth()):
            result += str(self._data[row][col]) + " "
        result += "\n"
    return result
```

Ragged Grids and Multidimensional Arrays

The grids discussed thus far in this section have been two-dimensional and rectangular. You can also create ragged grids and grids of more than two dimensions.

A ragged grid has a fixed number of rows, but the number of columns of data in each row can vary. An array of lists or arrays provides a suitable structure for implementing a ragged grid.

Dimensions can also be added to the definition of a grid when necessary; the only limit is the computer's memory. For example, you can visualize a three-dimensional array as a box filled with smaller boxes stacked neatly in rows and columns. This array is given a depth, height, and width when it is created. The array type now has a method getDepth as well as getWidth and getHeight to examine the dimensions. Each item is accessed with three integers as indexes, and processing is accomplished with a control statement structure that contains three loops.

Exercises 4.3

1. What are two-dimensional arrays or grids?

2. Describe an application in which a two-dimensional array might be used.

3. Write a code segment that searches a Grid object for a negative integer. The loop should terminate at the first instance of a negative integer in the grid, and the

variables `row` and `column` should be set to the position of that integer. Otherwise, the variables `row` and `column` should equal the number of rows and columns in the grid.

4. Describe the contents of the grid after you run the following code segment:

```
matrix = Grid(3, 3)
for row in range(matrix.getHeight()):
    for column in range(matrix.getWidth()):
        matrix[row][column] = row * column
```

5. Write a code segment that creates a ragged grid whose rows contain positions for three, six, and nine items, respectively.

6. Suggest a strategy for implementing a three-dimensional `array` class that uses the `Grid` class as a data structure.

7. Write a code segment that initializes each cell in a three-dimensional array with an integer that represents its three index positions. Thus, if a position is (depth, row, column), the integer datum at position (2, 3, 3) is 233.

8. Write a code segment that displays the items in a three-dimensional array. Each line of data should represent all the items at a given row and column, stretching back from the first depth position to the last one. The traversal should start at the first row, column, and depth positions and move through depths, columns, and rows.

LINKED STRUCTURES

After arrays, linked structures are probably the most commonly used data structures in programs. Like an array, a linked structure is a concrete data type that implements many types of collections, including lists. A thorough examination of the use of linked structures in collections such as lists and binary trees appears later in this book. This section discusses in detail several characteristics that programmers must keep in mind when using linked structures to implement any type of collection.

Singly Linked Structures and Doubly Linked Structures

As the name implies, a linked structure consists of items that are linked to other items. Although many links among items are possible, the two simplest linked structures are the *singly linked structure* and the *doubly linked structure*.

It is useful to draw diagrams of linked structures using a box and pointer notation. Figure 4.6 uses this notation to show examples of the two kinds of linked structures.

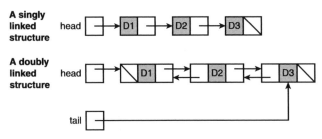

Figure 4.6

Two types of linked structures.

© 2014 Cengage Learning®

A user of a singly linked structure accesses the first item by following a single external *head link*. The user then accesses other items by chaining through the single links (represented by arrows in the figure) that emanate from the items. Thus, in a singly linked structure, it is easy to get to the successor of an item, but not so easy to get to the predecessor of an item.

A doubly linked structure contains links running in both directions. Thus, it is easy for the user to move to an item's successor or to its predecessor. A second external link, called the *tail link*, allows the user of a doubly linked structure to access the last item directly.

The last item in either type of linked structure has no link to the next item. The figure indicates the absence of a link, called an *empty link*, by means of a slash instead of an arrow. Note also that the first item in a doubly linked structure has no link to the preceding item.

Like arrays, these linked structures represent linear sequences of items. However, the programmer who uses a linked structure cannot immediately access an item by specifying its index position. Instead, the programmer must start at one end of the structure and follow the links until the desired position (or item) is reached. This property of linked structures has important consequences for several operations, as discussed shortly.

The way in which memory is allocated for linked structures is also quite unlike that of arrays and has two important consequences for insertion and removal operations:

■ Once an insertion or removal point has been found, the insertion or removal can take place with no shifting of data items in memory.

■ The linked structure can be resized during each insertion or removal with no extra memory cost and no copying of data items.

Now you'll learn the underlying memory support for linked structures that makes these advantages possible.

Noncontiguous Memory and Nodes

Recall that array items must be stored in contiguous memory. This means that the logical sequence of items in the array is tightly coupled to a physical sequence of cells in memory. By contrast, a linked structure decouples the logical sequence of items in the structure from any ordering in memory. That is, the cell for a given item in a linked structure can be found anywhere in memory as long as the computer can follow a link to its address or location. This kind of memory representation scheme is called *noncontiguous memory*.

The basic unit of representation in a linked structure is a *node*. A *singly linked node* contains the following components or fields:

- A data item
- A link to the next node in the structure

In addition to these components, a *doubly linked node* contains a link to the previous node in the structure.

Figure 4.7 shows a singly linked node and a doubly linked node whose internal links are empty.

Singly linked node

Doubly linked node

Figure 4.7
Two types of nodes with empty links.
© 2014 Cengage Learning®

Depending on the programming language, the programmer can set up nodes to use noncontiguous memory in several ways:

- In early languages such as FORTRAN, the only built-in data structure was the array. The programmer thus implemented nodes and their noncontiguous memory for a singly linked structure by using two parallel arrays. One array contained the data items. The other array contained the index positions, for corresponding items in the data array, of their successor items in the data array. Thus, following a link meant using a data item's index in the first array to access a value in the second array and then using that value as an index into another data item in the first array. The empty link was represented by the value –1. Figure 4.8 shows a linked structure and its array representation. As you can see, this setup effectively decouples the logical position of a data item in the linked structure from its physical position in the array.

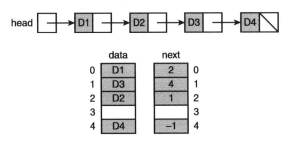

Figure 4.8

An array representation of a linked structure.

© 2014 Cengage Learning®

- In more modern languages, such as Pascal and C++, the programmer has direct access to the addresses of data in the form of *pointers*. In these more modern languages, a node in a singly linked structure contains a data item and a pointer value. A special value null (or nil) represents the empty link as a pointer value. The programmer does not use an array to set up the noncontiguous memory but simply asks the computer for a pointer to a new node from a built-in area of noncontiguous memory called the *object heap*. The programmer then sets the pointer within this node to another node, thus establishing a link to other data in the structure. The use of explicit pointers and a built-in heap represents an advance over the FORTRAN-style scheme because the programmer is no longer responsible for managing the underlying array representation of noncontiguous memory. (After all, the memory of any computer—RAM—is ultimately just a big array.) However, Pascal and C++ still require the programmer to manage the heap insofar as the programmer has to return unused nodes to it with a special dispose or delete operation.

- Python programmers set up nodes and linked structures by using *references* to objects. In Python, any variable can refer to anything, including the value None, which can mean an empty link. Thus, a Python programmer defines a singly linked node by defining an object that contains two fields: a reference to a data item and a reference to another node. Python provides dynamic allocation of noncontiguous memory for each new node object, as well as automatic return of this memory to the system (garbage collection) when the object no longer can be referenced by the application.

In the discussion that follows, the terms link, pointer, and reference are used interchangeably.

Defining a Singly Linked Node Class

Node classes are simple. Flexibility and ease of use are critical, so the instance variables of a node object are usually referenced without method calls, and constructors allow the user to set a node's link(s) when the node is created. As mentioned earlier, a singly linked node contains just a data item and a reference to the next node. Here is the code for a simple, singly linked node class:

```
class Node(object):
    """Represents a singly linked node."""

    def __init__(self, data, next = None):
        """Instantiates a Node with a default next of None."""
        self.data = data
        self.next = next
```

Using the Singly Linked Node Class

Node variables are initialized to either the None value or a new Node object. The next code segment shows some variations on these two options:

```
# Just an empty link
node1 = None

# A node containing data and an empty link
node2 = Node("A", None)

# A node containing data and a link to node2
node3 = Node("B", node2)
```

Figure 4.9 shows the state of the three variables after this code is run.

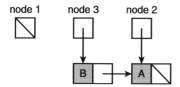

Figure 4.9

Three external links.

© 2014 Cengage Learning®

Note the following:

- node1 points to no node object yet (is None).
- node2 and node3 point to objects that are linked.
- node2 points to an object whose next pointer is None.

Now suppose you attempt to place the first node at the beginning of the linked structure that already contains node2 and node3 by running the following statement:

```
node1.next = node3
```

Python responds by raising an AttributeError. The reason for this response is that the variable node1 contains the value None and thus does not reference a node object containing a next field. To create the desired link, you could run either

```
node1 = Node("C", node3)
```

or

```
node1 = Node("C", None)
node1.next = node3
```

In general, you can guard against exceptions by asking whether a given node variable is None before attempting to access its fields:

```
if nodeVariable != None:
    <access a field in nodeVariable>
```

Like arrays, linked structures are processed with loops. You can use loops to create a linked structure and visit each node in it. The next tester script uses the Node class to create a singly linked structure and print its contents:

```
"""
File: testnode.py

Tests the Node class.
"""

from node import Node

head = None

# Add five nodes to the beginning of the linked structure
for count in range(1, 6):
    head = Node(count, head)

# Print the contents of the structure
while head != None:
    print(head.data)
    head = head.next
```

Note the following points about this program:

- One pointer, head, generates the linked structure. This pointer is manipulated in such a way that the most recently inserted item is always at the beginning of the structure.

- Thus, when the data are displayed, they appear in the reverse order of their insertion.

- Also, when the data are displayed, the head pointer is reset to the next node, until the head pointer becomes None. Thus, at the end of this process, the nodes are effectively deleted from the linked structure. They are no longer available to the program and are recycled during the next garbage collection.

Exercises 4.4

1. Using box and pointer notation, draw a picture of the nodes created by the first loop in the tester program.

2. What happens when a programmer attempts to access a node's data fields when the node variable refers to None? How do you guard against it?

3. Write a code segment that transfers items from a full array to a singly linked structure. The operation should preserve the ordering of the items.

OPERATIONS ON SINGLY LINKED STRUCTURES

Almost all the operations on arrays are already index based, because the indexes are an integral part of the array structure. The programmer must emulate index-based operations on a linked structure by manipulating links within the structure. This section explores how these manipulations are performed in common operations such as traversals, insertions, and removals.

Traversal

The second loop in the last tester program effectively removed each node from the linked structure after printing that node's data. However, many applications simply need to visit each node without deleting it. This operation, called a *traversal*, uses a temporary pointer variable. This variable is initialized to the linked structure's head pointer and then controls a loop as follows:

```
probe = head
while probe != None:
    <use or modify probe.data>
    probe = probe.next
```

Figure 4.10 shows the state of the pointer variables probe and head during each pass of the loop. Note that at the end of the process, the probe pointer is None, but the head pointer still references the first node.

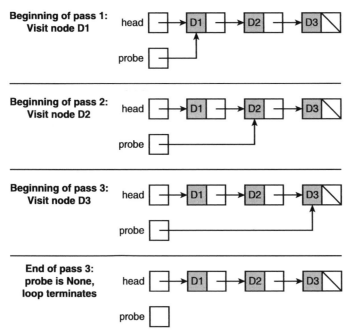

Figure 4.10

Traversing a linked structure.

© 2014 Cengage Learning®

In general, a traversal of a singly linked structure visits every node and terminates when an empty link is reached. Thus, the value None serves as a *sentinel* that stops the process.

Traversals are linear in time and require no extra memory.

Searching

Chapter 3, "Searching, Sorting, and Complexity Analysis," discussed the sequential search for a given item in a list. The sequential search of a linked structure resembles a traversal in that you must start at the first node and follow the links until you reach a sentinel. However, in this case, there are two possible sentinels:

■ The empty link, indicating that there are no more data items to examine

■ A data item that equals the target item, indicating a successful search

Here is the form of the search for a given item:

```
probe = head
while probe != None and targetItem != probe.data:
    probe = probe.next
if probe != None:
    <targetItem has been found>
else:
    <targetItem is not in the linked structure>
```

It is no surprise that, on the average, the sequential search is linear for singly linked structures.

Unfortunately, accessing the *i*th item of a linked structure is also a sequential search operation. This is because you must start at the first node and count the number of links until you reach the *i*th node. You can assume that $0 <= i < n$, where *n* is the number of nodes in the linked structure. Here is the form for accessing the *i*th item:

```
# Assumes 0 <= index < n
probe = head
while index > 0:
    probe = probe.next
    index -= 1
return probe.data
```

Unlike arrays, linked structures do not support random access. Thus, you cannot search a singly linked structure whose data are in sorted order as efficiently as you can search a sorted array. However, as you will see later in this book, there are ways to organize the data in other types of linked structures to remedy this defect.

Replacement

The replacement operations in a singly linked structure also employ the traversal pattern. In these cases, you search for a given item or a given position in the linked structure and replace the item with a new item. The first operation, replacing a given item, need not assume that the target item is in the linked structure. If the target item is not present, no replacement occurs and the operation returns False. If the target is present, the new item replaces it and the operation returns True. Here is the form of the operation:

```
probe = head
while probe != None and targetItem != probe.data:
    probe = probe.next
if probe != None:
    probe.data = newItem
    return True
else:
    return False
```

The operation to replace the *i*th item assumes that $0 <= i < n$. Here is the form:

```
# Assumes 0 <= index < n
probe = head
while index > 0:
    probe = probe.next
    index -= 1
probe.data = newItem
```

Both replacement operations are linear on the average.

Inserting at the Beginning

By now, you are probably wondering whether there is a better-than-linear operation on a linked structure. In fact, there are several. In some cases, these operations can make linked structures preferable to arrays. The first such case is the insertion of an item at the beginning of the structure. This is just what was done repeatedly in the tester program of the previous section. Here is the form:

```
head = Node(newItem, head)
```

Figure 4.11 traces this operation for two cases. The head pointer is None in the first case, so the first item is inserted into the structure. In the second case, the second item is inserted at the beginning of the same structure.

First case: head is None

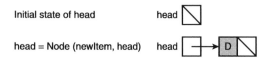

Second case: head is not None

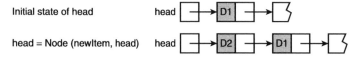

Figure 4.11

The two cases of inserting an item at the beginning of a linked structure.

© 2014 Cengage Learning®

Note that in the second case, there is no need to copy data to shift them down, and there is no need for extra memory. This means that inserting data at the beginning of a linked structure uses constant time and memory, unlike the same operation with arrays.

Inserting at the End

Inserting an item at the end of an array (used in the append operation of a Python list) requires constant time and memory, unless the array must be resized. The same process for a singly linked structure must consider two cases:

- The head pointer is None, so the head pointer is set to the new node.

- The head pointer is not None, so the code searches for the last node and aims its next pointer at the new node.

The second case returns you to the traversal pattern. Here is the form:

```
newNode = Node(newItem)
if head is None:
    head = newNode
else:
    probe = head
    while probe.next != None:
        probe = probe.next
    probe.next = newNode
```

Figure 4.12 traces the insertion of a new item at the end of a linked structure of three items. This operation is linear in time and constant in memory.

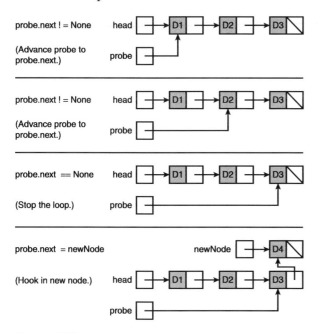

Figure 4.12

Inserting an item at the end of a linked structure.

© 2014 Cengage Learning®

Removing at the Beginning

In the tester program of the previous section, you repeatedly removed the item at the beginning of the linked structure. In this type of operation, you can typically assume that there is at least one node in the structure. The operation returns the removed item. Here is the form:

```
# Assumes at least one node in the structure
removedItem = head.data
head = head.next
return removedItem
```

Figure 4.13 traces the removal of the first node.

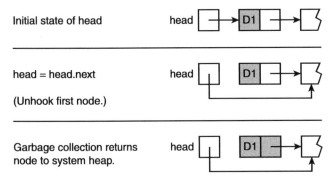

Figure 4.13

Removing an item at the beginning of a linked structure.

© 2014 Cengage Learning®

As you can see, the operation uses constant time and memory, unlike the same operation for arrays.

Removing at the End

Removing an item at the end of an array (used in the Python list method pop) requires constant time and memory, unless you must resize the array. The same process for a singly linked structure assumes at least one node in the structure. There are then two cases to consider:

■ There is just one node. The head pointer is set to None.

■ There is a node before the last node. The code searches for this second-to-last node and sets its next pointer to None.

In either case, the code returns the data item contained in the deleted node. Here is the form:

```
# Assumes at least one node in structure
removedItem = head.data
if head.next is None:
    head = None
else:
    probe = head
    while probe.next.next != None:
        probe = probe.next
    removedItem = probe.next.data
    probe.next = None
return removedItem
```

Figure 4.14 shows the removal of the last node from a linked structure of three items.

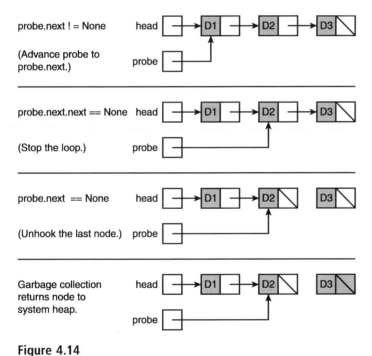

Figure 4.14

Removing an item at the end of a linked structure.

© 2014 Cengage Learning®

This operation is linear in time and constant in memory.

Inserting at Any Position

The insertion of an item at the *i*th position in an array requires shifting items from position *i* down to position $n - 1$. Thus, you actually insert the item before the item currently at position *i* so that the new item occupies position *i* and the old item occupies position $i + 1$. What about the cases of an empty array or an index that is greater than $n - 1$? If the array is empty, the new item goes at the beginning, whereas if the index is greater than or equal to *n*, the item goes at the end.

The insertion of an item at the *i*th position in a linked structure must deal with the same cases. The case of an insertion at the beginning uses the code presented earlier. In the case of an insertion at some other position *i*, however, the operation must first find the node at position $i - 1$ (if $i < n$) or the node at position $n - 1$ (if $i >= n$). Then there are two cases to consider:

■ That node's next pointer is None. This means that $i >= n$, so you should place the new item at the end of the linked structure.

■ That node's next pointer is not None. That means that $0 < i < n$, so you must place the new item between the node at position $i - 1$ and the node at position *i*.

As with a search for the *i*th item, the insertion operation must count nodes until the desired position is reached. However, because the target index might be greater than or equal to the number of nodes, you must be careful to avoid going off the end of the linked structure in the search. Thus, the loop has an additional condition that tests the current node's next pointer to see if it is the final node. Here is the form:

```
if head is None or index <= 0:
    head = Node(newItem, head)
else:
    # Search for node at position index - 1 or the last position
    probe = head
    while index > 1 and probe.next != None:
        probe = probe.next
        index -= 1
    # Insert new node after node at position index - 1
    # or last position
    probe.next = Node(newItem, probe.next)
```

Figure 4.15 shows a trace of the insertion of an item at position 2 in a linked structure containing three items.

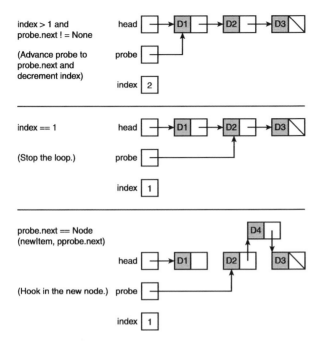

index > 1 and
probe.next ! = None

(Advance probe to
probe.next and
decrement index)

index == 1

(Stop the loop.)

probe.next == Node
(newItem, pprobe.next)

(Hook in the new node.) probe

Figure 4.15

Inserting an item between two items in a linked structure.

© 2014 Cengage Learning®

As with any singly linked structure operation that uses a traversal pattern, this operation has a linear time performance. However, the use of memory is constant.

The insertion of an item before a given item in a linked structure uses elements of this pattern and is left as an exercise for you.

Removing at Any Position

The removal of the ith item from a linked structure has three cases:

- $i <= 0$—You use the code to remove the first item.
- $0 < i < n$—You search for the node at position $i - 1$, as in insertion, and remove the following node.
- $i >= n$—You remove the last node.

Assume that the linked structure has at least one item. The pattern is similar to the one used for insertion in that you must guard against going off the end of the linked structure. However, you must allow the probe pointer to go no farther than the second node from the end of the structure. Here is the form:

```
# Assumes that the linked structure has at least one item
if index <= 0 or head.next is None
```

```
        removedItem = head.data
        head = head.next
        return removedItem
else:
        # Search for node at position index - 1 or
        # the next to last position
        probe = head
        while index > 1 and probe.next.next != None:
            probe = probe.next
            index -= 1
        removedItem = probe.next.data
        probe.next = probe.next.next
        return removedItem
```

Figure 4.16 shows a trace of the removal of the item at position 2 in a linked structure containing four items.

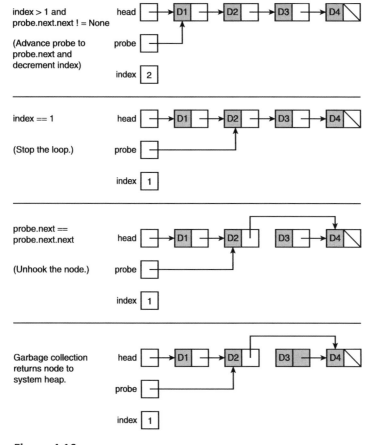

Figure 4.16

Removing an item between two items in a linked structure.

© 2014 Cengage Learning®

Complexity Trade-Off: Time, Space, and Singly Linked Structures

Singly linked structures present a different space/time trade-off than arrays. Table 4.3 provides a tally of the running times of the operations.

Table 4.3   The Running Times of Operations on Singly Linked Structures

Operation	Running Time
Access at ith position	O(n), average case
Replacement at ith position	O(n), average case
Insert at beginning	O(1), best and worst case
Remove from beginning	O(1), best and worst case
Insert at ith position	O(n), average case
Remove from ith position	O(n), average case

© 2014 Cengage Learning®

Surprisingly, this tally reveals that the only two linked structure operations that are not linear in time are the insertion and removal of the first item. You might be wondering why a linked structure is used instead of an array if so many of a linked structure's operations have linear behavior. Well, suppose you want to implement a collection that just inserts, accesses, or removes the first item. You will see such a collection in Chapter 7, "Stacks." Of course, you might also choose an array implementation that inserts or removes the last item with similar time performance. In Chapter 10, "Trees," you also look at linked structures that support logarithmic insertions and searches.

The main advantage of the singly linked structure over the array is not time performance but memory performance. Resizing an array, when this must occur, is linear in time and memory. Resizing a linked structure, which occurs upon each insertion or removal, is constant in time and memory. Moreover, no memory ever goes to waste in a linked structure. The physical size of the structure never exceeds the logical size. Linked structures do have an extra memory cost in that a singly linked structure must use n cells of memory for the pointers. This cost increases for doubly linked structures, whose nodes have two links.

Programmers who understand this analysis can pick the implementation that best suits their needs.

Exercises 4.5

1. Assume that the position of an item to be removed from a singly linked structure has been located. State the run-time complexity for completing the removal operation from that point.

2. Can a binary search be performed on items that are in sorted order within a singly linked structure? If not, why not?

3. Suggest a good reason that Python list uses an array rather than a linked structure to hold its items.

VARIATIONS ON A LINK

This section examines two types of linked structures with extra pointers that can help to improve performance and simplify code.

A Circular Linked Structure with a Dummy Header Node

The insertion and the removal of the first node are special cases of the insert *i*th and remove *i*th operations on singly linked structures. These cases are special because the head pointer must be reset. You can simplify these operations by using a *circular linked structure* with a *dummy header node*. A circular linked structure contains a link from the last node back to the first node in the structure. There is always at least one node in this implementation. This node, the dummy header node, contains no data but serves as a marker for the beginning and the end of the linked structure. Initially, in an empty linked structure, the head variable points to the dummy header node, and the dummy header node's next pointer points back to the dummy header node itself, as shown in Figure 4.17.

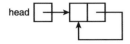

Figure 4.17
An empty circular linked structure with a dummy header node.
© 2014 Cengage Learning®

The first node to contain data is located after the dummy header node. This node's next pointer then points back to the dummy header node in a circular fashion, as shown in Figure 4.18.

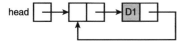

Figure 4.18

A circular linked structure after inserting the first node.

© 2014 Cengage Learning®

The search for the *i*th node begins with the node after the dummy header node. Assume that the empty linked structure is initialized as follows:

```
head = Node(None, None)
head.next = head
```

Here is the code for insertions at the *i*th position using this new representation of a linked structure:

```
# Search for node at position index - 1 or the last position
probe = head
while index > 0 and probe.next != head:
    probe = probe.next
    index -= 1
# Insert new node after node at position index - 1 or
# last position
probe.next = Node(newItem, probe.next)
```

The advantage of this implementation is that the insertion and removal operations have only one case to consider—the case in which the *i*th node lies between a prior node and the current *i*th node. When the *i*th node is the first node, the prior node is the header node. When *i* >= *n*, the last node is the prior node and the header node is the next node.

Doubly Linked Structures

A doubly linked structure has the advantages of a singly linked structure. In addition, it allows the user to do the following:

- Move left, to the previous node, from a given node.
- Move immediately to the last node.

Figure 4.19 shows a doubly linked structure that contains three nodes. Note the presence of two pointers, conventionally known as next and previous, in each node. Note also the presence of a second external tail pointer that allows direct access to the last node in the structure.

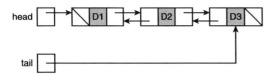

Figure 4.19

A doubly linked structure with three nodes.

© 2014 Cengage Learning®

The Python implementation of a node class for doubly linked structures extends the Node class discussed earlier by adding a field for the previous pointer. Here is the code for the two classes:

```
class Node(object):

    def __init__(self, data, next = None):
        """Instantiates a Node with default next of None"""
        self.data = data
        self.next = next

class TwoWayNode(Node):

    def __init__(self, data, previous = None, next = None):
        """Instantiates a TwoWayNode."""
        Node.__init__(self, data, next)
        self.previous = previous
```

The following tester program creates a doubly linked structure by adding items to the end. The program then displays the linked structure's contents by starting at the last item and working backward to the first item:

```
"""File: testtwowaynode.py
Tests the TwoWayNode class.
"""

from node import TwoWayNode

# Create a doubly linked structure with one node
head = TwoWayNode(1)
tail = head

# Add four nodes to the end of the doubly linked structure
for data in range(2, 6):
    tail.next = TwoWayNode(data, tail)
    tail = tail.next

# Print the contents of the linked structure in reverse order
probe = tail
while probe != None:
    print(probe.data)
    probe = probe.previous
```

Consider the following two statements in the first loop of the program:

```
tail.next = TwoWayNode(data, tail)
tail = tail.next
```

The purpose of these statements is to insert a new item at the end of the linked structure. You can assume that there is at least one node in the linked structure and that the `tail` pointer always points to the last node in the nonempty linked structure. You must set the three pointers, in the following order:

1. The previous pointer of the new node must be aimed at the current tail node. This is accomplished by passing `tail` as the second argument to the node's constructor.

2. The next pointer of the current tail node must be aimed at the new node. The first assignment statement accomplishes this.

3. The `tail` pointer must be aimed at the new node. The second assignment statement accomplishes this.

Figure 4.20 shows the insertion of a new node at the end of a doubly linked structure.

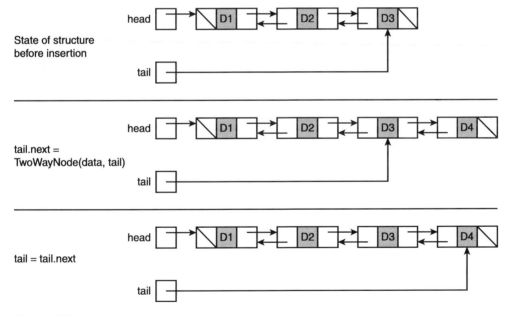

Figure 4.20

Inserting an item at the end of a doubly linked structure.

© 2014 Cengage Learning®

As you can see, insertions in the middle of a doubly linked structure would require the redirection of still more pointers. However, the redirected pointers are always constant in number no matter where the target position is.

The more general insertion and removal operations for doubly linked structures also have two special cases, as they did with singly linked structures. You can simplify these operations by resorting to a circular linked structure with a dummy header node. That's an exercise for you for later.

With the exception of insertions and removals at the tail of the structure, the run-time complexities of the operations on a doubly linked structure are the same as the corresponding operations on the singly linked structure. However, a linear amount of extra memory is required for the extra pointers of a doubly linked structure.

Another variation on a linked structure combines a doubly linked structure with a dummy header node. This option is used in Chapter 8, "Queues," to implement linked lists.

Exercises 4.6

1. What advantage does a circular linked structure with a dummy header node give the programmer?

2. Describe one benefit and one cost of a doubly linked structure, as compared to a singly linked structure.

Summary

- A data structure is an object that represents the data contained in a collection.

- The array is a data structure that supports random access, in constant time, to an item by position. An array is given a number of positions for data when it is created, and its length remains fixed. Insertions and removals require shifting of data elements and perhaps the creation of a new, larger or smaller array.

- A two-dimensional array locates each data value at a row and column in a rectangular grid.

- A linked structure is a data structure that consists of zero or more nodes. A node contains a data item and one or more links to other nodes.

- A singly linked structure's nodes contain a data item and a link to the next node. A node in a doubly linked structure also contains a link to the previous node.

■ Insertions or removals in linked structures require no shifting of data elements. At most, one node is created. However, insertions, removals, and accesses in linear linked structures require linear time.

■ Using a header node in a linked structure can simplify some of the operations, such as adding or removing items.

REVIEW QUESTIONS

1. Arrays and linked structures are examples of

   a. Abstract data types (ADTs)

   b. Data structures

2. An array's length

   a. Is fixed in size after it is created

   b. Can be increased or decreased after it is created

3. Random access supports

   a. Constant time access to data

   b. Linear time access to data

4. Data in a singly linked structure are contained in

   a. Cells

   b. Nodes

5. Most operations on singly linked structures run in

   a. Constant time

   b. Linear time

6. It requires constant time to remove the first item from a(n)

   a. Array

   b. Singly linked structure

PROJECTS

In the first six projects, you modify the Array class defined in this chapter to make it behave more like Python's list class. For each solution, include code that tests your modifications to the Array class.

1. Add an instance variable _logicalSize to the Array class. This variable is initially 0 and will track the number of items currently available to users of the array. Then add the method size() to the Array class. This method should return the array's logical size. The method __len__ should still return the array's capacity or physical size.

2. Add preconditions to the methods __getitem__ and __setitem__ of the Array class. The precondition of each method is 0 <= index < size(). Be sure to raise an exception if the precondition is not satisfied.

3. Add the methods grow and shrink to the Array class. These methods should use the strategies discussed in this chapter to increase or decrease the length of the list contained in the array. Make sure that the physical size of the array does not shrink below the user-specified capacity and that the array's cells use the fill value when the array's size is increased.

4. Add the methods insert and pop to the Array class. These methods should use the strategies discussed in this chapter, including adjusting the length of the array, if necessary. The insert method expects a position and an item as arguments and inserts the item at the given position. If the position is greater than or equal to the array's logical size, the method inserts the item after the last item currently available in the array. The pop method expects a position as an argument and removes and returns the item at that position. The pop method's precondition is 0 <= index < size(). The remove method should also reset the vacated array cell to the fill value.

5. Add the method __eq__ to the Array class. Python runs this method when an Array object appears as the left operand of the == operator. The method returns True if its argument is also an Array, it has the same logical size as the left operand, and the pair of items at each *logical* position in the two arrays are equal. Otherwise, the method returns False.

6. Jill tells Jack that he should now remove the current implementation of the __iter__ method from the Array class, if it's really behaving like a list. Explain why this is a good suggestion. Also explain how the __str__ method should be modified at this point.

7. A Matrix class can be used to perform some of the operations found in linear algebra, such as matrix arithmetic. Develop a Matrix class that uses the built-in operators for arithmetic. The Matrix class should extend the Grid class.

The next four projects ask you to define some functions for manipulating linked structures. You should use the Node and TwoWayNode classes, as defined in this chapter. Create a tester module that contains your function definitions and your code for testing them.

8. Define a function length (*not* len) that expects a singly linked structure as an argument. The function returns the number of items in the structure.

9. Define a function named insert that inserts an item into a singly linked structure at a given position. The function expects three arguments: the item, the position, and the linked structure. (The latter may be empty.) The function returns the modified linked structure. If the position is greater than or equal to the structure's length, the function inserts the item at its end. An example call of the function, where head is a variable that either is an empty link or refers to the first node of a structure, is head = insert(1, data, head).

10. Define a function named pop that removes the item at a given position from a singly linked structure. This function expects a position as a first argument, with the precondition 0 <= position < length of structure. Its second argument is the linked structure, which, of course, cannot be empty. The function returns a *tuple* containing the modified linked structure and the item that was removed. An example call is (head, item) = pop(1, head).

11. Define a function makeTwoWay that expects a singly linked structure as its argument. The function builds and returns a doubly linked structure that contains the items in the singly linked structure. (*Note*: The function should not alter the argument's structure.)

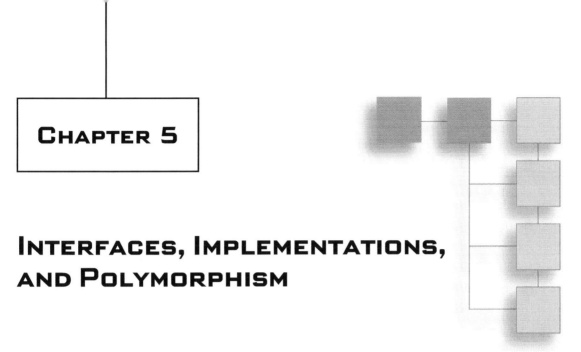

CHAPTER 5

INTERFACES, IMPLEMENTATIONS, AND POLYMORPHISM

The universal serial bus (USB) provides a standard *interface* to connect a wide range of devices to computers. As you probably know, a standard USB cable allows you to connect a computer to digital cameras, smart phones, printers, scanners, external storage disks, and many other devices. The common flash stick comes with an integrated USB connector.

Interfaces are just as common in software as they are in hardware. One of the hallmarks of well-designed software is the clean separation of interfaces from implementations. When programmers use a software resource, they need only be concerned with its interface—the set of methods, functions, and data type names available to them. Ideally, the details of how this resource is implemented—the underlying algorithmic code and data structures—lie hidden or encapsulated within an *abstraction barrier*. The barrier that separates an interface from an implementation

- Flattens the learning curve for a resource's users

- Allows users to quickly glue resources together in a plug-and-play fashion

- May give users the opportunity to choose among alternative implementations of the same resource

- Allows implementers to make changes to a resource's implementation without disturbing its users' code

This chapter examines how to design and implement a software resource by separating its interface from its implementations. In the process, it also explores another useful concept in software design, called *polymorphism*. In this context, polymorphism is just

133

the idea that multiple implementations of a resource conform to the same interface or set of methods.

DEVELOPING AN INTERFACE

Each time you run Python's `help` function to obtain information about a module, data type, method, or function, you are accessing documentation about that resource's interface. In the case of data types (or classes), you see a list of method headers, which include their names, the types of their arguments, a statement of what the methods do, and the values the methods return, if any. The documentation gives you enough information to know how to use or call a method and what to expect it to accomplish and return. That's it. Interfaces are concise and informative, allowing you to grasp the behavior of a resource just by glancing at its public, external "face."

In this section, you develop the interface for a simple collection type called a bag. As mentioned in the early survey of collections (Chapter 2, "An Overview of Collections"), a *bag* is a type of unordered collection. The bag interface allows clients to use bags effectively and allows implementers to produce new classes that implement this interface.

Designing the Bag Interface

The methods in a resource's interface express the behavior of that resource, the kinds of things it does, or the things that you can do to it. In the case of a new type of object like a bag, you can derive an interface from thinking about what bags can do in a real-world situation.

Obviously, a bag can contain any objects, such as tennis balls, clothing, groceries, or items purchased at an office supply store. You will want to know how many things are in a bag and how to add things to it or remove them from it. Unlike physical bags, these software bags can grow larger as more items are added, or they can shrink smaller as more items are removed.

For convenience, it's helpful to know whether a bag is empty, to empty a bag in a single operation, to determine whether a given item is in a bag, and to view each item in a bag without emptying it. The last such operation might take two forms: one would give you access to a bag's contents, and the other would give you a "printable" version of a bag's contents—a string.

Other useful operations determine whether two bags contain the same objects and combine the contents of two bags into a third bag (*concatenation*). Last but not least, you need to know how to create a bag—one that is initially empty or one that comes already filled with the contents of another collection.

The next step is to draw up a list of function names, method names, and operator symbols that meet the descriptions of these operations. These names typically are whole words or abbreviations of the actions performed or the properties being examined. You should strive to conform to common, conventional usage when selecting method or function names. For example, in the case of collections, the functions `len` and `str` always designate operations that return a collection's length and its string representation, respectively. The operator symbols +, ==, and `in` always stand for the operations of concatenation, equality, and item membership. A `for` loop is used to visit all of a collection's items. The methods `add` and `remove`, in addition to having the obvious meanings, also belong to the interfaces of other collections, such as sets. Where convention is lacking, use common sense: the meanings of the methods `isEmpty` and `clear` are immediately recognizable. (The latter empties a bag.)

Indeed, in the use of common names for operations on different types of collections, you see the first example of polymorphism (from the Greek term for *many bodies*) in action. Following are the function names, method names, and operators in the bag interface:

```
isEmpty
len
str
for …
in
+
==
clear
add
remove
```

Specifying Arguments and Return Values

The next refinement of the bag interface is to add arguments to the operations in the interface and to think about what values, if any, they return. Note that an interface never discloses how an operation performs its task; that's the job of its implementers.

Once again, you can return to a scenario for the use of bags in real life. For each operation, ask what, if any, objects it needs from you to perform its task, and what, if any, objects are returned to you when the task is completed. This information gives you the operation's arguments and return values, if any. A quick way to get clear on these matters is to imagine writing a short program that uses a bag of numbers. The next code segment illustrates such a daydream, where the variables b and c refer to bags:

```
b.clear()               # Make the bag empty
for item in range(10):  # Add 10 numbers to it
    b.add(item)
print(b)                # Print the contents (a string)
print(4 in b)           # Is 4 in the bag?
c = b + b               # Contents doubled in a new bag
print(len(c))           # 20 numbers
for item in c:          # Print them all individually
    print(item)
for item in range(10):  # Remove half of them
    c.remove(item)
print(c == b)           # Should be the same contents now
```

The isEmpty, len, and clear operations are the simplest, because each of them needs no information from us to do its work. len returns an integer, whereas str returns a string.

The add and remove operations need to know the item being added or removed, so each expects one argument: an item. One question that now arises is what remove should do when its argument is not in the bag. When this happens with Python's built-in collections, Python typically raises an exception. You can ignore this problem for now and return to it in the next subsection.

The in, +, and == operators each expect two operands, and each operator returns a single value. The two operands of the in operator are any Python object and a bag. The in operator returns a Boolean value. The + operator expects two bags as operands and returns a third bag. The == operator expects a bag and any Python object as operands and returns a Boolean value.

The for loop over a collection is what programmers call "syntactic sugar" for a more complex loop that uses an *iterator object*. This chapter examines iterators in more detail later. For now, just assume that this part of the bag interface relies upon a method named __iter__.

As mentioned earlier in this book, several Python functions and operator symbols are shorthand for certain standard methods in an implementing class. Table 5.1 adds these methods to the list in the previous section "Designing the Bag Interface," along with the relevant arguments. Note that b in column 1 refers to a bag, and self in column 2 refers to the object (a bag) on which the method is run. Note also that you can omit the __contains__ method if you include the __iter__ method.

Table 5.1   Arguments for Bag Operations and Their Methods

User's Bag Operation	Method in a Bag Class
b = <class name>(<optional collection>)	__init__(self, sourceCollection = None)
b.isEmpty()	isEmpty(self)
len(b)	__len__(self)
str(b)	__str__(self)
for item in b:	__iter__(self)
item in b	__contains__(self, item)
	Not needed if __iter__ is included
b1 + b2	__add__(self, other)
b == anyObject	__eq__(self, other)
b.clear()	clear(self)
b.add(item)	add(self, item)
b.remove(item)	remove(self, item)

© 2014 Cengage Learning®

Constructors and Implementing Classes

The first row in Table 5.1 shows an operation not named or included in the earlier list. This operation is the *constructor* for the particular type of bag being created. For the user of a bag, this constructor is just the name of the implementing bag class, followed by its arguments, if any. The syntactic form <class name> is used in Table 5.1 to indicate that this can be the name of any implementing bag class. The method in the right column is always named __init__. Note that this method takes an optional source collection as an argument, which defaults to None if the user does not provide it. This allows the user to create either an empty bag or a bag with the contents of another collection.

For example, assume that two implementing classes, ArrayBag and LinkedBag, are available to the programmer. The following code segment creates an empty linked bag and an array bag that contains the numbers in a given list:

```
from arraybag import ArrayBag
from linkedbag import LinkedBag

bag1 = LinkedBag()
bag2 = ArrayBag([20, 60, 100, 43])
```

Preconditions, Postconditions, Exceptions, and Documentation

The final step before expressing an interface in code is to describe clearly and concisely what each method does. This description includes not only what you expect to occur under normal conditions when a method is called, but also what will happen when something abnormal, such as an error, occurs. Such descriptions are brief and deal only with what a method does, not with how it does it. They form the basis for documenting the coded interface with docstrings, as you will see shortly.

As discussed in Chapter 1, "Basic Python Programming," a *docstring* is a string enclosed in triple quotes that will be displayed when Python's `help` function is run on a resource. A docstring for a method with no possible error conditions simply states what the method's parameters are, what its return value is, and what action is performed. Sometimes you can express this information in a single sentence, such as, "Returns the sum of the numbers in the list," or "Sorts the list's items in ascending order."

A more detailed form of documentation can include preconditions and postconditions.

A *precondition* is a statement of what must be true for a method to perform its actions correctly. Typically, this condition has to do with the state of the object on which the method is run. For example, an item must be in a collection before it can be accessed or removed.

A *postcondition* states what will be true after the method completes execution, assuming that its preconditions are also true. For example, the postcondition of clearing a collection is that the collection is empty. Postconditions are usually included in mutator methods, which modify the internal state of an object.

Documentation in an interface should also include a statement of any exceptions that could be raised, usually as the result of the failure to adhere to the preconditions of a method. For example, a bag's `remove` method might raise a `KeyError` if the target item is not in the bag.

Now you'll see what a bag's `remove` method does, under normal or abnormal circumstances. Here is a Python method header for this operation, which includes a detailed docstring that describes the method's argument, preconditions, postconditions, and possible exceptions. Note that `self` is the name of the bag object, from the method's perspective.

```python
def remove(self, item):
    """Precondition: item is in self.
    Raises: KeyError if item in not in self.
    Postcondition: item is removed from self."""
```

Coding an Interface in Python

Some languages, such as Java, provide syntax for coding an interface. A Java interface performs no actions by itself but provides a template of methods to which implementing classes must adhere. Python has no such feature, but you can emulate it for purposes of documenting and guiding the development of implementing classes. Although you will never use this pseudo-interface in a real application, it can serve as a useful blueprint for specifying operations and ensuring consistency among their implementations.

To create an interface, list each of the method headers with its documentation, and complete each method with a single pass or return statement. A pass statement is used in the mutator methods that return no value, whereas each accessor method returns a simple default value, such as False, 0, or None. So that the method headers can be checked with the compiler, place them within a class whose suffix is "Interface." Here is a listing of the bag interface, as defined in the class BagInterface:

```python
"""
File: baginterface.py
Author: Ken Lambert
"""

class BagInterface(object):
    """Interface for all bag types."""

    # Constructor
    def __init__(self, sourceCollection = None):
        """Sets the initial state of self, which includes the
        contents of sourceCollection, if it's present."""
        pass

    # Accessor methods
    def isEmpty(self):
        """Returns True if len(self) == 0,
        or False otherwise."""
        return True

    def __len__(self):
        """Returns the number of items in self."""
        return 0

    def __str__(self):
        """Returns the string representation of self."""
        return ""

    def __iter__(self):
        """Supports iteration over a view of self."""
        return None
```

```
def __add__(self, other):
    """Returns a new bag containing the contents
    of self and other."""
    return None

def __eq__(self, other):
    """Returns True if self equals other,
    or False otherwise."""
    return False

# Mutator methods
def clear(self):
    """Makes self become empty."""
    pass

def add(self, item):
    """Adds item to self."""
    pass

def remove(self, item):
    """Precondition: item is in self.
    Raises: KeyError if item in not in self.
    Postcondition: item is removed from self."""
    pass
```

Now that you have a handy blueprint for all bags, you are ready to consider some bag implementations. In the next two sections, you develop an array-based bag collection and a link-based bag collection.

Exercises 5.1

1. Do the items in a bag have a position, or are they unordered?

2. Which operations appear in the interface of any collection?

3. Which method is responsible for creating a collection object?

4. Give three reasons why interfaces are separated from implementations.

DEVELOPING AN ARRAY-BASED IMPLEMENTATION

In this section, you develop an array-based implementation of the bag interface, called ArrayBag.

Once the designer of a collection class has obtained its interface, the design and implementation of the class itself consists of two steps:

1. Choose an appropriate data structure to contain the collection's items, and determine any other data that might be needed to represent the state of the collection. These data are assigned to instance variables in the __init__ method.

2. Complete the code for the methods specified in the interface.

Choose and Initialize the Data Structures

Because this is an array-based implementation, each object of type ArrayBag contains an array of the items in the bag. This array can be an instance of the Array class discussed in Chapter 4, "Arrays and Linked Structures," or perhaps another array-based collection, such as Python's list type. To illustrate the use of an array, this example prefers it to a list. The module, named arraybag, thus imports the Array type from the arrays module.

As mentioned earlier, the __init__ method is responsible for setting up the initial state of a collection. Therefore, this method creates an array with an initial, default capacity and assigns this array to an instance variable named self._items. Because the default capacity is the same for all instances of ArrayBag, it's defined as a class variable. The default capacity is a fairly small value, such as 10, for reasons of economy.

Because the logical size of the bag will likely differ from the array's capacity, each ArrayBag object must track its logical size in a separate instance variable. Therefore, the __init__ method sets this variable, named self._size, to 0.

After initializing the two instance variables, the __init__ method must deal with the possibility that its caller has provided a source collection parameter. If that is the case, all the data in the source collection must be added to the new ArrayBag object. This process sounds harder than it really is. If you think about how to do it, you're really just looping through the source collection and adding each of its items to self (the new ArrayBag object). Because you can use a for loop on any collection, and because the bag interface already includes an add method, the code is straightforward.

The code for this part of the design is easy to create. You just make a copy of the bag interface file, baginterface.py, and rename it to arraybag.py. You then add an import statement for the array, rename the class to ArrayBag, add a class variable for the default capacity, and complete the __init__ method. Here is a snapshot of these changes:

```
"""
File: arraybag.py
Author: Ken Lambert
"""
```

```
from arrays import Array
class ArrayBag(object):
    """An array-based bag implementation."""

    # Class variable
    DEFAULT_CAPACITY = 10

    # Constructor
    def __init__(self, sourceCollection = None):
        """Sets the initial state of self, which includes the
        contents of sourceCollection, if it's present."""
        self._items = Array(ArrayBag.DEFAULT_CAPACITY)
        self._size = 0
        if sourceCollection:
            for item in sourceCollection:
                self.add(item)
```

You should now be able to load this module and create an instance of ArrayBag. But until you complete some of the other methods, you won't be able to view or modify its contents.

Complete the Easy Methods First

There are now nine methods left to complete in the ArrayBag class. When faced with a number of things to accomplish, try doing the easy things first and putting off the most difficult ones for last. Sometimes that policy does not work well in real life, but it normally works well in programming. Finishing several easy things quickly will build your confidence and help you conserve energy and brain power to solve the hard problems later.

The simplest methods in this interface are isEmpty, __len__, and clear. If you ignore the problem of the array becoming full for now, the add method is also fairly simple. Here is the new code for these four methods:

```
# Accessor methods
def isEmpty(self):
    """Returns True if len(self) == 0, or False otherwise."""
    return len(self) == 0

def __len__(self):
    """-Returns the number of items in self."""
    return self._size
```

```
# Mutator methods
def clear(self):
    """Makes self become empty."""
    self._size = 0
    self._items = Array(ArrayBag.DEFAULT_CAPACITY)

def add(self, item):
    """Adds item to self."""
    # Check array memory here and increase it if necessary
    self._items[len(self)] = item
    self._size += 1
```

You should call a method or function on self to get something done, whenever possible. For example, whenever you need to use the logical size of the bag, run `len(self)` instead of referring directly to the instance variable `self._size`.

The add method places the new item at the logical end of the array. This is not just for simplicity, but because it's a constant time operation. Of course, you'll have to return later to complete the code for resizing the array if it's full.

Now when you try out the ArrayBag class in the shell, you can observe changes to a bag's length with the isEmpty method and len function, but you still can't see its items.

Complete the Iterator

The methods __str__, __add__, and __eq__ all use a for loop on self. You could complete these methods now, but instead bite the bullet and compete the __iter__ method, which enables the other methods to work properly when they are run.

When Python sees a for loop on an iterable object, it runs that object's __iter__ method. If you glance back at the __iter__ method in the Array class for a moment (in Chapter 4), you notice that this method follows the rule of thumb of calling a function to get a job done. In that case, the iter function is called on the underlying list object, and the result is returned. Thus, in the __iter__ method of ArrayBag, you might be tempted just to return the result of calling the iter function on the bag's underlying array object. However, this would be a big mistake. The array might not be full, but its iterator always visits all its positions, including those that contain garbage values. Clearly, you need to be careful to visit only those positions in the array up to but not including the length of the bag.

To solve this problem, the new __iter__ method maintains a cursor that allows it to navigate through a sequence of objects. The caller's for loop drives this process. On each pass through the calling for loop, the item at the cursor is yielded to the caller, and then the cursor is advanced to the next object in the sequence. When the cursor reaches the length of the bag, the __iter__ method's while loop terminates, which in turn terminates the calling `for` loop. Here is the code for the `__iter__` method in `ArrayBag`, followed by a brief explanation:

```
def __iter__(self):
    """Supports iteration over a view of self."""
    cursor = 0
    while cursor < len(self):
        yield self._items[cursor]
        cursor += 1
```

Note that this method implements an index-based traversal of the underlying array object, up to but not including the length of the bag. The method uses a `yield` statement to send each item to the calling `for` loop. This pattern is quite standard for most iterators presented in this book.

Complete the Methods That Use the Iterator

The `__eq__` method follows the rules for the equality test discussed in Chapter 2, "An Overview of Collections." The `__add__` method follows the rules for the concatenation of two collections discussed in Chapter 2. The `__str__` method uses the map and join operations to build a string containing the string representations of the bag's items. Here is the code for these methods, followed by some comments:

```
def __str__(self):
    """Returns the string representation of self."""
    return "{" + ", ".join(map(str, self)) + "}"

def __add__(self, other):
    """Returns a new bag containing the contents
    of self and other."""
    result = ArrayBag(self)
    for item in other:
        result.add(item)
    return result

def __eq__(self, other):
    """Returns True if self equals other,
    or False otherwise."""
    if self is other: return True
    if type(self) != type(other) or \
        len(self) != len(other):
        return False
    for item in self:
        if not item in other:
            return False
    return True
```

Each of these methods relies on the fact that a bag object is iterable, or supports the use of a for loop. This is obvious in the case of the __add__ and __eq__ methods, which run explicit loops over bags. Each of these methods also runs a hidden loop over a bag. The __add__ method creates a clone of self, indirectly using the for loop in the ArrayBag constructor. The __add__ and __eq__ methods run the in operator on other (a bag), which must be iterable for in to work properly. The __str__ method generates a sequence of strings from a bag by using the map function, which in turn assumes that self (the bag) is iterable.

The in Operator and the __contains__ Method

When Python sees the in operator used with a collection, it runs the __contains__ method in the collection's class. However, if the author of this class does not include such a method, Python automatically generates a default method. This method performs a simple sequential search for the target item, using a for loop on self. Because the search of a bag can be no better than linear on the average, you rely on the default implementation of __contains__, omitting the method for it in the ArrayBag class. You will have occasion to include your own __contains__ method for a more efficient search in the next chapter.

Complete the remove Method

The remove method is the most challenging method to complete in the bag implementation. To begin with, you must check the preconditions and raise an exception if they are violated. Then you must search the underlying array for the target item. Finally, you must shift the items in the array to the left to close the hole left by the removed item, decrement the bag's size by one, and resize the array if necessary. Here is the code for the method, with each of these five steps flagged by a comment:

```
def remove(self, item):
    """Precondition: item is in self.
    Raises: KeyError if item in not in self.
    postcondition: item is removed from self."""
    # Check precondition and raise if necessary
    if not item in self:
        raise KeyError(str(item) + " not in bag")
    # Search for index of target item
    targetIndex = 0
    for targetItem in self:
        if targetItem == item:
            break
        targetIndex += 1
```

```
# Shift items to the left of target up by one position
for i in range(targetIndex, len(self) - 1):
    self._items[i] = self._items[i + 1]
# Decrement logical size
self._size -= 1
# Check array memory here and decrease it if necessary
```

As items are removed, more and more of the underlying array's space go to waste. You can remedy this problem by adding code to resize the array, as discussed in Chapter 4, when the array's load factor reaches an unacceptable threshold.

Exercises 5.2

1. Explain the responsibilities of the __init__ method of a collection class.

2. Why is it better to call methods than to refer to instance variables directly within a class?

3. Show how the code for the __init__ method of ArrayBag can be simplified by calling its clear method.

4. Explain why the __iter__ method might be the most useful method in a collection class.

5. Explain why you do not include a __contains__ method in the ArrayBag class.

DEVELOPING A LINK-BASED IMPLEMENTATION

To develop a link-based implementation of a bag collection, you need to focus on two things:

- You're using the same interface as before, with all the methods specified in the file baginterface.py.

- You need to shift your way of thinking from arrays to linked structures to represent the bag's data.

Your first impulse might be to create the new module, named linkedbag, by copying the contents of the baginterface module and editing the methods, as before. However, by glancing through the ArrayBag class, you should notice that several of the methods, such as isEmpty, __len__, __add__, __eq__, and __str__, do not directly access the array variable. Recall that you were encouraged to call other methods as much as possible and keep those variable references to a minimum. Now you can see the payoff of this policy: you don't have to change any of these methods in the least for your linked implementation!

If a method does not access the array variable, it does not have to access the linked structure variable either. Therefore, you can copy several completed methods from the ArrayBag class, without changes, to the LinkedBag class. As you can see, this is an important lesson to learn about the coding of methods: always try to hide the implementing data structures behind a wall of method calls on the object being implemented.

The only methods that will have different implementations in the LinkedBag class are those that cannot avoid this direct access to data: __init__, __iter__, clear, add, and remove. To these the chapter now turns.

Initialize the Data Structures

As in the ArrayBag class, the role of the __init__ method in LinkedBag is to create the instance variables and give them initial values. In this case, instead of an array and a logical size, the two pieces of data are a linked structure and a logical size. To maintain consistency, you can use the same variable names as before. However, self._items is now an external pointer instead of an array. This pointer is initially set to None, the state of an empty linked structure. When the structure is not empty, self._items refers to the first node in the linked structure.

The code to copy the items from the source collection to the new bag is the same as before (because you use a for loop with a method call, of course).

The linkedbag module now imports the singly linked Node type to represent nodes. The class variable for the default capacity is omitted, because it is not relevant in a linked implementation. Here is the code for these changes:

```
"""
File: linkedbag.py
Author: Ken Lambert
"""

from node import Node

class LinkedBag(object):
    """A link-based bag implementation."""

    # Constructor
    def __init__(self, sourceCollection = None):
        """Sets the initial state of self, which includes the
        contents of sourceCollection, if it's present."""
        self._items = None
        self._size = 0
        if sourceCollection:
            for item in sourceCollection:
                self.add(item)
```

Complete the Iterator

The __iter__ method for LinkedBag supports the same kind of traversal as it does in ArrayBag, so the structure of the two methods is quite similar. Both methods use a cursor-based loop that yields items. The primary change is that the cursor is now a pointer to nodes in the linked structure. The cursor is initially set to the external pointer, self._items, and stops the loop when it becomes None. Otherwise, the cursor is used to extract the data item from its current node, and is updated to point to the next node. Here is the code for the new method:

```
def __iter__(self):
    """Supports iteration over a view of self."""
    cursor = self._items
    while not cursor is None:
        yield cursor.data
        cursor = cursor.next
```

Complete the Methods clear and add

The method clear in LinkedBag is quite similar to its sister method in ArrayBag, so it's left as an exercise.

The method add in ArrayBag takes advantage of constant-time access to the logical end of the array, after adjusting the array size if needed. The method add in LinkedBag also leverages constant-time access by placing the new item at the head of the linked structure. However, because memory is only allocated for a new node, there is never an occasional large performance hit like the one taken to increase the array's size in ArrayBag. Here is the code for the new method add:

```
def add(self, item):
    """Adds item to self."""
    self._items = Node(item, self._items)
    self._size += 1
```

Complete the Method remove

Like the method remove in ArrayBag, the method remove in LinkedBag must first handle the precondition and then do a sequential search for the target item. When the node containing the target item is found, there are two cases to consider:

1. This is the node at the head of the linked structure. In that case, you must reset variable self._items to this node's next link.

2. This is some node after the first one: in that case, the next link of the node before it must be reset to the next link of the target item's node.

Either action unlinks the target item's node from the linked structure and frees it for the garbage collector.

As before, you want to try to borrow as much code from the ArrayBag implementation as possible, resorting to manipulating pointers in the linked structure only when necessary. The code for checking the precondition and the search loop has the same structure as before. The difference now is that you track two pointers during the search, named probe and trailer. probe is initially set to the head node, and trailer is set to None. As you move through the search loop, probe stays ahead of trailer by one node. At the end of the loop, when the target item is found, probe points to the item's node, and trailer points to the node before it, if there is one. If probe points to the node at the head of the linked structure, trailer will be None. Thus, at the end of the loop, you will be able to decide which pointer to reset. If it's the next pointer of the previous node, you will be able to access it. Here is the code for the new method remove:

```python
def remove(self, item):
    """Precondition: item is in self.
    Raises: KeyError if item is not in self.
    postcondition: item is removed from self."""
    # Check precondition and raise if necessary
    if not item in self:
        raise KeyError(str(item) + " not in bag")
    # Search for the node containing the target item
    # probe will point to the target node, and trailer
    # will point to the one before it, if it exists
    probe = self._items
    trailer = None
    for targetItem in self:
        if targetItem == item:
            break
        trailer = probe
        probe = probe.next
    # Unhook the node to be deleted, either the first one or the
    # one thereafter
    if probe == self._items:
        self._items = self._items.next
    else:
        trailer.next = probe.next
    # Decrement logical size
    self._size -= 1
```

Exercises 5.3

1. Let a be an array bag and b be a linked bag, both of which are empty. Describe the difference in their memory usage at this point.

2. Why does a linked bag still need a separate instance variable to track its logical size?

3. Why does the programmer not have to worry about wasting memory after an item is removed from a linked bag?

RUN-TIME PERFORMANCE OF THE TWO BAG IMPLEMENTATIONS

Surprisingly, the running times of the operations on the two implementations of bags are quite similar.

The in and remove operations take linear time in both implementations, because they incorporate a sequential search. The remove operation in ArrayBag must do the additional work of shifting data items in the array, but the cumulative effect is not worse than linear. The +, str, and iter operations are linear, as would be expected for any collection.

The running time of the == operation has several cases and is left as an exercise.

The remaining operations are constant time, although ArrayBag's add incurs an occasional linear time hit to resize the array.

The two implementations have the expected memory trade-offs. When the array within an ArrayBag is better than half full, it uses less memory than a LinkedBag of the same logical size. In the worst case, a LinkedBag uses twice as much memory as an ArrayBag whose array is full.

Because of these memory trade-offs, additions to an ArrayBag are generally faster, but removals are slower, than the corresponding operations on a LinkedBag.

TESTING THE TWO BAG IMPLEMENTATIONS

A critical part of software resource development is testing. This chapter has indicated in its narrative of program development that you can run the code as you go to try out the capabilities of each part. This kind of testing is all right for roughing out a resource and refining its implementation. But once the code is completed, you must run a thorough test to build confidence that the resource meets its requirements.

Unit testing with tools such as pyunit can provide such assurance, but an exploration of this type of testing is beyond the scope of this book. Instead, the approach used here is to include a tester function for each resource that you develop. This function both ensures that a new collection class conforms to a collection interface and checks to see that these operations do what they are supposed to do.

To illustrate the use of a tester function for your bag classes, here is the code for a stand-alone application that you can run with any bag class. The tester function expects a type as an argument and runs the tests on objects of that type.

```
"""
File: testbag.py
Author: Ken Lambert
A tester program for bag implementations.
"""

from arraybag import ArrayBag
from linkedbag import LinkedBag

def test(bagType):
    """Expects a bag type as an argument and runs some tests
    on objects of that type."""
    lyst = [2013, 61, 1973]
    print("The list of items added is:", lyst)
    b1 = bagType(lyst)
    print("Expect 3:", len(b1))
    print("Expect the bag's string:", b1)
    print("Expect True:", 2013 in b1)
    print("Expect False:", 2012 in b1)
    print("Expect the items on separate lines:")
    for item in b1:
        print(item)
    b1.clear()
    print("Expect {}:", b1)
    b1.add(25)
    b1.remove(25)
    print("Expect {}:", b1)
    b1 = bagType(lyst)
    b2 = bagType(b1)
    print("Expect True:", b1 == b2)
    print("Expect False:", b1 is b2)
    print("Expect two of each item:", b1 + b2)
    for item in lyst:
        b1.remove(item)
    print("Expect {}:", b1)
    print("Expect crash with KeyError:")
    b2.remove(99)

# test(ArrayBag)
test(LinkedBag)
```

Note that you can run the same methods—those in the bag interface—in this test program on any bag type. That's the whole point of an interface: it remains the same while the implementations can change.

DIAGRAMMING THE BAG RESOURCE WITH UML

As you add more resources to your software toolbox, it will help to catalog them with a set of visual aids called *class diagrams*. These diagrams are taken from a visual language called Unified Modeling Language (UML). Class diagrams show the relationships among classes at various levels of detail. The primary relationship concerning you in the present chapter has been that of a class implementing or realizing an interface. In fact, you now have two classes that realize the same interface, as depicted in the class diagram of Figure 5.1.

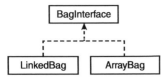

Figure 5.1

A class diagram with an interface and two implementing classes.

© 2014 Cengage Learning®

Two other important relationships among classes are aggregation and composition. Each LinkedBag object aggregates zero or more nodes, whereas each ArrayBag object is composed of a single Array object. Figure 5.2 adds these relationships to the resources depicted in Figure 5.1. Note that the * symbol in Figure 5.2 indicates zero or more instances of the Node class in the aggregation.

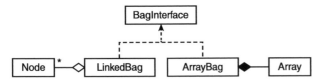

Figure 5.2

A class diagram with aggregation and composition relationships.

© 2014 Cengage Learning®

Informally, you can think of composition as a whole-to-part relationship, whereas aggregation is a one-to-many relationship. The next chapter introduces another important relationship, that of inheritance. Keep your bags packed until then!

SUMMARY

- An interface is the set of operations available to the user of a software resource.
- The items in an interface are the headers of functions and methods, together with their documentation.
- Preconditions state what must be true before a function or method can complete its task correctly.
- Postconditions state what must be true after a function or method completes its task correctly.
- A well-designed software system separates the interfaces from their implementations.
- An implementation is a function, method, or class that conforms to an interface.
- A collection type can be specified by an interface.
- A collection type can have several implementing classes.
- Polymorphism is the use of the same operator symbol, function name, or method name in two or more implementations. Examples of polymorphic functions are str and len. Examples of polymorphic operators are + and ==. Examples of polymorphic methods are add and isEmpty.
- A bag collection type is unordered and supports operations to add, remove, and visit its items.
- A class diagram is a visual notation for depicting relationships among classes.
- Composition relates two classes as part to whole.
- Aggregation relates a class to another class as one to many.
- The UML (unified modeling language) is a graphical notation for depicting the relationships among software resources.

REVIEW QUESTIONS

1. A bag is an example of
   a. A linear collection
   b. An unordered collection
2. The method that is responsible for setting the initial state of an object's instance variables is the
   a. __init__ method
   b. __str__ method

3. The method that allows a programmer to visit each item in a collection is the

   a. `__init__` method

   b. `__iter__` method

4. Methods that change the internal state of an object are its

   a. Accessor methods

   b. Mutator methods

5. The set of methods available to the user of a class is called its

   a. Implementation

   b. Interface

6. Polymorphism is a term that refers to the use of

   a. The same method names in multiple classes

   b. One class to represent the data contained in another class

7. Composition is a term that refers to a

   a. Part-whole relationship among two classes

   b. Many-to-one relationship among two classes

PROJECTS

1. Determine the running time of the $==$ operation for the two bag implementations. Be forewarned that there are several cases to analyze.

2. Complete the code for the `ArrayBag` methods `add` and `remove`, so that the array is resized when necessary.

3. A sorted bag behaves just like a regular bag but allows the user to visit its items in ascending order with the `for` loop. Therefore, the items added to this type of bag must have a natural ordering and recognize the comparison operators. Some examples of such items are strings and integers.
   Define a new class named `ArraySortedBag` that supports this capability. Like `ArrayBag`, this new class is array based, but its `in` operation can now run in logarithmic time. To accomplish this, `ArraySortedBag` must place new items into its array in sorted order. The most efficient way to do this is to modify the `add` method to insert new items in their proper places. You also have to include a `__contains__` method to implement the new, more efficient search. Finally, you must change all references to `ArrayBag` to be `ArraySortedBag`. (*Another hint*: copy the code from the `ArrayBag` class to a new file and begin making your changes from there.)

CHAPTER 6

INHERITANCE AND ABSTRACT CLASSES

When engineers design a product line, such as refrigerators, they start with a basic model. For example, a basic fridge comes with refrigeration and freezer compartments. When building the specialized model, such as a fridge with an icemaker in the freezer and an external cold-water dispenser, the engineers don't start a new model from scratch but instead customize an existing model with new features and behavior.

Software designers have a similar practice of reusing existing models rather than building entirely new models from scratch. For example, a function with parameters captures the idea of using a general algorithm in different situations. A class with its objects broadens this strategy to a set of methods and related data. But perhaps the most powerful way in which a programmer can reuse an existing model to build new models is by exploiting a feature of object-oriented languages called *inheritance*. When a new class is made a subclass of a more general class, the new class acquires all of an existing class's features and behavior by inheritance, like a windfall of free code. The reuse of existing code eliminates redundancy and eases the maintenance and verification of software systems.

This chapter explores the strategies for using inheritance in object-oriented software design, as well as one other mechanism for reusing code: abstract classes. In the process, the bag resources of Chapter 5, "Interfaces, Implementations, and Polymorphism," are placed in a new software framework that sets the stage for the examination of the other collection types later in this book.

USING INHERITANCE TO CUSTOMIZE AN EXISTING CLASS

By far the easiest and most straightforward way to take advantage of inheritance is to use it to customize an existing class. Ideally, the two classes will have the same interface, so clients can use them in the same way. But one of the two classes will give users some specialized behavior.

For example, consider the sorted bag class, `ArraySortedBag`, mentioned in Project 3 of Chapter 5. The sorted bag behaves just like a regular bag, but with three significant exceptions:

- The sorted bag allows the client to visit its elements in sorted order, via the `for` loop.
- The sorted bag's `in` operator runs in logarithmic time.
- The items added to the bag must be comparable with each other. This means that they recognize the comparison operators $<$, $<=$, $>$, and $>=$, and that they are of the same type.

Project 3 of Chapter 5 required you to write an entirely new class for the sorted bag, even though only three of the methods, `__init__`, `add`, and `__contains__`, are different from those in an existing bag class.

This section shows how to use inheritance to create a sorted bag class with just those three methods.

Subclassing an Existing Class

This section exploits the magic of inheritance by making the `ArraySortedBag` class a *subclass* of the `ArrayBag` class. `ArrayBag` is called the *parent* or *superclass* of `ArraySortedBag`. The relationship of subclass and superclass (inheritance) is depicted in the class diagram of Figure 6.1. In the diagram, a solid arrow indicates the subclass/superclass relation, whereas a dashed arrow indicates the class/interface relation.

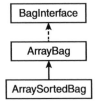

Figure 6.1
Depicting a subclass and inheritance in a class diagram.
© 2014 Cengage Learning®

Note that because the ArrayBag class implements BagInterface, the ArraySortedBag class also implements this interface, via inheritance.

When you began work on the ArraySortedBag class in Project 3 of Chapter 5, you copied the code from ArrayBag, the most similar class, to a new file. You then changed the name of the class throughout the file, modified the add method, and added a __contains__ method.

The strategy for creating a subclass of an existing class is dramatically different. You still work on a copy of the parent class's file, but you now perform the following steps:

1. Begin by *deleting* all the methods that do not have to change. They will be automatically included from the parent class, by the windfall mechanism of inheritance. However, note that you still need the __init__ method in the new class.

2. To guarantee that the inheritance happens, you must place the name of the parent class within the parentheses of the class header.

3. Modify the code for the methods that must change (including __init__).

4. Add any new methods.

Revising the __init__ Method

The ArraySortedBag class does not include any new instance variables, so it does not seem that its __init__ method would have anything to do. However, this method must at least call the __init__ method in the parent class, ArrayBag, so that it can initialize the data contained there. The syntax to call any method in one's parent class is

```
<parent class name>.<method name>(self, <other arguments>)
```

Note the additional argument, self, at the beginning of the argument list. Recall that when the __init__ method of ArrayBag executes, it may add items from a source collection to self. To enable Python to run the correct add method there, self must refer to an instance of ArraySortedBag, not ArrayBag. That's why self is passed as an additional argument to ArrayBag.__init__.

Because the user creates a sorted bag in the same manner as a regular bag, the sorted bag's __init__ method must have the same header as the __init__ method in the parent class.

Here is the code for the changes to ArraySortedBag discussed thus far:

```
"""
File: arraysortedbag.py
Author: Ken Lambert
"""
```

```
from arraybag import ArrayBag

class ArraySortedBag(ArrayBag):
    """An array-based sorted bag implementation."""

    # Constructor
    def __init__(self, sourceCollection = None):
        """Sets the initial state of self, which includes the
        contents of sourceCollection, if it's present."""
        ArrayBag.__init__(self, sourceCollection)
```

Adding a New __contains__ Method

There is no __contains__ method in ArrayBag. You can rely on Python to automatically generate a sequential search, using the ArrayBag iterator, when the in operator is used on a bag. To override this behavior for sorted bags, include a __contains__ method in ArraySortedBag. Now when Python sees the in operator used on a sorted bag, it also sees that bag's __contains__ method and calls it.

This method implements a binary search on the sorted bag's array of items. This array, named self._items and located in the ArrayBag class, is accessible in any of its subclasses. Thus, you can reference this variable directly during the search, as shown in the next code segment.

```
# Accessor methods
def __contains__(self, item):
"""Returns True if item is in self, or False otherwise."""
    left = 0
    right = len(self) - 1
    while left <= right:
        midPoint = (left + right) // 2
        if self._items[midPoint] == item:
            return True
        elif self._items[midPoint] > item:
            right = midPoint - 1
        else:
            left = midPoint + 1
    return False
```

Modifying the Existing add Method

The add method in ArraySortedBag must place a new item in the appropriate position in a sorted array. In many cases, you have to search for this position. However, there are two cases—when the bag is empty or when the new item is greater than or equal to the last item—in which this search is unnecessary. In those cases, you can add the new item by passing it along to the add method in the ArrayBag class. (Remember, whenever possible, to try to call a method to do something rather than doing it yourself.)

If you can't get away with passing the buck to ArrayBag, you must look in the array for the first item that's greater than or equal to the new item. Then open a hole for the new item, insert it, and increment the size of the bag.

Here is the code for the revised method add in ArraySortedBag:

```
# Mutator methods
def add(self, item):
    """Adds item to self."""
    # Empty or last item, call ArrayBag.add
    if self.isEmpty() or item >= self._items[len(self) - 1]:
        ArrayBag.add(self, item)
    else:
        # Resize the array if it is full here
        # Search for first item >= new item
        targetIndex = 0
        while item > self._items[targetIndex]:
            targetIndex += 1
        # Open a hole for new item
        for i in range(len(self), targetIndex, -1):
            self._items[i] = self._items[i - 1]
        # Insert item and update size
        self._items[targetIndex] = item
        self._size += 1
```

Note the different prefixes used in the method call to ArrayBag.add and the variable reference to self._items.

You need the class name to distinguish the ArrayBag version of add from the ArraySortedBag version of add, which, in this context, would be self.add.

Because ArraySortedBag does not introduce a new version of the instance variable _items, the reference to self._items here locates the variable directly in the ArrayBag class.

Although the syntax of calls to methods in a parent class is somewhat complicated, the calls themselves illustrate once more the intelligent reuse of code. Moreover, you now have an additional bag resource that adds great value at little cost to your collection framework.

Run-Time Performance of ArraySortedBag

The `in` operator, which uses the `__contains__` method in `ArraySortedBag`, has a worst-case running time of O(log$n$). This is a big improvement on the linear running time of the `in` operator for regular bags.

The improved search time also has an impact on the methods that use the new `in` operator, even though these methods are still defined in `ArrayBag`. For example, the `remove` method uses `in` to check its precondition. Although the improved search still leaves `remove` with a linear running time on average, less time is spent on the test of the precondition.

The performance improvement in the `__eq__` method is more dramatic. When this method is run on two regular bags of the same length, its average running time is O(n^2). When this method is run on two sorted bags of the same length, its average running time is O($n$log$n$).

If you are willing to include the `__eq__` method in `ArraySortedBag`, you can reduce its average running time to O(n). This implementation takes advantage of the fact that the pairs of items being compared in the two bags are located at the same positions in the underlying arrays. This new version of `__eq__` is left as an exercise for you.

A Note on Class Hierarchies in Python

Every data type in Python is actually a class, and all built-in classes reside in a hierarchy. The topmost or root class of this hierarchy is `object`. When you define a new class and omit the parent class from the syntax, Python automatically installs this class under the `object` class.

When you design a new set of collection classes, it's generally not a good idea to subclass under a built-in Python collection class, such as `str` or `list`. Instead, you should develop your own classes to conform to interfaces and place the topmost class in your hierarchy under the `object` class, as this book does.

Python supports subclassing and inheritance with multiple parent classes, a feature that is useful in some advanced applications. You will explore the use of multiple parent classes later in this book.

Exercises 6.1

1. Using the `ArrayBag` and `ArraySortedBag` classes as examples, explain how class inheritance helps to eliminate redundant code.

2. Explain why the `ArraySortedBag` class must still include an `__init__` method.

3. A programmer calls the `remove` method on an object of type `ArraySortedBag`, which is a subclass of `ArrayBag`. Explain how Python locates the correct method implementation to run in this case.

4. Explain why the `ArrayBag` method `add` is called within the code of the `ArraySortedBag` method `add`.

5. The method `add` is called within the code for the methods `__init__` and `__add__` in the `AbstractBag` class, but it is not defined in that class. To which class does this method belong, and how does Python locate its implementation?

USING ABSTRACT CLASSES TO ELIMINATE REDUNDANT CODE

It is exciting to discover that subclassing and inheritance allow you to omit some code from a new class instead of retaining it. To retain it, like you did in the sorted bag project of Chapter 5, would be to tolerate unnecessary redundancy.

Another place where you can see redundant code in your bag collections is in the `ArrayBag` and `LinkedBag` classes. Recall that when you created `LinkedBag` by copying code from `ArrayBag` in Chapter 5, several methods did not have to be changed. They look the same in both classes; therefore, they are by definition redundant.

You just learned how to avoid this problem with sorted bags by keeping the potentially redundant methods in a parent class and sharing them with another class via inheritance.

In this section, you learn how to eliminate redundant methods and data in a set of existing classes by factoring the code for them into a common superclass. Such a class is called an *abstract class* to indicate that it captures the common features and behavior of a set of related classes. An abstract class is not normally instantiated in client applications. Its subclasses are called *concrete classes* to indicate that they are the classes actually used to create objects in client applications.

Designing an AbstractBag Class

Programmers typically spot the need for an abstract class after they have developed two or more classes and notice some redundant methods and variables. In the case of your bag classes, the most obviously redundant methods are the ones that simply call other methods and do not directly access the instance variables. They include the methods `isEmpty`, `__str__`, `__add__`, and `__eq__`.

Redundant instance variables are a bit trickier to spot. Your bag classes use two instance variables, named self._items and self._size. To discover a redundancy, you must look at the types of data to which the variables refer. In each class, self._items refers to a different type of data structure. (That's why they're called different implementations.) By contrast, self._size refers to an integer value in every bag class. Therefore, only self._size is a redundant instance variable, and thus a safe candidate for movement to an abstract class.

Because the __len__ method accesses self._size but not self._items, it, too, counts as a redundant method.

You can remove the redundant methods from the bag classes and place them in a new class called AbstractBag. The bag classes then access these methods via inheritance by becoming subclasses of AbstractBag. The modified framework of your bag classes is depicted in the class diagram of Figure 6.2.

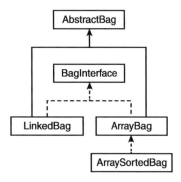

Figure 6.2
Adding an abstract bag class to the collection framework.
© 2014 Cengage Learning®

Note that the AbstractBag class does not implement the bag interface. That's because only a subset of the bag methods are included in AbstractBag. The other three bag classes continue to conform to the bag interface.

Note also that you now have a more obvious class hierarchy, with two levels of inheritance. The ArraySortedBag class now inherits some methods and data directly from its parent class ArrayBag, and other methods and data indirectly from its ancestor class AbstractBag. In general, the methods and variables of a class are available to any of its descendant classes.

To create the AbstractBag class, you start by copying the contents of one of its subclasses to a new file and save that file as abstractbag.py. Then perform the following steps:

1. Delete any irrelevant imports and rename the class AbstractBag.

2. Delete all the methods that directly access the instance variable self._items, except for the __init__ method. The next subsection shows you how to modify the __init__ method.

Redoing the __init__ Method in AbstractBag

The __init__ method in AbstractBag is responsible for performing two steps:

1. Introducing the variable self._size and initializing it to 0

2. Adding the items from the source collection to self, if necessary

Therefore, you delete the line of code that initializes the variable self._items. This code is still the responsibility of the subclasses.

Here is the code for these changes in AbstractBag:

```
"""
File: abstractbag.py
Author: Ken Lambert
"""
class AbstractBag(object):
    """An abstract bag implementation."""
    # Constructor

    def __init__(self, sourceCollection = None):
        """Sets the initial state of self, which includes the
        contents of sourceCollection, if it's present."""
        self._size = 0
        if sourceCollection:
            for item in sourceCollection:
                self.add(item)
```

Modifying the Subclasses of AbstractBag

Each subclass of AbstractBag must now import this class, place its name within the parentheses in the class header, omit the redundant methods mentioned earlier, and include a modified __init__ method.

Examine the changes to the __init__ method of ArrayBag. This method is still responsible for setting self._items to a new array, but that's the only line of code kept from before. After you run this code, run the __init__ method in AbstractBag, which initializes the bag's size and adds the items from the source collection if necessary. Here is the code for these changes to __init__:

```
""
File: arraybag.py
Author: Ken Lambert
"""
from arrays import Array
from abstractbag import AbstractBag

class ArrayBag(AbstractBag):
    """An array-based bag implementation."""

    # Class variable
    DEFAULT_CAPACITY = 10

    # Constructor
    def __init__(self, sourceCollection = None):
        """Sets the initial state of self, which includes the
        contents of sourceCollection, if it's present."""
        self._items = Array(ArrayBag.DEFAULT_CAPACITY)
        AbstractBag.__init__(self, sourceCollection)
```

Note the order in which the two statements are written in __init__. It is critical to initialize self._items to the new array before running the constructor in the superclass so that there will be storage for any items that are added to the new bag.

The changes to the LinkedBag class are similar and are left as an exercise for you.

Generalizing the __add__ Method in AbstractBag

If you test the bag classes with your tester function at this point, the + operator, which uses the __add__ method in AbstractBag, raises an exception. The exception states that AbstractBag does not know about ArrayBag (or LinkedBag, if that's the class from which you copied this method). Of course, AbstractBag cannot know anything about its subclasses. The cause of this error is that the __add__ method has attempted to create an instance of ArrayBag to hold its results, as shown in the next code segment:

```
def __add__(self, other):
    """Returns a new bag containing the contents
    of self and other."""
    result = ArrayBag(self)
    for item in other:
        result.add(item)
    return result
```

What you really want here is not an instance of a specific class, but an instance of the type of self, whatever type that happens to be.

To solve this problem, you can use Python's type function to access the type of self and then use the resulting type to create a clone of self in the usual manner. Here is the code for an __add__ method that works with all bag types:

```
def __add__(self, other):
    """Returns a new bag containing the contents
    of self and other."""
    result = type(self)(self)
    for item in other:
        result.add(item)
    return result
```

AN ABSTRACT CLASS FOR ALL COLLECTIONS

If you review the code for the AbstractBag class, you might notice something interesting about it. All of its methods, including __init__, run other methods or functions or simply access the variable self._size. They make no mention of bag classes. With the exception of the __str__ method, which creates a string with curly braces, and the __eq__ method, which does not compare pairs of items at given positions, the AbstractBag's methods are also methods that could be run on any other types of collections, such as lists, stacks, and queues. Finally, the one instance variable, self._size, could be used in the implementation of any collection as well.

This insight indicates that you would be well advised to factor these methods and data up to an even more general abstract class, where they would be available to other types of collections yet to be developed. Such a class, called AbstractCollection, would serve as the keystone class of your entire collection hierarchy.

Integrating AbstractCollection into the Collection Hierarchy

The AbstractCollection class is responsible for introducing and initializing the variable self._size. This variable is used by all the collection classes below it in the hierarchy.

The __init__ method of AbstractCollection can also add the items from the source collection to self, if necessary.

This class also includes the most general methods available to all collections: isEmpty, __len__, and __add__. "Most general" in this case means that their implementation need never be changed by a subclass.

Finally, AbstractCollection also includes default implementations of the __str__ and __eq__ methods. Their current form in AbstractBag is appropriate for unordered collections, but most collection classes are likely to be linear rather than unordered. Therefore, these two methods are left as is in AbstractBag, but new implementations are provided in AbstractCollection. The new __str__ method uses the square brackets to delimit the string, and the new __eq__ method compares pairs of items at given positions. New subclasses of AbstractCollection are still free to customize __str__ and __eq__ to suit their needs.

Figure 6.3 shows the integration of the new AbstractCollection class into your collection framework.

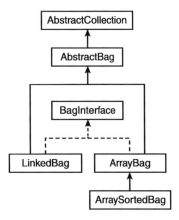

Figure 6.3

Adding an abstract collection class to the collection framework.

© 2014 Cengage Learning®

Note that the classes trend from the more general to the more specific in character, as your eyes move down through the hierarchy. Now when a new collection type, such as ListInterface, comes along, you can create an abstract class for it, place that under AbstractCollection, and begin with some data and methods ready to hand. The concrete implementations of lists would then go under the abstract list class.

To create the AbstractCollection class, you copy code as usual from another module, in this case, AbstractBag. You can now perform the following steps:

1. Rename the class to AbstractCollection.

2. Modify the __init__ method by removing the call to __init__ in a parent class.

3. Modify the __str__ and __eq__ methods to provide reasonable default behavior.

You then remove the isEmpty, __len__, and __add__ methods from AbstractBag. The implementation of AbstractCollection and the modification of AbstractBag are left as exercises for you.

Using Two Iterators in the __eq__ Method

The implementation of the __eq__ method in the AbstractCollection class compares pairs of items in the two collections. It does so by iterating through the sequences of items in both collections simultaneously. But how can this be accomplished, when one can run a for loop over only one collection at a time?

The answer to this question lies in manipulating the second collection's iterator object explicitly. When the programmer calls the iter function on a collection, the collection's iterator object is returned. When the programmer calls the next function on an iterator object, the function returns the current item in the iterator's sequence and advances to its next item, if there is one. If there is no current item in the sequence, the function next raises a StopIteration exception.

For example, the following two code segments perform the same task, but the first one uses Python's for loop and the second one manipulates the collection's iterator object:

```
# Print all the items in theCollection using a for loop
for item in theCollection:
    print(item)
```

```
# Print all the items in theCollection using an explicit iterator
iteratorObject = iter(theCollection)
try:
    while True:
        print(next(iteratorObject))
except StopIteration: pass
```

When you employ an explicit iterator in the __eq__ method of AbstractCollection, there is no need to trap a StopIteration exception. Because the two collections have the same length, the for loop on the first collection will stop when the iterator on the second collection reaches the end of its sequence of items. Here is the code for the new __eq__ method:

```
def __eq__(self, other):
    """Returns True if self equals other, or False otherwise."""
    if self is other: return True
    if type(self) != type(other) or \
        len(self) != len(other):
        return False
    otherIter = iter(other)
    for item in self:
        if item != next(otherIter):
            return False
    return True
```

Exercises 6.2

1. Using the AbstractBag class as an example, describe the purpose of an abstract class, and explain why no instance of it would ever be created.

2. The methods __init__, isEmpty, __len__, __str__, __eq__, and __add__ are defined in the AbstractCollection class. Which of these methods might be redefined in subclasses, and why?

3. Two methods are not defined in the AbstractCollection class but must be defined in its subclasses for its other methods to function properly. Which methods are these?

4. Write the code for a new method named clone, in the AbstractCollection class. This method expects no arguments and returns an exact copy of the object on which it is run.

Summary

- Two classes can be related as subclass and superclass. A subclass generally is a more specialized version of its superclass. The superclass is also called the parent of its subclasses.

- A subclass inherits all the methods and variables from its parent class, as well as any of its ancestor classes. Inheritance allows two classes—a subclass and a superclass—to share data and methods, thus eliminating potential redundancy.

- A subclass specializes the behavior of its superclass by modifying its methods or adding new methods.

- A class can call a method in its superclass by using the superclass name as a prefix to the method.

- An abstract class serves as a repository of data and methods that are common to a set of other classes. If these other classes are not also abstract, they are called concrete classes.

- Abstract classes are not instantiated.

- Python includes all classes in a hierarchy, with the object class as the topmost parent class.

- The methods with more general behavior should generally be located further up in a class hierarchy.

REVIEW QUESTIONS

1. A given class inherits all the methods and instance variables from its

   a. Descendant classes

   b. Ancestor classes

2. The number of methods available in a given class is generally

   a. Less than or equal to the number of methods available to its parent class

   b. Greater than or equal to the number of methods available to its parent class

3. A method in a given class can call the same method in an ancestor class by

   a. Using the prefix `self` with the method's name

   b. Using the ancestor class name as a prefix with the method's name

4. The name `self` always refers to

   a. The object of the class used when that object was instantiated

   b. The object of the class whose definition includes that use of `self`

5. The methods in an abstract class ideally

   a. Call other methods on `self` to do their work

   b. Include lots of references and assignments to instance variables

6. The methods most likely to be implemented in the `AbstractCollection` class are

   a. `__iter__`, add, and `remove`

   b. `isEmpty`, `__len__`, and `__add__`

7. The function that returns the type of an object is called

   a. `type`

   b. `getType`

PROJECTS

When you create or modify classes in the following projects, be sure to test your changes by running an appropriate tester program.

1. Add the `__eq__` method to the `ArraySortedBag` class discussed in this chapter. This method should run in no worse than linear time.

2. Modify the LinkedBag class discussed in Chapter 5, so that it becomes a subclass of AbstractBag. Be sure to retain in LinkedBag only those methods that cannot be moved to AbstractBag.

3. Complete the AbstractCollection class discussed in this chapter. Then revise the AbstractBag class so that it behaves as a subclass of AbstractCollection.

4. A set behaves just like a bag, except that a set cannot contain duplicate items. Some possible implementations are ArraySet and LinkedSet. Draw a class diagram that shows where you would place these new classes in the collection framework shown in Figure 6.3.

5. Complete the classes for ArraySet and LinkedSet.

6. A sorted set behaves just like a set, but allows the user to visit its items in ascending order with a for loop, and supports a logarithmic search for an item. Draw a class diagram that shows where you would place a new class for sorted sets in the collection framework shown in Figure 6.3.

7. Complete the new class for sorted sets.

8. Someone notices that the remove operation performs two searches of a bag: one during the test of the method's precondition (using the in operator) and the other to locate the position of the target item to actually remove it. One way to eliminate the redundant search is to track the position of the target item in an instance variable. In the case of an array-based bag, this position would be –1 at startup and whenever a target item is not found. If the in operator finds a target item, the position variable is set to that item's index in the array; otherwise, it is reset to –1. After the remove method checks its precondition, no search loop is necessary; the method can just close the hole in the array using the position variable. Modify the ArrayBag class to support this capability. Note that you will now have to add a __contains__ method to ArrayBag that performs this customized search.

9. The modified remove method of Project 8 no longer works correctly for a sorted bag. The reason for this is that the __contains__ method in ArraySortedBag does not update the new position variable in ArrayBag. Modify the method ArraySortedBag.__contains__ so that the remove method works correctly for sorted bags.

10. The remove method in the LinkedBag class has the redundant search described in Project 8. Modify this class so that this redundancy no longer exists.

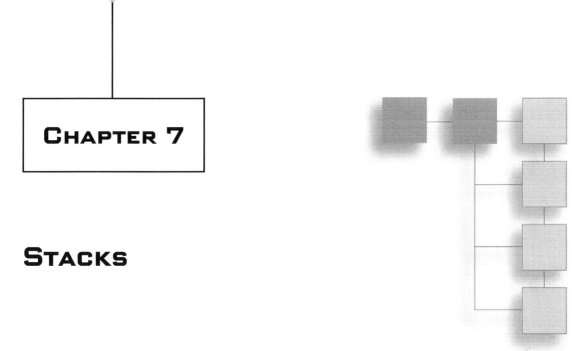

CHAPTER 7

STACKS

This chapter introduces the *stack*, a collection that has widespread use in computer science. The stack is the simplest collection to describe and implement. However, it has fascinating applications, three of which are discussed later in the chapter. This chapter also presents two standard implementations: one based on arrays and the other on linked structures. The chapter closes with a case study in which stacks play a central role—the translation and evaluation of arithmetic expressions.

OVERVIEW OF STACKS

Stacks are linear collections in which access is completely restricted to just one end, called the *top*. The classic analogous example is the stack of clean trays found in every cafeteria. Whenever a tray is needed, it is removed from the top of the stack, and whenever clean ones come back from the kitchen, they are again placed on the top. No one ever takes some particularly fine tray from the middle of the stack, and trays near the bottom might never be used. Stacks are said to adhere to a *last-in first-out* (LIFO) protocol. The last tray brought back from the dishwasher is the first one a customer takes.

The operations for putting items on and removing items from a stack are called push and pop, respectively. Figure 7.1 shows a stack as it might appear at various stages. The item at the top of the stack is shaded.

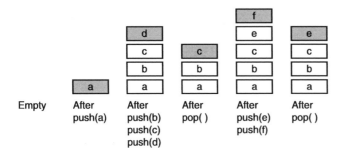

Figure 7.1

Some states in the lifetime of a stack.

© 2014 Cengage Learning®

Initially, the stack is empty, and then an item called a is pushed. Next, three more items called b, c, and d are pushed, after which the stack is popped, and so forth.

Other everyday examples of stacks include plates and bowls in a kitchen cupboard or a spindle of CDs. Although you continually add more papers to the top of the piles on your desk, these piles do not quite qualify because you often need to remove a long-lost paper from the middle. With a genuine stack, the item you get next is always the one added most recently.

Applications of stacks in computer science are numerous. Here are just a few, including three that are discussed in more detail later in this chapter:

- Translating infix expressions to postfix form and evaluating postfix expressions (discussed later in this chapter).

- Backtracking algorithms (discussed later in this chapter and occurring in problems such as automated theorem proving and game playing).

- Managing computer memory in support of function and method calls (discussed later in this chapter).

- Supporting the undo feature in text editors, word processors, spreadsheet programs, drawing programs, and similar applications.

- Maintaining a history of the links visited by a web browser.

USING A STACK

A stack type is not built into Python. In a pinch, Python programmers can use a Python list to emulate an array-based stack. If you view the end of a list as the top of a stack, the list method append pushes an element onto this stack, whereas the list method pop removes and returns the element at its top. The main drawback of this option is that all the other list operations can manipulate the stack as well. These include the insertion, replacement, and removal of an element at any position. These extra operations violate the spirit of a stack as an abstract data type. This section defines a more restricted interface for any authentic stack implementation and shows how these operations are used in a brief example.

The Stack Interface

In addition to the push and pop operations, a stack interface provides an operation named peek for examining the element at the top of a stack. Like other collections, the stack type can also include the clear, isEmpty, len, str, in, and + operations, as well as an iterator. These operations are listed as Python methods in Table 7.1, where the variable s refers to a stack.

Table 7.1   The Methods in the Stack Interface

Stack Method	What It Does
s.isEmpty()	Returns True if s is empty or False otherwise.
__len__(s)	Same as len(s). Returns the number of items in s.
__str__(s)	Same as str(s). Returns the string representation of s.
s.__iter__()	Same as iter(s), or for item in s:. Visits each item in s, from bottom to top.
c.__contains__(item)	Same as item in s. Returns True if item is in s or False otherwise.
s1__add__(s2)	Same as s1 + s2. Returns a new stack containing the items in s1 and s2.
s.__eq__(anyObject)	Same as s == anyObject. Returns True if s equals any Object or False otherwise. Two stacks are equal if the items at corresponding positions are equal.
s.clear()	Makes s become empty.
s.peek()	Returns the item at the top of s. *Precondition*: s must not be empty; raises a KeyError if the stack is empty.
s.push(item)	Adds item to the top of s.
s.pop()	Removes and returns the item at the top of s. *Precondition*: s must not be empty; raises a KeyError if the stack is empty.

Note that the methods `pop` and `peek` have an important precondition and raise an exception if the user of the stack does not satisfy that precondition. The advantage of this interface is that users will know which methods to use and what to expect from them, no matter which stack implementation is chosen.

Now that a stack interface has been defined, you will learn how to use it. Table 7.2 shows how the operations listed earlier affect a stack named s. The syntactic form `<Stack Type>` stands for any implementing class.

Table 7.2   The Effects of Stack Operations

Operation	State of the Stack After the Operation	Value Returned	Comment
s = <Stack Type>()			Initially, the stack is empty.
s.push(a)	a		The stack contains the single item a.
s.push(b)	a b		b is the top item.
s.push(c)	a b c		c is the top item.
s.isEmpty()	a b c	False	The stack is not empty.
len(s)	a b c	3	The stack contains three items.
s.peek()	a b c	c	Return the top item without removing it.
s.pop()	a b	c	Remove and return the top item. b is now the top item.
s.pop()	a	b	Remove and return the top item. a is now the top item.
s.pop()		a	Remove and return the top item.
s.isEmpty()		True	The stack is empty.
s.peek()		KeyError	Peeking at an empty stack raises an exception.
s.pop()		KeyError	Popping an empty stack raises an exception.
s.push(d)	d		d is the top item.

© 2014 Cengage Learning®

Instantiating a Stack

You can assume that any stack class that implements this interface also has a constructor that allows its user to create a new stack instance. Later in this chapter, two different implementations, named ArrayStack and LinkedStack, are considered. For now, assume that someone has coded these so you can use them. The next code segment shows how you might instantiate them:

```
s1 = ArrayStack()
s2 = LinkedStack([20, 40, 60])
```

Although the code of these two implementations need not be revealed to the implementation's users, it would be naïve to assume that the users know nothing at all about these implementations. As you have seen in Chapter 5, "Interfaces, Implementations, and Polymorphism," different implementations of the same interface likely have different performance trade-offs, and knowledge of these trade-offs is critical to users of the implementations. Users would base their choice of one implementation rather than another on the performance characteristics required by their applications. These characteristics in turn are implied by the very names of the classes (array or linked) and would likely be mentioned in the documentation of the implementations. But for now, assume that you have enough knowledge to use either implementation of stacks in the applications that follow.

Example Application: Matching Parentheses

Compilers need to determine if the bracketing symbols in expressions are balanced correctly. For example, every opening [should be followed by a properly positioned closing] and every (by a). Table 7.3 provides some examples.

Table 7.3   Balanced and Unbalanced Brackets in Expressions

Example Expression	Status	Reason
(...)...(...)	Balanced	
(...)...(...	Unbalanced	Missing a closing) at the end.
)...(...(...)	Unbalanced	The closing) at the beginning has no matching opening (and one of the opening parentheses has no closing parenthesis.
[...(...)...]	Balanced	
[...(...]...)	Unbalanced	The bracketed sections are not nested properly.

© 2014 Cengage Learning®

In these examples, three dots represent arbitrary strings that contain no bracketing symbols.

As a first attempt at solving the problem of whether brackets balance, you might simply count the number of left and right parentheses. If the expression balances, the two counts are equal. However, the converse is not true. If the counts are equal, the brackets do not necessarily balance. The third example provides a counterexample.

A more sophisticated approach, using a stack, does work. To check an expression, take the following steps:

1. Scan across the expression, pushing opening brackets onto a stack.

2. On encountering a closing bracket, if the stack is empty or if the item on the top of the stack is not an opening bracket of the same type, you know the brackets do not balance.

3. Pop an item off the top of the stack and, if it is the right type of bracket, continue scanning the expression.

4. When you reach the end of the expression, the stack should be empty, and if it is not, you know the brackets do not balance.

Here is a Python script that implements this strategy for the two types of brackets mentioned. Assume that the module linkedstack includes the class LinkedStack.

```
"""
File: brackets.py
Checks expressions for matching brackets
"""

from linkedstack import LinkedStack

def bracketsBalance(exp):
    """exp is a string that represents the expression"""
    stk = LinkedStack()                     # Create a new stack
    for ch in exp:                          # Scan across the expression
        if ch in ['[', '(']:               # Push an opening bracket
            stk.push(ch)
        elif ch in [']', ')']:             # Process a closing bracket
            if stk.isEmpty():                          # Not balanced
                return False
            chFromStack = stk.pop()
            # Brackets must be of same type and match up
            if ch == ']' and chFromStack != '[' or \
               ch == ')' and chFromStack != '(':
                return False
    return stk.isEmpty()                    # They all matched up
```

```
def main():
    exp = input("Enter a bracketed expression: ")
    if bracketsBalance(exp):
        print("OK")
    else:
        print("Not OK")
if __name__ == "__main__":
    main()
```

Exercises 7.1

1. Using the format of Table 7.2, complete a table that involves the following sequence of stack operations.

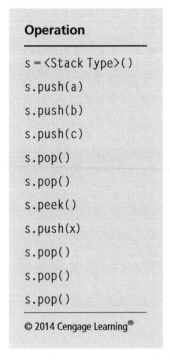

Operation
s = <Stack Type>()
s.push(a)
s.push(b)
s.push(c)
s.pop()
s.pop()
s.peek()
s.push(x)
s.pop()
s.pop()
s.pop()

© 2014 Cengage Learning®

The other columns are labeled State of the Stack After the Operation, Value Returned, and Comment.

2. Modify the bracketsBalance function so that the caller can supply the brackets to match as arguments to this function. The second argument should be a list of beginning brackets, and the third argument should be a list of ending brackets. The pairs of brackets at each position in the two lists should match; that is, position 0 in the two lists might have [and], respectively. You should be able to modify the code for the function so that it does not reference literal bracket symbols, but just uses the list arguments. (Hint: The method index returns the position of an item in a list.)

3. Someone suggests that you might not need a stack to match parentheses in expressions after all. Instead, you can set a counter to 0, increment it when a left parenthesis is encountered, and decrement it whenever a right parenthesis is seen. If the counter ever goes below 0 or remains positive at the end of the process, there was an error; if the counter is 0 at the end and never goes negative, the parentheses all match correctly. Where does this strategy break down? (*Hint*: There might be braces and brackets to match as well.)

THREE APPLICATIONS OF STACKS

Now you'll learn three other applications of stacks. First, you'll see algorithms for evaluating arithmetic expressions. These algorithms apply to problems in compiler design, and you will use them in the chapter's case study. Second, you'll learn a general technique for using stacks to solve backtracking problems. The programming projects explore applications of the technique. Third, you'll witness the role of stacks in computer memory management. Not only is this topic interesting in its own right, but it provides a foundation for understanding recursion.

Evaluating Arithmetic Expressions

In daily life, people are so accustomed to evaluating simple arithmetic expressions that they give little thought to the rules involved. So you might be surprised by the difficulty of writing an algorithm to evaluate arithmetic expressions. It turns out that an indirect approach to the problem works best. First, you transform an expression from its familiar *infix form* to a *postfix form*, and then you evaluate the postfix form. In the infix form, each operator is located between its operands, whereas in the postfix form, an operator immediately follows its operands. Table 7.4 gives several simple examples.

Table 7.4   Some Infix and Postfix Expressions

Infix Form	Postfix Form	Value
34	34	34
34 + 22	34 22 +	56
34 + 22 * 2	34 22 2 * +	78
34 * 22 + 2	34 22 * 2 +	750
(34 + 22) * 2	34 22 + 2 *	112

© 2014 Cengage Learning®

There are similarities and differences between the two forms. In both, operands appear in the same order. However, the operators do not. The infix form sometimes requires parentheses; the postfix form never does. Infix evaluation involves rules of precedence; postfix evaluation applies operators as soon as they are encountered. For instance, consider the steps in evaluating the infix expression 34 + 22 * 2 and the equivalent postfix expression 34 22 2 * +.

Infix evaluation: 34 + 22 * 2 → 34 + 44 → 78

Postfix evaluation:34 22 2 * + → 34 44 + → 78

The use of parentheses and operator precedence in infix expressions is for the convenience of the human beings who read them and write them. By eliminating these parentheses, the equivalent postfix expressions present a computer with a format that is much easier and more efficient for it to evaluate.

You'll now see stack-based algorithms for transforming infix expressions to postfix and for evaluating the resulting postfix expressions. In combination, these algorithms allow a computer to evaluate an infix expression. In practice, the conversion step usually occurs at compile time, whereas the evaluation step occurs at run time. In presenting the algorithms, you can ignore this difference and ignore the effects of syntax errors, but you'll return to the issue in the case study and the exercises. The evaluation of postfix expressions comes first; it is simpler than converting infix expressions to postfix expressions.

Evaluating Postfix Expressions

Evaluating a postfix expression involves three steps:

1. Scan across the expression from left to right.

2. On encountering an operator, apply it to the two preceding operands and replace all three by the result.

3. Continue scanning until you reach the expression's end, at which point only the expression's value remains.

To express this procedure as a computer algorithm, you use a stack of operands. In the algorithm, the term *token* refers to either an operand or an operator:

```
Create a new stack
While there are more tokens in the expression
    Get the next token
    If the token is an operand
        Push the operand onto the stack
    Else if the token is an operator
        Pop the top two operands from the stack
```

```
        Apply the operator to the two operands just popped
        Push the resulting value onto the stack
Return the value at the top of the stack
```

The time complexity of the algorithm is O(n), where n is the number of tokens in the expression (see the exercises). Table 7.5 shows a trace of the algorithm as it applies to the expression 4 5 6 * + 3 -.

Table 7.5 Tracing the Evaluation of a Postfix Expression

Postfix Expression: 4 5 6 * + 3 -		Resulting Value: 31
Portion of Postfix Expression Scanned So Far	**Operand Stack**	**Comment**
		No tokens have been scanned yet. The stack is empty.
4	4	Push the operand 4.
4 5	4 5	Push the operand 5.
4 5 6	4 5 6	Push the operand 6.
4 5 6 *	4 30	Replace the top two operands by their product.
4 5 6 * +	34	Replace the top two operands by their sum.
4 5 6 * + 3	34 3	Push the operand 3.
4 5 6 * + 3 -	31	Replace the top two operands by their difference.
		Pop the final value.

© 2014 Cengage Learning®

Exercises 7.2

1. Evaluate by hand the following postfix expressions:

   a. 10 5 4 + *

   b. 10 5 * 6 –

c. 22 2 4 * /

d. 33 6 + 3 4 / +

2. Perform a complexity analysis for postfix evaluation.

Converting Infix to Postfix

You now learn how to translate expressions from infix to postfix. For the sake of simplicity, you can restrict your attention to expressions involving the operators *, /, +, and -. (An exercise at the end of the chapter enlarges the set of operators.) As usual, multiplication and division have higher precedence than addition and subtraction, except when parentheses override the default order of evaluation.

In broad terms, the algorithm scans, from left to right, a sequence containing an infix expression and simultaneously builds a sequence containing the equivalent postfix expression. Operands are copied from the infix sequence to the postfix sequence as soon as they are encountered. However, operators must be held back on a stack until operators of greater precedence have been copied to the postfix string ahead of them. Here is a more detailed statement of the stepwise process:

1. Start with an empty postfix expression and an empty stack, which will hold operators and left parentheses.

2. Scan across the infix expression from left to right.

3. On encountering an operand, append it to the postfix expression.

4. On encountering a left parenthesis, push it onto the stack.

5. On encountering an operator, pop off the stack all operators that have equal or higher precedence, append them to the postfix expression, and then push the scanned operator onto the stack.

6. On encountering a right parenthesis, shift operators from the stack to the postfix expression until meeting the matching left parenthesis, which is discarded.

7. On encountering the end of the infix expression, transfer the remaining operators from the stack to the postfix expression.

Examples in Tables 7.6 and 7.7 illustrate the procedure.

Table 7.6 Tracing the Conversion of an Infix Expression to a Postfix Expression

Infix expression: 4 + 5 * 6 - 3   Postfix expression: 4 5 6 * + 3 -

Portion of Infix Expression So Far	Operator Stack	Postfix Expression	Comment
			No tokens have been seen yet. The stack and the PE are empty.
4		4	Append 4 to the PE.
4 +	+		Push + onto the stack.
4 + 5	+	4 5	Append 5 to the PE.
4 + 5 *	+ *	4 5	Push * onto the stack.
4 + 5 * 6	+ *	4 5 6	Append 6 to the PE.
4 + 5 * 6 −	-	4 5 6 * +	Pop * and +, append them to the PE, and push - onto the stack.
4 + 5 * 6 − 3	-	4 5 6 * + 3	Append 3 to the PE.
4 + 5 * 6 − 3		4 5 6 * + 3 -	Pop the remaining operators off the stack and append them to the PE.

Table 7.7 Tracing the Conversion of an Infix Expression to a Postfix Expression

Infix expression: (4 + 5) * (6 - 3)   Postfix expression: 4 5 + 6 3 - *

Portion of Infix Expression So Far	Operator Stack	Postfix Expression	Comment
			No tokens have been seen yet. The stack and the PE are empty.
(	(		Push (onto the stack.
(4	(	4	Append 4 to the PE.
(4 +	(+		Push + onto the stack.
(4 + 5	(+	4 5	Append 5 to the PE.

(4 + 5)		4 5 +	Pop the stack until (is encountered, and append operators to the PE.
(4 + 5) *	*	4 5 +	Push * onto the stack.
(4 + 5) * (	* (	4 5 +	Push (onto the stack.
(4 + 5) * (6	* (	4 5 + 6	Append 6 to the PE.
(4 + 5) * (6 −	* (-	4 5 + 6	Push - onto the stack.
(4 + 5) * (6 − 3	* (-	4 5 + 6 3	Append 3 to the PE.
(4 + 5) * (6 − 3)	*	4 5 + 6 3 −	Pop the stack until (is encountered, and append operators to the PE.
(4 + 5) * (6 − 3)		4 5 6 * + 3 − *	Pop the remaining operators off the stack, and append them to the PE.

© 2014 Cengage Learning®

It's left to you to determine the time complexity of this process. You'll see another example of this in the case study in this chapter, and then, in the end-of-chapter projects, you'll have a chance to incorporate the process into a programming project that extends the case study.

Exercises 7.3

1. Translate by hand the following infix expressions to postfix form:

    a. $33 - 15 * 6$

    b. $11 * (6 + 2)$

    c. $17 + 3 - 5$

    d. $22 - 6 + 33 / 4$

2. Perform a complexity analysis for a conversion of infix to postfix.

Backtracking

A *backtracking algorithm* begins in a predefined starting state and then moves from state to state in search of a desired ending state. At any point along the way, when there is a choice between several alternative states, the algorithm picks one, possibly at random, and continues. If the algorithm reaches a state that represents an undesirable outcome, it backs up to the last point at which there was an unexplored alternative and tries it. In this way, the algorithm either exhaustively searches all states, or it reaches the desired ending state.

There are two principal techniques for implementing backtracking algorithms: one uses stacks and the other uses recursion. The use of stacks is explored next.

The role of a stack in the process is to remember the alternative states that occur at each juncture. To be more precise, the role is the following:

```
Create an empty stack
Push the starting state onto the stack
While the stack is not empty
    Pop the stack and examine the state
     If the state represents an ending state
         Return SUCCESSFUL CONCLUSION
     Else if the state has not been visited previously
         Mark the state as visited
         Push onto the stack all unvisited adjacent states
Return UNSUCCESSFUL CONCLUSION
```

This general backtracking algorithm finds applications in many game-playing and puzzle-solving programs. Consider, for example, the problem of finding a path out of a maze. In one instance of this problem, a hiker must find a path to the top of a mountain. Assume that the hiker leaves a parking lot, marked P, and explores the maze until she reaches the top of a mountain, marked T. Figure 7.2 shows what one possible maze looks like.

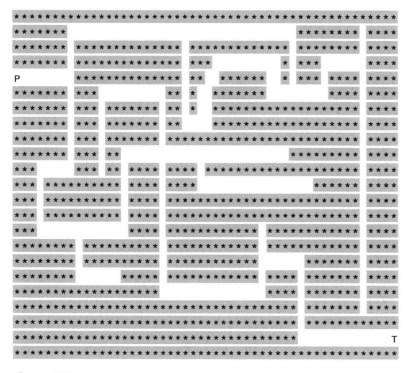

Figure 7.2

A maze problem.

Here's a program to solve this problem. At start-up, the program's data model inputs the maze as a grid of characters from a text file. The character * marks a barrier, and P and T mark the parking lot and mountaintop, respectively. A blank space marks a step along a path. After the maze is loaded from the file, the program should display it in the terminal window. The program should then ask the user to press the Enter or Return key to solve the maze. The model attempts to find a path through the maze and returns True or False to the view, depending on the outcome. In the model, the maze is represented as a grid of characters (P, T, *, or space). During the search, each visited cell is marked with a dot. At the end of the program, the grid is redisplayed with the dots included. Here is the backtracking algorithm that is at the core of the solution:

```
Instantiate a stack
Locate the character "P" in the grid
Push its location onto the stack
While the stack is not empty
    Pop a location, (row, column), off the stack
    If the grid contains "T" at this location, then
        A path has been found
        Return True
    Else if this location does not contain a dot
        Place a dot in the grid at this location
        Examine the adjacent cells to this one and
        for each one that contains a space,
            push its location onto the stack
Return False
```

It would be interesting to calculate the time complexity of the foregoing algorithm. However, two crucial pieces of information are missing:

- The complexity of deciding if a state has been visited
- The complexity of listing states adjacent to a given state

If, for the sake of argument, you assume that both of these processes are O(1), then the algorithm as a whole is O(n), where n represents the total number of states.

This discussion has been a little abstract, but at the end of the chapter, there is a programming project involving the application of stack-based backtracking to a maze problem.

Memory Management

During a program's execution, both its code and its data occupy computer memory. The computer's run-time system must keep track of various details that are invisible to the program's author. These include the following:

- Associating variables with data objects stored in memory so they can be located when these variables are referenced.

- Remembering the address of the instruction in which a method or function is called, so control can return to the next instruction when that function or method finishes execution.

- Allocating memory for a function's or a method's arguments and temporary variables, which exist only during the execution of that function or method.

Although the exact manner in which a computer manages memory depends on the programming language and operating system involved, there's a simplified, yet reasonably realistic, overview. The emphasis must be on the word *simplified*, because a detailed discussion is beyond the scope of this book.

As you probably already know, a Python compiler translates a Python program into bytecodes. A complex program called the Python Virtual Machine (PVM) then executes these. The memory, or *run-time environment*, controlled by the PVM is divided into six regions, as shown on the left side of Figure 7.3.

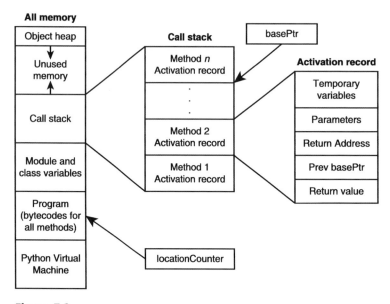

Figure 7.3

The architecture of a run-time environment.

© 2014 Cengage Learning®

In what follows, the term *subroutine* is used for either a Python function or a Python method. Working up from the bottom, these regions contain the following:

- The Python Virtual Machine (PVM), which executes a Python program. Internal to the PVM are two variables, called `locationCounter` and `basePtr`. The `location-Counter` points at the instruction the PVM will execute next. The `basePtr` points at the top activation record's base. More will be said about these variables soon.

- Bytecodes for all the subroutines of the program.

- The program's module and class variables.

- The call stack. Every time a subroutine is called, an activation record is created and pushed onto the call stack. When a subroutine finishes execution and returns control to the subroutine that called it, the activation record is popped off the stack. The total number of activation records on the stack equals the number of subroutine calls currently in various stages of execution. More will be said about activation records in a moment.

- Unused memory. This region's size grows and shrinks in response to the demands of the call stack and the object heap.

- The object heap. In Python, all objects exist in a region of memory called the heap. When an object is instantiated, the PVM must find space for the object on the heap, and when the object is no longer needed, the PVM's garbage collector recovers the space for future use. When low on space, the heap extends further into the region marked Unused Memory.

The activation records shown in the figure contain two types of information. The regions labeled Temporary Variables and Parameters hold data needed by the executing subroutine. The remaining regions hold data that allow the PVM to pass control backward from the currently executing subroutine to the subroutine that called it.

When a subroutine is called, the PVM performs the following steps:

1. Creates the subroutine's activation record and pushes it onto the call stack (the activation record's bottom-three regions are fixed in size, and the top two vary depending on the number of parameters and local variables used by the subroutine).

2. Saves the `basePtr`'s current value in the region labeled `Prev basePtr` and sets the `basePtr` to the new activation record's base.

3. Saves the `locationCounter`'s current value in the region labeled `Return Address` and sets the `locationCounter` to the first instruction of the called subroutine.

4. Copies the calling parameters into the region labeled `Parameters`.

5. Starts executing the called subroutine at the location indicated by the `locationCounter`.

While a subroutine is executing, adding an offset to the `basePtr` references temporary variables and parameters in the activation record. Thus, regardless of an activation record's location in memory, you can correctly access the local variables and parameters, provided the `basePtr` has been initialized properly.

Just before returning, a subroutine stores its return value in the location labeled `Return Value`. Because the return value always resides at the bottom of the activation record, the calling subroutine knows exactly where to find it.

When a subroutine has finished executing, the PVM performs the following steps:

1. Reestablishes the settings needed by the calling subroutine by restoring the values of the `locationCounter` and the `basePtr` from values stored in the activation record.

2. Pops the activation record from the call stack.

3. Resumes execution of the calling subroutine at the location indicated by the `locationCounter`.

IMPLEMENTATIONS OF STACKS

Because of their simple behavior and linear structure, stacks are implemented easily using arrays or linked structures. The two implementations of stacks here illustrate the typical trade-offs involved in using these two recurring approaches.

Test Driver

Your two stack implementations are the classes `ArrayStack` and `LinkedStack`. Before you develop these, write a short tester program that shows how you can test them immediately. The code in this program exercises all the methods in any stack implementation and gives you an initial sense that they are working as expected. Here is the code for the program:

```
"""
File: teststack.py
Author: Ken Lambert
A tester program for stack implementations.
"""

from arraystack import ArrayStack
from linkedstack import LinkedStack
```

```
def test(stackType):
    # Test any implementation with the same code
    s = stackType()
    print("Length:", len(s))
    print("Empty:", s.isEmpty())
    print("Push 1-10")
    for i in range(10):
        s.push(i + 1)
    print("Peeking:", s.peek())
    print("Items (bottom to top):", s)
    print("Length:", len(s))
    print("Empty:", s.isEmpty())
    theClone = stackType(s)
    print("Items in clone (bottom to top):", theClone)
    theClone.clear()
    print("Length of clone after clear:", len(theClone))
    print("Push 11")
    s.push(11)
    print("Popping items (top to bottom):", end="")
    while not s.isEmpty(): print(s.pop(), end=" ")
    print("\nLength:", len(s))
    print("Empty:", s.isEmpty())

# test(ArrayStack)
test(LinkedStack)
```

Here is a transcript of the output of this program:

```
Length: 0
Empty: True
Push 1-10
Peeking: 10
Items (bottom to top): 1 2 3 4 5 6 7 8 9 10
Length: 10
Empty: False
Push 11
Popping items (top to bottom): 11 10 9 8 7 6 5 4 3 2 1
Length: 0
Empty: True
```

Note that the items in the stack print from bottom to top in the stack's string representation. In contrast, when they are popped, they print from top to bottom. You can do further testing to check the preconditions on the pop and peek methods.

Adding Stacks to the Collection Hierarchy

As you saw in Chapter 6, "Inheritance and Abstract Classes," a collection implementation can acquire some functionality for free by becoming part of a hierarchy of collections. For example, the three implementations of bags—LinkedBag, ArrayBag, and ArraySortedBag—are descendants of two abstract classes, AbstractBag and Abstract-Collection, which define some of the data and methods that all types of bags use.

The two stack implementations, ArrayStack and LinkedStack, are in a similar situation and can be treated in a similar manner. They implement the same interface, called StackInterface, whose methods are listed in Table 7.1. They are subclasses of the AbstractStack class, which in turn is a subclass of AbstractCollection. They inherit the add method from the AbstractStack class, and the _size variable and the methods isEmpty, __len__, __str__, __add__, and __eq__ from AbstractCollection. Therefore, the only methods that need to be implemented in ArrayStack and LinkedStack are __init__, peek, push, pop, clear, and __iter__.

The hierarchy of stack resources is shown in Figure 7.4.

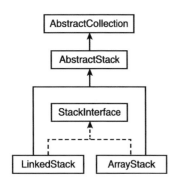

Figure 7.4

The stack resources in the collection hierarchy.

© 2014 Cengage Learning®

Array Implementation

The first implementation is built around an array called self._items and an integer called self._size. Initially, the array has a default capacity of 10 positions, and self._size equals 0. The top item, if there is one, will always be at location self._size - 1. To push an item onto the stack, store the item at the location self._items[len(self)] and increment self._size. To pop the stack, return self._items[len(self) -1] and decrement self._size. Figure 7.5 shows how self._items and self._size appear when four items are on the stack.

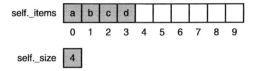

Figure 7.5

An array representation of a stack with four items.

© 2014 Cengage Learning®

The array, as shown, has a current capacity of 10 positions. How do you avoid the problem of stack overflow? As discussed in Chapter 4, "Arrays and Linked Structures," you create a new array when the existing array is about to overflow or when it becomes underutilized. Following the analysis in Chapter 4, you double the array's capacity after push fills it and halve it when pop leaves it three-quarters empty.

The array-based stack implementation uses the Array class developed in Chapter 4 and is quite similar to the ArrayBag class developed in Chapter 6. Like ArrayBag, ArrayStack is subclassed under an abstract class. In this case, the parent class is called AbstractStack. As mentioned earlier, the only operations you need to provide in ArrayStack are __init__, clear, push, pop, peek, and __iter__.

Here is the code for ArrayStack, with some parts to be completed in the exercises:

```
"""
File: arraystack.py
"""

from arrays import Array
from abstractstack import AbstractStack

class ArrayStack(AbstractStack):
    """An array-based stack implementation."""

    DEFAULT_CAPACITY = 10 # For all array stacks

    def __init__(self, sourceCollection = None):
        """Sets the initial state of self, which includes the
        contents of sourceCollection, if it's present."""
        self._items = Array(ArrayStack.DEFAULT_CAPACITY)
        AbstractStack.__init__(self, sourceCollection)

    # Accessors
    def __iter__(self):
        """Supports iteration over a view of self.
        Visits items from bottom to top of stack."""
        cursor = 0
```

```
        while cursor < len(self):
            yield self._items[cursor]
            cursor += 1
    def peek(self):
        """Returns the item at top of the stack.
        Precondition: the stack is not empty.
        Raises KeyError if the stack is empty."""
        return self._items[len(self) - 1]
    # Mutators
    def clear(self):
        """Makes self become empty."""
        self._size = 0
        self._items = Array(ArrayStack.DEFAULT_CAPACITY)
    def push(self, item):
        """Inserts item at top of the stack."""
        # Resize array here if necessary
        self._items[len(self)] = item
        self._size += 1
    def pop(self):
        """Removes and returns the item at top of the stack.
        Precondition: the stack is not empty.
        Raises KeyError if the stack is empty.
        Postcondition: the top item is removed from the stack."""
        oldItem = self._items[len(self) - 1]
        self._size -= 1
        # Resize the array here if necessary
        return oldItem
```

Note the preconditions on the methods peek and pop. A safe implementation would enforce these preconditions by raising exceptions when they are violated. That's left as an exercise for you. Likewise, the inclusion of code to resize the array in push and pop is left as an exercise.

Linked Implementation

Like the linked bag implementation of Chapter 6, the linked implementation of a stack uses a singly linked sequence of nodes. Efficient pushing and popping require adding and removing of nodes at the head of the linked sequence. The instance variable self._items now refers to the node at the head of this sequence, if there is one. Otherwise, when the stack is empty, self._items is None. Figure 7.6 illustrates a linked stack containing three items.

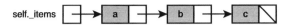

Figure 7.6
A linked representation of a stack with three items.

The linked implementation requires two classes: `LinkedStack` and `Node`. The `Node` class, as defined in Chapter 4, contains two fields:

- `data`—An item on the stack

- `next`—A pointer to the next node

Because new items are added to and removed from just one end of the linked structure, the methods `pop` and `push` are easy to implement, as shown in the next two figures. Figure 7.7 shows the sequence of steps required to push an item onto a linked stack. To perform these steps, you pass the `self._items` pointer to the `Node` constructor and assign the new node to `self._items`.

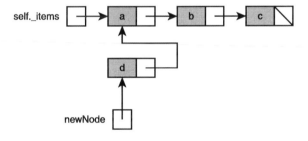

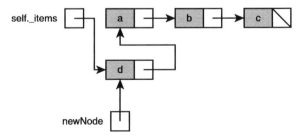

Figure 7.7
Pushing an item onto a linked stack.

Figure 7.8 shows the single step necessary to pop an item from a linked stack.

set self._items to self._items.next

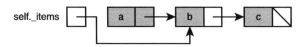

Figure 7.8

Popping an item from a linked stack.

© 2014 Cengage Learning®

Although the linked structure supports a simple push and pop, the implementation of the __iter__ method is complicated by the fact that the items must be visited from the tail of the linked structure to its head. Unfortunately, to traverse a singly linked structure, you must begin at its head and follow the next links to its tail.

Happily, recursion can come to the rescue. Within the __iter__ method, you create a temporary list and define a recursive helper function that expects a node as an argument. On the function's initial call, the argument node is the head of the stack's linked structure (the variable self._items). If this node is not None, you call the function recursively with the next field of the node to advance toward the tail of the structure. When this call returns, you append the node's data to the temporary list. When the top-level call of the helper function returns, you return an iterator on the list.

Here is the code for LinkedStack:

```
from node import Node
from abstractstack import AbstractStack

class LinkedStack(AbstractStack):
    """ Link-based stack implementation."""

    def __init__(self, sourceCollection = None):
        self._items = None
        AbstractStack.__init__(self, sourceCollection)

    # Accessors
    def __iter__(self):
        """Supports iteration over a view of self.
        Visits items from bottom to top of stack."""
        def visitNodes(node):
            if not node is None:
                visitNodes(node.next)
                tempList.append(node.data)
        tempList = list()
        visitNodes(self._items)
        return iter(tempList)

    def peek(self):
        """Returns the item at top of the stack.
```

```
            Precondition: the stack is not empty."""
        if self.isEmpty():
            raise KeyError("The stack is empty.")
        return self._items.data
    # Mutators
    def clear(self):
        """Makes self become empty."""
        self._size = 0
        self._items = None

    def push(self, item):
        """Inserts item at top of the stack."""
        self._items = Node(item, self._items)
        self._size += 1

    def pop(self):
        """Removes and returns the item at top of the stack.
        Precondition: the stack is not empty."""
        if self.isEmpty():
            raise KeyError("The stack is empty.")
        oldItem = self._items.data
        self._items = self._items.next
        self._size -= 1
        return oldItem
```

The Role of the Abstract Stack Class

The implementations of the methods in the stack interface are divided evenly between a concrete class (either ArrayStack or LinkedStack) and AbstractCollection. This might leave you wondering what would be left over for the AbstractStack class, which lies between the concrete stack classes and AbstractCollection.

If you review the stack interface listed earlier, you notice the absence of a critical method—add. Although the stack interface already includes a method push that does the same thing as add, there might be many clients, including an important one in the collection framework itself, who would prefer to use add.

As you have seen in Chapter 6, the __init__ method in AbstractCollection uses the add method to add items in a source collection to self. If self is a stack, Python raises an exception, stating that the add method is undefined for stacks.

To remedy this problem and maintain consistency with the interfaces of other collections, you need to include an add method with your stack types. The logical place to put this method, so that all stack types can use it, is in the AbstractStack class. Because self is always a stack in that context, the add method can simply call self.push to perform the desired task.

Here is the code for `AbstractStack`:

```
"""
File: abstractstack.py
Author: Ken Lambert
"""

from abstractcollection import AbstractCollection

class AbstractStack(AbstractCollection):
    """An abstract stack implementation."""

    # Constructor
    def __init__(self, sourceCollection = None):
        """Sets the initial state of self, which includes the
        contents of sourceCollection, if it's present."""
        AbstractCollection.__init__(self, sourceCollection)

    # Mutator methods
    def add(self, item):
        """Adds item to self."""
        self.push(item)
```

Time and Space Analysis of the Two Implementations

With the exception of the __iter__ method, all the stack methods are simple and have a maximum running time of O(1). In the array implementation, the analysis becomes more complex. At the moment of doubling, the push method's running time jumps to $O(n)$, but the rest of the time it remains at O(1). Similar remarks can be made about the pop method. On average, both are still O(1), as shown in Chapter 4. However, the programmer must decide if a fluctuating response time is acceptable and choose an implementation accordingly.

The __iter__ method runs in linear time in both implementations. However, the recursive function used in the linked implementation causes a linear growth of memory because of its use of the system call stack. You can avoid this problem by using a doubly linked structure; the iterator can begin at the last node and follow links to previous nodes. Chapter 9, "Lists," examines such a structure in detail.

A collection of n objects requires at least enough space to hold the n object references. Let us now see how our two stack implementations compare to this ideal. A linked stack of n items requires n nodes, each containing two references: one to an item and the other to the next node. In addition, there must be a variable that points to the top node and a variable for the size, yielding a total space requirement of $2n + 2$.

For an array implementation, a stack's total space requirement is fixed when the stack is instantiated. The space consists of an array with an initial capacity of 10 references and variables to track the stack's size and to refer to the array itself. Assuming that an integer and a reference occupy the same amount of space, the total space requirement is the array's capacity + 2. As discussed in Chapter 4, an array implementation is more space-efficient than a linked implementation whenever the load factor is greater than ½. The load factor for an array implementation normally varies between ¼ and 1, although obviously it can sink to 0.

Exercises 7.4

1. Discuss the difference between using an array and using a Python list to implement the class `ArrayStack`. What are the trade-offs?

2. Add code to the methods `peek` and `pop` in `ArrayStack` so that they raise an exception if their preconditions are violated.

3. Modify the method `pop` in `ArrayStack` so that it reduces the capacity of the array if it is underutilized.

CASE STUDY: EVALUATING POSTFIX EXPRESSIONS

The case study presents a program that evaluates postfix expressions. The program allows the user to enter an arbitrary postfix expression and then displays the expression's value or an error message if the expression is invalid. The stack-based algorithm for evaluating postfix expressions is at the heart of the program.

Request

Write an interactive program for evaluating postfix expressions.

Analysis

There are many possibilities for the user interface. Considering the educational setting, it would be good for the user to experiment with numerous expressions while retaining a transcript of the results. Errors in an expression should not stop the program but should generate messages that give insight into where the evaluation process breaks down. With these requirements in mind, a user interface like the one shown in this session is proposed:

```
Enter a postfix expression: 6 2 5 + *
6 2 5 + *
42
Enter a postfix expression: 10 2 300 *+ 20/
10 2 300 * + 20 /
```

```
30
Enter a postfix expression: 3 + 4
3 + 4
Error:
Too few operands on the stack
Portion of the expression processed: 3 +
Operands on the stack:              : 3
Enter a postfix expression: 5 6 %
5 6 %
Error:
Unknown token type
Portion of the expression processed: 5 6 %
Operands on the stack:              : 5 6
Enter a postfix expression:
>>>
```

The user enters an expression at a prompt, and the program displays the results. The expression, as entered, is confined to one line of text, with arbitrary spacing between tokens, provided that the adjacent operands have some white space between them. After the user presses Enter or Return, the expression is redisplayed with exactly one space between each token and is followed on the next line by its value or an error message. A prompt for another expression is then displayed. The user quits by pressing a simple Enter or Return at the prompt.

The program should detect and report all input errors, be they intentional or unintentional. Some common errors are the following:

- The expression contains too many operands; in other words, there is more than one operand left on the stack when the end of the expression is encountered.

- The expression contains too few operands; in other words, an operator is encountered when there are fewer than two operands on the stack.

- The expression contains unrecognizable tokens. The program expects the expression to be composed of integers, four arithmetic operators (+, -, *, /), and white space (a space or a tab). Anything else is unrecognizable.

- The expression includes division by 0.

Here are examples that illustrate each type of error with an appropriate error message:

```
Expression:
Error: Expression contains no tokens
Portion of expression processed: none
The stack is empty
```

```
Expression: 1 2 3 +
Error: Too many operands on the stack
Portion of expression processed: 1 2 3 +
Operands on the stack: 1 5

Expression: 1 + 2 3 4 *
Error: Too few operands on the stack
Portion of expression processed: 1 +
Operands on the stack: 1

Expression: 1 2 % 3 +
Error: Unknown token type
Portion of expression processed: 1 2 %
Operands on the stack: 1 2

Expression: 1 2 0 / +
Error: divide by zero
Portion of expression processed: 1 2 0 /
Operands on the stack: 1
```

As always, the existence of a view and a data model is assumed. In what follows, the prefix *PF* is short for the word *postfix*.

The view class is named `PFView`. When the user presses Enter or Return, the view runs three methods defined in the model:

1. The view asks the model to format the expression string with exactly one space between each token, and then it displays the formatted string.

2. The view asks the model to evaluate the expression, and then it displays the value returned.

3. The view catches any exceptions thrown by the model, asks the model for the conditions that were pertinent when the error was detected, and displays appropriate error messages.

The model class is named `PFEvaluatorModel`. It must be able to format and evaluate an expression string, raise exceptions in response to syntax errors in the string, and report on its internal state. To meet these responsibilities, the model can divide its work between the following two major processes:

1. Scan a string and extract the tokens.

2. Evaluate a sequence of tokens.

The output of the first process becomes the input to the second. These processes are complex, and they recur in other problems. For both reasons, they are worth encapsulating in separate classes, called `Scanner` and `PFEvaluator`.

Considering the manner in which it will be used, the scanner takes a string as input and returns a sequence of tokens as output. Rather than return these tokens all at once, the scanner responds to the methods hasNext and next.

The evaluator takes a scanner as input, iterates across the scanner's tokens, and either returns an expression's value or raises an exception. In the process, the evaluator uses the stack-based algorithm described earlier in the chapter. At any time, the evaluator can provide information about its internal state.

If the scanner is to return tokens, a Token class is needed. An instance of the Token class has a value and a type. The possible types are represented by arbitrarily chosen integer constants with the names PLUS, MINUS, MUL, DIV, and INT. The values of the first four integer constants are the corresponding characters +, -, *, and /. The value of an INT is found by converting a substring of numeric characters, such as "534", to its internal integer representation. A token can provide a string representation of itself by converting its value to a string.

Figure 7.9 is a class diagram that shows the relationships between the proposed classes. Notice that both the model and the evaluator use the scanner. You've already read why the evaluator needs the scanner. The model uses the scanner to format the expression string. Although you could accomplish this task by manipulating the expression string directly, it is easier to use the scanner, and the performance penalty is negligible.

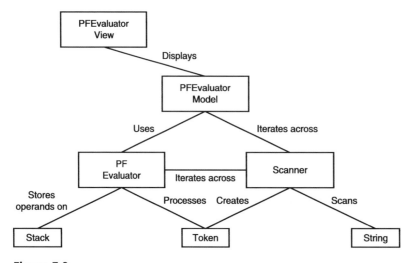

Figure 7.9

A class diagram for the expression evaluator.

© 2014 Cengage Learning®

Design

Now you'll see more closely the inner workings of each class. Figure 7.10 is an interaction diagram that summarizes the methods run among the classes:

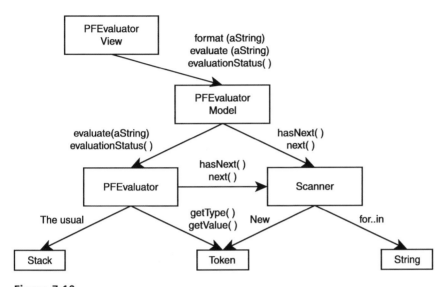

Figure 7.10

An interaction diagram for the expression evaluator.

© 2014 Cengage Learning®

What follows is a list of each class's instance variables and methods.

Instance Variables and Methods for Class PFEvaluatorView

The attribute is a model. The methods are the following:

```
PFEvaluatorView()
    Creates and saves a reference to the model.

run()
    While True:
        Retrieve the expression string from the keyboard.
        If the string is empty, return.
        Send it to the model for formatting.
        Send it to the model for evaluation.
        Either print the value or catch exceptions raised by the evaluator,
        ask the model for the associated details, and display error
        messages.
```

Instance Variables and Methods for Class PFEvaluatorModel

The model communicates with the scanner and the evaluator, so it needs references to both. The evaluator must be an instance variable because it is referenced in more than one method. However, the scanner can be local to the format method. The public methods are the following:

```
format(expressionStr)
    Instantiate a scanner on the expression string.
    Build a response string by iterating across the scanner and appending a
    string representation of each token to the response string.
    Return the response string.

evaluate(expressionStr)
    Ask the evaluator to evaluate the expression string.
    Return the value.

evaluationStatus()
    Ask the evaluator for its status.
    Return the status.
```

Instance Variables and Methods for Class PFEvaluator

The evaluator's attributes include a stack, a scanner, and a string variable called expressionSoFar, which holds the portion of the expression string processed so far. The stack is an ArrayStack. The public methods are the following:

```
PFEvaluator(scanner)
    Initialize expressionSoFar.
    Instantiate an ArrayStack.
    Save a reference to the scanner.

evaluate()
    Iterate across the scanner and evaluate the expression.
    Raise exceptions in the following situations:
        The scanner is None or empty.
        There are too many operands.
        There are too few operands.
        There are unrecognizable tokens.
        A divide by 0 exception is raised by the PVM.

evaluationStatus()
    Return a multipart string that contains the portion of the expression
    processed and the contents of the stack.
```

Instance Variables and Methods for Class Scanner

Suppose that a third party has provided the scanner. Consequently, you do not need to consider its inner workings, and its public methods are just next() and hasNext(). For those who are interested, the complete source code is available from your instructor or on the companion website at www.cengageptr.com/downloads.

Scanner(sourceStr)
> Save a reference to the string that will be scanned and tokenized.

hasNext()
> Return True if the string contains another token and False otherwise.

next()
> Return the next token. Raise an exception if hasNext() returns False.

Instance and Class Variables and Methods for Class Token

A token's attributes are type and value. Both are integers. The type is one of the following Token class variables:

```
UNKNOWN  = 0        # unknown
INT      = 4        # integer
MINUS    = 5        # minus    operator
PLUS     = 6        # plus     operator
MUL      = 7        # multiply operator
DIV      = 8        # divide   operator
```

The actual values of the symbolic constants are arbitrary. A token's value is the following:

- A number for integer operands.

- A character code for operators; for instance, '*' corresponds to the multiplication operator.

The methods are the following:

Token(value)
> Construct a new integer token with the specified value.

Token(ch)
> If ch is an operator (+, -, *, /), then construct a new operator token; otherwise, construct a token of unknown type.

getType()
> Return a token's type.

getValue()
> Return a token's value.

isOperator()
    Return True if the token is an operator, and False otherwise.

__str__()
    Return the token's numeric value as a string if the token is an
    integer; otherwise, return the token's character representation.

Implementation

The code for the view class is routine, except for the minor complication of using a try-except statement. The internal workings of the scanner are not presented here but can be found in the code file available from your instructor or on the companion website at www.cengageptr.com/downloads. That leaves the token and the evaluator classes, which are presented next:

```python
"""
File: tokens.py
Tokens for processing expressions.
"""

class Token(object):

    UNKNOWN  = 0         # unknown

    INT      = 4         # integer

    MINUS    = 5         # minus     operator
    PLUS     = 6         # plus      operator
    MUL      = 7         # multiply  operator
    DIV      = 8         # divide    operator

    FIRST_OP = 5         # first operator code

    def __init__(self, value):
        if type(value) == int:
            self._type = Token.INT
        else:
            self._type = self._makeType(value)
        self._value = value

    def isOperator(self):
        return self._type >= Token.FIRST_OP

    def __str__(self):
        return str(self._value)

    def getType(self):
        return self._type

    def getValue(self):
        return self._value
```

```
        def _makeType(self, ch):
            if   ch == '*': return Token.MUL
            elif ch == '/': return Token.DIV
            elif ch == '+': return Token.PLUS
            elif ch == '-': return Token.MINUS
            else:           return Token.UNKNOWN;
"""
File: model.py
Defines PFEvaluatorModel and PFEvaluator
"""

from tokens import Token
from scanner import Scanner
from arraystack import ArrayStack

class PFEvaluatorModel(object):

    def evaluate(self, sourceStr):
        self._evaluator = PFEvaluator(Scanner(sourceStr))
        value = self._evaluator.evaluate()
        return value

    def format(self, sourceStr):
        normalizedStr = ""
        scanner = Scanner(sourceStr);
        while scanner.hasNext():
            normalizedStr += str(scanner.next()) + " "
        return normalizedStr;

    def evaluationStatus(self):
        return str(self._evaluator)

class PFEvaluator(object):

    def __init__(self, scanner):
        self._expressionSoFar = ""
        self._operandStack = ArrayStack()
        self._scanner = scanner

    def evaluate(self):
        while self._scanner.hasNext():
            currentToken = self._scanner.next()
            self._expressionSoFar += str(currentToken) + " "
            if currentToken.getType() == Token.INT:
                self._operandStack.push(currentToken)
            elif currentToken.isOperator():
                if len(self._operandStack) < 2:
                    raise AttributeError ( \
                        "Too few operands on the stack")
```

```python
                t2 = self._operandStack.pop()
                t1 = self._operandStack.pop()
                result = \
                    Token(self._computeValue(currentToken,
                                             t1.getValue(),
                                             t2.getValue()))
                self._operandStack.push(result)

            else:
                raise AttributeError ("Unknown token type")
        if len(self._operandStack) > 1:
            raise AttributeError (
                "Too many operands on the stack")
        result = self._operandStack.pop()
        return result.getValue();

    def __str__(self):
        result = "\n"
        if self._expressionSoFar == "":
            result += \
                "Portion of expression processed: none\n"
        else:
            result += "Portion of expression processed: " + \
                self._expressionSoFar + "\n"
        if self._operandStack.isEmpty():
            result += "The stack is empty"
        else:
            result += "Operands on the stack : " + \
                    str(self._operandStack)
        return result

    def _computeValue(self, op, value1, value2):
        result = 0;
        theType = op.getType()
        if theType == Token.PLUS:
            result = value1 + value2;
        elif theType == Token.MINUS:
            result = value1 - value2;
        elif theType == Token.MUL:
            result = value1 * value2;
        elif theType == Token.DIV:
            result = value1 // value2;
        else:
            raise AttributeError ("Unknown operator")
        return result
```

SUMMARY

- A stack is a linear collection that allows access to one end only, called the top. Elements are pushed onto the top or popped from it.

- Other operations on stacks include peeking at the top element, determining the number of elements, determining whether the stack is empty, and returning a string representation.

- Stacks are used in applications that manage data items in a last-in, first-out manner. These applications include matching bracket symbols in expressions, evaluating postfix expressions, backtracking algorithms, and managing memory for subroutine calls on a virtual machine.

- Arrays and singly linked structures support simple implementations of stacks.

REVIEW QUESTIONS

1. Examples of stacks are

   a. Customers waiting in a checkout line

   b. A deck of playing cards

   c. A file directory system

   d. A line of cars at a tollbooth

   e. Laundry in a hamper

2. The operations that modify a stack are called

   a. Add and remove

   b. Push and pop

3. Stacks are also known as

   a. First-in, first-out data structures

   b. Last-in, first-out data structures

4. The postfix equivalent of the expression 3 + 4 * 7 is

   a. 3 4 + 7 *

   b. 3 4 7 * +

5. The infix equivalent of the postfix expression 22 45 11 * − is

   a. 22 − 45 * 11

   b. 45 * 11 − 22

6. The value of the postfix expression 5 6 + 2 ∗ is

   a. 40

   b. 22

7. Memory for function or method parameters is allocated on the

   a. Object heap

   b. Call stack

8. The running time of the two stack-mutator operations is

   a. Linear

   b. Constant

9. The linked implementation of a stack uses nodes with

   a. A link to the next node

   b. Links to the next and previous nodes

10. The array implementation of a stack places the top element at the

    a. First position in the array

    b. Position after the last element that was inserted

PROJECTS

1. Complete and test the linked and array implementations of the stack collection type discussed in this chapter. Verify that exceptions are raised when preconditions are violated and that the array-based implementation adds or removes storage as needed.

2. Write a program that uses a stack to test input strings to determine whether they are palindromes. A palindrome is a sequence of words that reads the same as the sequence in reverse: for example, *noon.*

3. Complete the classes needed to run the expression evaluator discussed in the case study.

4. Add the ^ operator to the language of expressions processed by the expression evaluator of the case study. This operator has the same semantics as Python's exponentiation operator ∗∗. Thus, the expression 2 4 3 ∗ ^ evaluates to 4096.

5. Write a program that converts infix expressions to postfix expressions. This program should use the Token and Scanner classes developed in the case study. The program should consist of a main function that performs the inputs and outputs,

and a class named IFToPFConverter. The main function receives an input string and creates a scanner with it. The scanner is then passed as an argument to the constructor of the converter object. The converter object's convert method is then run to convert the infix expression using the algorithm described in this chapter. This method returns a list of tokens that represent the postfix string. The main function then displays this string. You should also define a new method in the Token class, getPrecedence(), which returns an integer that represents the precedence level of an operator. (*Note*: You should assume for this project that the user always enters a syntactically correct infix expression.)

6. Add the ^ operator to the expression language processed by the infix to postfix converter developed in Project 5. This operator has a higher precedence than either * or /. Also, this operator is right associative, which means that consecutive applications of this operator are evaluated from right to left rather than from left to right. Thus, the value of the expression 2 ^ 2 ^ 3 is equivalent to 2 ^ (2 ^ 3) or 256, not (2 ^ 2) ^ 3 or 64. You must modify the algorithm for infix to postfix conversion to place the operands as well as the operators in the appropriate positions in the postfix string.

7. Modify the program of Project 6 so that it checks the infix string for syntax errors as it converts to postfix. The error-detection and recovery strategy should be similar to the one used in the case study. Add a method named conversionStatus to the IFToPFConverter class. When the converter detects a syntax error, it should raise an exception, which the main function catches in a try-except statement. The main function can then call conversionStatus to obtain the information to print when an error occurs. This information should include the portion of the expression scanned until the error is detected. The error messages should also be as specific as possible.

8. Integrate the infix to postfix converter from one of the earlier projects into the expression evaluator of the case study. Thus, the input to the program is a purported infix expression, and its output is either its value or an error message. The program's main components are the converter and the evaluator. If the converter detects a syntax error, the evaluator is not run. Thus, the evaluator can assume that its input is a syntactically correct postfix expression (which may still contain semantic errors, such as the attempt to divide by 0).

9. Write a program that solves the maze problem discussed earlier in this chapter. You should use the Grid class developed in Chapter 4 in this problem. The program should input a description of the maze from a text file at start-up. The program then displays this maze, attempts to find a solution, displays the result, and displays the maze once more.

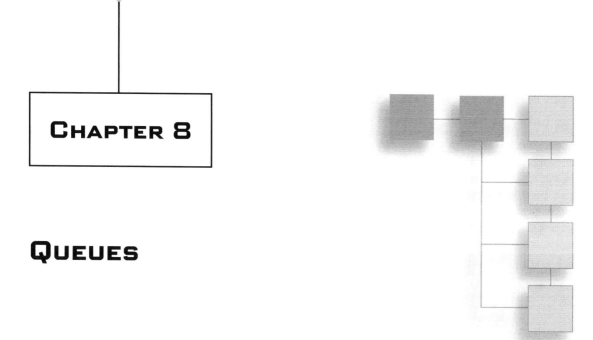

CHAPTER 8

QUEUES

This chapter explores the queue, another linear collection that has widespread use in computer science. There are several implementation strategies for queues—some based on arrays, and others based on linked structures. To illustrate the application of a queue, this chapter develops a case study that simulates a supermarket checkout line. The chapter closes with an examination of a special kind of queue, known as a priority queue, and shows how it is used in a second case study.

OVERVIEW OF QUEUES

Like stacks, queues are linear collections. However, with queues, insertions are restricted to one end, called the *rear*, and removals to the other end, called the *front*. A queue thus supports a first-in first-out (FIFO) protocol. Queues are omnipresent in everyday life and occur in any situation where people or things are lined up for service or processing on a first-come, first-served basis. Checkout lines in stores, highway tollbooth lines, and airport baggage check-in lines are familiar examples of queues.

Queues have two fundamental operations: add, which adds an item to the rear of a queue, and pop, which removes an item from the front. Figure 8.1 shows a queue as it might appear at various stages in its lifetime. In the figure, the queue's front is on the left, and its rear is on the right.

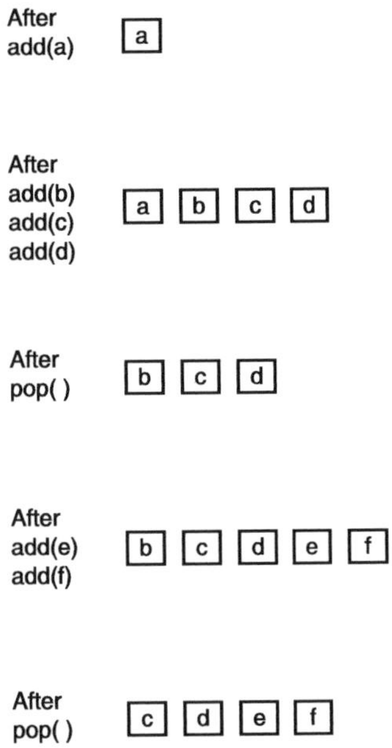

After
add(a)   a

After
add(b)
add(c)   a b c d
add(d)

After
pop( )   b c d

After
add(e)   b c d e f
add(f)

After
pop( )   c d e f

Figure 8.1

The states in the lifetime of a queue.

© 2014 Cengage Learning®

Initially, the queue is empty. Then an item called a is added. Next, three more items called b, c, and d are added, after which an item is popped, and so forth.

Related to queues is a collection called a *priority queue.* In a queue, the item popped, or served next, is always the item that has been waiting the longest. But in some circumstances, this restriction is too rigid, and it's preferable to combine the idea of waiting with a notion of priority. In a priority queue, higher-priority items are popped before those of lower priority, and items of equal priority are popped in FIFO order. Consider, for example, the manner in which passengers board an aircraft. The first-class passengers line up and board first, and the lower-priority coach-class passengers line up and board second. However, this is not a true priority queue because after the first-class queue has emptied and the coach-class queue starts boarding, late-arriving first-class passengers usually go to the end of the second queue. In a true priority queue, they would immediately jump ahead of all the coach-class passengers.

Most queues in computer science involve scheduling access to shared resources. The following list describes some examples:

- **CPU access**—Processes are queued for access to a shared CPU.
- **Disk access**—Processes are queued for access to a shared secondary storage device.
- **Printer access**—Print jobs are queued for access to a shared laser printer.

Process scheduling can involve either simple queues or priority queues. For example, processes requiring keyboard input and screen output are often given higher-priority access to the CPU than those that are computationally intensive. The result is that human users, who tend to judge a computer's speed by its response time, are given the impression that the computer is fast.

Processes that are waiting for a shared resource can also be prioritized by their expected duration, with short processes given higher priority than longer ones, again with the intent of improving the apparent response time of a system. Imagine 20 print jobs queued up for access to a printer. If 19 jobs are 1 page long and 1 job is 200 pages long, more users will be happy if the short jobs are given higher priority and printed first.

THE QUEUE INTERFACE AND ITS USE

If they are in a hurry, Python programmers can use a Python list to emulate a queue. Although it does not matter which ends of the list you view as the front and rear of the queue, the simplest strategy is to use the list method append to add an item to the rear of this queue, and to use the list method pop(0) to remove and return the item at the front of its queue. As you saw in the case of stacks, the main drawback of this option is that all the other list operations can manipulate the queue as well. These include the insertion, replacement, and removal of an item at any position. These extra operations violate the spirit of a queue as an abstract data type. Moreover, removing an item at the beginning of a Python list object is a linear time operation. This section defines a more restricted interface, or set of operations, for any queue implementation and shows how these operations are used.

Aside from the add and pop operations, it will be useful to have a peek operation, which returns the item at the front of the queue. The remaining operations in the queue interface are standard for any collection. Table 8.1 lists them all.

Table 8.1   The Methods in the Queue Interface

Queue Method	What It Does
q.isEmpty()	Returns True if q is empty or False otherwise.
__len__(q)	Same as len(q). Returns the number of items in q.
__str__(q)	Same as str(q). Returns the string representation of q.
q.__iter__()	Same as iter(q), or for item in q:. Visits each item in q, from front to rear.
q.__contains__(item)	Same as item in q. Returns True if item is in q or False otherwise.

(Continued)

Table 8.1   The Methods in the Queue Interface (*Continued*)

Queue Method	What It Does
q1__add__(q2)	Same as q1 + q2. Returns a new queue containing the items in q1 and q2.
q.__eq__(anyObject)	Same as q == anyObject. Returns True if q equals anyObject or False otherwise. Two queues are equal if the items at corresponding positions are equal.
q.clear()	Makes q become empty.
q.peek()	Returns the item at the front of q. *Precondition*: q must not be empty; raises a KeyError if the queue is empty.
q.add(item)	Adds item to the rear of q.
q.pop()	Removes and returns the item at the front of q. *Precondition*: q must not be empty; raises a KeyError if the queue is empty.

© 2014 Cengage Learning®

Note that the methods pop and peek have an important precondition and raise an exception if the user of the queue does not satisfy that precondition.

Now that a queue interface has been defined, you'll see how to use it. Table 8.2 shows how the operations listed earlier affect a queue named q.

Table 8.2   The Effects of Queue Operations

Operation	State of the Queue After the Operation	Value Returned	Comment
Q = <Queue Type>()			Initially, the queue is empty.
q.add(a)	a		The queue contains the single item a.
q.add(b)	a b		a is at the front of the queue and b is at the rear.
q.add(c)	a b c		c is added at the rear.
q.isEmpty()	a b c	False	The queue is not empty.
len(q)	a b c	3	The queue contains three items.

q.peek()	a b c	a	Return the front item on the queue without removing it.
q.pop()	b c	a	Remove the front item from the queue and return it. b is now the front item.
q.pop()	c	b	Remove and return b.
q.pop()		c	Remove and return c.
q.isEmpty()		True	The queue is empty.
q.peek()		exception	Peeking at an empty queue throws an exception.
q.pop()		exception	Trying to pop an empty queue throws an exception.
q.add(d)	d		d is the front item.

© 2014 Cengage Learning®

Assume that any queue class that implements this interface will also have a constructor that allows its user to create a new queue instance. Later in this chapter, two different implementations, named ArrayQueue and LinkedQueue, are considered. For now, assume that someone has coded these so you can use them. The next code segment shows how they might be instantiated:

```
q1 = ArrayQueue()             # Create empty array queue
q2 = LinkedQueue([3, 6, 0])   # Create linked queue with given items
```

Exercises 8.1

1. Using the format of Table 8.2, complete a table that involves the following sequence of queue operations.

Operation	State of Queue After Operation	Value Returned
Create q		
q.add(a)		
q.add(b)		
q.add(c)		
q.pop()		

(Continued)

Operation	State of Queue After Operation	Value Returned
q.pop()		
q.peek()		
q.add(x)		
q.pop()		
q.pop()		
q.pop()		

© 2014 Cengage Learning®

2. Define a function named stackToQueue. This function expects a stack as an argument. The function builds and returns an instance of LinkedQueue that contains the items in the stack. The function assumes that the stack has the interface described in Chapter 7, "Stacks." The function's postconditions are that the stack is left in the same state as it was before the function was called, and that the queue's front item is the one at the top of the stack.

Two Applications of Queues

This chapter now looks briefly at two applications of queues: one involving computer simulations and the other involving round-robin CPU scheduling.

Simulations

Computer simulations are used to study the behavior of real-world systems, especially when it is impractical or dangerous to experiment with these systems directly. For example, a computer simulation could mimic traffic flow on a busy highway. Urban planners could then experiment with factors that affect traffic flow, such as the number and types of vehicles on the highway, the speed limits for different types of vehicles, the number of lanes in the highway, and the frequency of tollbooths. Outputs from such a simulation might include the total number of vehicles able to move between designated points in a designated period and the average duration of a trip. By running the simulation with many combinations of inputs, the planners could determine how best to upgrade sections of the highway, subject to the ever-present constraints of time, space, and money.

As a second example, consider the problem faced by the manager of a supermarket who is trying to determine the number of checkout cashiers to schedule at various times of the day. Some important factors in this situation are the following:

- The frequency with which new customers arrive
- The number of checkout cashiers available
- The number of items in a customer's shopping cart
- The period of time considered

These factors could be inputs to a simulation program, which would then determine the total number of customers processed, the average time each customer waits for service, and the number of customers left standing in line at the end of the simulated period. By varying the inputs, particularly the frequency of customer arrivals and the number of available checkout cashiers, a simulation program could help the manager make effective staffing decisions for busy and slow times of the day. By adding an input that quantifies the efficiency of different checkout equipment, the manager can even decide whether it is more cost effective to add more cashiers or buy better, more efficient equipment.

A common characteristic of both examples, and of simulation problems in general, is the moment-by-moment variability of essential factors. Consider the frequency of customer arrivals at checkout stations. If customers arrived at precise intervals, each with the same number of items, it would be easy to determine how many cashiers to have on duty. However, such regularity does not reflect the reality of a supermarket. Sometimes several customers show up at practically the same instant, and at other times no new customers arrive for several minutes. In addition, the number of items varies from customer to customer; therefore, so does the amount of service that each customer requires. All this variability makes it difficult to devise formulas to answer simple questions about the system, such as how a customer's waiting time varies with the number of cashiers on duty. A simulation program, on the other hand, avoids the need for formulas by imitating the actual situation and collecting pertinent statistics.

Simulation programs use a simple technique to mimic variability. For instance, suppose new customers are expected to arrive on average once every 4 minutes. Then, during each minute of simulated time, a program can generate a random number between 0 and 1. If the number is less than 1/4, the program adds a new customer to a checkout line; otherwise, it does not. More sophisticated schemes based on probability distribution functions produce even more realistic results. Obviously, each time the program runs, the results change slightly, but this only adds to the realism of the simulation.

Now you'll learn the common role played by queues in these examples. Both examples involve service providers and service consumers. In the first example, service providers include tollbooths and traffic lanes, and service consumers are the vehicles waiting at the tollbooths and driving in the traffic lanes. In the second example, cashiers provide a service that is consumed by waiting customers. To emulate these conditions in a program, associate each service provider with a queue of service consumers.

Simulations operate by manipulating these queues. At each tick of an imaginary clock, a simulation adds varying numbers of consumers to the queues and gives consumers at the head of each queue another unit of service. Once a consumer has received the needed quantity of service, it leaves the queue and the next consumer steps forward. During the simulation, the program accumulates statistics such as how many ticks each consumer waited in a queue and the percentage of time each provider is busy. The duration of a tick is chosen to match the problem being simulated. It could represent a millisecond, a minute, or a decade. In the program itself, a tick probably corresponds to one pass through the program's major processing loop.

You can use object-oriented methods to implement simulation programs. For instance, in a supermarket simulation, each customer is an instance of a Customer class. A customer object keeps track of when the customer starts standing in line, when service is first received, and how much service is required. Likewise, a cashier is an instance of a Cashier class, and each cashier object contains a queue of customer objects. A simulator class coordinates the activities of the customers and cashiers. At each clock tick, the simulation object does the following:

- Generates new customer objects as appropriate

- Assigns customers to cashiers

- Tells each cashier to provide one unit of service to the customer at the head of the queue

In this chapter's first case study, you develop a program based on the preceding ideas. In the exercises, you extend the program.

Round-Robin CPU Scheduling

Most modern computers allow multiple processes to share a single CPU. There are various techniques for scheduling these processes. The most common, called *round-robin scheduling*, adds new processes to the end of a *ready queue*, which consists of processes waiting to use the CPU. Each process on the ready queue is popped in turn and given a slice of CPU time. When the time slice runs out, the process is returned to the rear of the queue, as shown in Figure 8.2.

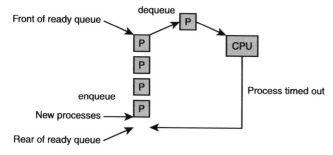

Figure 8.2

Scheduling processes for a CPU.

© 2014 Cengage Learning®

Generally, not all processes need the CPU with equal urgency. For instance, user satisfaction with a computer is greatly influenced by the computer's response time to keyboard and mouse inputs. Thus, it makes sense to give precedence to processes that handle these inputs. Round-robin scheduling adapts to this requirement by using a priority queue and assigning each process an appropriate priority. As a follow-up to this discussion, the second case study in this chapter shows how you can use a priority queue to schedule patients in an emergency room.

Exercises 8.2

1. Suppose customers in a 24-hour supermarket are ready to be checked out at the precise rate of one every two minutes. Suppose also that it takes exactly five minutes for one cashier to process one customer. How many cashiers need to be on duty to meet the demand? Will customers need to wait in line? How much idle time will each cashier experience per hour?

2. Now suppose that the rates—one customer every two minutes and five minutes per customer—represent averages. Describe in a qualitative manner how this will affect customer wait time. Will this change affect the average amount of idle time per cashier? For both situations, describe what happens if the number of cashiers is decreased or increased.

IMPLEMENTATIONS OF QUEUES

This chapter's approach to the implementation of queues is similar to the one that was used for stacks. The structure of a queue lends itself to either an array implementation or a linked implementation. To obtain some default behavior for free, subclass each queue implementation under the AbstractCollection class in your collection framework (see Chapter 6, "Inheritance and Abstract Classes"). Because the linked implementation is somewhat more straightforward, consider it first.

A Linked Implementation of Queues

The linked implementations of stacks and queues have much in common. Both classes, LinkedStack and LinkedQueue, use a singly linked Node class to implement nodes. The operation pop removes the first node in the sequence in both collections. However, LinkedQueue.add and LinkedStack.push differ. The operation push adds a node at the head of the sequence, whereas add adds a node at the tail. To provide fast access to both ends of a queue's linked structure, there are external pointers to both ends. Figure 8.3 shows a linked queue containing four items.

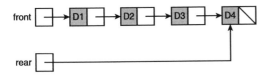

Figure 8.3

A linked queue with four items.

© 2014 Cengage Learning®

The instance variables front and rear of the LinkedQueue class are given an initial value of None. A variable named size, already defined in the collection framework, tracks the number of elements currently in the queue.

During an add operation, create a new node, set the next pointer of the last node to the new node, and set the variable rear to the new node, as shown in Figure 8.4.

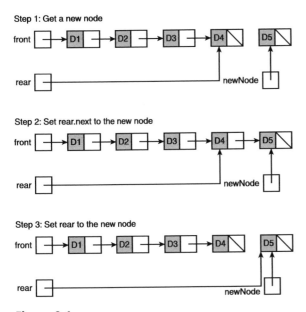

Figure 8.4

Adding an item to the rear of a linked queue.

© 2014 Cengage Learning®

Here is the code for the add method:

```
def add(self, newItem):
    """Adds newItem to the rear of the queue."""
    newNode = Node(newItem, None)
    if self.isEmpty():
        self._front = newNode
    else:
        self._rear.next = newNode
    self._rear = newNode
    self._size += 1
```

As mentioned earlier, LinekdQueue.pop is similar to LinkedStack.pop. However, if the queue becomes empty after a pop operation, the front and rear pointers must both be set to None. Here is the code:

```
def pop(self):
    """Removes and returns the item at front of the queue.
    Precondition: the queue is not empty."""
    # Check precondition here
    oldItem = self._front.data
    self._front = self._front.next
    if self._front is None:
        self._rear = None
    self._size -= 1
    return oldItem
```

Completion of the LinkedQueue class, including the enforcement of the preconditions on the methods pop and peek, is left as an exercise for you.

An Array Implementation

The array implementations of stacks and queues have less in common than the linked implementations. The array implementation of a stack needs to access items at only the logical end of the array. However, the array implementation of a queue must access items at the logical beginning and the logical end. Doing this in a computationally effective manner is complex, so it's best to approach the problem in a sequence of three attempts.

First Attempt

The first attempt at implementing a queue fixes the front of the queue at index position 0 and maintains an index variable, called rear, that points to the last item at position $n - 1$, where n is the number of items in the queue. A picture of such a queue, with four data items in an array of six cells, is shown in Figure 8.5.

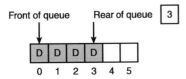

Figure 8.5

An array implementation of a queue with four items.

© 2014 Cengage Learning®

For this implementation, the add operation is efficient. However, the pop operation entails shifting all but the first item in the array to the left, which is an O(*n*) process.

Second Attempt

You can avoid pop's linear behavior by not shifting items left each time the operation is applied. The modified implementation maintains a second index, called front, that points to the item at the front of the queue. The front pointer starts at 0 and advances through the array as items are popped. Figure 8.6 shows such a queue after five add and two pop operations.

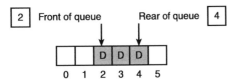

Figure 8.6

An array implementation of a queue with a front pointer.

© 2014 Cengage Learning®

Notice that, in this scheme, cells to the left of the queue's front pointer are unused until you shift all elements left, which you do whenever the rear pointer is about to run off the end. Now the maximum running time of pop is O(1), but it comes at the cost of boosting the maximum running time of add from O(1) to O(*n*).

Third Attempt

By using a *circular array implementation*, you can simultaneously achieve good running times for both add and pop. The implementation resembles the previous one in one respect: the front and rear pointers both start at the beginning of the array.

However, the front pointer now "chases" the rear pointer through the array. During the add operation, the rear pointer moves farther ahead of the front pointer, and during the pop operation, the front pointer catches up by one position. When either pointer is about to run off the end of the array, that pointer is reset to 0. This has the effect of wrapping the queue around to the beginning of the array without the cost of moving any items.

As an example, assume that an array implementation uses six cells, that six items have been added, and that two items have then been popped. According to this scheme, the next add resets the rear pointer to 0. Figure 8.7 shows the state of the array before and after the rear pointer is reset to 0 by the last add operation.

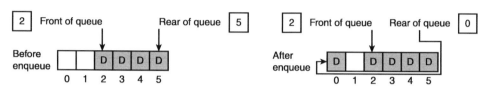

Figure 8.7

Wrapping data around a circular array implementation of a queue.

© 2014 Cengage Learning®

The rear pointer now appears to chase the front pointer until the front pointer reaches the end of the array, at which point it, too, is reset to 0. As you can readily see, the maximum running times of both add and pop are now O(1).

You will naturally wonder what happens when the queue becomes full and how the implementation can detect this condition. By maintaining a count of the items in the queue, you can determine whether the queue is full or empty. When this count equals the size of the array, you know it's time to resize.

After resizing, you would like the queue to occupy the initial segment of the array, with the front pointer set to 0. To achieve this, consider two cases at the beginning of the resizing process:

1. The front pointer is less than the rear pointer. In this case, you loop from front to rear in the original array and copy to positions 0 through size - 1 in the new array.

2. The rear pointer is less than the front pointer. In this case, you loop from front to size - 1 in the original array and copy to positions 0 through size - front in the new array. You then loop from 0 through rear in the original array and copy to positions size - front + 1 through size - 1 in the new array.

The resizing code for an array-based queue is more complicated than the code for an array-based stack, but the process is still linear. Completion of the circular array implementation of the class ArrayQueue is left as an exercise for you.

Time and Space Analysis for the Two Implementations

The time and space analysis for the two queue classes parallels that for the corresponding stack classes, so you do not dwell on the details. Consider first the linked implementation of queues. The running time of the __str__, __add__, and __eq__ methods is O(n). The maximum running time of all the other methods is O(1). In particular, because there are external links to the head and tail nodes in the queue's linked structure, you can access these nodes in constant time. The total space requirement is $2n + 3$, where n is the size of the queue. There is a reference to a datum and a pointer to the next node in each of the n nodes, and there are three cells for the queue's logical size and head and tail pointers.

For the circular array implementation of queues, if the array is static, the maximum running time of all methods other than __str__, __add__, and __eq__ is O(1). In particular, no items in the array are shifted during add or pop. If the array is dynamic, add and pop jump to O(n) anytime the array is resized but retain an average running time of O(1). Space utilization for the array implementation again depends on the load factor, as discussed in Chapter 4, "Arrays and Linked Structures." For load factors above ½, an array implementation makes more efficient use of memory than a linked implementation, and for load factors below ½, memory use is less efficient.

Exercises 8.3

1. Write a code segment that uses an if statement during an add to adjust the rear index of the circular array implementation of ArrayQueue. You may assume that the queue implementation uses the variables self._rear and self._items to refer to the rear index and array, respectively.

2. Write a code segment that uses the % operator during an add to adjust the rear index of the circular array implementation of ArrayQueue to avoid the use of an if statement. You can assume that the queue implementation uses the variables self._rear and self._items to refer to the rear index and array, respectively.

CASE STUDY: SIMULATING A SUPERMARKET CHECKOUT LINE

In this case study, you develop a program to simulate supermarket checkout stations. To keep the program simple, some important factors found in a realistic supermarket situation have been omitted; you're asked to add them back as part of the exercises.

Request

Write a program that allows the user to predict the behavior of a supermarket checkout line under various conditions.

Analysis

For the sake of simplicity, the following restrictions are imposed:

- There is just one checkout line, staffed by one cashier.

- Each customer has the same number of items to check out and requires the same processing time.

- The probability that a new customer will arrive at the checkout does not vary over time.

The inputs to the simulation program are the following:

- The total time, in abstract minutes, that the simulation is supposed to run.

- The number of minutes required to serve an individual customer.

- The probability that a new customer will arrive at the checkout line during the next minute. This probability should be a floating-point number greater than 0 and less than or equal to 1.

The program's outputs are the total number of customers processed, the number of customers left in the line when the time runs out, and the average waiting time for a customer. Table 8.3 summarizes the inputs and outputs.

Table 8.3   Inputs and Outputs of the Supermarket Checkout Simulator

Inputs	Range of Values for Inputs	Outputs
Total minutes	0 <= total <= 1000	Total customers processed
Average minutes per customer	0 < average <= total	Customers left in line
Probability of a new arrival in the next minute	0 < probability <= 1	Average waiting time

© 2014 Cengage Learning®

The User Interface

The following user interface for the system has been proposed:

```
Welcome the Market Simulator

Enter the total running time: 60
Enter the average time per customer: 3
Enter the probability of a new arrival: 0.25
TOTALS FOR THE CASHIER
Number of customers served: 16
Number of customers left in queue: 1
Average time customers spend
Waiting to be served: 2.38
```

Classes and Responsibilities

As far as classes and their overall responsibilities are concerned, the system is divided into a main function and several model classes. The main function is responsible for interacting with the user, validating the three input values, and communicating with the model. The design and implementation of this function require no comment, and the function's code is not presented. The classes in the model are listed in Table 8.4.

Table 8.4   The Classes in the Model

Class	Responsibilities
MarketModel	A market model does the following: 1. Runs the simulation. 2. Creates a cashier object. 3. Sends new customer objects to the cashier. 4. Maintains an abstract clock. 5. During each tick of the clock, tells the cashier to provide another unit of service to a customer.
Cashier	A cashier object does the following: 1. Contains a queue of customer objects. 2. Adds new customer objects to this queue when directed to do so. 3. Removes customers from the queue in turn. 4. Gives the current customer a unit of service when directed to do so and releases the customer when the service has been completed.

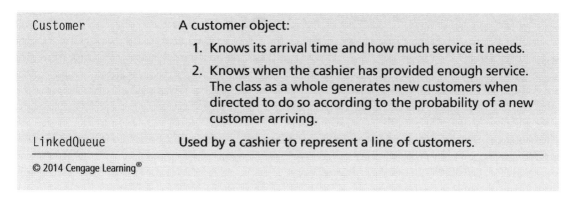

Customer	A customer object:
	1. Knows its arrival time and how much service it needs.
	2. Knows when the cashier has provided enough service. The class as a whole generates new customers when directed to do so according to the probability of a new customer arriving.
LinkedQueue	Used by a cashier to represent a line of customers.

© 2014 Cengage Learning®

The relationships among these classes are shown in Figure 8.8.

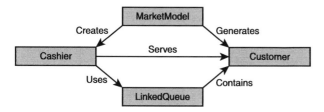

Figure 8.8

A class diagram of the supermarket checkout simulator.

© 2014 Cengage Learning®

The overall design of the system is reflected in the collaboration diagram shown in Figure 8.9.

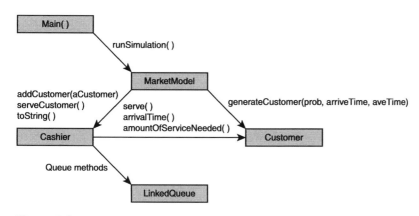

Figure 8.9

A collaboration diagram for the supermarket checkout simulator.

© 2014 Cengage Learning®

You can now design and implement each class in turn.

Because the checkout situation has been restricted, the design of the class MarketModel is fairly simple. The constructor does the following:

1. Saves the inputs—probability of new arrival, length of simulation, and average time per customer.

2. Creates the single cashier.

The only other method needed is runSimulation. This method runs the abstract clock that drives the checkout process. On each tick of the clock, the method does three things:

1. Asks the Customer class to generate a new customer, which it may or may not do, depending on the probability of a new arrival and the output of a random number generator.

2. If a new customer is generated, sends the new customer to the cashier.

3. Tells the cashier to provide a unit of service to the current customer.

When the simulation ends, the runSimulation method returns the cashier's results to the view. Here is the pseudocode for the method:

```
for each minute of the simulation
    ask the Customer class to generate a new customer
    if a customer is generated
        cashier.addCustomer(customer)
        cashier.serveCustomers(current time)
return cashier's results
```

Note that the pseudocode algorithm asks the Customer class for an instance of itself. Because it is only probable that a customer will arrive at any given minute, occasionally a customer will not be generated. Rather than code the logic for making this choice at this level, you can bury it in a *class method* in the Customer class. From the model, the Customer class method generateCustomer receives the probability of a new customer arriving, the current time, and the average time needed per customer. The method uses this information to determine whether to create a customer and, if it does, how to initialize the customer. The method returns either the new Customer object or the value None. The syntax of running a class method is just like that of an instance method, except that the name to the left of the dot is the class's name.

Here is a complete listing of the class `MarketModel`:

```
"""
File: marketmodel.py
"""

from cashier import Cashier
from customer import Customer

class MarketModel(object):

    def __init__(self, lengthOfSimulation, averageTimePerCus,
                 probabilityOfNewArrival):
        self._probabilityOfNewArrival = \
            probabilityOfNewArrival
        self._lengthOfSimulation = lengthOfSimulation
        self._averageTimePerCus = averageTimePerCus
        self._cashier = Cashier()

    def runSimulation(self):
        """Run the clock for n ticks."""
        for currentTime in range(self._lengthOfSimulation):
            # Attempt to generate a new customer
            customer = Customer.generateCustomer(
                self._probabilityOfNewArrival,
                currentTime,
                self._averageTimePerCus)

            # Send customer to cashier if successfully
            # generated
            if customer != None:
                self._cashier.addCustomer(customer)

            # Tell cashier to provide another unit of service
            self._cashier.serveCustomers(currentTime)

    def __str__(self):
        return str(self._cashier)
```

A cashier is responsible for serving a queue of customers. During this process, the cashier tallies the customers served and the minutes they spend waiting in line. At the end of the simulation, the class's __str__ method returns these totals as well as the number of customers remaining in the queue. The class has the following instance variables:

```
totalCustomerWaitTime
customersServed
queue
currentCustomer
```

The last variable holds the customer currently being processed.

To allow the market model to send a new customer to a cashier, the class implements the method addCustomer. This method expects a customer as a parameter and adds the customer to the cashier's queue.

The method serveCustomers handles the cashier's activity during one clock tick. The method expects the current time as a parameter and responds in one of several different ways, as listed in Table 8.5.

Table 8.5 Responses of a Cashier During a Clock Tick

Condition	What It Means	Action to Perform
The current customer is None and the queue is empty.	There are no customers to serve.	None; just return.
The current customer is None and the queue is not empty.	There is a customer waiting at the front of the queue.	1. Pop a customer and make it the current customer. 2. Ask it when it was instantiated, determine how long it has been waiting, and add that time to the total waiting time for all customers. 3. Increment the number of customers served. 4. Give the customer a unit of service and dismiss it if it is finished.
The current customer is not None.	Serve the current customer.	Give the customer one unit of service and dismiss it if it is finished.

© 2014 Cengage Learning®

Here is pseudocode for the method serveCustomers:

```
if currentCustomer is None
    if queue is empty
        return
    else
        currentCustomer = queue.pop()
        totalCustomerWaitTime = totalCustomerWaitTime +
            currentTime - currentCustomer.arrivalTime()
        increment customersServed
```

```
        currentCustomer.serve()
        if currentCustomer.amountOfServiceNeeded() == 0
            currentCustomer = None
```

Here is the code for the Cashier class:

```
"""
File: cashier.py
"""

from linkedqueue import LinkedQueue

class Cashier(object):

    def __init__(self):
        self._totalCustomerWaitTime = 0
        self._customersServed = 0
        self._currentCustomer = None
        self._queue = LinkedQueue()

    def addCustomer(self, c):
        self._queue.add(c)

    def serveCustomers(self, currentTime):
        if self._currentCustomer is None:
            # No customers yet
            if self._queue.isEmpty():
                return
            else:
                # Pop first waiting customer
                # and tally results
                self._currentCustomer = self._queue.pop()
                self._totalCustomerWaitTime += \
                    currentTime - \
                    self._currentCustomer.arrivalTime()
                self._customersServed += 1

        # Give a unit of service
        self._currentCustomer.serve()

        # If current customer is finished, send it away
        if self._currentCustomer.amountOfServiceNeeded() == \
            0:
            self._currentCustomer = None

    def __str__(self):
        result = "TOTALS FOR THE CASHIER\n" + \
                 "Number of customers served:       " + \
                 str(self._customersServed) + "\n"
        if self._customersServed != 0:
```

```
        aveWaitTime = self._totalCustomerWaitTime / \
            self._customersServed
        result += "Number of customers left in queue: " \
            + str(len(self._queue)) + "\n" + \
                "Average time customers spend\n" + \
                "waiting to be served:              " \
                + "%5.2f" % aveWaitTime
    return result
```

The `Customer` class maintains a customer's arrival time and the amount of service needed. The constructor initializes these with data provided by the market model. The instance methods include the following:

- `arrivalTime()`—Returns the time at which the customer arrived at a cashier's queue.

- `amountOfServiceNeeded()`—Returns the number of service units left.

- `serve()`—Decrements the number of service units by one.

The remaining method, `generateCustomer`, is a class method. It expects as arguments the probability of a new customer arriving, the current time, and the number of service units per customer. The method returns a new instance of `Customer` with the given time and service units, provided the probability is greater than or equal to a random number between 0 and 1. Otherwise, the method returns `None`, indicating that no customer was generated. The syntax for defining a class method in Python is the following:

```
@classmethod
def <method name>(cls, <other parameters>):
    <statements>
```

Here is the code for the `Customer` class:

```
"""
File: customer.py
"""

import random

class Customer(object):

    @classmethod
    def generateCustomer(cls, probabilityOfNewArrival,
                        arrivalTime,
                        averageTimePerCustomer):
        """Returns a Customer object if the probability
        of arrival is greater than or equal to a random number.
        Otherwise, returns None, indicating no new customer.
        """
```

```
        if random.random() <= probabilityOfNewArrival:
            return Customer(arrivalTime,
                                averageTimePerCustomer)
        else:
            return None
    def __init__(self, arrivalTime, serviceNeeded):
        self._arrivalTime = arrivalTime
        self._amountOfServiceNeeded = serviceNeeded

    def arrivalTime(self):
        return self._arrivalTime

    def amountOfServiceNeeded(self):
        return self._amountOfServiceNeeded

    def serve(self):
        """Accepts a unit of service from the cashier."""
        self._amountOfServiceNeeded -= 1
```

PRIORITY QUEUES

As mentioned earlier, a priority queue is a specialized type of queue. When items are added to a priority queue, they are assigned an order of rank. When they are removed, items of higher priority are removed before those of lower priority. Items of equal priority are removed in the usual FIFO order. An item A has a higher priority than an item B if A < B. Thus, integers, strings, or any other objects that recognize the comparison operators can be ordered in priority queues. If an object does not recognize these operators, it can be wrapped, or bundled, with a priority number in another object that does recognize these operators. The queue will then recognize this object as comparable with others of its type.

Because a priority queue closely resembles a queue, the two have the same interface or set of operations (see Table 8.1). Table 8.6 shows the states in the lifetime of a priority queue. Note that the items are integers, so the smaller integers are the items with the higher priority.

Table 8.6   States in the Lifetime of a Priority Queue

Operation	State of the Queue after the Operation	Value Returned	Comment
q = <Priority queue type>()			Initially, the queue is empty.
q.add(3)	3		The queue contains the single item 3.

(Continued)

Table 8.6   States in the Lifetime of a Priority Queue (Continued)

Operation	State of the Queue after the Operation	Value Returned	Comment
q.add(1)	1 3		1 is at the front of the queue and 3 is at the rear of the queue because 1 has a higher priority.
q.add(2)	1 2 3		2 is added but has a higher priority than 3, so 2 moves ahead of 3.
q.pop()	2 3	1	Remove the front item from the queue and return it. 2 is now the front item.
q.add(3)	2 3 3		The new 3 is inserted after the existing 3, in FIFO order.
q.add(5)	2 3 3 5		5 has the lowest priority, so it goes to the rear.

As mentioned earlier, when an object is not intrinsically comparable, it can be wrapped with a priority in another object that is comparable. The *wrapper class* used to build a comparable item from one that is not already comparable is named Comparable. This class includes a constructor that expects an item and its priority as arguments. The priority must be an integer, a string, or another object that recognizes the comparison operators. Recall that Python looks for an object's comparison methods when the comparison operators are used. After a wrapper object has been created, the methods getItem, getPriority, __str__, __eq__, __le__, and __lt__ can be used to extract the item or its priority, return its string representation, and support comparisons based on the priority, respectively. Here is the code for the Comparable class:

```python
class Comparable(object):
    """Wrapper class for items that are not comparable."""

    def __init__(self, data, priority = 1):
        self._data = data
        self._priority = priority
```

```python
    def __str__(self):
        """Returns the string rep of the contained datum."""
        return str(self._data)

    def __eq__(self, other):
        """Returns True if the contained priorities are equal
        or False otherwise."""
        if self is other: return True
        if type(self) != type(other): return False
        return self._priority == other._priority

    def __lt__(self, other):
        """Returns True if self's priority < other's priority,
        or False otherwise."""
        return self._priority < other._priority

    def __le__(self, other):
        """Returns True if self's priority <= other's priority,
        or False otherwise."""
        return self._priority <= other._priority

    def getData(self):
        """Returns the contained datum."""
        return self._data

    def getPriority(self):
        """Returns the contained priority."""
        return self._priority
```

Note that the __str__method is also included in the Comparable class so that the queue's __str__ method will have the expected behavior with these items.

During insertions, a priority queue does not know whether it is comparing items in wrappers or just items. When a wrapped item is accessed with the method peek or pop or in the context of a for loop, it must be unwrapped with the method getItem before processing. For example, assume that the items labeled a, b, and c are not comparable but should have the priorities 1, 2, and 3, respectively, in a queue. Then the code to add them to a priority queue named queue and retrieve them from it is as follows:

```python
queue.add(Comparable(a, 1))
queue.add(Comparable(b, 2))
queue.add(Comparable(c, 3))
while not queue.isEmpty():
    item = queue.pop().getItem()
    <do something with item>
```

This book discusses two implementations of a priority queue. One uses a data structure called a heap, which is examined in Chapter 10, "Trees." The other extends the LinkedQueue class presented earlier. This one is called the sorted list implementation.

A sorted list is a list of comparable elements that are maintained in a natural order. A priority queue's list should be arranged so that the minimum element is always accessed at or removed from just one end of the list. The elements are inserted in their proper places in the ordering.

A singly linked structure represents this type of list well if the minimum element is always removed from the head of the structure. If this structure is inherited from the singly linked structure used in the LinkedQueue class, you can continue to remove an element by running that class's pop method. Only the add method needs to change. Its definition is overridden in the new subclass, called LinkedPriorityQueue.

The new implementation of add conducts a search for the new item's position in the list. It considers the following cases:

■ If the queue is empty or the new item is greater than or equal to the item at the rear, add it as before. (It will be placed at the rear.)

■ Otherwise, begin at the head and move forward through the nodes until the new item is less than the item in the current node. At that point, a new node containing the item must be inserted between the current node and the previous node, if there is one. To accomplish this insertion, the search uses two pointers, named probe and trailer. When the search stops, probe points to the node *after* the position of the new item. If that node is not the first one, trailer points to the node *before* the position of the new item. The new node's next pointer is then set to the probe pointer. The previous node's next pointer is then set to the new node, if probe does not point to the first node. Otherwise, the queue's front pointer is set to the new node.

To illustrate the process described in Case 2, Figure 8.10 depicts the state of a priority queue containing the three integers 1, 3, and 4 during the add of the value 2. Note the adjustments of the probe and trailer pointers during this process.

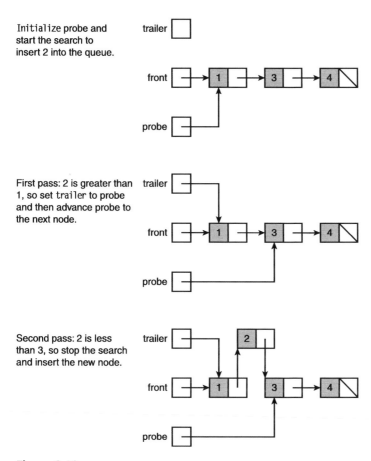

Initialize probe and start the search to insert 2 into the queue.

First pass: 2 is greater than 1, so set trailer to probe and then advance probe to the next node.

Second pass: 2 is less than 3, so stop the search and insert the new node.

Figure 8.10

Inserting an item into a priority queue.

© 2014 Cengage Learning®

Although the code for add is complicated, you don't have to write other methods in the new class. Moreover, the use of LinkedQueue's add earlier in Case 1 simplifies the new method somewhat.

Here is the code for the class LinkedPriorityQueue:

```
"""
File: linkedpriorityqueue.py
"""

from node import Node
from linkedqueue import LinkedQueue

class LinkedPriorityQueue(LinkedQueue):
    """A link-based priority queue implementation."""
```

```python
def __init__(self, sourceCollection = None):
    """Sets the initial state of self, which includes the
    contents of sourceCollection, if it's present."""
    LinkedQueue.__init__(self, sourceCollection)

def add(self, newItem):
    """Inserts newItem after items of greater or equal
    priority or ahead of items of lesser priority.
    A has greater priority than B if A < B."""
    if self.isEmpty() or newItem >= self._rear.data:
        # New item goes at rear
        LinkedQueue.add(self, newItem)
    else:
        # Search for a position where it's less
        probe = self._front
        while newItem >= probe.data:
            trailer = probe
            probe = probe.next
        newNode = Node(newItem, probe)
        if probe == self._front:
            # New item goes at front
            self._front = newNode
        else:
            # New item goes between two nodes
            trailer.next = newNode
    self._size += 1
```

The time and space analysis for `LinkedPriorityQueue` is the same as that of `LinkedQueue`, with the exception of the `add` method. This method now must search for the proper place to insert an item. Rearranging the links once this place is found is a constant time operation, but the search itself is linear, so `add` is now O(n).

Exercise 8.4

Suggest a strategy for an array-based implementation of a priority queue. Will its space/time complexity be any different from the linked implementation? What are the trade-offs?

CASE STUDY: AN EMERGENCY ROOM SCHEDULER

As anyone who has been to a busy hospital emergency room knows, people must wait for service. Although everyone might appear to be waiting in the same place, they are actually in separate groups and scheduled according to the seriousness of their condition. This case study develops a program that performs this scheduling with a priority queue.

Request

Write a program that allows a supervisor to schedule treatments for patients coming into a hospital's emergency room. Assume that, because some patients are in more critical condition than others, patients are not treated on a strictly first-come, first-served basis, but are assigned a priority when admitted. Patients with a high priority receive attention before those with a lower priority.

Analysis

Patients come into the emergency room in one of three conditions. In order of priority, the conditions are ranked as follows:

1. Critical

2. Serious

3. Fair

When the user selects the Schedule option, the program allows the user to enter a patient's name and condition, and the patient is placed in line for treatment according to the severity of his condition. When the user selects the Treat Next Patient option, the program removes and displays the patient first in line with the most serious condition. When the user selects the Treat All Patients option, the program removes and displays all patients in order from patient to serve first to patient to serve last.

Each command button produces an appropriate message in the output area. Table 8.7 lists the interface's responses to the commands.

Table 8.7 Commands of the Emergency Room Program

User Command	Program Response
Schedule	Prompts the user for the patient's name and condition, and then prints `<patient name> is added to the <condition> list`.
Treat Next Patient	Prints `<patient name> is being treated`.
Treat All Patients	Prints `<patient name> is being treated`. ... Prints `<patient name> is being treated`.

© 2014 Cengage Learning®

Here is an interaction with the terminal-based interface:

```
Main menu
  1 Schedule a patient
  2 Treat the next patient
  3 Treat all patients
  4 Exit the program

Enter a number [1-4]: 1

Enter the patient's name: Bill
Patient's condition:
  1 Critical
  2 Serious
  3 Fair

Enter a number [1-3]: 1
Bill is added to the critical list.

Main menu
  1 Schedule a patient
  2 Treat the next patient
  3 Treat all patients
  4 Exit the program

Enter a number [1-4]: 3

Bill / critical is being treated.
Martin / serious is being treated.
Ken / fair is being treated.
No patients available to treat.
```

Classes

The application consists of a view class, called ERView, and a set of model classes. The view class interacts with the user and runs methods with the model. The class ERModel maintains a priority queue of patients. The class Patient represents patients, and the class Condition represents the three possible conditions. The relationships among the classes are shown in Figure 8.11.

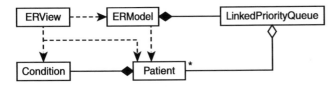

Figure 8.11

The classes in the ER scheduling system.

© 2014 Cengage Learning®

Design and Implementation

The `Patient` and `Condition` classes maintain a patient's name and condition. You can compare (according to their conditions) and view them as strings. Here is the code for these two classes:

```python
class Condition(object):

    def __init__(self, rank):
        self._rank = rank

    def __ge__(self, other):
        """Used for comparisons."""
        return self._rank >= other._rank

    def __str__(self):
        if    self._rank == 1: return "critical"
        elif self._rank == 2:  return "serious"
        else:                  return "fair"

class Patient(object):

    def __init__(self, name, condition):
        self._name = name
        self._condition = condition

    def __ge__(self, other):
        """Used for comparisons."""
        return self._condition >= other._condition

    def __str__(self):
        return self._name + " / " + str(self._condition)
```

The class `ERView` uses a typical menu-driven loop. You structure the code using several helper methods. Here is a complete listing:

```python
"""
File: erapp.py
The view for an emergency room scheduler.
"""

from model import ERModel, Patient, Condition

class ERView(object):
    """The view class for the ER application."""

    def __init__(self, model):
        self._model = model

    def run(self):
        """Menu-driven command loop for the app."""
```

```
            menu = "Main menu\n" + \
                " 1 Schedule a patient\n" + \
                " 2 Treat the next patient\n" + \
                " 3 Treat all patients\n" \
                " 4 Exit the program\n"
        while True:
            command = self._getCommand(4, menu)
            if   command == 1: self._schedule()
            elif command == 2: self._treatNext()
            elif command == 3: self._treatAll()
            else: break

    def treatNext(self):
        """Treats one patient if there is one."""
        if self.model.isEmpty():
            print("No patients available to treat")
        else:
            patient = self.model.treatNext()
            print(patient, "is being treated.")

    def treatAll(self):
        """Treats all the remaining patients."""
        if self.model.isEmpty():
            print("No patients available to treat.")
        else:
            while not self.model.isEmpty():
                self.treatNext()

    def _schedule(self):
        """Obtains patient info and schedules patient."""
        name = input("\nEnter the patient's name: ")
        condition = self._getCondition()
        self._model.schedule(Patient(name, condition))
        print(name, "is added to the", condition, "list\n")

    def _getCondition(self):
        """Obtains condition info."""
        menu = "Patient's condition:\n" + \
                " 1 Critical\n" + \
                " 2 Serious\n" + \
                " 3 Fair\n"
        number = self._getCommand(3, menu)
        return Condition(number)

    def _getCommand(self, high, menu):
        """Obtains and returns a command number."""
```

```
        prompt = "Enter a number [1-" + str(high) + "]: "
        commandRange = list(map(str, range(1, high + 1)))
        error = "Error, number must be 1 to " + str(high)
        while True:
            print(menu)
            command = input(prompt)
            if command in commandRange:
                return int(command)
            else:
                print(error)
# Main function to start up the application
def main():
    model = ERModel()
    view = ERView(model)
    view.run()
if __name__ == "__main__":
    main()
```

The class ERModel uses a priority queue to schedule the patients. Its implementation is left as a programming project for you.

SUMMARY

- A queue is a linear collection that adds elements to one end, called the rear, and removes them from the other end, called the front. Thus, they are accessed in first-in, first-out (FIFO) order.

- Other operations on queues include peeking at the top element, determining the number of elements, determining whether the queue is empty, and returning a string representation.

- Queues are used in applications that manage data items in a FIFO order. These applications include scheduling items for processing or access to resources.

- Arrays and singly linked structures support simple implementations of queues.

- Priority queues schedule their elements using a rating scheme as well as a FIFO order. If two elements have equal priority, they are scheduled in FIFO order. Otherwise, elements are ranked from smallest to largest, according to some attribute, such as a number or an alphabetical content. In general, elements with the smallest priority values are removed first, no matter when they are added to the priority queue.

REVIEW QUESTIONS

1. Examples of queues are (choose all that apply)

   a. Customers waiting in a checkout line

   b. A deck of playing cards

   c. A file directory system

   d. A line of cars at a tollbooth

   e. Laundry in a hamper

2. The operations that modify a queue are called

   a. Add and remove

   b. Add and pop

3. Queues are also known as

   a. First-in, first-out data structures

   b. Last-in, first-out data structures

4. The front of a queue containing the items a b c is on the left. After two pop operations, the queue contains

   a. a

   b. c

5. The front of a queue containing the items a b c is on the left. After the operation add(d), the queue contains

   a. a b c d

   b. d a b c

6. Memory for objects such as nodes in a linked structure is allocated on

   a. The object heap

   b. The call stack

7. The running time of the three queue mutator operations is

   a. Linear

   b. Constant

8. The linked implementation of a queue uses

   a. Nodes with a link to the next node

   b. Nodes with links to the next and previous nodes

c. Nodes with a link to the next node and an external pointer to the first node and an external pointer to the last node

9. In the circular array implementation of a queue

 a. The front index chases the rear index around the array

 b. The front index is always less than or equal to the rear index

10. The items in a priority queue are ranked from

 a. Smallest (highest priority) to largest (lowest priority)

 b. Largest (highest priority) to smallest (lowest priority)

PROJECTS

1. Complete the linked implementation of the queue collection discussed in this chapter. Verify that exceptions are raised when preconditions are violated.

2. Complete and test the circular array implementation of the queue collection discussed in this chapter. Verify that exceptions are raised when preconditions are violated and that the implementation adds or removes storage as needed.

3. When you send a file to be printed on a shared printer, it is put onto a print queue with other jobs. Anytime before your job prints, you can access the queue to remove it. Thus, some queues support a remove operation. Add this method to the queue implementations. The method should expect an integer index as an argument. It should then remove and return the item in the queue at that position (counting from position 0 at the front to position $n - 1$ at the rear).

4. Modify the supermarket checkout simulator so that it simulates a store with many checkout lines. Add the number of cashiers as a new user input. At instantiation, the model should create a list of these cashiers. When a customer is generated, it should be sent to a cashier randomly chosen from the list of cashiers. On each tick of the abstract clock, each cashier should be told to serve its next customer. At the end of the simulation, the results for each cashier should be displayed.

5. In real life, customers do not choose a random cashier when they check out. They typically base their choice on at least the following two factors:

 a. The length of a line of customers waiting to check out.

 b. The physical proximity of a cashier.

 Modify the simulation of Project 5 so that it takes account of the first factor.

6. Modify the simulation of Project 5 so that it takes account of both factors listed in that project. You should assume that a customer initially arrives at the checkout line of a random cashier and then chooses a cashier who is no more than two lines away from this spot. This simulation should have at least four cashiers.

7. The simulator's interface asks the user to enter the average number of minutes required to process a customer. However, as written, the simulation assigns the same processing time to each customer. In real life, processing times vary around the average. Modify the Customer class's constructor so that it randomly generates service times between 1 and (average * 2 + 1).

8. Complete the emergency room scheduler application as described in the case study.

9. Modify the maze-solving application of Chapter 7 so that it uses a queue instead of a stack. Run each version of the application on the same maze and count the number of choice points required by each version. Can you conclude anything from the differences in these results? Are there best cases and worst cases of maze problems for stacks and queues?

CHAPTER 9

LISTS

This chapter covers lists, the last of the three major linear collections discussed in this book (the other two being stacks and queues). Lists support a much wider range of operations than stacks and queues and, consequently, are both more widely used and more difficult to implement. Although Python includes a built-in list type, there are several possible implementations, of which Python's is only one. To make sense of a list's profusion of fundamental operations, you classify them into three groups: index-based operations, content-based operations, and position-based operations. This chapter discusses the two most common list implementations: arrays and linked structures. You develop a special type of object called a list iterator to support position-based operations. This chapter's case study shows how to develop a special type of list called a sorted list.

OVERVIEW OF LISTS

A list supports manipulation of items at any point within a linear collection. Some common examples of lists include the following:

- A recipe, which is a list of instructions
- A string, which is a list of characters
- A document, which is a list of words
- A file, which is a list of data blocks on a disk

In all these examples, order is critically important, and shuffling the items renders the collections meaningless. However, the items in a list are not necessarily sorted. Words in a dictionary and names in a phone book are examples of sorted lists, but the words in this paragraph equally form a list and are unsorted. Although the items in a list are always logically contiguous, they need not be physically contiguous in memory. Array implementations of lists use physical positions to represent logical order, but linked implementations do not.

The first item in a list is at its *head*, whereas the last item in a list is at its *tail*. Items in a list retain position relative to each other over time, and additions and deletions affect predecessor/successor relationships only at the point of modification. Computer scientists typically count positions from 0 through the length of the list minus 1. Each numeric position is also called an *index*. When a list is visualized, the indices decrease to the left and increase to the right. Figure 9.1 shows how a list changes in response to a succession of operations. The operations, which represent just a small subset of those possible for lists, are described in Table 9.1.

Table 9.1   The Operations Used in Figure 9.1

Operation	What It Does
add(item)	Adds item to the tail of the list.
insert(index, item)	Inserts item at position index, shifting other items to the right by one position if necessary.
replace(index, item)	Replaces the item at position index with item.
pop(index)	Removes the item at position index, shifting other items to the left by one position if necessary.

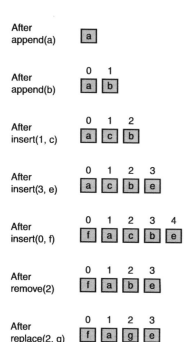

Empty

After
append(a)

0   1
After
append(b)

0   1   2
After
insert(1, c)

0   1   2   3
After
insert(3, e)

0   1   2   3   4
After
insert(0, f)

0   1   2   3
After
remove(2)

0   1   2   3
After
replace(2, g)

Figure 9.1

The states in the lifetime of a list.

© 2014 Cengage Learning®

Using Lists

If you look at most textbooks on data structures and at the list class provided in Python, you can discern two broad categories of operations, which are called index-based operations and content-based operations. To these, you can add a third category of operations that are position-based. Before learning the uses of lists, you'll read about these categories.

Index-Based Operations

Index-based operations manipulate items at designated indices within a list. In the case of array-based implementations, these operations also provide the convenience of random access. Suppose a list contains n items. Because a list is ordered linearly, you can refer unambiguously to an item in a list via its relative position from the head of the list using an index that runs from 0 to $n - 1$. Thus, the head is at index 0 and the tail is at index $n - 1$. Table 9.2 lists some fundamental index-based operations for any list named L.

Table 9.2   Index-Based Operations for a List

List Method	What It Does
L.insert(i, item)	Adds item at index i, after shifting items to the right by one position.
L.pop(i = None)	Removes and returns the item at index i. If i is absent, removes and returns the last item. *Precondition*: 0 <= i <= len(L).
L.[i]	Returns the item at index i. *Precondition*: 0 <= i <= len(L).
L.[i] = item	Replaces the item at index i with item. *Precondition*: 0 <= i <= len(L).

© 2014 Cengage Learning®

When viewed from this perspective, lists are sometimes called *vectors* or *sequences*, and in their use of indices, they are reminiscent of arrays. However, an array is a concrete data structure with a specific and unvarying implementation based on a single block of physical memory. A list is an abstract data type that can be represented in a variety of ways, only one of which uses an array. In addition, a list has a much larger repertoire of basic operations than an array, even though suitable sequences of array operations can mimic all list operations.

Content-Based Operations

Content-based operations are based not on an index, but on the content of a list. These operations usually expect an item as an argument and do something with it and the list. Some of these operations search for an item equal to a given item before taking further action. Table 9.3 lists three basic content-based operations for a list named L. Note that add is used instead of append, for consistency with other collections.

Table 9.3 Content-Based Operations for a List

List Method	What It Does
L.add(item)	Adds item after the list's tail.
L.remove(item)	Removes item from the list. *Precondition*: item is in the list.
L.index(item)	Returns the position of the first instance of item in the list. *Precondition*: item is in the list.

© 2014 Cengage Learning®

Position-Based Operations

Position-based operations are performed relative to a currently established position called the *cursor*. The operations allow the programmer to navigate through a list by moving this cursor. In some programming languages, a separate object called a *list iterator* provides these operations. That policy is adopted here. Although a list already supports an iterator, which allows the programmer to visit a list's items with a for loop, a list iterator is more powerful. Unlike a simple iterator, a list iterator supports movement to previous positions, directly to the first position, and directly to the last position. Aside from these navigational operations, a list iterator also supports insertions, replacements, and removals of items at cursor positions. A list iterator implementation is developed later in this chapter, but at this point, you can examine its logical structure and behavior.

The programmer creates a list iterator object by running the listIterator method on a list, as follows:

```
listIterator = aList.listIterator()
```

At this point, there are two objects—the list iterator and the list—connected by the list interface, as shown in Figure 9.2. The list is sometimes called the list iterator's *backing store*.

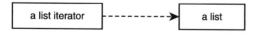

Figure 9.2

A list iterator attached to its backing store (a list).

© 2014 Cengage Learning®

With respect to the items in its backing store, a list iterator's cursor is always in one of three places:

- Just before the first item
- Between two adjacent items
- Just after the last item

Initially, when a list iterator is first instantiated, its cursor is undefined. After one or more items have been inserted into the list, the user can establish the position of the cursor by moving it to the beginning or to the end of the list. From these positions, the user can navigate to another position in some way. Table 9.4 lists the navigational operations for a list iterator named LI.

Table 9.4   Navigational Operations for a List Iterator

Operation	What It Does
LI.hasNext()	Returns True if there is an item after the cursor. Returns False if the cursor is undefined or is positioned after the last item.
LI.next()	Returns the next item and moves the cursor to the right by one position. *Preconditions*: hasNext returns True. There have been no intervening mutations on the list since the most recent next or previous operation.
LI.hasPrevious()	Returns True if there is an item before the cursor. Returns False if the cursor is undefined or is positioned before the first item.
LI.previous()	Returns the previous item and moves the cursor to the left by one position. *Preconditions*: hasPrevious returns True. There have been no intervening mutations on the list since the most recent next or previous operation.
LI.first()	Moves the cursor before the first item, if there is one.
LI.last()	Moves the cursor after the last item, if there is one.

© 2014 Cengage Learning®

The remaining position-based operations are used to modify the list. Table 9.5 lists mutator operations that work at the currently established position in the list iterator named LI.

Table 9.5   Mutator Operations for a List Iterator

Operation	What It Does
LI.insert(item)	If the cursor is defined, inserts item after it; otherwise, inserts item at the tail of the list.
LI.remove()	Removes the item returned by the most recent next or previous operation. *Precondition*: there have been no intervening mutations on the list since the most recent next or previous operation.
LI.replace(item)	Replaces the item returned by the most recent call of next or previous operation. *Precondition*: there have been no intervening mutations on the list since the most recent next or previous operation.

© 2014 Cengage Learning®

Table 9.6 presents a sequence of operations on a list iterator and indicates the state of its associated list after each operation. You can assume that this list is empty when the list iterator is opened on it.

Remember that a list iterator's cursor, once it is established, is located before the first item, after the last item, or between two items. In the table, the cursor is indicated by a comma and by an integer variable called the *current position*. If the list contains n items, the following applies:

- Current position = i if it is located before the item at index i, where $i = 0, 1, 2, ... ,$ $n - 1$.

- Current position = n if it is located after the last item.

Notice in Table 9.6 that there is no current position until there is at least one item in the list and the method first or last has been run. Until that point, the methods hasNext and hasPrevious return False and the methods next, previous, remove, and replace should not be run.

From the specification for the operations, you know that remove and replace operate on the last item returned by a successful next or previous operation, provided there have been no intervening insert or remove operations. The table highlights this last item returned in boldface. If no item is highlighted, remove and replace are invalid. The highlighted item, when present, can be on either side of the cursor—on the left after a next operation or on the right after a previous operation.

When a list becomes empty, its cursor is once again undefined.

Table 9.6 The Effects of List Iterator Operations on a List

Operation	Position After the Operation	The List After the Operation	Value Returned	Comment
Instantiation	Undefined	Empty		A new list iterator.
insert(a)	Undefined	a		When the cursor is undefined, each item inserted goes at the tail of the list.
insert(b)	Undefined	a b		
hasNext()	Undefined		False	When the cursor is undefined, there is no next or previous item.
first()	0	, a b		Establish the cursor before the first item, if there is one.
hasNext()	0		True	There is an item to the right of the cursor, so there is a next item.
next()	1	a , b	a	Return a and move the cursor to the right.
replace(c)	1	c , b		Replace a, the item most recently returned by next, with c.
next()	2	c b ,	b	Return b and move the cursor to the right.
next()	2	c b ,	Exception	The cursor is at the tail of the list, so it is impossible to move to the next item.
hasNext()	2	c b ,	False	The cursor is at the tail of the list; therefore, there is no next item.

hasPrevious()	2	c b ,	True	There is an item to the left of the cursor, so there is a previous item.
previous()	1	c, **b**	b	Return b and move the cursor to the left.
insert(e)	1	c, **e** b		Inserts e to the right of the cursor position.
remove()	1	c, **e** b	Exception	An insert has occurred since the most recent next or previous.
previous()	0	, **c** e b	c	Return c and move the cursor to the left.
remove()	0	, e b		Remove c, the item most recently returned by previous.

© 2014 Cengage Learning®

The next code segment also illustrates the use of a list iterator. You can assume that someone has defined the class ArrayList that supports the operations mentioned earlier.

```
print("Create a list with 1-9")
lyst = ArrayList(range(9))
print("Length:", len(lyst))
print("Items (first to last): ", lyst)

# Create and use a list iterator
listIterator = lyst.listIterator()
print("Forward traversal: ", end = "")
listIterator.first()
while listIterator.hasNext():
    print (listIterator.next(), end = " ")

print("\nBackward traversal: ", end = "")
listIterator.last()
while listIterator.hasPrevious():
    print(listIterator.previous(), end = " ")

print("\nInserting 10 before 3: ", end = "")
listIterator.first()
for count in range(2):
    listIterator.next()
```

```
listIterator.insert(10)
print(lyst)

print("Removing 2: ", end = "")
listIterator.first()
for count in range(3):
    listIterator.next()
listIterator.remove()
print(lyst)

print("Removing all items")
listIterator.first()
while listIterator.hasNext():
    listIterator.next()
    listIterator.remove()
print("Length:", len(lyst))
```

Here is the output of the code segment:

```
Create a list with 1-9
Length: 9
Items (first to last): 1 2 3 4 5 6 7 8 9
Forward traversal: 1 2 3 4 5 6 7 8 9
Backward traversal: 9 8 7 6 5 4 3 2 1
Inserting 10 before 3: 1 2 10 3 4 5 6 7 8 9
Removing 2: 1 10 3 4 5 6 7 8 9
Removing all items
Length: 0
```

Note that a traversal with a list iterator begins by moving the cursor to the first position or to the last position. Remember that there are additional restrictions on some operations. For example, replace and remove require establishing a current position with an immediately preceding next or previous operation. These two operations, in turn, assume that hasNext and hasPrevious return True, respectively. These operations are discussed in detail later in this chapter.

Interfaces for Lists

Although there are a breathtaking number of list operations, the classification scheme helps to reduce the potential confusion. Table 9.7 gives a recap. In this table, L refers to a list and LI refers to a list iterator opened on a list.

Table 9.7 Summary of Basic List Operations

Index-Based Operation	Content-Based Operation	Position-Based Operation
L.insert(i, item)	L.add(item)	LI.hasNext()
L.pop(i)	L.remove(item)	LI.next()
L[i]	L.index(item)	LI.hasPrevious()
L[i] = item		LI.first()
		LI.last()
		LI.insert(item)
		LI.remove(item)
		LI.replace(item)

© 2014 Cengage Learning®

Based on the foregoing discussion of list operations, it's proposed that you split these operations into two interfaces. The first interface includes the index-based and content-based operations that are similar to those of Python's list class. Later in this chapter, you develop two implementations called ArrayList and LinkedList. The second interface contains operations for list iterators. Each implementation of a list iterator is associated with a given list implementation. Although the two interfaces are just sets of operations, you can give them names, such as ListInterface and ListIteratorInterface, to identify them.

The UML diagram in Figure 9.3 shows how the implementing classes are related to the two interfaces. To the list interface, you also add the basic methods common to all collections, namely, isEmpty, __len__, __str__, __iter__, __add__, __eq__, and clear, as well as the listIterator method. The arrows drawn from the list iterator classes to the list classes indicate a relationship of dependency.

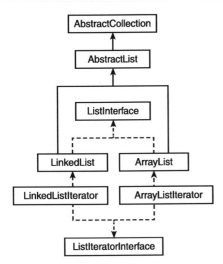

Figure 9.3

The interfaces and implementing classes for lists and list iterators.

© 2014 Cengage Learning®

Exercises 9.1

1. What are the restrictions on index-based operations with a list?

2. How does the position-based operation `insert` differ from an index-based operation `insert`?

APPLICATIONS OF LISTS

Lists are probably the most widely used collections in computer science. This section examines three important applications: heap-storage management, disk file management, and the implementation of other collections.

Heap-Storage Management

When you read Chapter 7, "Stacks," you learned about one aspect of Python memory management: the call stack. Now you will learn the other aspects by reading about how you can manage free space in the object heap, also introduced in Chapter 7, using a linked list. Recall that the object heap is an area of memory from which the Python virtual machine allocates segments of various sizes for all new data objects. When an object no longer can be referenced from a program, the Python Virtual Machine (PVM) can return that object's memory segment to the heap for use by other objects. Heap-management schemes can have a significant impact on an application's overall performance, especially if the application creates and abandons many objects during the course of its execution. PVM implementers, therefore, are willing to expend a great deal of effort to organize the heap in the most efficient manner possible. Their elaborate solutions are beyond this book's scope, so a simplified scheme is presented here.

In this scheme, contiguous blocks of free space on the heap are linked in a free list. When an application instantiates a new object, the PVM searches the free list for the first block large enough to hold the object. When the object is no longer needed, the garbage collector returns the object's space to the free list.

This scheme has two defects. First, over time, large blocks on the free list become fragmented into many smaller blocks. Second, searching the free list for blocks of sufficient size can take $O(n)$ running time, where n is the number of blocks in the list. To counteract fragmentation, the garbage collector periodically reorganizes the free list by recombining adjacent blocks. To reduce search time, you can use multiple free lists. For instance, if an object reference requires 4 bytes, list 1 could consist of blocks of size 4; list 2, blocks of size 8; list 3, blocks of size 9; list 4, blocks of size 32; and so on. The last list would contain all blocks larger than some designated size.

In this scheme, space is always allocated in units of 4 bytes, and space for a new object is taken from the head of the first nonempty list containing blocks of sufficient size. Because access and removal from the head is $O(1)$, allocating space for a new object now takes $O(1)$ time unless the object requires more space than is available in the first block of the last list. At that point, the last list must be searched, giving the operation a maximum running time of $O(n)$, where n is the size of the last list.

For the sake of simplicity in this discussion, two difficult problems have been completely ignored. The first problem has to do with deciding when to run the garbage collector. Running the garbage collector takes time away from the application, but not running it means the free lists are never replenished. The second problem concerns how the garbage collector identifies objects that are no longer referenced and, consequently, no longer needed. (A solution to these problems is outside the scope of this book.)

Organization of Files on a Disk

A computer's file system has three major components: a directory of files, the files themselves, and free space. To understand how these work together to create a file system, first consider a disk's physical format. Figure 9.4 shows a standard arrangement. The disk's surface is divided into concentric tracks, and each track is further subdivided into sectors. The numbers of these tracks vary depending on the disk's capacity and physical size. However, all tracks contain the same number of sectors, and all sectors contain the same number of bytes. For the sake of this discussion, suppose that a sector contains 8 kilobytes of data plus a few additional bytes reserved for a pointer. A sector is the smallest unit of information transferred to and from the disk, regardless of its actual size, and a pair of numbers (*t*, *s*) specifies a sector's location on the disk, where *t* is the track number and *s* the sector number. Figure 9.4 shows a disk with *n* tracks. The *k* sectors in track 0 are labeled from 0 to *k* – 1.

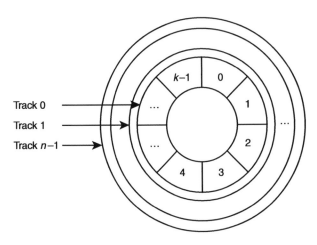

Figure 9.4

Tracks and sectors on the surface of a disk.

© 2014 Cengage Learning®

A file system's directory is organized as a hierarchical collection. It's unnecessary to go into the details of that structure here. For these purposes, just assume that the directory occupies the first few tracks on the disk and contains an entry for each file. This entry holds the file's name, creation date, size, and so forth. In addition, it holds the address of the sector containing the first bytes in the file. Depending on its size, a file might be completely contained within a single sector or it might span several sectors. Usually, the last sector is only partially full, and no attempt is made to recover the unused space. The sectors that make up a file do not need to be physically adjacent because each sector except the last one ends with a pointer to the sector containing the next portion of the file. Finally, sectors that are not in use are linked together in a free list. When new files are created, they are allocated space from this list, and when old files are deleted, their space is returned to the list.

Because all sectors are the same size and because space is allocated in sectors, a file system does not experience the same fragmentation problem encountered in Python's object heap. Nonetheless, there is still a difficulty. To transfer data to or from the disk, read/write heads must first be positioned to the correct track, the disk must rotate until the desired sector is under the heads, and then the transfer of data takes place. Of these three steps, the transfer of data takes the least time. Fortunately, data can be transferred to or from several adjacent sectors during a single rotation without the need to reposition the heads. Thus, a disk system's performance is optimized when multisector files are not scattered across the disk. Over time, however, as files of varying sizes are created and destroyed, this sort of scattering becomes frequent, and the file system's performance degrades. As a countermeasure, file systems include a utility, run either automatically or at the explicit request of the user, which reorganizes the file system so that the sectors in each file are contiguous and have the same physical and logical order.

Implementation of Other Collections

Lists are frequently used to implement other collections, such as stacks and queues. There are two ways to do this:

- Extend the list class, making the new class a subclass of the list class.
- Use an instance of the list class within the new class and let the list contain the data items.

For example, you might implement a stack class by extending a list class. Extension is not a wise choice in this case, however, because this version of a stack inherits the methods from the list that allow users to access items at positions other than the top, thus violating the spirit of the stack abstract data type. In the case of stacks and queues, a better design decision is to contain a list within the stack or queue. In that case, all the list operations are available to the implementer of the stack or queue, but only the essential stack or queue operations are available to its users.

Collections that use lists also inherit their performance characteristics. For example, a stack that uses an array-based list has the performance characteristics of an array-based list, whereas a stack that uses a link-based list has characteristics of a link-based list.

The primary advantage of using a list to implement another collection is that coding becomes easier. Instead of operating on a concrete array or linked structure, the implementer of a stack needs only call the appropriate list methods.

Chapter 10, "Trees," and Chapter 11, "Sets and Dictionaries," showcase other situations in which you can use lists in the implementation of collections.

LIST IMPLEMENTATIONS

Earlier in this chapter, it was mentioned that there are two common data structures to implement lists: arrays and linked structures. This section develops array-based and linked implementations.

The Role of the AbstractList Class

The list implementations follow the pattern established by the bag, stack, and queue classes discussed in Chapters 6 through 8. Rather than start from scratch, each concrete list class is subclassed under an abstract class, called AbstractList. Because this class is a subclass of AbstractCollection, the list classes inherit the usual collection methods, as well as the variable self._size. Can you also include some other list methods in AbstractList to reduce the number of methods you need to define in the concrete classes?

The answer is "Of course." Recall that the content-based method index is a search for the position of a given item. Because the search can use a simple for loop, you can define this method in AbstractList. Moreover, the content-based methods remove and add can call the index-based methods pop and insert, respectively, to delete or add an item after locating its position with a call to index. Thus, you can define these two content-based methods in AbstractList as well.

In addition to these methods, the AbstractList class maintains a new instance variable called self._modCount. The list iterators use this variable to enforce preconditions on certain methods, as discussed later in this chapter. Here is the code for the AbstractList class:

```
"""
File: abstractlist.py
Author: Ken Lambert
"""

from abstractcollection import AbstractCollection

class AbstractList(AbstractCollection):
    """An abstract list implementation."""

    def __init__(self, sourceCollection):
        """Maintains a count of modifications to the list."""
        self._modCount = 0
        AbstractCollection.__init__(self, sourceCollection)

    def getModCount(self):
        """Returns the count of modifications to the list."""
        return self._modCount

    def incModCount(self):
        """Increments the count of modifications
        to the list."""
        self._modCount += 1

    def index(self, item):
        """Precondition: item is in the list.
        Returns the position of item.
```

```
        Raises: ValueError if the item is not in the list."""
        position = 0
        for data in self:
            if data == item:
                return position
            else:
                position += 1
        if position == len(self):
            raise ValueError(str(item) + " not in list.")

    def add(self, item):
        """Adds the item to the end of the list."""
        self.insert(len(self), item)

    def remove(self, item):
        """Precondition: item is in self.
        Raises: ValueError if item in not in self.
        Postcondition: item is removed from self."""
        position = self.index(item)
        self.pop(position)
```

An Array-Based Implementation

The array-based implementation of the list interface is a class called ArrayList. An ArrayList maintains its data items in an instance of the Array class introduced in Chapter 4, "Arrays and Linked Structures." An ArrayList has an initial default capacity that is automatically increased when necessary.

Because the ArrayList class is a subclass of AbstractList, only the index-based methods, the __iter__ method, and the listIterator methods are defined here.

The index-based operations __getitem__ and __setitem__ simply use the subscript operator on the array variable self._items. The insert and pop methods shift the items in the array using the techniques described in Chapter 4. A discussion of the ArrayListIterator class is deferred to a later section of this chapter. Here is the code for the class ArrayList:

```
"""
File: arraylist.py
Author: Ken Lambert
"""

from arrays import Array
from abstractlist import AbstractList
from arraylistiterator import ArrayListIterator
```

```python
class ArrayList(AbstractList):
    """An array-based list implementation."""

    DEFAULT_CAPACITY = 10

    def __init__(self, sourceCollection = None):
        """Sets the initial state of self, which includes the
        contents of sourceCollection, if it's present."""
        self._items = Array(ArrayList.DEFAULT_CAPACITY)
        AbstractList.__init__(self, sourceCollection)

    # Accessor methods
    def __iter__(self):
        """Supports iteration over a view of self."""
        cursor = 0
        while cursor < len(self):
            yield self._items[cursor]
            cursor += 1

    def __getitem__(self, i):
        """Precondition: 0 <= i < len(self)
        Returns the item at position i.
        Raises: IndexError."""
        if i < 0 or i >= len(self):
            raise IndexError("List index out of range")
        return self._items[i]

    # Mutator methods
    def __setitem__(self, i, item):
        """Precondition: 0 <= i < len(self)
        Replaces the item at position i.
        Raises: IndexError."""
        if i < 0 or i >= len(self):
            raise IndexError("List index out of range")
        self._items[i] = item

    def insert(self, i, item):
        """Inserts the item at position i."""
        # Resize array here if necessary
        if i < 0: i = 0
        elif i > len(self): i = len(self)
        if i < len(self):
            for j in range(len(self), i, -1):
                self._items[j] = self._items[j - 1]
        self._items[i] = item
        self._size += 1
        self.incModCount()
```

```
def pop(self, i = None):
    """Precondition: 0 <= i < len(self).
    Removes and returns the item at position i.
    If i is None, i is given a default of len(self) - 1.
    Raises: IndexError."""
    if i == None: i = len(self) - 1
    if i < 0 or i >= len(self):
        raise IndexError("List index out of range")
    item = self._items[i]
    for j in range(i, len(self) - 1):
        self._items[j] = self._items[j + 1]
    self._size -= 1
    self.incModCount()
    # Resize array here if necessary
    return item

def listIterator(self):
    """Returns a list iterator."""
    return ArrayListIterator(self)
```

A Linked Implementation

You used linked structures to implement bags, stacks, and queues earlier in this book. The structure used for a linked stack (see Chapter 7), which has a pointer to its head but not to its tail, would be an unwise choice for a linked list. The list's add method would have to chain through the entire sequence of nodes to locate the tail of the list.

The singly linked structure used for the linked queue (see Chapter 8, "Queues") would work better, because a pointer is maintained to the structure's tail as well as its head. The list method add puts the new item at the tail of the linked structure and adjusts the head link, if necessary.

However, a singly linked structure is not the ideal one to support a list iterator. The list iterator allows cursor movement in either direction, but a singly linked structure supports movement to the next node only. You can solve this problem by using a doubly linked structure, where each node has a pointer to the previous node as well as a pointer to the next node.

The code needed to manipulate a doubly linked structure can be simplified if one extra node is added at the head of the structure, as mentioned in Chapter 4. This node is called a *sentinel node*, and it points forward to the first data node and backward to the last data node. The head pointer points to the sentinel node. The resulting structure resembles the circular linked structure introduced in Chapter 4. The sentinel node does not contain a list item, and when the list is empty, the sentinel remains. Figure 9.5 shows an empty circular linked structure and a circular linked structure containing one data item.

An empty, circular, doubly
linked structure with
a dummy header code

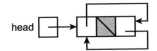

The linked structure after inserting
the first data node

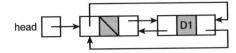

Figure 9.5
Two circular, doubly linked structures with sentinel nodes.
© 2014 Cengage Learning®

As you can see from the figure, the sentinel node's next pointer locates the first data node, whereas its previous pointer locates the last data node. Thus, there is no need for a separate tail pointer in the implementation. Moreover, as you shall soon see, when the first or last data node is inserted or removed, there is no need to reset the implementation's head pointer.

The basic building block of a doubly linked structure is a node with two pointers: next, which points right; and previous, which points left. This type of node, called TwoWayNode, is a subclass of the Node class defined in Chapter 4.

The next code segment shows the setup code for the LinkedList class, as well as its __iter__ method:

```
"""
File: linkedlist.py
Author: Ken Lambert
"""

from node import TwoWayNode
from abstractlist import AbstractList

class LinkedList(AbstractList):
    """A link-based list implementation."""

    def __init__(self, sourceCollection = None):
        """Sets the initial state of self, which includes the
        contents of sourceCollection, if it's present."""
        # Uses a circular structure with a sentinel node
        self._head = TwoWayNode()
        self._head.previous = self._head.next = self._head
```

```
        AbstractList.__init__(self, sourceCollection)
    #Accessor methods
    def __iter__(self):
        """Supports iteration over a view of self."""
        cursor = self._head.next
        while cursor != self._head:
            yield cursor.data
            cursor = cursor.next
```

Note that the __init__ method creates a node with no data—this is the sentinel node. The __iter__ method then sets its cursor not to the head node, which is the sentinel, but to its next node, which is the first node containing data, if that node exists. When the cursor cycles around to the head node, the iterator's loop terminates.

Remaining to be developed are the index-based methods __getitem__, __setitem__, insert, and pop. Each of these methods must chain through the nodes in the linked structure, beginning with the node after the head node, until the *i*th node is reached. At that point, the datum contained in that node is returned or modified (__getitem__ or __setitem__), or the node is removed (pop), or a new node is inserted before that node (insert). Because the search for the *i*th node is an operation that all four methods must perform, you include a helper method, named _getNode, that does this. This method expects the index position of the target node as an argument and returns a pointer to the *i*th node. The four calling methods can then use this pointer to manipulate the linked structure accordingly.

Here is the code for the methods _getNode, __setitem__, and insert. The remaining methods are left as exercises for you.

```
# Helper method returns node at position i
def _getNode(self, i):
    """Helper method: returns a pointer to the node
    at position i."""
    if i == len(self):      # Constant-time access to head node
        return self._head
    if i == len(self) - 1:  # or last data node
        return self._head.previous
    probe = self._head.next
    while i > 0:
        probe = probe.next
        i -= 1
    return probe
# Mutator methods
```

```
def __setitem__(self, i, item):
    """Precondition: 0 <= i < len(self)
    Replaces the item at position i.
    Raises: IndexError."""
    if i < 0 or i >= len(self):
        raise IndexError("List index out of range")
    self._getNode(i).data = item

def insert(self, i, item):
    """Inserts the item at position i."""
    if i < 0: i = 0
    elif i > len(self): i = len(self)
    theNode = self._getNode(i)
    newNode = TwoWayNode(item, theNode.previous, theNode)
    theNode.previous.next = newNode
    theNode.previous = newNode
    self._size += 1
    self.incModCount()
```

Note the use of the method _getNode in both __setitem__ and insert. Each of these methods makes sure that the index of the item is in range before calling _getNode to locate the node. Furthermore, because the linked structure includes a sentinel node, the insert method does not have to handle the special cases of insertions at the beginning and the end of the structure.

Time and Space Analysis for the Two Implementations

The running times of the list methods follow the pattern already established for arrays and linked structures in Chapter 4. The difference in performance is seen most clearly in the access and replacement methods, __getitem__ and __setitem__. In ArrayList, these methods simply run the array's subscript operation in constant time, whereas in LinkedList, these methods must perform a linear search for the *i*th node in the linked structure.

The two other index-based methods, insert and pop, exhibit the expected trade-offs in the two implementations, although their running times are linear in both cases. The ArrayList methods locate the position of the target item in constant time but require linear time to shift items to complete the process. Conversely, the LinkedList methods require linear time to locate the target item but need only constant time to insert or remove a node.

The content-based method index is $O(n)$ for both implementations. The content-based method remove runs the index method, followed by the pop method. Thus, this method is no worse than linear in both implementations. However, some extra work is done to repeat the search for the position in `LinkedList.pop`. You could eliminate this waste of work by including the `remove` method, with its own search process, in `LinkedList`.

The `add` method, which also calls the `insert` method, appears to run in linear time. However, the `insert` method in both implementations runs in constant time when the position is at or beyond the end of the list. Therefore, `add` also is O(1).

Table 9.8 lists the runtime complexity of the list methods.

Table 9.8   Average Running Times for List Operations

List Method	ArrayList	LinkedList
__getitem__(i)	O(1)	O(n)
__setitem__(i, item)	O(1)	O(n)
insert(i, item)	O(n)	O(n)
pop(i)	O(n)	O(n)
add(item)	O(1)	O(1)
remove(item)	O(n)	O(n)
index(item)	O(n)	O(n)

© 2014 Cengage Learning®

A space analysis for list implementations follows the pattern already established for stacks and queues. A minimal array implementation requires memory for the following items:

- An array that can hold `capacity` references, where `capacity` >= n
- A reference to the array
- Variables for the number of items and the mod count

Thus, the total space requirement for the minimal array implementation is `capacity` + 3.

The linked implementation requires memory for the following items:

- n + 1 nodes, where each node contains three references
- A reference to the head node
- Variables for the number of items and the mod count

Thus, the total space requirement for the linked implementation is $3n + 6$.

When comparing the memory requirements of the two implementations, you must remember that the space utilization for the array implementation depends on the load factor. For load factors above 1/3, the array implementation makes more efficient use of memory than a linked implementation, and for load factors below 1/3, an array is less efficient.

Exercises 9.2

1. Which list implementations would work well for implementing bags, stacks, and queues?

2. Someone suggests that `ArrayList` should be a subclass of `ArrayBag` and `LinkedList` should be a subclass of `LinkedBag`. Discuss the advantages and disadvantages of this proposal.

IMPLEMENTING A LIST ITERATOR

As mentioned earlier, a list iterator is an object attached to a list that provides positional operations on that list. These operations, listed in Table 9.4 and 9.5, allow the programmer to view and modify a list by moving a cursor. In this section, you develop a list iterator for an array-based list; the link-based version is left as an exercise for you.

Role and Responsibilities of a List Iterator

When the programmer runs the `listIterator` method on a list, this method returns a new instance of a list iterator class. The list iterator object depends on the associated list, in that the former needs to access the latter to locate items, replace them, insert them, or remove them. Thus, the list iterator will maintain a reference to its list or backing store, which it receives when it is created.

Aside from supporting its basic operations, the list iterator also must enforce their preconditions. There are three types of preconditions:

- A programmer cannot run a `next` or a `previous` operation if the `hasNext` or the `hasPrevious` operation returns `False`, respectively.

- A programmer cannot run consecutive mutator methods on a list iterator. A `next` or a `previous` must first be run before each mutation to establish a cursor position.

- A programmer cannot run mutations on the list itself, with the list's mutator methods, while using a list iterator on that list.

To help determine some of these preconditions, the list iterator maintains two additional variables. The first one is its own mod count variable. This variable is set to the value of the list's mod count when the list iterator is created. Thus, the list and the list iterator each have their own "notion" of the mod count. Whenever a list's own mutator is run, it increments the list's mod count to record the modification to the list. When certain methods, such as next and previous, are run on the list iterator, the list iterator compares its own mod count with the mod count of the list. If the two values are different, someone has run a list mutator in the wrong context; an exception is then raised. When a list iterator method mutates the list, the list iterator increments its own mod count to keep the two mod counts consistent.

The second variable tracks the position at which the list iterator can perform a mutation on the list. In the array-based implementation, this variable is –1 whenever the position has not yet been established. Its value becomes an index into the list whenever the programmer successfully runs a next or previous operation on the list iterator. Thus, the mutator methods insert and remove in the list iterator can check this variable for their precondition and reset it to –1 after they successfully mutate the list.

Setting Up and Instantiating a List Iterator Class

The list iterator class for array lists is called ArrayListIterator. This class includes the following instance variables:

- self._backingStore—The list on which the iterator is opened.
- self._modCount—The iterator's notion of the mod count.
- self._cursor—The cursor position manipulated by the iterator's navigational methods first, last, hasNext, next, hasPrevious, and previous.
- self._lastItemPos—The cursor position used by the iterator's mutator methods insert, remove, and replace. This position is established by running next or previous and is undefined after running insert or remove.

Recall that the ArrayList method listIterator passes the backing store (self) to the list iterator during its instantiation. The list iterator can then run the list methods on this object to manipulate it. Here is the code for this portion of the ArrayListIterator class.

```
"""
File: arraylistiterator.py
Author: Ken Lambert
"""

class ArrayListIterator(object):
    """Represents the list iterator for an array list."""

    def __init__(self, backingStore):
        """Set the initial state of the list iterator."""
```

```
        self._backingStore = backingStore
        self._modCount = backingStore.getModCount()
        self.first()

    def first(self):
        """Resets the cursor to the beginning
        of the backing store."""
        self._cursor = 0
        self._lastItemPos = -1
```

The Navigational Methods in the List Iterator

The navigational methods hasNext and next work with a cursor that is moving from the beginning of an array-based list to its end. This cursor is initially 0 and is reset to 0 when the programmer runs the first method on the list iterator. The method hasNext returns True as long as the cursor is less than the backing store's length.

The method next must check two preconditions before advancing the cursor and returning an item from the backing store. First, the method hasNext must return True. Second, the two mod counts—one belonging to the list iterator and the other to the backing store—must be equal. If all goes well, the method next sets self._lastItemPos to self._cursor, increments the latter by 1, and returns the item at self._lastItemPos in the backing store. Here is the code for these two methods:

```
def hasNext(self):
    """Returns True if the iterator has
    a next item or False otherwise."""
    return self._cursor < len(self._backingStore)

def next(self):
    """Preconditions: hasNext returns True.
    The list has not been modified except by this
    iterator's mutators.
    Returns the current item and advances the cursor.
    to the next item."""
    if not self.hasNext():
        raise ValueError("No next item in list iterator")
    if self._modCount != self._backingStore.getModCount():
        raise AttributeError(
            "Illegal modification of backing store")
    self._lastItemPos = self._cursor
    self._cursor += 1
    return self._backingStore[self._lastItemPos]
```

The methods last, hasPrevious, and previous work with a cursor that is moving from the end of an array-based list to its beginning. The method last sets the position of the cursor to the right of the last item in the list. This position will be equal to the length of the list. The method hasPrevious returns True if the cursor is greater than position 0. The method previous checks the same two preconditions as the method next. It then decrements the cursor by 1, sets self._lastItemPos to self._cursor, and returns the item at self._lastItemPos in the backing store. Here is the code for the three methods:

```
def last(self):
    """Moves the cursor to the end of the backing store."""
    self._cursor = len(self._backingStore)
    self._lastItemPos = -1

def hasPrevious(self):
    """Returns True if the iterator has a
    previous item or False otherwise."""
    return self._cursor > 0

def previous(self):
    """Preconditions: hasPrevious returns True.
    The list has not been modified except
    by this iterator's mutators.
    Returns the current item and moves
    the cursor to the previous item."""
    if not self.hasPrevious():
        raise ValueError("No previous item in list iterator")
    if self._modCount != self._backingStore.getModCount():
        raise AttributeError(
            "Illegal modification of backing store")
    self._cursor -= 1
    self._lastItemPos = self._cursor
    return self._backingStore[self._lastItemPos]
```

The Mutator Methods in the List Iterator

The mutator methods remove and replace must check two preconditions. First, the cursor must be established, meaning that the variable self._lastItemPos must not equal –1. Second, the two mod counts must be equal. The method insert checks only the precondition on the mod counts. These methods accomplish their tasks as follows:

■ The method replace has the easiest job. The item is replaced at the current position in the backing store, and self._lastItemPos is reset to –1. The list iterator's mod count is not incremented during a replacement operation.

■ If the cursor is defined, the method `insert` inserts the item into the backing store at the current position and resets `self._lastItemPos` to –1. Otherwise, the item is added to the end of the backing store. In either case, the list iterator's mod count is incremented.

■ The method `remove` pops the item from the backing store at the current position and increments the list iterator's mod count by 1. If `self._lastItemPos` is less than `self._cursor`, this means that `remove` was run after a `next` operation, so the cursor is decremented by 1. Finally, `self._lastItemPos` is reset to –1.

Here is the code for the three mutator methods:

```
def replace(self, item):
    """Preconditions: the current position is defined.
    The list has not been modified except by this
    iterator's mutators."""
    if self._lastItemPos == -1:
        raise AttributeError(
            "The current position is undefined.")
    if self._modCount != self._backingStore.getModCount():
        raise AttributeError(
            "List has been modified illegally.")
    self._backingStore[self._lastItemPos] = item
    self._lastItemPos = -1

def insert(self, item):
    """Preconditions:
    The list has not been modified except by this
    iterator's mutators."""
    if self._modCount != self._backingStore.getModCount():
        raise AttributeError(
            "List has been modified illegally.")
    if self._lastItemPos == -1:
    # Cursor not defined, so add item to end of list
        self._backingStore.add(item)
    else:
        self._backingStore.insert(self._lastItemPos, item)
    self._lastItemPos = -1
    self._modCount += 1

def remove(self):
    """Preconditions: the current position is defined.
    The list has not been modified except by this
    iterator's mutators."""
    if self._lastItemPos == -1:
```

```
        raise AttributeError(
            "The current position is undefined.")
    if self._modCount != self._backingStore.getModCount():
        raise AttributeError(
            "List has been modified illegally.")
    item = self._backingStore.pop(self._lastItemPos)

    # If the item removed was obtained via next,
    # move cursor back
    if self._lastItemPos < self._cursor:
        self._cursor -= 1
    self._modCount += 1
    self._lastItemPos = -1
```

Design of a List Iterator for a Linked List

It is possible to use the ListIterator class just described with a linked list. However, because this implementation of the list iterator runs the index-based methods __getitem__ and __setitem__ on the backing store, the next, previous, and replace operations will run in linear time when this backing store is a linked list. This performance penalty is unacceptable.

The cursor in an alternative implementation tracks nodes within the backing store's linked structure. The navigational methods adjust the cursor by setting it to the next node or the previous node. Because these are constant time operations, the positional navigation through a linked list is no less efficient than that through an array-based list. Direct access to the backing store's linked structure also makes possible the insertion, removal, or replacement of an item in constant time. The implementation of a list iterator for a linked list is left as an exercise for you.

Time and Space Analysis of List Iterator Implementations

The running times of all the methods in the linked implementation of a list iterator are O(1). That alone makes it a clear winner over the array-based implementation, whose insert and remove methods are both O(n).

Case Study: Developing a Sorted List

This case study explores the development of a useful type of collection: the sorted list.

Request

Develop a sorted list collection.

Analysis

When you developed a sorted bag class in Chapter 6, "Inheritance and Abstract Classes," you were able to subclass the sorted bag class under a bag class, because the two classes had the same interface. Do a sorted list and a regular list have the same interface? If the answer is "yes," the path to design and implementation will parallel the one you took for the sorted bag.

Unfortunately, the answer is "no." A sorted list does include most of the methods in a regular list, but there are two important exceptions. The insert and __setitem__ methods place an item in a list at a given position. However, you cannot allow a programmer to place an item at an arbitrary position in a sorted list. If that were allowed, the programmer could place a larger item before a smaller one, or conversely. Therefore, you must exclude these two methods from the sorted list interface.

This restriction on item placement within the list likewise has consequences for the interface of the list iterator on a sorted list. The programmer should be able to navigate and remove items as before, but you cannot allow insertions or replacements with a list iterator on a sorted list.

Two methods in the sorted list, add and index, behave in a different manner than they do for regular lists. The add method now searches for the proper place to insert the item among the items already in the list. The index operation can now take advantage of the fact that the list is sorted by performing a binary search for the given item.

Lastly, you assume that items can be compared using the standard comparison operators. Thus, any class of an item that goes into a sorted list should include the __le__ and __gt__ methods.

The list-specific operations in the interface for sorted lists, which are called SortedList Interface, are summarized in Table 9.9.

Table 9.9   The Sorted List Operations

Sorted List Method	What It Does
L.add(item)	Inserts item into its proper place in L.
L.remove(item)	Removes item from L. *Precondition*: item is in L.
L.index(item)	Returns the position of the first instance of item in L. *Precondition*: item is in L.
L.__getitem__(i)	Returns the item from L at position i. *Precondition*: 0 <= i < len(L).
L.pop(i = None)	If *i* is omitted, removes and returns the last item in L. Otherwise, removes and returns the item from L at position i. *Precondition*: 0 <= i < len(L).

© 2014 Cengage Learning®

Design

Because you would like to support binary search, you develop just an array-based implementation, named ArraySortedList.

The ArraySortedList class cannot be a subclass of the ArrayList class, because then ArraySortedList would inherit the two unusable methods mentioned earlier (see Figure 9.6).

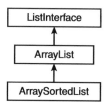

Figure 9.6

The rejected implementation strategy for an array-based sorted list.
© 2014 Cengage Learning®

When these situations arise, most programming textbooks suggest that you use an instance of the class you would have subclassed as the container for the items. This strategy would make ArrayList the type of collection used to hold the items within the ArraySortedList object (see Figure 9.7).

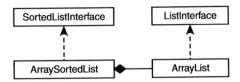

Figure 9.7

A better implementation strategy for an array-based sorted list.

© 2014 Cengage Learning®

Unfortunately, the second design does not exploit the reuse of code in the manner to which you are accustomed. Every method in ArrayList must be redone in ArraySortedList, and the size variable in one of the two classes goes to waste.

A better design comes from the insight that a list is actually a sorted list with two additional methods: insert and __setitem__. Put another way, the list interface is an extension of the sorted list interface; thus, the array-based list class can extend the array-based sorted list class. With a bit of effort, you can refactor your list hierarchy by subclassing ArrayList under ArraySortedList, as shown in the class diagram of Figure 9.8.

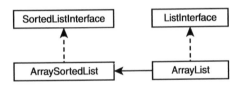

Figure 9.8

A still better implementation strategy for an array-based sorted list.

© 2014 Cengage Learning®

In this new arrangement, the ArraySortedList class maintains the array, as referenced by the variable self._items. This class also implements the allowable index-based methods pop and __getitem__, and it overrides the methods add and index inherited from the AbstractList class. The ArrayList class overrides the add and index methods inherited from the ArraySortedList class, includes the index-based methods insert and __setitem__, and inherits the remaining methods from its ancestors.

One other method is also included in the ArraySortedList class. This class now needs the __contains__ method. Recall that when Python sees the in operator, it looks for a __contains__ method in the second operand's class. If this method does not exist, Python automatically performs a linear search with the operand's for loop. Because you now want Python to select a given collection's index method to perform the search, you must include an implementation of __contains__. This method can easily trap the exceptions raised by index when a target item is not in a list. Table 9.10 shows how the list methods are distributed among the implementing classes. Note that uniquely defined methods are shaded; also, note that the ArrayList methods index and add call their namesakes in the AbstractList class.

Table 9.10   The Distribution of the List Methods Among the List Classes

AbstractList	ArraySortedList	ArrayList
getModCount	__iter__	__setitem__
incModCount	__getitem__	insert
remove	__contains__	index
index	clear	add
add	pop	listIterator
	index	
	add	
	listIterator	

© 2014 Cengage Learning®

You can use a similar strategy to design the list iterator classes for the array-based list and array-based sorted list. The list iterator class for an array-based list is a subclass of the list iterator class for an array-based sorted list. The ArraySortedListIterator class includes all the navigational methods and the remove method. Its subclass, the ArrayListIterator class, includes just the insert and replace methods. The relationship between these two classes is shown in Figure 9.9.

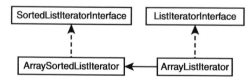

Figure 9.9

An implementation strategy for array-based list iterators.

© 2014 Cengage Learning®

Implementation (Coding)

Here is the code for the refactored `ArrayList` class. Note that its `add` and `index` methods call the same methods in `AbstractList` to retain their behavior from the earlier implementation. Otherwise, only the methods `insert`, `__setitem__`, and `listIterator` are included.

```
"""
File: arraylist.py
Author: Ken Lambert
"""

from arrays import Array
from abstractlist import AbstractList
from arraysortedlist import ArraySortedList
from arraylistiterator import ArrayListIterator

class ArrayList(ArraySortedList):
    """An array-based list implementation."""

    def __init__(self, sourceCollection = None):
        """Sets the initial state of self, which includes the
        contents of sourceCollection, if it's present."""
        ArraySortedList.__init__(self, sourceCollection)

    # Accessor methods
    def index(self, item):
        """Precondition: item is in the list.
        Returns the position of item.
        Raises: ValueError if the item is not in the list."""
        return AbstractList.index(self, item)

    # Mutator methods
    def __setitem__(self, i, item):
        """Precondition: 0 <= i < len(self)
        Replaces the item at position i.
        Raises: IndexError if i is out of range."""
        if i < 0 or i >= len(self):
            raise IndexError("List index out of range")
        self._items[i] = item

    def insert(self, i, item):
        """Inserts the item at position i."""
        # Resize the array here if necessary
        if i < 0: i = 0
        elif i > len(self): i = len(self)
        if i < len(self):
            for j in range(len(self), i, -1):
```

```
            self._items[j] = self._items[j - 1]
        self._items[i] = item
        self._size += 1
        self.incModCount()
    def add(self, item):
        """Adds item to self."""
        AbstractList.add(self, item)
    def listIterator(self):
        """Returns a list iterator."""
        return ArrayListIterator(self)
```

The code for the `ArraySortedList` class is left as an exercise for you.

SUMMARY

- A list is a linear collection that allows users to insert, remove, access, and replace elements at any position.

- Operations on lists are index based, content based, or position based. An index-based operation allows access to an element at a specified integer index. A position-based list lets the user scroll through it by moving a cursor.

- List implementations are based on arrays or on linked structures. A doubly linked structure is more convenient and faster when used with a list iterator than a singly linked structure.

- A sorted list is a list whose elements are always in ascending or descending order.

REVIEW QUESTIONS

1. Examples of lists are (choose all that apply)

   a. Customers waiting in a checkout line

   b. A deck of playing cards

   c. A file directory system

   d. A line of cars at a tollbooth

   e. The roster of a football team

2. Operations that access list elements at integer positions are called

   a. Content-based operations

   b. Index-based operations

   c. Position-based operations

3. Operations that access list elements by moving a cursor are called
   a. Content-based operations
   b. Index-based operations
   c. Position-based operations

4. The index-based operations on a linked implementation of a list run in
   a. Constant time
   b. Linear time

5. The operation that inserts an element after the tail of a list is called
   a. pop
   b. add

6. Most of the operations on a list iterator connected to a linked list run in
   a. Constant time
   b. Linear time

7. The insert and remove operations on an array-based indexed list run in
   a. Constant time
   b. Linear time

8. The positional list operation next has
   a. No preconditions
   b. One precondition—that hasNext returns True

9. A linked list is best implemented with a
   a. Singly linked structure
   b. Doubly linked structure

10. The index operation on an array-based sorted list uses
    a. Binary search
    b. Sequential search

PROJECTS

1. Complete the list iterator for the linked list implementation that was discussed in this chapter. Verify that exceptions are raised when preconditions are violated.

2. Complete the array sorted list implementation discussed in the case study. You may defer the completion of the list iterator for sorted lists until Project 3.

3. Complete the two list iterators for the array list and the array sorted list using the design strategy discussed in the case study.

4. Write a program that inserts lines of text from a file into a list and allows the user to view any line of text from the file. The program should present a menu of options that allow the user to enter a filename and to navigate to the first line, the last line, the next line, and the previous line.

5. Add commands to the program of Project 4 so that the user can delete the currently selected line, replace it with a new line, or insert a line at the current cursor position. The user should also be able to save the current file.

6. Most word processors have a feature called word wrap, which automatically moves the user's next word down a line when the right margin is reached. To explore how this feature works, write a program that allows the user to reformat the text in a file. The user should input the line width in characters and input the names of the input and output files. The program should then input the words from the file into a list of sublists. Each sublist represents a line of text to be output to the file. As the words are input into each sublist, the program tracks the length of that line to ensure that it is less than or equal to the user's line length. When all the words have been entered into the sublists, the program should traverse them to write their contents to the output file.

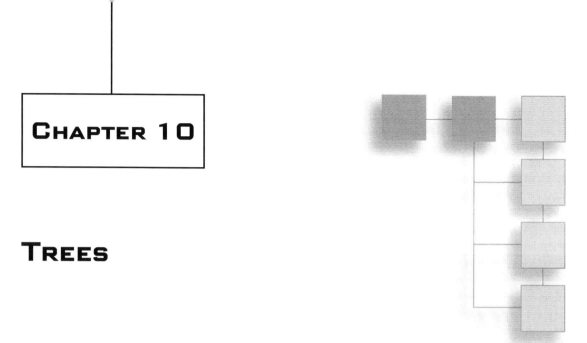

CHAPTER 10

TREES

A third major category of collections, which was called *hierarchical* in Chapter 2, "An Overview of Collections," consists of various types of tree structures. Most programming languages do not include trees as a standard type. Nonetheless, trees have widespread uses. They represent collections of objects, such as a file directory structure and a book's table of contents, quite naturally. Trees can also be used for implementing other collections, such as sorted sets and sorted dictionaries, that require efficient searching, or that, like priority queues, must impose some priority order on their elements. This chapter examines the properties of trees that make them useful data structures and explores their role in implementing several types of collections.

AN OVERVIEW OF TREES

In the linear data structures you have studied thus far, all items except for the first have a distinct predecessor, and all items except the last have a distinct successor. In a tree, the ideas of predecessor and successor are replaced with those of *parent* and *child*. Trees have two main characteristics:

- Each item can have multiple children.
- All items, except a privileged item called the *root*, have exactly one parent.

Tree Terminology

Tree terminology is a peculiar mix of biological, genealogical, and geometric terms. Table 10.1 provides a quick summary of these terms. Figure 10.1 shows a tree and some of its properties.

Table 10.1   A Summary of Terms Used to Describe Trees

Term	Definition
Node	An item stored in a tree.
Root	The topmost node in a tree. It is the only node without a parent.
Child	A node immediately below and directly connected to a given node. A node can have more than one child, and its children are viewed as organized in left-to-right order. The leftmost child is called the first child, and the rightmost is called the last child.
Parent	A node immediately above and directly connected to a given node. A node can have only one parent.
Siblings	The children of a common parent.
Leaf	A node that has no children.
Interior node	A node that has at least one child.
Edge/Branch/Link	The line that connects a parent to its child.
Descendant	A node's children, its children's children, and so on, down to the leaves.
Ancestor	A node's parent, its parent's parent, and so on, up to the root.
Path	The sequence of edges that connect a node and one of its descendants.
Path length	The number of edges in a path.
Depth or level	The depth or level of a node equals the length of the path connecting it to the root. Thus, the root depth or level of the root is 0. Its children are at level 1, and so on.
Height	The length of the longest path in the tree; put differently, the maximum level number among leaves in the tree.
Subtree	The tree formed by considering a node and all its descendants.

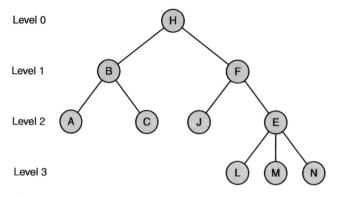

PROPERTY	VALUE
Number of nodes	10
Height	3
Root node	H
Leaves	A, C, J, L, M, N
Interior nodes	H, B, F, E
Nodes at level 2	A, C, J, E
Ancestors of E	F, H
Descendants of F	J, E, L, M, N
Node in the rightmost subtree of F	E, L, M, N

Figure 10.1

Some properties of a tree.

© 2014 Cengage Learning®

Note that the height of a tree is different from the number of nodes contained in it. The height of a tree containing one node is 0, and, by convention, the height of an empty tree is −1.

General Trees and Binary Trees

The tree shown in Figure 10.1 is sometimes called a *general tree* to distinguish it from a special category called a *binary tree*. In a binary tree, each node has at most two children, referred to as the *left child* and the *right child*. In a binary tree, when a node has only one child, you distinguish it as being either a left child or a right child. Thus, the two trees shown in Figure 10.2 are not the same when they are considered binary trees, although they are the same when they are considered general trees.

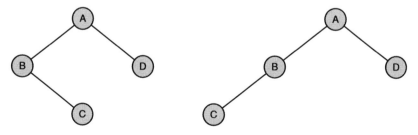

Figure 10.2

Two unequal binary trees that have the same sets of nodes.

© 2014 Cengage Learning®

Recursive Definitions of Trees

Now you'll see more formal definitions of general trees and binary trees. As is often the case, it's not possible to understand the formal definition without an intuitive grasp of the concept being defined. The formal definition is important, however, because it provides a precise basis for further discussion. Furthermore, because recursive processing of trees is common, here are recursive definitions of both types of tree:

- **General tree**—A general tree is either empty or consists of a finite set of nodes T. One node r is distinguished from all others and is called the root. In addition, the set $T - \{r\}$ is partitioned into disjointed subsets, each of which is a general tree.

- **Binary tree**—A binary tree is either empty or consists of a root plus a left subtree and a right subtree, each of which is a binary tree.

Exercises 10.1

Use the following tree to answer the next six questions.

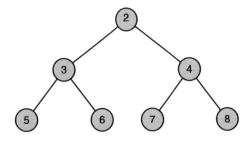

© 2014 Cengage Learning®

1. What are the leaf nodes in the tree?

2. What are the interior nodes in the tree?

3. What are the siblings of node 7?

4. What is the height of the tree?

5. How many nodes are in level 2?

6. Is the tree a general tree, a binary tree, or both?

WHY USE A TREE?

As mentioned earlier, trees nicely represent hierarchical structures. For example, *parsing* is the process of analyzing the syntax of a particular sentence in a language. A *parse tree* describes the syntactic structure of a sentence in terms of its component parts, such as noun phrases and verb phrases. Figure 10.3 shows the parse tree for the following sentence: "The girl hit the ball with a bat."

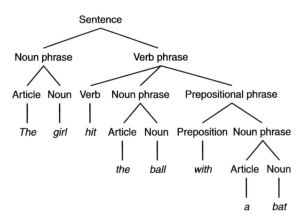

Figure 10.3

A parse tree for a sentence.

© 2014 Cengage Learning®

The root node of this tree, labeled "Sentence," represents the top-level phrase in this structure. Its two children, labeled "Noun phrase" and "Verb phrase," represent the constituent phrases of this sentence. The node labeled "Prepositional phrase" is a child of "Verb phrase," which indicates that the prepositional phrase "with a bat" modifies the verb "hit" rather than the noun phrase "the ball." At the bottom level, the leaf nodes such as "ball" represent the words within the phrases.

As you will see later in this chapter, computer programs can construct parse trees during the analysis of arithmetic expressions. You can then use these trees for further processing, such as checking expressions for grammatical mistakes and interpreting them for their meaning or values.

File system structures are also tree-like. Figure 10.4 shows one such structure, in which the directories are labeled "D" and the files are labeled "F."

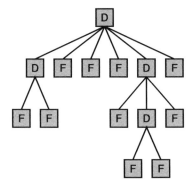

Figure 10.4

A file system structure.

© 2014 Cengage Learning®

Note that the root node represents the root directory. The other directories are either interior nodes when they are nonempty or leaves when they are empty. All the files are leaves.

Some sorted collections can also be represented as tree-like structures. This type of tree is called a *binary search tree*, or BST for short. Each node in the left subtree of a given node is less than that node, and each node in the right subtree of a given node is greater than that node. Figure 10.5 shows a binary search tree representation of a sorted collection that contains the letters *A* through *G*.

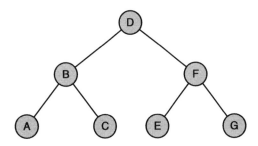

Figure 10.5
A sorted collection as a binary search tree.
© 2014 Cengage Learning®

Unlike the sorted bag discussed in Chapter 6, "Inheritance and Abstract Classes," a binary search tree can support not only logarithmic searches, but logarithmic insertions and removals.

These three examples show that the most important and useful feature of a tree is not the positions of its items, but the relationships between parents and children. These relationships are essential to the meaning of the structure's data. They may indicate alphabetical ordering, phrase structure, containment in a subdirectory, or any one-to-many relationship in a given problem domain. The processing of the data within trees is based on the parent/child relationships among the data.

The sections that follow restrict your attention to different types, applications, and implementations of binary trees.

THE SHAPE OF BINARY TREES

Trees in nature come in various shapes and sizes, and trees as data structures come in various shapes and sizes. Speaking informally, some trees are vine-like and almost linear in shape, whereas others are bushy. The two extremes of these shapes are shown in Figure 10.6.

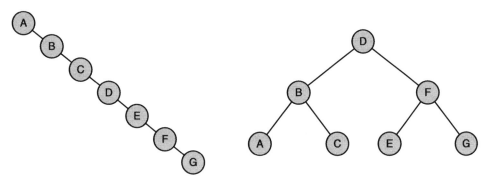

Figure 10.6
A vine-like tree and a bushy tree.
© 2014 Cengage Learning®

The shape of a binary tree can be described more formally by specifying the relationship between its height and the number of nodes contained in it. This relationship also provides information about the potential efficiency of some operations on the tree.

At one extreme, a binary tree can be vine-like, with N nodes and a height of $N - 1$. (See the left side of Figure 10.6.) Such a tree resembles a linear chain of nodes in a linked list. An access, an insertion, or a removal of a node in this structure would therefore be linear in the worst case.

At the other extreme, consider a *full binary tree*, which contains the maximum number of nodes for a given height H. (See the right side of Figure 10.6.) A tree of this shape contains the full complement of nodes at each level. All the interior nodes have two children, and all the leaves are on the lowest level. Table 10.2 lists the height and number of nodes for full binary trees of four heights.

Table 10.2   The Relationship Between the Height and the Number of Nodes in Full Binary Tree

Height of the Tree	Number of Nodes in the Tree
0	1
1	3
2	7
3	15

© 2014 Cengage Learning®

Let's generalize from this table. What is the number of nodes, N, contained in a full binary tree of height H? To express N in terms of H, you start with the root (1 node), add its children (2 nodes), add their children (4 nodes), and so on, as follows:

$$N = 1 + 2 + 4 + \cdots + 2^H$$
$$= 2^{H+1} - 1$$

And what is the height, H, of a full binary tree with N nodes? Using simple algebra, you get

$$H = \log_2(N + 1) - 1$$

Because the number of nodes on a given path from the root to a leaf is close to $\log_2(N)$, the maximum amount of work that it takes to access a given node in a full binary tree is $O(\log N)$.

Not all bushy trees are full binary trees. However, a *perfectly balanced binary tree*, which includes a complete complement of nodes at each level but the last one, is bushy enough to support worst-case logarithmic access to leaf nodes. A *complete binary tree*, in which any nodes on the last level are filled in from left to right, is, like a full binary tree, a special case of a perfectly balanced binary tree. Figure 10.7 summarizes these types of shapes of binary trees with some examples.

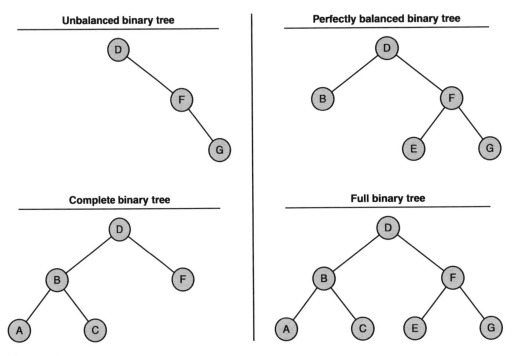

Figure 10.7
Four types of shapes of binary trees.
© 2014 Cengage Learning®

Generally speaking, as a binary tree becomes more balanced, the performance of accesses, insertions, and removals improves.

Exercises 10.2

1. What is the difference between a perfectly balanced binary tree and a complete binary tree?

2. What is the difference between a complete binary tree and a full binary tree?

3. A full binary tree has a height of 5. How many nodes does it contain?

4. A complete binary tree contains 125 nodes. What is its height?

5. How many nodes are on a given level L in a full binary tree? Express your answer in terms of L.

THREE COMMON APPLICATIONS OF BINARY TREES

As mentioned earlier, trees emphasize the parent/child relationship, which allows users to order data according to criteria other than position. This section introduces three special uses of binary trees that impose an ordering on their data: heaps, binary search trees, and expression trees.

Heaps

The data in binary trees are often drawn from ordered sets whose items can be compared. A *min-heap* is a binary tree in which each node is less than or equal to both of its children. A *max-heap* places the larger nodes nearer to the root. Either constraint on the order of the nodes is called the *heap property*. You should not confuse this kind of heap with the heap that a computer uses to manage dynamic memory. Figure 10.8 shows two examples of min-heaps.

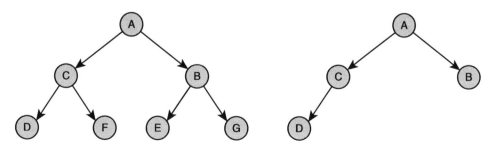

Figure 10.8
Examples of min-heaps.

As the figure shows, the smallest item is in the root node, and the largest items are in the leaves. Note that the heaps in Figure 10.8 have the shape of a complete binary tree, according to the definition given earlier. This arrangement of data in a heap supports an efficient sorting method called the *heap sort*. The heap sort algorithm builds a heap from a set of data and then repeatedly removes the root item and adds it to the end of a list. Heaps are also used to implement priority queues. You will develop an implementation of a heap later in this chapter.

Binary Search Trees

As mentioned earlier, a BST imposes a sorted ordering on its nodes. The manner in which it does so differs from that of a heap, however. In a BST, the nodes in the left subtree of a given node are less than the given node, and the nodes in its right subtree are greater than the given node. When the shape of a BST approaches that of a perfectly balanced binary tree, searches and insertions are O(log *n*) in the worst case.

Figure 10.9 shows all the possible search paths for the binary search of a sorted list, although only one of these paths is taken on any given search. The items visited for comparison in each sublist are shaded.

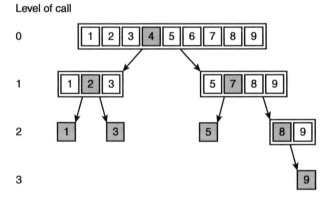

Figure 10.9
The possible search paths for the binary search of a sorted list.
© 2014 Cengage Learning®

As the figure shows, the longest search path (items 5-7-8-9) requires four comparisons in the list of eight items. Because the list is sorted, the search algorithm reduces the search space by one-half after each comparison.

Now you can transfer the items that are shaded to an explicit binary tree structure, as shown in Figure 10.10.

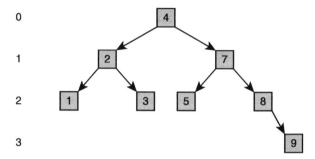

Figure 10.10
A binary search tree.
© 2014 Cengage Learning®

The search algorithm, which you develop later in this chapter, follows an explicit path from the root node to the target node. In this case, a perfectly balanced tree yields a logarithmic search time. Unfortunately, not all BSTs are perfectly balanced. In the worst case, they become linear and support linear searches. Fortunately, the worst case rarely occurs in practice.

Expression Trees

Chapter 7, "Stacks," showed how to use a stack to convert infix expressions to postfix form and examined how to use a stack to evaluate postfix expressions. In that chapter, you also developed a translator and an evaluator for a language of *arithmetic* expressions. The process of translating sentences in a language is also called *parsing*. Yet another way to process sentences is to build a parse tree during parsing. For a language of expressions, this structure is also called an *expression tree*. Figure 10.11 shows several expression trees that result from parsing infix expressions.

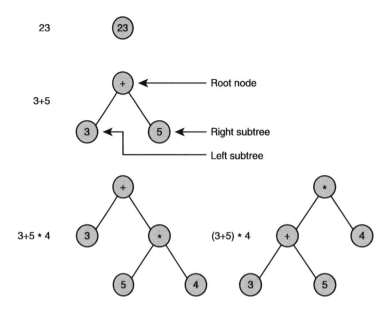

Figure 10.11

Some expression trees.

© 2014 Cengage Learning®

Note the following points:

- An expression tree is never empty.

- Each interior node represents a compound expression, consisting of an operator and its operands. Thus, each interior node has exactly two children, which represent its operands.

- Each leaf node represents an atomic, numeric operand.

- Operands of higher precedence usually appear near the bottom of the tree, unless they are overridden in the source expression by parentheses.

If you assume that an expression tree represents the structure of an infix expression, you can make the following requests of an expression tree:

- Ask for the expression's value.

- Ask for the expression in postfix form.

- Ask for the expression in prefix form.

- Ask for the expression in infix form.

This chapter's case study develops an expression tree type and incorporates it into a program for performing these operations.

Exercises 10.3

1. What is the heap property for a min-heap?

2. How is a binary search tree different from a binary tree?

3. Write the expression represented by the following expression tree in infix, prefix, and postfix notations. (*Hint*: Use the inorder, preoder, and postorder traversals described in this section to obtain your answers.)

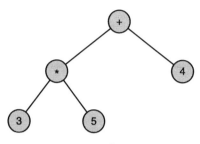

© 2014 Cengage Learning®

4. Draw diagrams of the expression trees for the following expressions:

   a. 3 * 5 + 6

   b. 3 + 5 * 6

   c. 3 * 5 ** 6

BINARY TREE TRAVERSALS

In earlier chapters, you saw how to traverse the items in linear collections using a `for` loop or an iterator. There are four standard types of traversals for binary trees, called preorder, inorder, postorder, and level order. Each type of traversal follows a particular path and direction as it visits the nodes in the tree. This section shows diagrams of each type of traversal on binary search trees; algorithms for the traversals are developed later in this chapter.

Preorder Traversal

The *preorder traversal* algorithm visits a tree's root node and then traverses the left subtree and the right subtree in a similar manner. The sequence of nodes visited by a preorder traversal is illustrated in Figure 10.12.

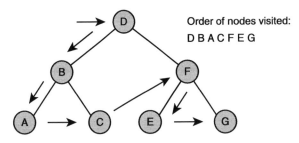

Figure 10.12
A preorder traversal.
© 2014 Cengage Learning®

Inorder Traversal

The *inorder traversal* algorithm traverses the left subtree, visits the root node, and traverses the right subtree. This process moves as far to the left in the tree as possible before visiting a node. The sequence of nodes visited by an inorder traversal is illustrated in Figure 10.13.

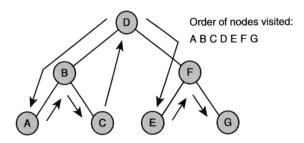

Figure 10.13
An inorder traversal.
© 2014 Cengage Learning®

Postorder Traversal

The *postorder traversal* algorithm traverses the left subtree, traverses the right subtree, and visits the root node. The path traveled by a postorder traversal is illustrated in Figure 10.14.

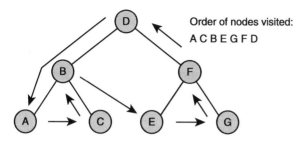

Figure 10.14

A postorder traversal.

© 2014 Cengage Learning®

Level Order Traversal

Beginning with level 0, the *level order traversal* algorithm visits the nodes at each level in left-to-right order. The path traveled by a level order traversal is illustrated in Figure 10.15.

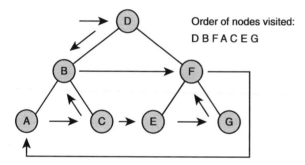

Figure 10.15

A level order traversal.

© 2014 Cengage Learning®

As you can see, an inorder traversal is appropriate for visiting the items in a binary search tree in sorted order. The preorder, inorder, and postorder traversals of expression trees can be used to generate the prefix, infix, and postfix representations of the expressions, respectively.

DEVELOPING A BINARY SEARCH TREE

A binary search tree imposes a special ordering on the nodes in a binary tree, so it supports logarithmic searches and insertions. This section develops a binary search tree collection and assesses its performance.

The Binary Search Tree Interface

The interface for a binary search tree should include a constructor and the basic operations common to all collections (isEmpty, len, str, +, ==, in, and add).

As with bags and sets, insertions and removals are accomplished by the add and remove methods. The method __contains__, which is run when Python sees the in operator, performs a binary search in any BST implementation.

To allow users to retrieve and replace items in a binary search tree, the methods find and replace are included also. The method find expects an item as an argument and returns the item matching it in the tree, or None otherwise. The method replace expects two items as arguments. If the method locates a match in the tree for the first argument, it replaces the item in that node with the second argument and returns the replaced item. Otherwise, the method returns None. These two methods will be useful for lookups and modifications of items such as dictionary entries, when you use a binary search tree to implement a sorted dictionary.

Because there are four ways to traverse a binary tree, you include methods for each one. Each traversal method returns an iterator. The tree's __iter__ method supports a preorder traversal. The choice of this type of traversal for the standard iterator enables the user to create a clone of a binary search tree with the same shape as the original and to produce a similarly shaped tree from the concatenation of two trees.

Two trees are considered equal if they contain the same items in the same positions. The str operation returns a string that shows the shape of the tree.

The methods included in any binary search tree class are described in Table 10.3.

Table 10.3   The Methods in the Binary Search Tree Interface

BST Method	What It Does
tree.isEmpty()	Returns True if tree is empty or False otherwise.
tree.__len__()	Same as len(tree). Returns the number of items in tree.
tree.__str__()	Same as str(tree). Returns a string that shows the shape of the tree.
tree.__iter__()	Same as iter(tree) or for item in tree:. Performs a preorder traversal on the tree.
tree.__contains__(item)	Same as item in tree. Returns True if item is in the tree or False otherwise.
tree.__add__(otherTree)	Same as tree + otherTree. Returns a new tree containing the items in tree and otherTree.

`tree.__eq__(anyObject)`	Same as tree == anyObject. Returns True if tree equals anyObject or False otherwise. Two trees are equal if they have the same items in corresponding positions.
`tree.clear()`	Makes tree become empty.
`tree.add(item)`	Adds item to its proper place in the tree.
`tree.remove(item)`	Removes item from the tree. *Precondition*: item is in the tree.
`tree.find(item)`	If an item matching item is in the tree, returns the matched item. Otherwise, returns None.
`tree.replace(item, newItem)`	If item equals another item in the tree, replaces the matched item in the tree with newItem and returns the matched item. Otherwise, returns None.
`tree.inorder()`	Returns an iterator that performs an inorder traversal on the tree.
`tree.postorder()`	Returns an iterator that performs a postorder traversal on the tree.
`tree.levelorder()`	Returns an iterator that performs a level order traversal on the tree.

The next Python script assumes that the LinkedBST class has been defined in the linkedbst module. The script creates a BST containing the letters shown in Figure 10.15 and prints its shape.

```
from linkedbst import LinkedBST

tree = LinkedBST()
print("Adding D B A C F E G")
tree.add("D")
tree.add("B")
tree.add("A")
tree.add("C")
tree.add("F")
tree.add("E")
tree.add("G")

# Display the structure of the tree
print("\nTree structure:\n")
print(tree)
```

Here is the output of the script:

```
Adding D B A C F E G

Tree structure:

| | G
| F
| | E
D
| | C
| B
| | A
```

Data Structure for the Linked Implementation

Your implementation of the binary search tree, called LinkedBST, is a subclass of AbstractCollection, which provides the basic collection methods and the variable self._size. The container for each item in a tree is a node object of type BSTNode. This type of node contains a data field and two link fields, named left and right. The external link to this structure is named self._root. On instantiation, this variable is set to None. Here is the code for the part of the LinkedBST class that creates a tree.

```
"""
File: linkedbst.py
Author: Ken Lambert
"""

from abstractCollection import AbstractCollection
from bstnode import BSTNode

class LinkedBST (AbstractCollection):
    """A link-based binary search tree implementation."""

    def __init__(self, sourceCollection = None):
        """Sets the initial state of self, which includes the
        contents of sourceCollection, if it's present."""
        self._root = None
        AbstractCollection.__init__(sourceCollection)

    # Remaining method definitions go here
```

Several other methods are now examined in more detail.

Searching a Binary Search Tree

The find method returns the first matching item if the target item is in the tree; otherwise, it returns None. You can use a recursive strategy that takes advantage of the recursive structure of the underlying binary tree. Following is a pseudocode algorithm for this process:

```
if the tree is empty
    return None
else if the target item equals the root item
    return the root item
else if the target item is less than the root item
    return the result of searching the left subtree
else
    return the result of searching the right subtree
```

Because the recursive search algorithm requires a parameter for a tree node, you cannot define it as a top-level method. Instead, the algorithm is defined as a nested helper function that is called within the top-level `find` method. Following is the code for the two routines:

```
def find(self, item):
    """Returns data if item is found or None otherwise."""

    # Helper function to search the binary tree
    def recurse(node):
        if node is None:
            return None
        elif item == node.data:
            return node.data
        elif item < tree.data:
            return recurse(node.left)
        else:
            return recurse(node.right)

    # Top-level call on the root node
    return recurse(self._root)
```

Traversing a Binary Search Tree

There are four methods for traversing a binary search tree—inorder, postorder, level-order, and __iter__ (the preorder traversal). Each method returns an iterator that allows the user to visit the sequence of the tree's items in the specified order. This section shows examples of recursive and iterative strategies for two of the traversals, while leaving the others as exercises for you.

Here is a general recursive strategy for an inorder traversal of a binary tree:

```
if the tree is not empty
    visit the left subtree
```

```
visit the item at the root of the tree
visit the right subtree
```

You can embed this strategy in a recursive helper function within the `inorder` method. The method creates an empty list and then passes the root node to the helper function. When this function visits an item, it's added to the list. The `inorder` method returns an iterator on the list. Here is the code for the recursive implementation of the `inorder` method:

```
def inorder(self):
    """Supports an inorder traversal on a view of self."""
    lyst = list()
    def recurse(node):
        if node != None:
            recurse(node.left)
            lyst.append(node.data)
            recurse(node.right)
    recurse(self._root)
    return iter(lyst)
```

The postorder traversal can use a quite similar recursive strategy, but it places the visit to an item in a different position in the code.

The level order traversal guides the visits to items from left to right through the levels of the tree, much like reading lines of text in a document. A recursive strategy for this process employs a list and a queue. The helper function in this case takes no arguments. The `levelorder` method creates the list and the queue and adds the root node, if there is one, to the queue. The helper function is then called. In this function, if the queue is not empty, the front node is popped and its item is added to the list. This node's left and right children, if they exist, are then added to the queue, and the function is called recursively. The method then returns an iterator on the list.

The `__iter__` method, which runs a preorder traversal, is run so frequently that a more efficient strategy would be desirable. You could build a list as before and return an iterator on it, but that strategy would require linear running time and linear memory usage before the user ever visits the items. An alternative strategy would use a probe-based loop to visit the nodes, along with a stack to support returns to parent nodes during the traversal. Upon each visit to a node, its item is yielded, as you have done in your implementations of this method for other collections. The new strategy is as follows:

```
create a stack
push the root node, if there is one, onto the stack
while the stack is not empty
    pop a node from the stack
    yield the item in the node
```

```
push the node's right and left children, if they exist,
in that order onto the stack
```

This implementation incurs no extra overhead in running time, and its memory growth is no worse than the depth of the tree (ideally, O(log$n$)).

The String Representation of a Binary Search Tree

You can view the items in a binary search tree by running any of the traversals. However, because you use the __str__ method primarily in testing and debugging, your implementation returns a string of "ASCII art" that displays the tree's shape as well as its items. A convenient way to do this for a text-only display is to "rotate" the tree 90 degrees counterclockwise and display vertical bars between the interior nodes. The following code builds the appropriate string by first recursing with the right subtree, then visiting an item, and finally recursing with the left subtree.

```
def __str__(self):
    """Returns a string representation with the tree rotated
    90 degrees counterclockwise."""

    def recurse(node, level):
        s = ""
        if node != None:
            s += recurse(node.right, level + 1)
            s += "| " * level
            s += str(node.data) + "\n"
            s += recurse(node.left, level + 1)
        return s

    return recurse(self._root, 0)
```

Inserting an Item into a Binary Search Tree

The add method inserts an item into its proper place in the binary search tree.

In general, an item's proper place will be in one of three positions:

- The root node, if the tree is already empty

- A node in the current node's left subtree, if the new item is less than the item in the current node

- A node in the current node's right subtree, if the new item is greater than or equal to the item in the current node

For the second and third options, the add method uses a recursive helper function named recurse. This function, which takes a node as an argument, searches for the new item's spot in the node's left or right children. The recurse function looks to the left or to the right of the current node, depending on whether the new item is less than (left) or greater than or equal to (right) the item in the current node. If the appropriate child node is None, the new item is placed in a new node and attached at that position. Otherwise, recurse is called recursively with that child node to continue the search for the appropriate position.

Following is the code for the add method:

```
def add(self, item):
    """Adds item to the tree."""

    # Helper function to search for item's position
    def recurse(node):
        # New item is less; go left until spot is found
        if item < node.data:
            if node.left == None:
                node.left = BSTNode(item)
            else:
                recurse(node.left)
        # New item is greater or equal;
        # go right until spot is found
        elif node.right == None:
            node.right = BSTNode(item)
        else:
            recurse(node.right)
        # End of recurse

    # Tree is empty, so new item goes at the root
    if self.isEmpty():
        self._root = BSTNode(item)
    # Otherwise, search for the item's spot
    else:
        recurse(self._root)
    self._size += 1
```

Note that, in all cases, an item is added in a leaf node.

Removing an Item from a Binary Search Tree

Recall that removing an item from an array causes a shift of items to fill the hole. Removing an item from a linked list requires rearranging a few pointers. Removing an item from a binary search tree can require both of the preceding actions. Following is an outline of the strategy for this process:

1. Save a reference to the root node.

2. Locate the node to be removed, its parent, and its parent's reference to this node.

3. If the node has a left child and a right child, replace the node's value with the largest value in the left subtree and delete that value's node from the left subtree.

4. Otherwise, set the parent's reference to the node to the node's only child.

5. Reset the root node to the saved reference.

6. Decrement the size and return the item.

Step 3 in this process is complex, so you can factor it into a helper function, which takes the node to be deleted as a parameter. The outline for this function follows. In this outline, the node containing the item to be removed is referred to as the *top node*.

1. Search the top node's left subtree for the node containing the largest item. This is in the rightmost node of the subtree (the node at the end of the rightmost path in this subtree). Be sure to track the parent of the current node during the search.

2. Replace the top node's value with the item.

3. If the top node's left child contained the largest item (for example, that node had no right subtree, so the parent reference still refers to the top node), set the top node's left child to its left child's left child.

4. Otherwise, set the parent node's right child to that right child's left child.

The code for these two routines is available from your instructor or on the companion website at www.cengageptr.com/downloads.

Complexity Analysis of Binary Search Trees

As you might have expected, binary search trees are set up with the intent of replicating the O(log$n$) behavior for the binary search of a sorted list. In addition, a binary search tree can provide fast insertions. Unfortunately, as mentioned earlier, this intent is not always realized. Optimal behavior depends on the height of the tree. A perfectly balanced tree (one with a height of log(n)) supports logarithmic searches. In the worst case, when the items are inserted in sorted order (either ascending or descending), the tree's height becomes linear, as does its search behavior. Surprisingly, insertions in random order result in a tree with close-to-optimal search behavior.

The run time of insertions is also highly dependent on the height of the tree. Recall that an insertion involves a search for the item's spot, which is always a leaf node. Thus, the run time of an insertion into a perfectly balanced tree is close to logarithmic. Removals also require a search for the target item, with behavior similar to that of the other operations.

Strategies for maintaining a tree structure that supports optimal insertions and searches in all cases are the subject of advanced computer science courses. However, if you assume that a tree is relatively balanced already, there is one technique that you can apply immediately to preserve the tree's shape, if your application must transfer BSTs to and from text files. Consider the output operation. The only way to obtain the tree's items is to run one of the traversals. The worst possible choice would be an inorder traversal. Because this traversal visits the nodes in sorted order, the items in the tree are saved in sorted order. Then, when the items are input from the file to another tree, they are inserted in sorted order, leaving behind a tree with a linear shape. Alternatively, if you select a preorder traversal (by using the simple for loop), the items are output to the file, starting with each parent node and moving down to its left and right children. The input of the items from such a file then generate a new tree whose shape is the same as the original tree.

The programming projects include exercises to construct methods to determine if a tree is balanced and rebalance it.

Exercises 10.4

1. Describe how insertions can have a negative effect on subsequent searches of a binary search tree.

2. Discuss the trade-offs between the array-based implementation of a sorted bag presented in Chapter 6 and a binary search tree implementation of a sorted bag.

RECURSIVE DESCENT PARSING AND PROGRAMMING LANGUAGES

Chapter 7 discussed algorithms that use a stack to convert expressions from infix to postfix and then evaluate the postfix form. Recursive algorithms are also used in processing languages, whether they are programming languages such as Python or natural languages such as English. This section gives a brief overview of some resources for processing languages, including grammars, parsing, and a recursive descent-parsing strategy. The next section illustrates their application in a case study.

Introduction to Grammars

Most programming languages, no matter how small or large they are, have a precise and complete definition called a *grammar*. A grammar consists of a few parts:

■ A *vocabulary* (or *dictionary* or *lexicon*) consisting of words and symbols allowed in sentences in the language.

- A set of *syntax rules* that specify how symbols in the language are combined to form sentences.

- A set of *semantic rules* that specify how sentences in the language should be interpreted. For example, the statement x = y might mean "copy the value of y to the variable x."

Computer scientists have developed several notations for expressing grammars. For example, suppose you want to define a language for representing simple arithmetic expressions such as the following:

```
4 + 2
3 * 5
6 - 3
10 / 2
(4 + 5) * 10
```

Now suppose you don't want to allow expressions, such as 4 + 3 − 2 or 4 ∗ 3 / 2, that contain consecutive adding operations or consecutive multiplying operations. The following grammar defines the syntax and vocabulary of this new little language:

```
expression = term [ addingOperator term ]

term = factor [ multiplyOperator factor ]

factor = number | "(" expression ")"

number = digit { digit }

digit = "0" | "1" | "2" | "3" | "4" | "5" | "6" | "7" | "8" | "9"

addingOperator = "+" | "-"

multiplyingOperator = "*" | "/"
```

This type of grammar is called an Extended Backus-Naur Form (EBNF) grammar. An EBNF grammar uses three kinds of symbols:

- **Terminal symbols**—These symbols are in the vocabulary of the language and literally appear in programs in the language—for instance, + and ∗ in the preceding examples.

- **Nonterminal symbols**—These symbols name phrases in the language, such as expression or factor in the preceding examples. A phrase usually consists of one or more terminal symbols or the names of other phrases.

- **Metasymbols**—These symbols are used to organize the rules in the grammar. Table 10.4 lists the metasymbols used in EBNF.

Table 10.4   Metasymbols in EBNF

Metasymbols	Use
" "	Enclose literal items
=	Means "is defined as"
[ ]	Enclose optional items
{ }	Enclose zero or more items
( )	Group together required choices (same as parentheses)
|	Indicates a choice

© 2014 Cengage Learning®

Thus, the rule

```
expression = term [ addingOperator term ]
```

means "an expression is defined as a term, which might or might not be followed by an adding operator and another term." The symbol to the left of the = in a rule is called the left side of the rule; the set of items to the right of the = is called the right side of the rule.

The grammar just discussed does not allow expressions such as 45 ∗ 22 ∗ 14 / 2, thus forcing programmers to use parentheses if they want to form an equivalent expression, such as ((45 ∗ 22) ∗ 14) / 2. The next grammar solves this problem by allowing iteration over terms and factors:

```
expression = term { addingOperator term }
term = factor { multiplyOperator factor }
factor = number | "(" expression ")"
number = digit { digit }
digit = "0" | "1" | "2" | "3" | "4" | "5" | "6" | "7" | "8" | "9"
addingOperator = "+" | "-"
multiplyingOperator = "*" | "/"
```

In any grammar, there is one privileged symbol known as the *start symbol*. In the two example grammars, the start symbol is expression. The use of this symbol is discussed shortly.

You might have noticed that the foregoing grammars have a recursive quality. For instance, an expression consists of terms, a term consists of factors, and a factor can be a number or an expression within parentheses. Thus, an expression can contain another expression.

Recognizing, Parsing, and Interpreting Sentences in a Language

To process the sentences in a language, you use recognizers, parsers, and interpreters. A *recognizer* analyzes a string to determine if it is a sentence in a given language. The inputs to the recognizer are the grammar and a string. The outputs are "Yes" or "No" and appropriate syntax error messages. If there are one or more syntax errors, you get "No," and the string is not a sentence.

A *parser* has all the features of a recognizer and returns information about the syntactic and semantic structure of the sentence. This information is used in further processing and is contained in a parse tree.

An *interpreter* carries out the actions specified by a sentence. In other words, an interpreter runs the program. Occasionally, parsing and interpreting occur at the same time. Otherwise, the input to the interpreter is the data structure that results from parsing.

From now on, there's no distinction between a recognizer and a parser, but *parser* refers to both.

Lexical Analysis and the Scanner

When developing a parser, it is convenient to assign the task of recognizing symbols in a string to a lower-level module called a scanner. The scanner performs *lexical analysis*, in which individual words are picked out of a stream of characters. The scanner also outputs lexical error messages as needed. Examples of lexical errors are inappropriate characters in a number and unrecognized symbols (ones not in the vocabulary).

The output of the scanner is a stream of words called *tokens*. These become the input to another module called the *syntax analyzer*. This module uses the tokens and the grammar rules to determine whether the program is syntactically correct. Thus, the lexical analyzer determines if characters go together to form correct words, whereas the syntax analyzer determines if words go together to form correct sentences. For simplicity, the lexical analyzer is referred to as the scanner and the syntax analyzer is referred to as the parser. The connection between the scanner and parser is shown in Figure 10.16.

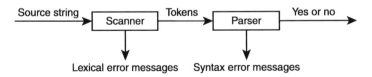

Figure 10.16

A scanner and parser working in tandem.

© 2014 Cengage Learning®

Parsing Strategies

You can use several strategies for parsing. One of the simplest is called *recursive descent parsing*. A recursive descent parser defines a function for each rule in the grammar. Each function processes the phrase or portion of the input sentence covered by its rule. The top-level function corresponds to the rule that has the start symbol on its left side. When this function is called, it calls the functions corresponding to the non-terminal symbols on the right side of its rule. For example, here is the top-level rule and the associated parsing function for the original grammar shown in this section:

```
# Syntax rule:
# expression = term [ addingOperator term ]

# Parsing function:
def expression():
    term()
    token = scanner.get()
    if token.getType() in (Token.PLUS, Token.MINUS):
        scanner.next()
        term()
        token = scanner.get()
```

Note the following points:

- Each nonterminal symbol in the grammar becomes the name of a function in the parser.

- The body of a function processes the phrases on the right side of the rule.

- To process a nonterminal symbol, you simply invoke a function.

- To process an optional item, you use an if statement.

- You observe the current token by calling the method get on the scanner object.

- You scan to the next token by calling the method next on the scanner object.

Your parser descends through the grammar rules, starting with the top-level function and working its way down to lower-level functions, which can then recursively call functions at a higher level.

You can easily extend recursive descent parsers to interpret as well as parse programs. In the case of your languages, for example, each parsing function could compute and return the value represented by the associated phrase in the expression. The value returned by the topmost function would be the value of the entire expression. Alternatively, as shown in the next case study, a recursive descent parser can build and return a parse tree. Another module then traverses this tree to compute the value of the expression.

CASE STUDY: PARSING AND EXPRESSION TREES

As mentioned earlier, expression trees are binary trees that contain the operands and operators of expressions. Because an expression tree is never empty, it lends itself to a particularly elegant kind of recursive processing. In this section, you design and implement an expression tree to support the processing of arithmetic expressions.

Request

Write a program that uses an expression tree to evaluate expressions or convert them to alternative forms.

Analysis

The program parses an input expression and prints syntax error messages if errors occur. If the expression is syntactically correct, the program prints its value and its prefix, infix, and postfix representations. The next session shows an interaction with the program. As you can see, the infix output is placed in parentheses to show the precedence of the operators explicitly.

```
Enter an infix expression: 4 + 5 * 2
Prefix: + 4 * 5 2
Infix: (4 + (5 * 2))
Postfix: 4 5 2 * +
Value: 14
Enter an infix expression: (4 + 5) * 2
Prefix: * + 4 5 2
Infix: ((4 + 5) * 2)
Postfix: 4 5 + 2 *
Value: 18
```

The program includes the Scanner and Token classes discussed earlier. To these, three new classes are added. The Parser class performs the parsing, and the LeafNode and InteriorNode classes represent expression trees. Leaf nodes represent integer operands in an expression, whereas interior nodes represent an operator and its two operands. The structure of the system is shown in the class diagram of Figure 10.17.

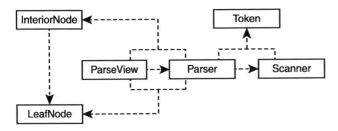

Figure 10.17

The classes for the parsing system.

© 2014 Cengage Learning®

Design and Implementation of the Node Classes

The parser builds an expression tree in two ways:

- It builds a leaf node containing a number.

- It builds an interior node whose value is an operator and whose left and right subtrees are nodes representing the operand expressions.

A simple and elegant design results from partitioning the nodes into two types. The first type of node, called LeafNode, contains an integer. The second type of node, called InteriorNode, contains an operator and two other nodes. The latter nodes can be either leaf nodes or interior nodes.

Both types of nodes recognize the same methods, which are listed in Table 10.5.

Table 10.5   Methods for the Node Classes

Method	What It Does
N.prefix()	Returns the string representation of the node's expression in prefix form
N.infix()	Returns the string representation of the node's expression in infix form
N.postfix()	Returns the string representation of the node's expression in postfix form
N.value()	Returns the value of the node's expression

© 2014 Cengage Learning®

The constructor for LeafNode expects an integer as an argument, whereas the constructor for InteriorNode expects a character-based operator symbol and two other nodes as arguments.

Here is a short tester program that illustrates the use of the node classes:

```
from expressiontree import LeafNode, InteriorNode

a = LeafNode(4)
b = InteriorNode('+', LeafNode(2), LeafNode(3))
c = InteriorNode('*', a, b)
c = InteriorNode('-', c, b)

print("Expect ((4 * (2 + 3)) - (2 + 3)) :", c.infix())
print("Expect - * 4 + 2 3 + 2 3        :", c.prefix())
print("Expect 4 2 3 + * 2 3 + -        :", c.postfix())
print("Expect 15                       :", c.value())
```

You now develop one of the traversal methods for both classes and leave the others as exercises for you. The method postfix returns the string representation of an expression in postfix form. In the case of a LeafNode, that is the string representation of the node's integer.

```
class LeafNode(object):
    """Represents an integer."""

    def __init__(self, data):
        self._data = data

    def postfix(self):
        return str(self)

    def __str__(self):
        return str(self._data)
```

An InteriorNode's postfix string contains the postfix strings of its two operand nodes, followed by the node's operator.

```
class InteriorNode(object):
    """Represents an operator and its two operands."""

    def __init__(self, op, leftOper, rightOper):
        self._operator = op
        self._leftOperand = leftOper
        self._rightOperand = rightOper

    def postfix(self):
        return self._leftOperand.postfix() + " " + \
               self._rightOperand.postfix() + " " + \
               self._operator
```

The design pattern of the `postfix` methods of `InteriorNode` and `LeafNode` is like the one used for the traversals of binary trees. The only difference is that in this application, an expression tree is never empty, so a leaf node is the base case. The other expression tree traversals have a similar design and are left as exercises for you.

Design and Implementation of the Parser Class

It is easiest to build an expression tree with a parser that uses the recursive descent strategy described earlier. Because they are embedded in a class, the parsing functions described in the previous section are redefined as methods.

The top-level method `parse` returns an expression tree to its caller, which uses that tree to obtain information about the expression. Each parsing method that handles a syntactic form in the language builds and returns an expression tree. That tree represents the phrase of the expression parsed by the method. You develop two of these methods; the others are left as exercises.

The method `factor` processes either a number or an expression nested in parentheses. When the token is a number, the method creates a leaf node containing the number and returns it. Otherwise, if the token is a left parenthesis, the method calls the method `expression` to parse the nested expression. This method returns a tree representing the results, and `factor` passes this tree back to its caller. Here is the revised code for `factor`:

```
# Syntax rule:
# factor = number | "(" expression ")"

def factor(self):
    token = self.scanner.get()
    if token.getType() == Token.INT:
        tree = LeafNode(token.getValue())
        self.scanner.next()
    elif token.getType() == Token.L_PAR:
        self.scanner.next()
        tree = self.expression()
        self.accept(self._scanner.get(),
                    Token.R_PAR,
                    "')' expected")
        self.scanner.next()
    else:
        tree = None
        self.fatalError(token, "bad factor")
    return tree
```

The method expression processes a term followed by zero or more adding operators and terms. You begin by calling the method term, which returns a tree representing the term. If the current token is not an adding operator, expression just passes the tree back to its caller. Otherwise, expression enters a loop. In this loop, expression builds an interior node whose value is the adding operator, whose left subtree is the tree just received from the last call to term, and whose right subtree is the tree received from a new call to term. This process ends when expression does not see an adding operator. By this point, a complex tree might have built up, and expression returns it. Here is the code for expression:

```
# Syntax rule:
# expression = term { addingOperator term }

def expression(self):
    tree = self.term()
    token = self.scanner.get()
    while token.getType() in (Token.PLUS, Token.MINUS):
        op = str(token)
        self.scanner.next()
        tree = InteriorNode(op, tree, self.term())
        token = self.scanner.get()
    return tree
```

The other parsing methods build their trees in a similar manner. The completion of the program is left as an exercise for you.

An Array Implementation of Binary Trees

An array-based implementation of a binary tree is also possible, but it is difficult to define and practical only in some special situations. Mapping stacks, queues, and lists to arrays is straightforward because all are linear and support the same notion of adjacency, each element having an obvious predecessor and successor. But given a node in a tree, what would be its immediate predecessor in an array? Is it the parent or a left sibling? What is its immediate successor? Is it a child or a right sibling? Trees are hierarchical and resist being flattened. Nevertheless, for complete binary trees, there is an elegant and efficient array-based representation.

Consider the complete binary tree in Figure 10.18.

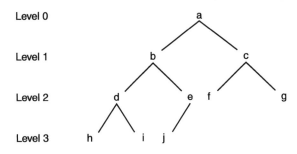

Figure 10.18

A complete binary tree.

© 2014 Cengage Learning®

In an array-based implementation, the elements are stored by level, as shown in Figure 10.19.

```
 0  1  2  3  4  5  6  7  8  9
[a][b][c][d][e][f][g][h][i][j]
```

Figure 10.19

An array representation of a complete binary tree.

© 2014 Cengage Learning®

Given an arbitrary item at position i in the array, it is easy to determine the location of related items, as shown in Table 10.6.

Table 10.6 The Locations of Items in an Array Representation of a Complete Binary Tree	
Item	**Location**
Parent	$(i - 1) / 2$
Left sibling, if there is one	$i - 1$
Right sibling, if there is one	$i + 1$
Left child, if there is one	$i * 2 + 1$
Right child, if there is one	$i * 2 + 2$

© 2014 Cengage Learning®

Thus, for item d at location 3, you get the results shown in Table 10.7.

Table 10.7 The Relatives of Item d in an Array Representation of a Complete Binary Tree

Item	Location
Parent	b at 1
Left sibling, if there is one	Not applicable
Right sibling, if there is one	e at 4
Left child, if there is one	h at 7
Right child, if there is one	i at 8

© 2014 Cengage Learning®

You might naturally ask why the array representation does not work for incomplete binary trees. The reason is not hard to see. In an incomplete binary tree, some levels are not filled above others. But the calculation of a node's relatives in an array is based on being able to multiply or divide its index by 2, which you cannot do when levels are not filled in a top-down manner.

The array representation of a binary tree is pretty rare and is used mainly to implement a heap, which is discussed in the next section.

Exercises 10.5

Assume that a node is at position 12 in an array representation of a binary tree. Give the positions of that node's parent, left child, and right child.

What are the constraints on a binary tree that is contained in an array?

IMPLEMENTING HEAPS

You will use a heap to implement a priority queue, so the heap interface should include methods to return its size, add an item, remove an item, and peek at an item (see Table 10.8).

Table 10.8   The Methods in the Heap Interface

Method	What It Does
heap.isEmpty()	Returns True if heap is empty or False otherwise.
heap.__len__()	Same as len(heap). Returns the number of items in heap.
heap.__iter__()	Same as iter(heap) or for item in heap:. Visits the items from least to greatest.
heap.__str__()	Same as str(heap). Returns a string that shows the shape of the heap.
heap.__contains__(item)	Same as item in heap. Returns True if item is in the heap or False otherwise.
heap.__add__(otherHeap)	Same as heap + otherHeap. Returns a new heap with the contents of heap and otherHeap.
heap.__eq__(anyObject)	Same as heap == anyObject. Returns True if heap equals anyObject or False otherwise. Two heaps are equal if they contain the same items.
heap.peek()	Returns the topmost item in heap.*Precondition*: heap is not empty.
(heap.add(item)	Inserts item in its proper place in heap.
heap.pop()	Removes and returns the topmost item in heap. *Precondition*: heap is not empty.

The two most critical heap operations are add and pop. The add method expects a comparable element as an argument and inserts the element into its proper place in the heap. That place is generally at a level above an element that is larger and below an element that is smaller. Duplicate elements are placed below previously entered ones. The pop method deletes the topmost node in the heap, returns the element contained there, and maintains the heap property. The peek operation returns but does not remove the topmost element in a heap.

The methods add (insertion) and pop (removal), which are used throughout the heap implementation, are defined in the class ArrayHeap. In the array-based implementation, both methods need to maintain the structure of the heap within the array. (You actually use a Python list, but refer to the structure as an array in the following discussion.) This structure is similar to the array representation of a binary tree discussed earlier, but it has the constraint that each node is less than either of its children.

Consider insertion first. The goal is to find the new element's proper place in the heap and insert it there. Following is your strategy for insertions:

1. Begin by inserting the element at the bottom of the heap. In the array implementation, this is the position after the last element currently in the array.

2. Then enter a loop that "walks" the new element up the heap while the new element's value is less than that of its parent. Each time this relationship is true, you swap the new element with its parent. When this process stops (either the new element is greater than or equal to its parent or you will have reached the top node), the new element is in its proper place.

Recall that the position of an element's parent in the array is computed by subtracting 1 from the element's position and dividing the result by 2. The top of the heap is at position 0 in the array. In the implementation, the instance variable _heap refers to a Python list. Following is the code for the add method:

```
def add(self, item):
    self._size += 1
    self._heap.append(item)
    curPos = len(self._heap) - 1
    while curPos > 0:
        parent = (curPos - 1) // 2            # Integer quotient!
        parentItem = self._heap[parent]
        if parentItem <= item:
            break
        else:
            self._heap[curPos] = self._heap[parent]
            self._heap[parent] = item
            curPos = parent
```

A quick analysis of this method reveals that, at most, you must make $\log_2 n$ comparisons to walk up the tree from the bottom, so the add operation is $O(\log n)$. The method occasionally triggers a doubling in the size of the underlying array. When doubling occurs, this operation is $O(n)$, but amortized over all additions, the operation is $O(1)$ per addition.

The goal of a removal is to return the element in the root node after deleting this node and adjusting the positions of other nodes to maintain the heap property. Following is your strategy for removals:

1. Begin by saving pointers to the top element and the bottom element in the heap and by moving the element from the bottom of the heap to the top.

2. Walk down the heap from the top, moving the smallest child up one level, until the bottom of the heap is reached.

Following is the code for the pop method:

```
def pop(self):
    if self.isEmpty():
        raise Exception, "Heap is empty"

    self._size -= 1
    topItem = self._heap[0]
    bottomItem = self._heap.pop(len(self._heap) - 1)
    if len(self._heap) == 0:
        return bottomItem

    self._heap[0] = bottomItem
    lastIndex = len(self._heap) - 1
    curPos = 0
    while True:
        leftChild = 2 * curPos + 1
        rightChild = 2 * curPos + 2
        if leftChild > lastIndex:
            break
        if rightChild > lastIndex:
            maxChild = leftChild;
        else:
            leftItem  = self._heap[leftChild]
            rightItem = self._heap[rightChild]
            if leftItem < rightItem:
                maxChild = leftChild
            else:
                maxChild = rightChild
        maxItem = self._heap[maxChild]
        if bottomItem <= maxItem:
            break
        else:
            self._heap[curPos] = self._heap[maxChild]
            self._heap[maxChild] = bottomItem
            curPos = maxChild
    return topItem
```

Once again, analysis shows that the number of comparisons required for a removal is at most $\log_2 n$, so the pop operation is $O(\log n)$. The method pop occasionally triggers a halving in the size of the underlying array. When halving occurs, this operation is $O(n)$, but amortized over all removals, the operation is $O(1)$ per removal.

Exercises 10.6

1. How do the run times of the heap operations differ from their counterparts in binary search trees?

2. What is the advantage of using a list over using an array to implement a heap?

3. The heap sort uses a heap to sort a list of items. The strategy of this sort is to add the items in the list to a heap and then remove all of them from the heap as they are transferred back to the list. What is the run time and memory complexity of the heap sort?

SUMMARY

■ Trees are hierarchical collections. The topmost node in a tree is called its root. In a general tree, each node below the root has at most one predecessor, or parent node, and zero or more successors, or child nodes. Nodes without children are called leaves. Nodes that have children are called interior nodes. The root of a tree is at level 0, its children are at level 1, and so on.

■ In a binary tree, a node can have at most two children. A complete binary tree fills each level of nodes before moving to the next level. A full binary tree includes all the possible nodes at each level.

■ There are four standard types of tree traversals: preorder, inorder, postorder, and levelorder.

■ An expression tree is a type of binary tree in which the interior nodes contain operators and the successor nodes contain their operands. Atomic operands are contained in the leaf nodes. Expression trees represent the structure of expressions in programming language parsers and interpreters.

■ A binary search tree is a type of binary tree in which each nonempty left subtree contains data that are less than the datum in its parent node, and each nonempty right subtree contains data that are greater than the datum in its parent node.

■ A binary search tree supports logarithmic searches and insertions if it is close to complete.

■ A heap is a type of binary tree in which smaller data items are located near the root. You can use a heap to implement the $n \log n$ heap sort algorithm and a priority queue.

REVIEW QUESTIONS

1. The distinguished node at the beginning or top of a tree is called the
   a. Head node
   b. Root node
   c. Leaf node

2. A node without children is called a
   a. Single node
   b. Leaf node

3. Each level k in a full binary tree contains
   a. $2k$ nodes
   b. $2^k + 1$ nodes
   c. $2^k - 1$ nodes

4. Assume that data are inserted into a binary search tree in the order D B A C F E G. A preorder traversal would return these data in the order
   a. D B A C F E G
   b. A B C D E F G

5. Assume that data are inserted into a binary search tree in the order D B A C F E G. An inorder traversal would return these data in the order
   a. D B A C F E G
   b. A B C D E F G

6. Assume that data are inserted into a binary search tree in the order A B C D E F G. The structure of this tree resembles that of a
   a. Full binary tree
   b. List

7. The item removed from a min-heap is always the
   a. Smallest item
   b. Largest item

8. A postorder traversal of an expression tree returns the expression in
   a. Infix form
   b. Prefix form
   c. Postfix form

9. The worst-case behavior of the search of a binary search tree is
   a. O(log*n*)
   b. O(*n*)
   c. O(*n*²)

10. Insertions and removals from a heap are
    a. Linear operations
    b. Logarithmic operations

PROJECTS

1. Complete the implementation of the LinkedBST class discussed in this chapter, and test it with a tester program.

2. Add the methods height and isBalanced to the LinkedBST class. The height method returns the height of the tree, as defined in this chapter. The isBalanced method returns True if the height of the tree is less than twice the log₂ of its number of nodes, or False otherwise.

3. Add the method rebalance to the LinkedBST class. The method copies the tree's items to a list during an inorder traversal and then clears the tree. The method then copies the items from the list back to the tree in such a manner that the shape of the tree is balanced. *Hint*: Use a recursive helper function that repeatedly visits the items at the midpoints of portions of the list.

4. Add the methods successor and predecessor to the LinkedBST class. Each method expects an item as an argument and returns an item or None. A successor is the smallest item in the tree that is greater than the given item. A predecessor is the largest item in the tree that is less than the given item. Note that the successor may exist even if the given item is not present in the tree.

5. Add a method rangeFind to the LinkedBST class. This method expects two items as arguments that specify the bounds of a range of items to be found in the tree. The method traverses the tree and builds and returns a list of the items found within the specified range.

6. The ArraySortedBag class discussed in Chapter 6 is an array-based implementation of a sorted bag collection. A linked implementation, named TreeSortedBag, uses a binary search tree. Complete and test this new implementation of a sorted bag collection. Compare the run-time performance of the add, remove, and in operations of the two implementations of sorted bags.

7. Complete and test the node classes for the expression tree developed in this chapter.

8. Add and test the ^ operator for exponentiation to the expression tree developed in this chapter.

9. Complete the parser developed in the case study of this chapter. The parser should also handle the exponentiation operator ^. Recall that this operator has a higher precedence than * and / and is right associative. This means that the expression 2 ^ 3 ^ 4 is equivalent to 2 ^ (3 ^ 4), not (2 ^ 3) ^ 4. To handle this syntax and semantics, rename the rule (and method in the parser) for factor to primary. Then add a new rule named factor to the grammar, and a corresponding method to the parser. A factor now is a primary, followed by an optional ^ operator and another factor. You will also have to modify the Token class to include the new ^ operator.

10. Implement and test a heapSort function that is based on the heap class developed in this chapter. Profile this function using the technology developed in Chapter 3, "Searching, Sorting, and Complexity Analysis," to verify its run-time complexity.

11. Modify the emergency room scheduler case study program from Chapter 8, "Queues," so that it uses a heap-based priority queue called HeapPriorityQueue.

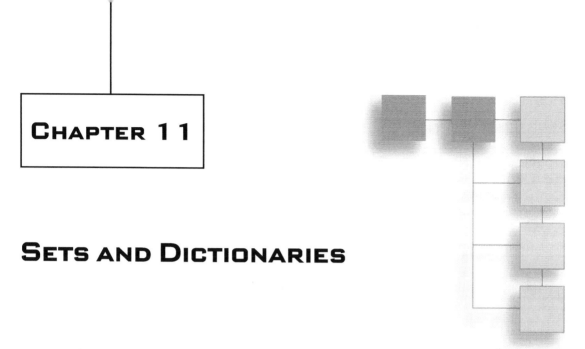

CHAPTER 11

SETS AND DICTIONARIES

In an ordered collection, both the value and the position of each item are significant, and each item is accessed by its position. This chapter looks at unordered collections and focuses particularly on their implementation. From the user's perspective, only the items' values matter; to the user, an item's position is not an issue. Thus, none of the operations on an unordered collection are position based. Once added, an item is accessed by its value. Users can insert, retrieve, or remove items from unordered collections, but they cannot access the ith item, the next item, or the previous item. Some examples of unordered collections are bags, sets, and dictionaries. Chapters 5, "Interfaces, Implementations, and Polymorphism," and 6, "Inheritance and Abstract Classes," explored various types of bags, and you may already have experience working with Python sets and dictionaries. This chapter introduces some efficient implementation strategies for sets and dictionaries.

USING SETS

As you have learned from your study of mathematics, a *set* is a collection of items in no particular order. From the user's perspective, the items in a set are unique. That is, there are no duplicate items in a set. In mathematics, you perform many operations on sets. Some of the most typical operations are the following:

- Return the number of items in the set.
- Test for the empty set (a set that contains no items).
- Add an item to the set.
- Remove an item from the set.

- Test for set membership (whether or not a given item is in the set).

- Obtain the union of two sets. The union of two sets A and B is a set that contains all the items in A and all the items in B.

- Obtain the intersection of two sets. The intersection of two sets A and B is the set of items in A that are also items in B.

- Obtain the difference of two sets. The difference of two sets A and B is the set of items in A that are not also items in B.

- Test a set to determine whether or not another set is its subset. The set B is a subset of set A if and only if B is an empty set or all the items in B are also in A.

Note that the difference and subset operations (the last two bullets) are not symmetric. For example, the difference of sets A and B is not always the same as the difference of sets B and A.

To describe the contents of a set, you use the notation {<item-1> … <item-n>} but assume that the items are in no particular order. Table 11.1 shows the results of some operations on example sets.

Table 11.1   Results of Some Typical Set Operations

Sets A and B	Union	Intersection	Difference	Subset
{12 5 17 6} {42 17 6}	{12 5 42 17 6}	{17 6}	{12 5}	False
{21 76 10 3 9} {}	{21 76 10 3 9}	{}	{21 76 10 3 9}	True
{87} {22 87 23}	{22 87 23}	{87}	{}	False
{22 87 23} {87}	{22 87 23}	{87}	{22 23}	True

THE PYTHON SET CLASS

Python includes a set class. The most commonly used methods in this class are listed in Table 11.2.

Table 11.2   The Commonly Used Operations on the Set Type

Set Method	What It Does
s = set()	Creates an empty set and assigns it to s.
s = set(anIterable)	Creates a set that contains the unique items in anIterable object (such as a string, a list, or a dictionary) and assigns it to s.
s.add(item)	Adds item to s if it is not already in s.
s.remove(item)	Removes item from s. *Precondition*: item must be in s.
s.__len__()	Same as len(s). Returns the number of items currently in s.
s.__iter__()	Returns an iterator on s. Supports a for loop with s. Items are visited in an unspecified order.
s.__str__()	Same as str(s). Returns a string containing the string representation of the items in s.
s.__contains__(item)	Same as item in s. Returns True if item is in s, or False otherwise.
s1.__or__(s2)	Set union. Same as s1 | s2. Returns a set containing the items in s1 and s2.
s1.__and__(s2)	Set intersection. Same as s1 & s2. Returns a set containing the items in s1 that are also in s2.
s1.__sub__(s2)	Set difference. Same as s1 - s2. Returns a set containing the items in s1 that are not in s2.
s1.issubset(s2)	Returns True if s1 is a subset of s2, or False otherwise.

A Sample Session with Sets

In the next example, you create two sets named A and B and perform some operations on them. When the set constructor receives a list as an argument, the list's items are copied to the set, omitting duplicate items. Note that Python prints a set value using braces instead of brackets.

```
>>> A = set([0, 1, 2])
>>> B = set()
>>> 1 in A
True
>>> A & B
{}
>>> B.add(1)
```

```
>>> B.add(1)
>>> B.add(5)
>>> B
{1, 5}
>>> A & B
{1}
>>> A | B
{0, 1, 2, 5}
>>> A - B
{0, 2}
>>> B.remove(5)
>>> B
{1}
>>> B.issubset(A)
True
>>> for item in A:
        print(item, end="")

0 1 2
>>>
```

Applications of Sets

Aside from their role in mathematics, sets have many applications in the area of data processing. For example, in the field of database management, the answer to a query that contains the conjunction of two keys could be constructed from the intersection of the sets of items associated with those keys.

Relationship Between Sets and Bags

As you learned in Chapter 5, a bag is an unordered collection of elements. The primary difference between sets and bags is that sets contain unique items, whereas bags can contain multiple instances of the same item. A set type also includes operations, such as intersection, difference, and subset, not typically associated with bags. The similarity of sets and bags has consequences for some implementation strategies, as you shall see shortly.

Relationship Between Sets and Dictionaries

As you learned in Chapter 2, "An Overview of Collections," a *dictionary* is an unordered collection of elements called *entries*. Each entry consists of a key and an associated value. Operations for adding, modifying, and removing entries use a key to locate an entry and its value. A dictionary's keys must be unique, but its values may be duplicated. Thus, you can think of a dictionary as having a set of keys. The differences and similarities between dictionaries and sets will come into play as you examine implementation strategies later in this chapter.

Implementations of Sets

You can use arrays or linked structures to contain the data items of a set. A linked structure has the advantage of supporting constant-time removals of items, once they are located in the structure. However, as you shall see shortly, adding and removing items require linear searches. Another strategy, called *hashing*, attempts to approximate random access into an array for insertions, removals, and searches. You explore all three implementation strategies later in this chapter.

Exercises 11.1

1. In what ways does a set differ from a list?

2. Assume that the set s contains the number 3. Write the sequence of sets resulting from the following operations:

    a. s.add(4)

    b. s.add(4)

    c. s.add(5)

    d. s.remove(3)

3. How do you visit all the items in a set?

ARRAY-BASED AND LINKED IMPLEMENTATIONS OF SETS

As mentioned earlier, a set is really just a bag containing unique data items and a few additional methods. Therefore, the simplest implementations of sets are subclasses of the bag classes discussed in Chapter 6. These set implementations, called ArraySet, LinkedSet, and ArraySortedSet, support the methods in the set interface but receive most of their code, via inheritance, from their parent classes ArrayBag, LinkedBag, and ArraySortedBag.

The set-specific methods __and__, __or__, __sub__, and issubset could be included in each set class. However, because these methods only run other methods in the set interface, they have the same code in all implementations. Therefore, they can be implemented in a second parent class named AbstractSet. Figure 11.1 shows these relationships among the set classes.

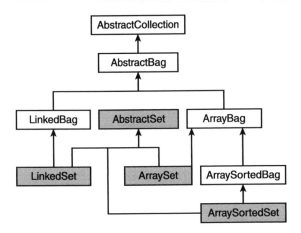

Figure 11.1

Array-based and linked set implementations.

© 2014 Cengage Learning®

Note that each concrete set class is a subclass of two classes, one of which is AbstractSet. Python supports multiple inheritance, meaning that a given class can have more than one parent class, as long as the items being inherited are distinct.

Note also that AbstractSet, unlike AbstractBag, is not a subclass of AbstractCollection. You now explore the array-based implementation to clarify who is inheriting what from whom in this hierarchy.

The AbstractSet Class

The AbstractSet class is just a repository of the generic set methods __and__, __or__, __sub__, and issubset. This class is a subclass of object, because the other set classes already inherit the other collection resources from the bag classes. Here is the code for this class:

```
"""
File: abstractset.py
Author: Ken Lambert
"""

class AbstractSet(object):
    """Generic set method implementations."""

    # Accessor methods
    def __or__(self, other):
        """Returns the union of self and other."""
        return self + other
```

```
def __and__(self, other):
    """Returns the intersection of self and other."""
    intersection = type(self)()
    for item in self:
        if item in other:
            intersection.add(item)
    return intersection

def __sub__(self, other):
    """Returns the difference of self and other."""
    difference = type(self)()
    for item in self:
        if not item in other:
            difference.add(item)
    return difference

def issubset(self, other):
    """Returns True if self is a subset of other
    or False otherwise."""
    for item in self:
        if not item in other:
            return False
    return True
```

This design allows you to add any other generic set methods to this class.

The ArraySet Class

The ArraySet class inherits the methods isEmpty, __len__, __iter__, __add__, __eq__, add, and remove from one parent, ArrayBag. From the other parent, AbstractSet, the ArraySet class inherits the methods __and__, __or__, __sub__, and issubset. The ArraySet class essentially mixes these methods together to support a new type of object. Along the way, however, ArraySet must override the add method in ArrayBag by preventing the insertion of duplicate items. Here is the code for ArraySet:

```
"""
File: arrayset.py
Author: Ken Lambert
"""

from arraybag import ArrayBag
from abstractset import AbstractSet


class ArraySet(ArrayBag, AbstractSet):
    """An array-based implementation of a set."""

    def __init__(self, sourceCollection = None):
        ArrayBag.__init__(self, sourceCollection)
```

```
def add(self, item):
    """Adds item to the set if it is not in the set."""
    if not item in self:
        ArrayBag.add(self, item)
```

Note the listing of the two parent classes in the class header and the call of the add method in ArrayBag if the item is not in the set. The code for the LinkedSet and ArraySortedSet classes is quite similar to ArraySet, and its completion is left as an exercise for you.

USING DICTIONARIES

You can view a dictionary as a set of key/value pairs called *items*. However, a dictionary's interface is rather different from that of a set. As you know from using Python's dict type, values are inserted or replaced at given keys using the subscript operator []. The method pop removes a value at a given key, and the methods keys and values return iterators on a dictionary's set of keys and collection of values, respectively. The __iter__ method supports a for loop over a dictionary's keys. The common collection methods are also supported. Table 11.3 lists the dictionary-specific methods in the dictionary interface that you will implement in this chapter.

Table 11.3   The Interface for Dictionary Collections

Method	What It Does
d = <dictionary type>(sourceCollection = None)	Creates a dictionary and assigns it to d. Copies key/value pairs from sourceCollection if it is present. *Precondition*: sourceCollection must be either another dictionary or a list of key/value tuples.
d.__getitem__(key)	Same as d[key]. Returns the value associated with key if key exists, or raises a KeyError otherwise.
d.__setitem__(key, value)	Same as d[key] = value. If key exists, replaces its associated value with value; otherwise, inserts a new key/value entry.
d.pop(key)	Removes the key/value entry and returns the associated value if key exists, or raises a KeyError otherwise.
d.__iter__()	Same as iter(d) or for key in d:. Returns an iterator on the keys in d.
d.keys()	Returns an iterator on the keys in d.
d.values()	Returns an iterator on the values in d.
d.items()	Returns an iterator on the items (key/value pairs) in d.

Note that unlike the constructor methods of other collection types, the dictionary constructor expects its optional collection argument to be an iterable object over key/value pairs.

ARRAY-BASED AND LINKED IMPLEMENTATIONS OF DICTIONARIES

The first two implementations of dictionaries are array based and linked. This design strategy is similar to the one you've used for other collections in this book:

- Place the new classes in the collections framework so that they get some data and methods for free.

- If other methods in the new interface have the same implementation in all classes, place them in a new abstract class.

To achieve these design goals, add an AbstractDict class to the framework, as a subclass of AbstractCollection. This new class is responsible for the methods __str__, __add__, __eq__, __contains__, __iter__, keys, values, and items.

The concrete classes ArrayDict and LinkedDict then appear as subclasses of Abstract-Dict. They are responsible for the methods __iter__, clear, __getitem__, __setitem__, and pop. Figure 11.2 shows the relationships among these classes.

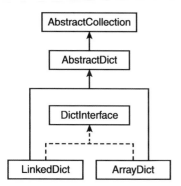

Figure 11.2
Array-based and linked dictionary implementations.
© 2014 Cengage Learning®

The Item Class

The items in a dictionary consist of two parts: a key and a value. Figure 11.3 shows one such item, whose key is "age" and whose value is 39.

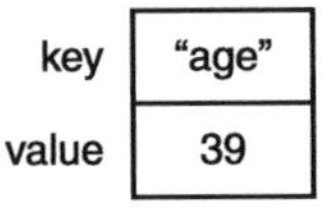

key	"age"
value	39

Figure 11.3

An item for a dictionary.

Each implementation of a dictionary contains items. Each key/value pair is packaged in an Item object. The Item class includes some comparison methods. It allows the programmer to test two entries for equality or to order them in a sorted dictionary. Here is the code for this class:

```
class Item(object):
    """Represents a dictionary item.
    Supports comparisons by key."""

    def __init__(self, key, value):
        self.key = key
        self.value = value

    def __str__(self):
        return str(self.key) + ":" + str(self.value)

    def __eq__(self, other):
        if type(self) != type(other): return False
        return self.key == other.key

    def __lt__(self, other):
        if type(self) != type(other): return False
        return self.key < other.key

    def __le__(self, other):
        if type(self) != type(other): return False
        return self.key <= other.key
```

For convenience, this class is placed in the same module, abstractdict as the AbstractDict class.

The AbstractDict Class

The AbstractDict class includes all the methods that call other dictionary methods to do their work. These methods also include some AbstractCollection methods, such as __str__, __add__, and __eq__, which must be overridden to support dictionary-like behavior.

In addition, the __init__ method in AbstractDict must now do the work of copying items from the optional source collection, which must be a collection of key/value pairs, to the new dictionary object. Note that this is done after the __init__ method in AbstractCollection is called with no collection argument.

Here is the code for the AbstractDict class:

```
"""
File: abstractdict.py
Author: Ken Lambert
"""

from abstractcollection import AbstractCollection

class AbstractDict(AbstractCollection):
    """Common data and method implementations
    for dictionaries."""

    def __init__(self, sourceCollection):
        """Will copy items to the collection
        from sourceCollection if it's present."""
        AbstractCollection.__init__(self)
        if sourceCollection:
            for key, value in sourceCollection:
                self[key] = value

    def __str__(self):
        return "{" + ", ".join(map(str,
                                   self.items())) + "}"

    def __add__(self, other):
        """Returns a new dictionary containing the contents
        of self and other."""
        result = type(self)(map(lambda item: (item.key, item.value),
                                self.items()))
        for key in other:
            result[key] = other[key]
        return result

    def __eq__(self, other):
        """Returns True if self equals other,
        or False otherwise."""
        if self is other: return True
        if type(self) != type(other) or \
           len(self) != len(other):
            return False
        for key in self:
            if not key in other:
                return False
        return True

    def keys(self):
        """Returns a iterator on the keys in
```

```
            the dictionary."""
            return iter(self)

    def values(self):
        """Returns an iterator on the values in
        the dictionary."""
        return iter(map(lambda key: self[key], self))

    def items(self):
        """Returns an iterator on the items in
        the dictionary."""
        return iter(map(lambda key: Item(key,
                                         self[key]),
                    self))
```

The ArrayDict Class

Like other concrete classes, the ArrayDict class is responsible for initializing the collection's container object and implementing the methods that must directly access this container. For convenience, you choose Python's array-based list as the container object and implement the methods __iter__, __getitem__, __setitem__, and pop in the dictionary interface. The helper method _index is called to locate a target key in the methods __getitem__, __setitem__, and pop.

Here is the code for the ArrayDict class:

```
"""
File: arraydict.py
Author: Ken Lambert
"""

from abstractdict import AbstractDict, Item

class ArrayDict(AbstractDict):
    """Represents an array-based dictionary."""

    def __init__(self, sourceCollection = None):
        """Will copy items to the collection
        from sourceDictionary if it's present."""
        self._items = list()
        AbstractDict.__init__(self, sourceCollection)

    # Accessors
    def __iter__(self):
        """Serves up the keys in the dictionary."""
        cursor = 0
        while cursor < len(self):
            yield self._items[cursor].key
            cursor += 1
```

```python
def __getitem__(self, key):
    """Precondition: the key is in the dictionary.
    Raises: a KeyError if the key is not in
    the dictionary.
    Returns the value associated with the key."""
    index = self._index(key)
    if index == -1:
        raise KeyError("Missing: " + str(key))
    return self._items[index].value

# Mutators
def __setitem__(self, key, value):
    """If the key is not in the dictionary,
    adds the key and value to it.
    Otherwise, replaces the old value with the new
    value."""
    index = self._index(key)
    if index == -1:
        self._items.append(Entry(key, value))
        self._size += 1
    else:
        self._items[index].value = value

def pop(self, key):
    """Precondition: the key is in the dictionary.
    Raises: a KeyError if the key is not in
    the dictionary.
    Removes the key and returns the associated
    value if the key is in the dictionary,
    or returns the default value otherwise."""
    index = self._index(key)
    if index == -1:
        raise KeyError("Missing: " + str(key))
    self._size -= 1
    return self._items.pop(index).value

def _index(self, key):
    """Helper method for key search."""
    index = 0
    for entry in self._items:
        if entry.key == key:
            return index
        index += 1
    return -1
```

The implementation of the LinkedDict class is similar and is left as an exercise for you.

Complexity Analysis of the Array-Based and Linked Implementations of Sets and Dictionaries

The array-based implementations of sets and dictionaries require little programmer effort, but unfortunately they do not perform well. A quick inspection of the basic accessing methods shows that each one must perform a linear search of the underlying array, so each basic accessing method is $O(n)$.

Because items are in no particular order from the user's perspective, you cannot resort to implementations that support logarithmic access and insertions, such as the binary search trees discussed in Chapter 10, "Trees." However, as you shall see in the next section, there are strategies for implementations of sets and dictionaries that are faster than linear implementations.

Exercises 11.2

1. The `ArraySet` method `add` searches the entire set. Discuss the consequences of this search of the entire set for the performance of the methods `union`, `intersection`, and `difference` and give the big-O complexity of each of these methods.

2. Jill proposes a more efficient strategy for the `ArraySet` method `add`. Her strategy is not to check for a duplicate, but simply to add it to the list. Discuss the consequences of this strategy for the other `ArraySet` methods.

HASHING STRATEGIES

As you learned in Chapter 4, "Arrays and Linked Structures," the fastest way to access items in a collection is via random access supported by arrays and array-based lists. Start with the assumption, then, that the underlying data structure for a set or a dictionary is an array; see if you can find a way to approximate random access to the items or keys in the set or dictionary. In an ideal world, the items or keys in a set or dictionary are consecutive numbers from 0 to the size of the structure minus 1. Then their positions in an underlying array are accessible in constant time. In the actual world of data processing, where the keys are large numbers or people's names or other attributes, this is rarely the case.

However, suppose the first key is the number 15,000, and the following keys are numbered consecutively. The position of a given key in an array could then be computed with the expression `key - 15000`. This type of computation is known as a *key-to-address transformation* or a *hashing function*. A hashing function acts on a given key by returning its relative position in an array. The array used with a hashing strategy is called a *hash table.* If the hashing function runs in constant time, insertions, accesses, and removals of the associated keys are O(1).

The first example of a hashing function is still rather unrealistic. Suppose that the keys are not consecutive numbers, and that the length of the array structure is 4. Then the hashing function key % 4 produces a distinct index into the array for each of the keys 3, 5, 8, and 10, as shown in Figure 11.4.

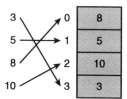

Figure 11.4
Placement of the keys 3, 5, 8, and 10 using the hashing function key % 4.
© 2014 Cengage Learning®

Unfortunately, the keys 3, 4, 8, and 10 do not find unique positions in the array, because both 4 and 8 hash to an index of 0 (Figure 11.5).

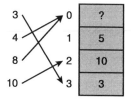

Figure 11.5
Placement of the keys 3, 4, 8, and 10 using the hashing function key % 4.
© 2014 Cengage Learning®

The hashing of the keys 4 and 8 to the same index is called a *collision.*

The rest of this section explores the development of techniques related to hashing that minimize collisions and increase the potential for constant-time access to items in unordered collections. It also examines strategies for dealing with collisions when they occur.

The Relationship of Collisions to Density

In Figure 11.5, you saw an example of data collision during hashing into an array that becomes full. Do collisions occur when extra cells (beyond those needed for the data) are available in the array? To answer this question, you'll write a Python function, keysToIndexes, which generates the indexes in an array of size *N* from a list of keys. A key in this context is just a positive integer. The array index corresponding to the key is the remainder after dividing the key by the length of the array (for any positive number c, c % n is a number from 0 through n − 1). The definition of keysToIndexes follows, and then a following session shows the indexes for the two data sets discussed earlier:

```
def keysToIndexes(keys, n):
    """Returns the indexes corresponding to
    the keys for an array of length n."""
    return list(map(lambda key: key % n, keys))
>>> keysToIndexes([3, 5, 8, 10], 4)    # No collisions
[3, 1, 0, 2]
>>> keysToIndexes([3, 4, 8, 10], 4)    # One collision
[3, 0, 0, 2]
```

Runs of both sets of keys with increasing array lengths show that no collisions occur when the array length reaches 8:

```
>>> keysToIndexes([3, 5, 8, 10], 8)
[3, 5, 0, 2]
>>> keysToIndexes([3, 4, 8, 10], 8)
[3, 4, 0, 2]
```

There might be other sets of four keys that would cause collisions with an array of length 8, but it's clear that if you're willing to waste some array memory, the likelihood of collisions during hashing decreases. Put another way, as the *density*, or number of keys relative to the length of an array decreases, so does the probability of collisions. The load factor of an array, introduced in Chapter 4, is a measure of its data density (number of items/length of the array). For example, when the load factor in the examples just discussed exceeds .5, a collision occurs. Keeping the load factor even lower (say, below .2) seems like a good way to avoid collisions, but the cost of memory incurred by load factors below .5 is probably prohibitive for data sets of millions of items.

Even load factors below .5 cannot prevent many collisions from occurring for some data sets. Consider the set of seven keys 10, 20, 30, 40, 50, 60, and 70. If you hash them into an array of length 15, none of them finds a unique index, as shown in the next session:

```
>>> keysToIndexes([10, 20, 30, 40, 50, 60, 70], 15)
[10, 5, 0, 10, 5, 0, 10]
```

However, if you choose a prime number, such as 11, for the array length, the results are much better:

```
>>> keysToIndexes([10, 20, 30, 40, 50, 60, 70], 11)
[10, 9, 8, 7, 6, 5, 4]
```

A small load factor and an array length that is a prime number help, but you must develop other techniques to handle collisions when they occur.

Hashing with Nonnumeric Keys

The preceding examples all used integer keys for data. How do you generate integer keys for other types of data, such as names or item codes with letters in them?

Consider strings in general. The goal is to obtain a unique integer key from each unique string. You might try returning the sum of the ASCII values in the string. However, this method produces the same keys for *anagrams*, or strings that contain the same characters, but in different order, such as "cinema" and "iceman." Another problem is that the first letters of many words in English are unevenly distributed; more words begin with the letter S, rather than the letter X, for example. This might have the effect of weighting or biasing the sums generated so that the keys will be clustered in certain ranges within the entire key set. These clusters can, in turn, result in clusters of keys in the array, when ideally it would be best to evenly distribute the keys in the array. To reduce the potential bias of the first letters and reduce the effect produced by anagrams, if the length of the string is greater than a certain threshold, you could drop the first character from the string before computing the sum. In addition, you could subtract the ASCII value of the last character if the string exceeds a certain length. The definition of this function, called stringHash, follows and is, in turn, followed by a demonstration of how it handles the anagrams:

```
def stringHash(item):
    """Generates an integer key from a string."""
    if len(item) > 4 and \
       (item[0].islower() or item[0].isupper()):
        item = item[1:]             # Drop first letter
    sum = 0
    for ch in item:
        sum += ord(ch)
    if len(item) > 2:
        sum -= 2 * ord(item[-1])   # Subtract last ASCII
    return sum
>>> stringHash("cinema")
328
>>> stringHash("iceman")
296
```

To test the adequacy of your new hashing function, you can update the `keysToIndexes` function to receive a hashing function as an optional third argument. The default of this hashing function, which covers the cases of integer keys seen earlier, is to simply return the key.

```
def keysToIndexes(keys, n, hash = lambda key: key):
    """Returns the array indexes corresponding to the
    hashed keys for an array of length n."""
    return list (map(lambda key: hash(key) % n, keys))
```

The tester function now works as before with lists of integer keys, but also with a list of strings, as shown in the next session:

```
# First example
>>> keysToIndexes([3, 5, 8, 10], 4)
[3, 1, 0, 2]
# Collision
>>> keysToIndexes(["cinema", "iceman"], 2, stringHash)
[0, 0]
# n is prime
>>> keysToIndexes(["cinema", "iceman"], 3, stringHash)
[1, 2]
```

Python also includes a standard `hash` function for use in hashing applications. This function can receive any Python object as an argument and returns a unique integer. Because the integer might be negative, you must take its absolute value before applying the remainder operator to the integer to compute an index. Compare the results of using `hash` with those of your `stringHash` function:

```
>>> list(map(lambda x: abs(hash(x)), ["cinema", "iceman"]))
[1338503047, 1166902005]
>>> list(map(stringHash, ["cinema", "iceman"]))
[328, 296]
>>> keysToIndexes(["cinema", "iceman"], 3,
                  lambda x: abs(hash(x)))
[1, 0]
>>> keysToIndexes(["cinema", "iceman"], 3, stringHash)
[1, 2]
>>>
```

More sophisticated hashing functions are the subject of advanced courses and are beyond the scope of this book. In the rest of this chapter, you use Python's hash function and the remainder method.

No matter how advanced the hashing functions, the potential remains for collisions in a hash table. Computer scientists have developed many methods for resolving collisions. The following subsections examine some of them.

Linear Probing

For insertions, the simplest way to resolve a collision is to search the array, starting from the collision spot, for the first available position; this process is referred to as *linear probing*. Each position in the array is in one of three distinguishable states: occupied, never occupied, or previously occupied. A position is considered to be available for the insertion of a key if it has never been occupied or if a key has been deleted from it (previously occupied). The values EMPTY and DELETED designate these two states, respectively. At start-up, the array cells are filled with the EMPTY value. The value of a cell is set to DELETED when a key is removed. At the start of an insertion, the hashing function is run to compute the *home index* of the item. The home index is the position where the item should go if the hash function works perfectly (this position will be unoccupied in this case). If the cell at the home index is not available, the algorithm moves the index to the right to probe for an available cell. When the search reaches the last position of the array, the probing wraps around to continue from the first position. If you assume the array does not become full and there are no duplicate items, the code for insertions into an array named table is as follows:

```
# Get the home index
index = abs(hash(item)) % len(table)

# Stop searching when an empty cell is encountered
while not table[index] in (EMPTY, DELETED):

    # Increment the index and wrap around to first
    # position if necessary
    index = (index + 1) % len(table)

# An empty cell is found, so store the item
table[index] = item
```

Retrievals and removals work in a similar manner. For retrievals, you stop the probing process when the current array cell is empty or it contains the target item. This allows you to step over the previously occupied cells as well as the currently occupied cells. For removals, you also probe, as in retrievals. If the target item is found, its cell is set to DELETED.

One problem with this method of resolving collisions is that after several insertions and removals, a number of cells marked DELETED may lie between a given item and its home index. This means that this item is farther away from its home index than it really needs to be, thus increasing the average overall access time. There are two ways to deal with this problem:

1. After a removal, shift the items that are on the cell's right over to the cell's left until an empty cell, a currently occupied cell, or the home indexes for each item are reached. If removing items leaves gaps, this process closes those gaps.

2. Regularly rehash the table, say, when its load factor becomes .5. Doing so converts all previously occupied cells into either currently occupied cells or empty cells. If the table has some way to track the frequency of accesses to given items, the items can be reinserted in decreasing order of frequency. This places more frequently accessed items closer to their home indexes.

Because the table has to be rehashed when the array becomes full (or its load factor exceeds an acceptable limit) in any case, you might prefer the second strategy.

Linear probing is prone to a second problem known as *clustering*. This situation occurs when the items that cause a collision are relocated to the same region (a cluster) within the array. Figure 11.6 shows an example of this situation after several insertions of keys, for the data set 20, 30, 40, 50, 60, 70. Note that probing is not done until the keys 60 and 70 are inserted, but a cluster has formed at the bottom of the array.

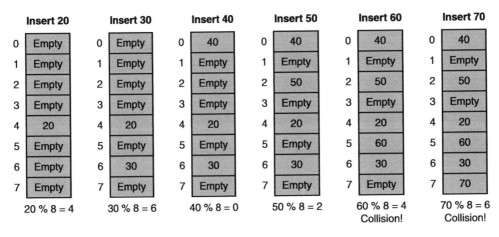

Figure 11.6
Clustering during linear probing.
© 2014 Cengage Learning®

This clustering usually leads to collisions with other relocated items. During the course of an application, several clusters may develop and coalesce into larger clusters. As the clusters become larger, the average distance incurred by probing from a home index to an available position becomes greater, and so does the average running time.

Quadratic Probing

One way to avoid the clustering associated with linear probing is to advance the search for an empty position a considerable distance from the collision point. *Quadratic probing* accomplishes this by incrementing the home index by the square of a distance on each attempt. If the attempt fails, you increment the distance and try again. Put another way, if you begin with home index k and a distance d, the formula used on each pass is $k + d^2$. Thus, if probing is necessary, the probe starts at the home index plus 1 and then moves distances of 4, 9, 25, and so on from the home index.

Here is the code for insertions, updated to use quadratic probing:

```
# Set the initial key, index, and distance
key = abs(hash(item))
distance = 1
homeIndex = key % len(table)
index = homeIndex

# Stop searching when an unoccupied cell is encountered
while not table[index] in (EMPTY, DELETED):

    # Increment the index and wrap around to the
    # first position if necessary
    index = (homeIndex + distance ** 2) % len(table)
    distance += 1

# An empty cell is found, so store the item
table[index] = item
```

The major problem with this strategy is that by jumping over some cells, one or more of them might be missed. This can lead to some wasted space.

Chaining

In a collision-processing strategy known as *chaining*, the items are stored in an array of linked lists, or *chains*. Each item's key locates the *bucket*, or index, of the chain in which the item already resides or is to be inserted. The retrieval and removal operations each perform the following steps:

1. Compute the item's home index in the array.

2. Search the linked list at that index for the item.

If the item is found, you can return it or remove it. Figure 11.7 shows an array of linked lists with five buckets and eight items.

index

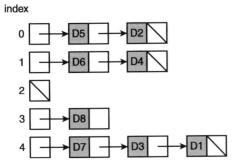

Figure 11.7

Chaining with five buckets.

© 2014 Cengage Learning®

The home index of each item is the index of its linked list in the array. For example, the items D7, D3, and D1 have the home index of 4.

To insert an item into this structure, you perform the following steps:

1. Compute the item's home index in the array.

2. If the array cell is empty, create a node with the item and assign the node to the cell. Otherwise, a collision occurs. The existing item is the head of a linked list or chain of items at that position. Insert the new item at the head of this list.

Borrowing the `Node` class discussed in Chapter 4, here is the code for inserting an item using chaining:

```
# Get the home index
index = abs(hash(item)) % len(table)

# Access a bucket and store the item at the head
# of its linked list
table[index] = Node(item, table[index])
```

Complexity Analysis

As you have seen, the complexity of linear collision processing depends on the load factor as well as the tendency of relocated items to cluster. In the worst case, when the method must traverse the entire array before locating an item's position, the behavior is linear. One study of the linear method (Donald E. Knuth, *The Art of Computer Programming, Volume 3, Searching and Sorting*, Menlo Park, CA: Addison-Wesley, 1973) showed that its average behavior in searching for an item that cannot be found is

$$(1/2) \left[1 + 1/(1 - D)^2\right]$$

where D is the density ratio or load factor.

Because the quadratic method tends to mitigate clustering, you can expect its average performance to be better than that of the linear method. According to Knuth (cited earlier), the average search complexity for the quadratic method is

$$1 - \log_e(1 - D) - (D / 2)$$

for the successful case and

$$1 / (1 - D) - D - \log_e(1 - D)$$

for the unsuccessful case.

Analysis of the bucket/chaining method shows that the process of locating an item consists of two parts:

1. Computing the home index
2. Searching a linked list when collisions occur

The first part has constant-time behavior. The second part has linear behavior. The amount of work is $O(n)$ in the worst case. In this case, all the items that have collided with each other are in one chain, which is a linked list. However, if the lists are evenly distributed throughout the array and the array is fairly large, the second part can be close to constant as well. In the best case, a chain of length 1 occupies each array cell, so the performance is exactly $O(1)$. Random insertion of items tends to result in an even distribution. As the load factor increases past 1, however, the lengths of the chains also increase, resulting in degraded performance. Unlike the other methods, chaining need not resize and rehash the array.

Other trade-offs and optimizations of various hashing strategies are the subject of later courses in computer science and are beyond the scope of this book.

Exercises 11.3

1. Explain how hashing can provide constant-time access to a data structure.
2. What is a home index?
3. What causes collisions?
4. How does the linear method of resolving collisions work?
5. What causes clustering?
6. How does the quadratic method of resolving collisions work, and how does it mitigate clustering?

7. Compute the load factors for the following situations:

   a. An array of length 30 with 10 items.

   b. An array of length 30 with 30 items.

   c. An array of length 30 with 100 items.

8. Explain how chaining works.

CASE STUDY: PROFILING HASHING STRATEGIES

In the case study in Chapter 3, "Searching, Sorting, and Complexity Analysis," you developed a profiler, or software tool, to help measure the performance of some sort algorithms. You now develop a similar tool to assess the performance of some of the hashing strategies discussed in the previous section.

Request

Write a program that allows a programmer to profile different hashing strategies.

Analysis

The profiler should allow a programmer to gather statistics on the number of collisions caused by different hashing strategies. Other useful information to be obtained includes a hash table's load factor and the number of probes needed to resolve collisions during linear probing or quadratic probing. The profiler assumes that a programmer has defined a HashTable class that includes the methods listed in Table 11.4.

Table 11.4 The Methods in the HashTable Class

HashTable Method	What It Does
T = HashTable(capacity = 29, hashFunction = hash, linear = True)	Creates and returns a hash table with the given initial capacity, hash function, and collision resolution strategy. If linear is False, uses a quadratic probing strategy.
T.insert(item)	Inserts item into the table.
T.__len__()	Same as len(T). Returns the number of items in the table.
T.loadFactor()	Returns the table's current load factor (number of items divided by capacity).

`T.homeIndex()`	Returns the home index of the item most recently inserted, removed, or accessed.
`T.actualIndex()`	Returns the actual index of the item most recently inserted, removed, or accessed.
`T.probeCount()`	Returns the number of probes required to resolve a collision during the most recent insertion, removal, or access.
`T.__str__()`	Same as `str(T)`. Returns a string representation of the table's array. Cells that are empty show the value `None`. Cells that have been previously occupied show the value `True`.

For purposes of this case study, this simple table allows the programmer to insert items and determine the array's length and load factor, the most recent insertion's home index and actual index, and the number of probes required following a collision. Note that when a table is created, the programmer can supply its initial capacity and a hash function. The programmer can also state whether or not a linear probing strategy should be used. The default hashing function is Python's own `hash`, but the programmer can supply a different hashing function during instantiation of the table. If linear probing is not desired, the table uses quadratic probing. The default capacity of a table is 29 cells, but the programmer can adjust this capacity when creating the table.

The information supplied to the profiler is a hash table and a list of items in its data set. The information returned is a string. This string represents a formatted table whose columns list the load factor, item inserted, home index and eventual position of the insertion in the hash table, and number of probes required. The total number of collisions, the total number of probes, and the average probes per collision follow this table in the string. The programmer runs the profiler on a hash table and its data set by supplying these data as arguments to a `test` method. The total collisions and probes can be obtained individually by calling the appropriate profiler methods or by printing the profiler object. Table 11.5 lists the methods in the `Profiler` class.

Table 11.5   The Methods in the Profiler Class

Profiler Method	What It Does
P = profiler()	Creates and returns a profiler object.
p.test(aTable, aList)	Runs the profiler on a table with the given data set.
p.__str__()	Same as str(p). Returns a formatted table of results.
p.collisions()	Returns the total number of collisions.
p.probeCount()	Returns the total number of probes required to resolve the collisions.

© 2014 Cengage Learning®

The following `main` function profiles the table used in an earlier example with linear probing:

```
def main():
    # Create a table with 8 cells, an identity hash function,
    # and linear probing.
    table = HashTable(8, lambda x: x)
    # The data are the numbers from 10 through 70, by 10s
    data = list(range(10, 71, 10))
    profiler = Profiler()
    profiler.test(table, data)
    print(profiler)
```

Here are the profiler's results:

```
Load Factor   Item Inserted   Home Index   Actual Index   Probes
   0.000           10              2             2            0
   0.125           20              4             4            0
   0.250           30              6             6            0
   0.375           40              0             0            0
   0.500           50              2             3            1
   0.625           60              4             5            1
   0.750           70              6             7            1
Total collisions: 3
Total probes: 3
Average probes per collision: 1.0
```

Design

The HashTable class requires instance variables for its array of cells, its size, its hash function, its collision strategy, the most recent home and actual indexes, and the probe count. The insert method employs the strategy discussed in the previous section, with the following two embellishments:

- The home index and probe count are updated.

- When the index is incremented during probing, the method used is determined by the strategy assigned to the table, either linear or quadratic.

As before, the insert method assumes that there is room for the new item in the array and that the new item does not duplicate an existing item. The remaining HashTable methods call for no comment.

The Profiler class requires instance variables to track a table, the total number of collisions, and the total number of probes. The test method inserts the items in the order given and accumulates the statistics following each insertion. This method also creates and builds a formatted string with the results. This string is saved in another instance variable, for reference when the str function is called on the profiler. The remaining methods simply return individual statistics.

Implementation

The partial listings of the code for the two classes follow. Their completion is left as an exercise for you. Here is the HashTable class:

```
"""
File: hashtable.py
Case study for Chapter 11.
"""

from arrays import Array

class HashTable(object):
    "Represents a hash table."""

    EMPTY = None
    DELETED = True

    def __init__(self, capacity = 29,
                 hashFunction = hash,
                 linear = True):
        self._table = Array(capacity, HashTable.EMPTY)
        self._size = 0
        self._hash = hashFunction
        self._homeIndex = -1
        self._actualIndex = -1
        self._linear = linear
        self._probeCount = 0
```

```
def insert(self, item):
    """Inserts item into the table
    Preconditions: There is at least one empty cell or
    one previously occupied cell.
    There is not a duplicate item."""
    self._probeCount = 0
    # Get the home index
    self._homeIndex = abs(self._hash(item)) % \
                      len(self._table)
    distance = 1
    index = self._homeIndex

    # Stop searching when an empty cell is encountered
    while not self._table[index] in (HashTable.EMPTY,
                                     HashTable.DELETED):

        # Increment the index and wrap around to first
        # position if necessary
        if self._linear:
            increment = index + 1
        else:
            # Quadratic probing
            increment = self._homeIndex + distance ** 2
            distance += 1
        index = increment % len(self._table)
        self._probeCount += 1

    # An empty cell is found, so store the item
    self._table[index] = item
    self._size += 1
    self._actualIndex = index
```

Here is the Profiler class:

```
"""
File: profiler.py

Case study for Chapter 11.
"""

from hashtable import HashTable

class Profiler(object):
    "Represents a profiler for hash tables."""

    def __init__(self):
        self._table = None
        self._collisions = 0
        self._probeCount = 0
```

```
def test(self, table, data):
    """Inserts the data into table and gathers statistics."""
    self._table = table
    self._collisions = 0
    self._probeCount = 0
    self._result = "Load Factor   Item Inserted " + \
                "Home Index   Actual Index    Probes\n"
    for item in data:
        loadFactor = table.loadFactor()
        table.insert(item)
        homeIndex = table.homeIndex()
        actualIndex = table.actualIndex()
        probes = table.probeCount()
        self._probeCount += probes
        if probes > 0:
            self._collisions += 1
        line = "%8.3f%14d%12d%12d%14d" % (loadFactor,
                                          item,
                                          homeIndex,
                                          actualIndex,
                                          probes)
        self._result += line + "\n"
    self._result += "Total collisions: " + \
                str(self._collisions) + \
                "\nTotal probes: " + \
                str(self._probeCount) + \
                "\nAverage probes per collision: " + \
                str(self._probeCount / self._collisions)

def __str__(self):
    if self._table is None:
        return "No test has been run yet."
    else:
        return self._result
```

HASHING IMPLEMENTATION OF SETS

In this section and the next one, hashing is used to construct efficient implementations of unordered collections. This hashing implementation of a set is called HashSet, and it uses the bucket/chaining strategy described earlier. Thus, the implementation must maintain an array and represent entries in such a manner as to allow chaining. To manage the array, you include three instance variables: _items (the array), _size (the number of items in the set), and _capacity (the number of cells in the array). The items are contained in singly linked nodes of the type introduced in Chapter 4. The value of _capacity is by default a constant, which is defined as 3 to ensure frequent collisions.

Because you use the same technique to locate the position of a node for insertions and removals, you can implement it in one method: __contains__. From the user's perspective, this method just searches for a given item and returns True or False. From the implementer's perspective, this method also sets the values of some instance variables to information that can be used during insertions, retrievals, and removals. Table 11.6 gives the variables and their roles in the implementation.

Table 11.6   The Variables Used for Accessing Entries in the Class HashSet

Instance Variable	Purpose
self._foundNode	Refers to the node just located, or is None otherwise.
self._priorNode	Refers to the node prior to the one just located, or is None otherwise.
self._index	Refers to the index of the chain in which the node was just located, or is –1 otherwise.

© 2014 Cengage Learning®

Now you'll discover how __contains__ locates a node's position and sets these variables. Following is the pseudocode for this process:

```
__contains__ (item)
    Set index to the hash code of the item
    Set priorNode to None
    Set foundNode to table[index]
    while foundNode != None
        if foundNode.data == item
            return true
        else
            Set priorNode to foundNode
            Set foundNode to foundNode.next
    return false
```

As you can see, the algorithm uses index, foundNode, and priorNode during the search. If the algorithm hashes to an empty array cell, then no node was found, but index contains the bucket for a subsequent insertion of the first item. If the algorithm hashes to a nonempty array cell, then the algorithm loops down the chain of nodes until it finds a matching item or runs off the chain. In either case, the algorithm leaves foundNode and priorNode set to the appropriate values for a subsequent insertion or removal of the item.

Otherwise, the design of the class HashSet is similar to the design of the classes ArraySet and LinkedSet. To get the maximum mileage from inheritance, the HashSet class is a subclass of the classes AbstractCollection and AbstractSet. The Node class is used to represent an item and a pointer to the next item in a chain.

Following is a partial implementation of the class HashSet:

```
from node import Node
from arrays import Array
from abstractset import AbstractSet

class HashSet(AbstractCollection, AbstractSet):
    """A hashing implementation of a set."""

    DEFAULT_CAPACITY = 3

    def __init__(self, sourceCollection = None,
                 capacity = None):
        if capacity is None:
            self._capacity = HashSet.DEFAULT_CAPACITY
        else:
            self._capacity = capacity
        self._items = Array(self._capacity)
        self._foundNode = self._priorNode = None
        self._index = -1
        AbstractCollection.__init__(self, sourceCollection)

    # Accessor methods
    def __contains__(self, item):
        """Returns True if item is in the set or
        False otherwise."""
        self._index = abs(hash(item)) % len(self._items)
        self._priorNode = None
        self._foundNode = self._items[self._index]
        while self._foundNode != None:
            if self._foundNode.data == item:
                return True
            else:
                self._priorNode = self._foundNode
                self._foundNode = self._foundNode.next
        return False

    def __iter__(self):
        """Supports iteration over a view of self."""
        # Exercise

    def __str__(self):
        """Returns the string representation of self."""
        # Exercise

    # Mutator methods
```

```
def clear(self):
    """Makes self become empty."""
    self._size = 0
    self._array = Array(HashSet.DEFAULT_CAPACITY)

def add(self, item):
    """Adds item to the set if it is not in the set."""
    if not item in self:
        newNode = Node(item,
                          self._items[self._index])
        self._items[self._index] = newNode
        self._size += 1

def remove(self, item):
    """Precondition: item is in self.
    Raises: KeyError if item in not in self.
    Postcondition: item is removed from self."""
    # Exercise
```

HASHING IMPLEMENTATION OF DICTIONARIES

This hashing implementation of a dictionary is called HashDict. It uses a bucket/chaining strategy quite similar to that of the HashSet class. To represent a key/value entry, you use the Item class defined earlier in the other implementations. The data field of each node in a chain now contains an Item object.

The __contains__ method now looks for a key in the underlying structure and updates the pointer variables as in the HashSet implementation.

The method __getitem__ simply calls __contains__ and returns the value contained in foundNode.data if the key was found.

```
__getitem__(key)
    if key in self
        return foundNodedata.value
    else
        raise KeyError
```

The method __setitem__ calls __contains__ to determine whether or not an entry exists at the target key's position. If the entry is found, __setitem__ replaces its value with the new value. Otherwise, __setitem__ performs the following steps:

1. Creates a new item object containing the key and value.

2. Creates a new node whose data is the item and whose next pointer is the node at the head of the chain.

3. Sets the head of the chain to the new node.

4. Increments the size.

Following is the pseudocode for __setitem__:

```
__setitem__(key, value)
    if key in self
        foundNode.data.value = value
    else
        newNode = Node(Item(key, value), items[index])
        items[index] = newNode
        size = size + 1
```

The strategy of the method pop is similar. The major difference is that pop uses the variable priorNode when the entry to be removed comes after the head of the chain. Following is the partially completed code of the class HashDict:

```
"""
File: hashdict.py
Author: Ken Lambert
"""

from abstractdict import AbstractDict, Item
from node import Node
from arrays import Array

class HashDict(AbstractDict):
    """Represents a hash-based dictionary."""

    DEFAULT_CAPACITY = 9

    def __init__(self, sourceDictionary = None):
        """Will copy items to the collection from
        sourceDictionary if it's present."""
        self._array = Array(HashDict.DEFAULT_CAPACITY)
        self._foundNode = self._priorNode = None
        self._index = -1
        AbstractDict.__init__(self, sourceDictionary)

    # Accessors
    def __contains__(self, key):
        """Returns True if key is in self
        or False otherwise."""
        self._index = abs(hash(key)) % len(self._array)
        self._priorNode = None
        self._foundNode = self._array[self._index]
        while self._foundNode != None:
            if self._foundNode.data.key == key:
                return True
            else:
                self._priorNode = self._foundNode
```

```
                    self._foundNode = self._foundNode.next
            return False

    def __iter__(self):
        """Serves up the keys in the dictionary."""
        # Exercise

    def __getitem__(self, key):
        """Precondition: the key is in the dictionary.
        Raises: a KeyError if the key is not in the
        dictionary.
        Returns the value associated with the key."""
        if key in self:
            return self._foundNode.data.value
        else:
            raise KeyError("Missing: " + str(key))

    # Mutators
    def __setitem__(self, key, value):
        """If the key is in the dictionary,
        replaces the old value with the new value.
        Otherwise, adds the key and value to it."""
        if key in self:
            self._foundNode.data.value = value
        else:
            newNode = Node(Item(key, value),
                           self._array[self._index])
            self._array[self._index] = newNode
            self._size += 1

    def pop(self, key):
        """Removes the key and returns the associated value
        if the key in in the dictionary, or returns the
        default value otherwise."""
        if not key in self:
            raise KeyError("Missing: " + str(key))
        elif self._priorNode == None:
            self._array[self._index] = self._foundNode.next
        else:
            self._priorNode.next = self._foundNode.next
        self._size -= 1
        return self._foundNode.data.value
```

Exercises 11.4

You can modify the __setitem__ method to take advantage of the dictionary's knowledge of the current load factor. Suggest a strategy for implementing this change in
__setitem__.

SORTED SETS AND DICTIONARIES

Although the data in sets and dictionaries are not ordered by position, it is possible and often convenient to be able to view them in sorted order. A *sorted set* and a *sorted dictionary* have the behaviors of a set and a dictionary, respectively, but the user can visit their data in sorted order. Each item added to a sorted set must be comparable with its other items, and each key added to a sorted dictionary must be comparable with its other keys. The iterator for each type of collection guarantees its users access to the items or the keys in sorted order. The discussion that follows focuses on sorted sets, but everything also applies to sorted dictionaries.

The requirement that the data be sorted has important consequences for the two implementations discussed in this chapter. A list-based implementation must now maintain a sorted list of the items. This improves the run-time performance of the __contains__ method from linear to logarithmic, because it can do a binary search for a given item. Unfortunately, the hashing implementation must be abandoned altogether, because there is no way to track the sorted order of a set's items.

Earlier in this chapter, you examined a simple array-based implementation of a sorted set. Another common implementation of sorted sets uses a binary search tree. As discussed in Chapter 10, this data structure supports logarithmic searches and insertions when the tree remains balanced. Thus, sorted sets (and sorted dictionaries) that use a tree-based implementation generally provide logarithmic access to data items.

The next code segment shows the use of the LinkedBST class from Chapter 10 in a partially defined sorted set class called TreeSortedSet. Its completion is left as an exercise for you.

```
from linkedbst import LinkedBST
from abstractCollection import AbstractCollection
from abstractset import AbstractSet

class TreeSortedSet(AbstractCollection, AbstractSet):
    """A tree-based implementation of a sorted set."""

    def __init__(self, sourceCollection = None):
        self._items = LinkedBST()
        AbstractCollection.__init__(self, sourceCollection)

    def __contains__(self, item):
        """Returns True if item is in the set or
        False otherwise."""
        return item in self._items

    def add(self, item):
        """Adds item to the set if it is not in the set."""
```

```
        if not item in self:
            self._items.add(item)
            self._size += 1
    # Remaining methods are exercises
```

SUMMARY

- A set is an unordered collection of items. Each item is unique. Items may be added, removed, or tested for membership in the set. A set can be traversed with an iterator.

- A list-based implementation of a set supports linear-time access. A hashing implementation of a set supports constant-time access.

- The items in a sorted set can be visited in sorted order. A tree-based implementation of a sorted set supports logarithmic-time access.

- A dictionary is an unordered collection of entries, where each entry consists of a key and a value. Each key in a dictionary is unique, but its values may be duplicated. Accesses, replacements, insertions, and removals of values are accomplished by providing the associated keys.

- A sorted dictionary imposes an ordering by comparison on its keys.

- Implementations of both types of dictionaries are similar to those of sets.

- Hashing is a technique for locating an item in constant time. This technique uses a hash function to compute the index of an item in an array.

- When using hashing, the position of a new item can collide with the position of an item already in an array. Several techniques exist to resolve collisions. Among these are linear collision processing, quadratic collision processing, and chaining.

- Chaining employs an array of buckets, which are linked structures that contain the items.

- The run-time and memory aspects of hashing methods involve the load factor of the array. When the load factor (logical size/physical size) approaches 1, the likelihood of collisions, and thus of extra processing, increases.

REVIEW QUESTIONS

1. The run-time complexity of the __or__, __and__, and __sub__ methods for array-based sets is

   a. $O(n)$

   b. $O(n \log n)$

   c. $O(n^2)$

2. The intersection of the two sets {A, B, C} and {B, C, D} is

   a. {A, B, C, D}

   b. {B, C}

3. The load factor of an array of 10 positions that contains 3 items is

   a. 3.0

   b. 0.33

   c. 0.67

4. The linear method of resolving collisions

   a. Searches for the next available empty position in the array

   b. Selects a position at random until the position is empty

5. When the load factor is small, a hashing implementation of a set or a dictionary provides

   a. Logarithmic-time access

   b. Constant-time access

6. The best implementation of a sorted set uses a

   a. Hash table

   b. Sorted list

   c. Balanced binary search tree

7. Assume that the function hash generates a large number (positive or negative) based on the content of its argument. The position of this argument in an array of capacity positions can then be determined by the expression

   a. `abs(hash(item)) // capacity`

   b. `abs(hash(item)) % capacity`

8. The worst-case access time of a chaining/hashing implementation of sets or dictionaries is

   a. Constant

   b. logarithmic

   c. Linear

9. A dictionary has

   a. A single method that supports an iterator

   b. Two methods that support iterators: one for the keys and one for the values

10. A method to avoid clustering is

   a. Linear probing

   b. Quadratic probing

Projects

1. Complete the profiler for hash tables begun in the case study.

2. Using a data set and load factor that cause several collisions, run the profiler with three different hashing functions and linear collision processing and compare the results.

3. Add the methods get and remove to the HashTable class developed in the case study.

4. Modify the profiler class to allow the programmer to study the behavior of the HashTable method get. Recall that this method must skip over previously occupied cells when probing for a target item. This profiler should insert a set of data items into the table, remove a specified number of them, and run get with the remaining items. The programmer should be able to view results such as the total number of probes and average number of probes for this process.

5. Complete the hashing implementation of a set and test it with an appropriate tester program.

6. Add methods to the hashing implementation of a set to compute the load factor, adjust the capacity of the array, and rehash the items if the array's load factor becomes greater than .80. The load factor in this case is the number of occupied array cells divided by the array's capacity.

7. Complete the hashing implementations of a dictionary and test it with an appropriate tester program.

8. Modify the ArraySortedSet class of Chapter 6, programming Project 7, so that it supports the set-specific operations discussed in this chapter. Then complete a tree-based implementation of a sorted set by using the tree-based implementation of a sorted bag developed in Chapter 10, programming Project 6. Set both sorted set implementations with an appropriate tester program.

9. Complete a tree-based implementation of a sorted dictionary.

CHAPTER 1 2

GRAPHS

This chapter covers one of the most general and useful collections: the graph. It begins by introducing some terms used to talk about graphs. It then considers two common representations of graphs: the adjacency matrix representation and the adjacency list representation. Next, it discusses some widely used and well-known graph-based algorithms. The algorithms of principal interest deal with graph traversals, minimal spanning trees, topological sorting, and shortest-path problems. Finally, this chapter introduces a class for graphs and concludes with a case study.

GRAPH TERMINOLOGY

Mathematically, a graph is a set V of *vertices* and a set E of *edges*, such that each edge in E connects two of the vertices in V. The term *node* is also used here as a synonym for vertex.

Vertices and edges can be labeled or unlabeled. When the edges are labeled with numbers, the numbers can be viewed as *weights*, and the graph is said to be a *weighted graph*. Figure 12.1 shows examples of unlabeled, labeled, and weighted graphs.

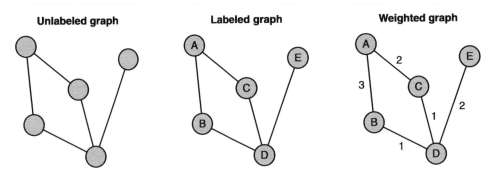

Figure 12.1

Unlabeled, labeled, and weighted graphs.

© 2014 Cengage Learning®

One vertex is *adjacent* to another vertex if there is an edge connecting the two vertices. These two vertices are also called *neighbors*. A *path* is a sequence of edges that allows one vertex to be reached from another vertex in a graph. Thus, a vertex is *reachable* from another vertex if and only if there is a path between the two. The *length of a path* is the number of edges on the path. A graph is *connected* if there is a path from each vertex to every other vertex. A graph is *complete* if there is an edge from each vertex to every other vertex. Figure 12.2 shows graphs that are disconnected, connected but not complete, and complete.

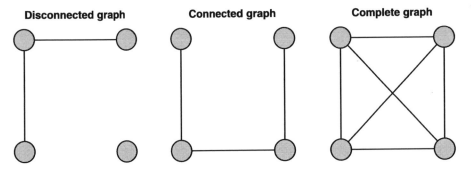

Figure 12.2

Disconnected, connected but not complete, and complete graphs.

© 2014 Cengage Learning®

The *degree of a vertex* is equal to the number of edges connected to it. For example, the degree of each vertex in a complete graph (see Figure 12.2) is equal to the number of vertices minus one.

A *subgraph* of a given graph consists of a subset of that graph's vertices and the edges connecting those vertices. A *connected component* is a subgraph consisting

of the set of vertices that are reachable from a given vertex. Figure 12.3 shows a disconnected graph with vertices A, B, C, D, and E and the connected component that contains the vertex B.

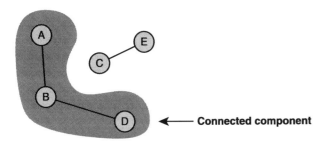

Figure 12.3
A connected component of a graph.
© 2014 Cengage Learning®

A *simple path* is a path that does not pass through the same vertex more than once. By
contrast, a *cycle* is a path that begins and ends at the same vertex. Figure 12.4 shows a
graph with a simple path and a graph with a cycle.

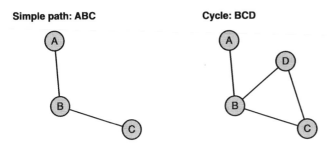

Figure 12.4
A simple path and a cycle.
© 2014 Cengage Learning®

The graphs shown in Figures 12.1 through 12.4 are *undirected,* which means that their
edges indicate no direction. That is, a graph-processing algorithm can move in either
direction along an edge that connects two vertices. There can be at most one edge connecting any two vertices in an undirected graph. By contrast, the edges in a *directed
graph,* or *digraph,* specify an explicit direction, as shown in Figure 12.5.

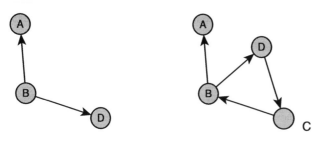

Figure 12.5
Directed graphs (digraphs).
© 2014 Cengage Learning®

Each edge in a digraph is called a *directed edge*. Such an edge has a *source vertex* and a *destination vertex*. When there is only one directed edge connecting two vertices, the vertices are in the relation of predecessor (the source vertex) and successor (the destination vertex). However, the relation of adjacency between them is asymmetric; the source vertex is adjacent to the destination vertex, but the converse is not true. To convert an undirected graph to an equivalent directed graph, you replace each edge in the undirected graph with a pair of edges pointing in opposite directions, as shown in Figure 12.6. The edges emanating from a given source vertex are called its *incident edges*.

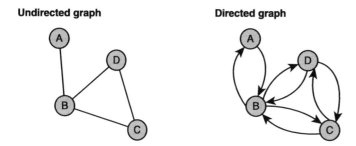

Figure 12.6
Converting an undirected graph to a directed graph.
© 2014 Cengage Learning®

A special case of digraph that contains no cycles is known as a *directed acyclic graph*, or DAG. The second directed graph in the previous figure contains a cycle. In the graph on the right side of Figure 12.7, the direction of one edge (between B and C) is reversed to produce a DAG.

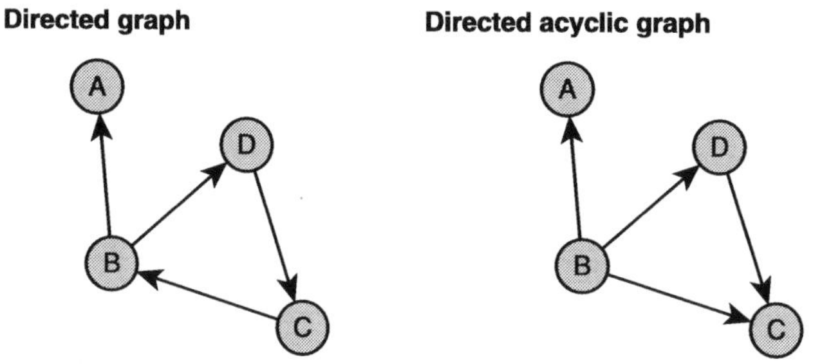

Directed graph

Directed acyclic graph

Figure 12.7

A directed graph and a directed acyclic graph (DAG).

© 2014 Cengage Learning®

Lists and trees are special cases of directed graphs. The nodes in a list are related as predecessors and successors, whereas the nodes in a tree are related as parents and children.

Speaking informally, a connected graph that has relatively many edges is called a *dense graph*, whereas one that has relatively few edges is called a *sparse graph*. There are two limiting cases. The number of edges in a complete directed graph with N vertices is $N * (N - 1)$, and the number of edges in a complete undirected graph is $N * (N - 1) / 2$. Thus, the limiting case of a dense graph has approximately N^2 edges. By contrast, the limiting case of a sparse graph has approximately N edges.

Hereafter, "connected graph" in this context means an undirected graph, unless it's explicitly stated otherwise. Also, when the text refers to "component," it means a connected component in an undirected graph.

Exercises 12.1

1. The course prerequisites for a computer science major at a local college are numbered as follows: 111 is required for 112 and 210; 112 is required for 312, 313, 209, and 211; and 210 is required for 312. Draw a directed graph that represents this numbering structure.

2. How many edges are in a complete, undirected graph with six vertices?

3. A star configuration of a network represents its structure as a graph with an edge from a single, central node to each remaining node. A point-to-point configuration represents a network as a complete graph. Draw a picture of an example of each kind of configuration with four nodes, and use big-O notation to state the efficiency of adding or removing a given node in each type of configuration. You can assume for now that removing each edge is a constant-time operation.

WHY USE GRAPHS?

Graphs serve as models of a wide range of objects. Among them are the following:

- A roadmap
- A map of airline routes
- A layout of an adventure game world
- A schematic of the computers and connections that make up the Internet
- The links between pages on the web
- The relationship between students and courses
- The prerequisite structure of courses in a computer science department
- A diagram of the flow capacities in a communications or transportation network

REPRESENTATIONS OF GRAPHS

To represent graphs, you need a convenient way to store the vertices and the edges that connect them. The two commonly used representations of graphs are the *adjacency matrix* and the *adjacency list.*

Adjacency Matrix

The adjacency matrix representation stores the information about a graph in a matrix or grid, as introduced in Chapter 4, "Arrays and Linked Structures." Recall that a matrix has two dimensions, and each cell is accessed at a given row and column position. Assume that a graph has N vertices labeled 0, 1,..., $N - 1$, and then the following applies:

- The adjacency matrix for the graph is a grid G with N rows and N columns.
- The cell $G[i][j]$ contains 1 if there is an edge from vertex i to vertex j in the graph. Otherwise, there is no edge, and that cell contains 0.

Figure 12.8 shows a directed graph and its adjacency matrix. Each node in the graph is labeled with a letter. Next to each node is its row number in the adjacency matrix.

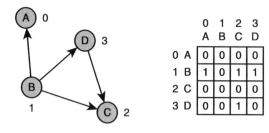

Figure 12.8

A directed graph and its adjacency matrix.

© 2014 Cengage Learning®

The matrix itself is the 4-by-4 grid of cells containing the 1s and 0s in the lower-right corner of the table. The two columns of numbers and letters to the left of the matrix contain the row positions and the labels of the vertices, respectively. The vertices represented in these two columns are considered the source vertices of potential edges. The numbers and letters above the matrix represent the destination vertices of potential edges.

Note that there are four edges in this graph, so only 4 of the 16 matrix cells are occupied by 1: cells (1,0), (1,2), (1,3), and (3,2). This is an example of a sparse graph, which produces a sparse adjacency matrix. If the graph is undirected, then four more cells are occupied by 1 to account for the bidirectional character of each edge (see Figure 12.9).

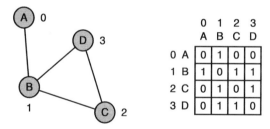

Figure 12.9

An undirected graph and its adjacency matrix.

© 2014 Cengage Learning®

If the edges have weights, the weight values can occupy the matrix cells. The cells that indicate no edges must then have some value that is not within the range of the allowable weights. If the vertices are labeled, the labels can be stored in a separate one-dimensional array (as shown in the second row of Figures 12.8 and 12.9).

Adjacency List

Figure 12.10 shows a directed graph and its adjacency list representation. An adjacency list representation stores the information about a graph in an array of lists. You can use either linked or array-based list implementations. This example uses a linked list implementation. Assume that a graph has N vertices labeled 0, 1,..., $N - 1$, and then the following applies:

■ The adjacency list for the graph is an array of N linked lists.

■ The ith linked list contains a node for vertex j if and only if there is an edge from vertex i to vertex j.

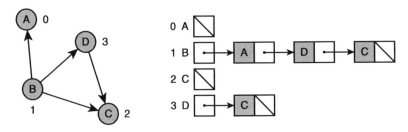

Figure 12.10

A directed graph and its adjacency list.

© 2014 Cengage Learning®

Note that the labels of the vertices are included in the nodes for each edge. Naturally, there would be twice as many nodes in an undirected graph (see Figure 12.11).

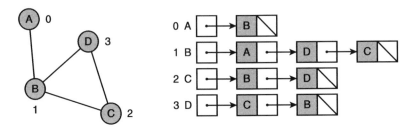

Figure 12.11

An undirected graph and its adjacency list.

© 2014 Cengage Learning®

When the edges have weights, the weights can also be included as a second data field in the nodes, as shown in Figure 12.12.

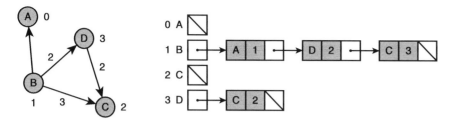

Figure 12.12
A weighted, directed graph and its adjacency list.
© 2014 Cengage Learning®

Analysis of the Two Representations

As far as running time is concerned, the behavior of two commonly used graph operations illustrates the difference in computational efficiency between the adjacency matrix and the adjacency list. These operations are the following:

- Determine whether or not there is an edge between two given vertices.
- Find all the vertices adjacent to a given vertex.

The adjacency matrix supports the first operation in constant time because it requires just an index operation into a two-dimensional array. By contrast, the linked adjacency list requires an index into an array of linked lists and then a search of a linked list for a target vertex. The running time is linear with the length of this list, on the average. The use of an array-based adjacency list can improve this performance to logarithmic time, if the vertices can be sorted in the lists.

The adjacency list tends to support the second operation more efficiently than the adjacency matrix. In the adjacency list, the set of adjacent vertices for a given vertex is simply the list for that vertex, which can be located with one index operation. In contrast, the set of adjacent vertices for a given vertex in the adjacency matrix must be computed by traversing that vertex's row in the matrix and accumulating just those positions that contain 1. The operation must always visit N cells in the adjacency matrix, whereas the operation typically visits much fewer than N nodes in an adjacency list. The limiting case is that of a complete graph. In this case, each cell in the matrix is occupied by 1, each linked list has $N - 1$ nodes, and the performance is a toss-up.

The linked adjacency list and the array-based adjacency list exhibit performance trade-offs for insertions of edges into the lists. The array-based insertion takes linear time, whereas the linked-based insertion requires constant time.

As far as memory usage is concerned, the adjacency matrix always requires N^2 cells, no matter how many edges connect the vertices. Thus, the only case in which no cells are wasted is that of a complete graph. In contrast, the adjacency list requires an array of N pointers and a number of nodes equal to twice the number of edges in the case of an undirected graph. The number of edges typically is much smaller than N^2, although as the number of edges increases, the extra memory required for the pointers in the linked adjacency list becomes a significant factor.

Further Run-Time Considerations

Another commonly performed operation in graph algorithms is to iterate across all the neighbors of a given vertex. Let N = number of vertices and M = number of edges. Then the following applies:

■ Using an adjacency matrix to iterate across all neighbors, you must traverse a row in a time that is $O(N)$. To repeat this for all rows is $O(N^2)$.

■ Using an adjacency list, the time to traverse across all neighbors depends on the number of neighbors. On the average, this time is $O(M/N)$. To repeat this for all vertices is $O(\max(M, N))$, which for a dense graph is $O(N^2)$ and for a sparse graph is $O(N)$. Thus, adjacency lists can provide a run-time advantage when working with sparse graphs.

Exercises 12.2

1. Make a table showing the adjacency matrix for the following directed graph with edge costs.

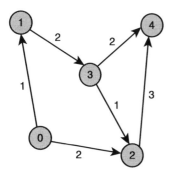

2. Draw a picture showing the adjacency list for the above directed graph with edge costs. You should assume that the edges in a list are ordered from least cost to greatest cost.

3. State one advantage and one disadvantage of the adjacency matrix representation and the adjacency list representation of graphs.

GRAPH TRAVERSALS

As in a tree, you get to a given item in a graph by following a link to it from another item. Often, you need to follow several links, from one item to another, in a path to get to a given item. In addition to the insertion and removal of items, important graph-processing operations include the following:

- Finding the shortest path to a given item in a graph
- Finding all the items to which a given item is connected by paths
- Traversing all the items in a graph

This section examines several types of graph traversals. One starts at a given vertex and, from there, visits all vertices to which it connects. Graph traversals are thus different from tree traversals, which visit all the nodes in a given tree.

A Generic Traversal Algorithm

Graph traversal algorithms start at a given vertex and move outward to explore paths to neighboring vertices. Iterative (nonrecursive) versions of these algorithms schedule vertices to be visited on a separate, temporary collection. As you shall see, the type of collection used for the scheduling influences the order in which vertices are visited. For now, you'll use a generic function that performs a graph traversal that starts at an arbitrary vertex startVertex and uses a generic collection to schedule the vertices. Here is the pseudocode for this function:

```
traverseFromVertex(graph, startVertex, process):
    mark all vertices in the graph as unvisited
    add the startVertex to an empty collection
    while the collection is not empty:
        pop a vertex from the collection
        if the vertex has not been visited:
            mark the vertex as visited
            process(vertex)
            add all adjacent unvisited vertices to the collection
```

In the foregoing function, for a graph that contains N vertices, the following applies:

1. All vertices reachable from startVertex are processed exactly once.

2. Determining all the vertices adjacent to a given vertex is straightforward:

  a. When an adjacency matrix is used, you iterate across the row corresponding to the vertex.

    ■ This is an $O(N)$ operation.

    ■ Repeating this for all rows is $O(N^2)$.

  b. When an adjacency list is used, you traverse the vertex's linked list.

    ■ Performance depends on how many vertices are adjacent to the given vertex.

    ■ Repeating this for all vertices is $O(\max(M, N))$, where M is the number of edges.

Breadth-First and Depth-First Traversals

There are two common orders in which vertices can be visited during a graph traversal. The first, called a *depth-first traversal*, uses a stack as the collection in the generic algorithm. The use of a stack forces the traversal process to go deeply into the graph before backtracking to another path. Put another way, the use of a stack constrains the algorithm to move from a vertex to one of its neighbors, and then to one of this neighbor's neighbors, and so on.

The second kind of traversal, called a *breadth-first traversal*, uses a queue as the collection in the generic algorithm. The use of a queue forces the traversal process to visit every vertex adjacent to a given vertex before it moves deeper into the graph. In this respect, a breadth-first traversal of a graph is similar to a level order traversal of a tree, as discussed in Chapter 10, "Trees."

Figure 12.13 shows a graph and the vertices or nodes visited during these two types of traversals. The start vertex is shaded, and the vertices are numbered in the order in which they are visited during the traversals.

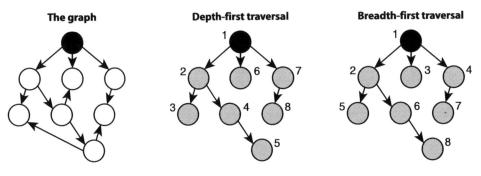

Figure 12.13
Depth-first and breadth-first traversals of a given graph.

You can also implement a depth-first traversal recursively. This fact should not be too surprising; remember the relationship between stacks and recursion established in Chapter 7, "Stacks." Here is a function for recursive depth-first traversal. It uses an auxiliary function called dfs (short for depth-first search). Here is the pseudocode for the two functions:

```
traverseFromVertex(graph, startVertex, process):
    mark all vertices in the graph as unvisited
    dfs(graph, startVertex, process)

dfs(graph, v, process):
    mark v as visited
    process(v)
    for each vertex, w, adjacent to v:
        if w has not been visited:
            dfs(graph, w, process)
```

As just presented, a traversal starting at a vertex v is limited to the vertices reachable from v, which in an undirected graph is the component containing v. If you desire to traverse all the vertices of an undirected graph component by component, these functions can be extended, as is illustrated next. Here is the iterative version:

```
traverseAll(graph, process):
    mark all vertices in the graph as unvisited
    instantiate an empty collection
    for each vertex in the graph:
        if the vertex has not been visited:
            add the vertex to the collection
        while the collection is not empty:
            pop a vertex from the collection
            if the vertex has not been visited:
                mark the vertex as visited
                process(vertex)
                add all adjacent unvisited vertices to the collection
```

And here is the recursive version:

```
traverseAll(graph, process):
    mark all vertices in the graph as unvisited
    for each vertex, v, in the graph:
        if v is unvisited:
            dfs(graph, v, process)

dfs(graph, v, process):
    mark v as visited
    process(v)
```

```
for each vertex, w, adjacent to v:
    if w is unvisited
        dfs(graph, w, process)
```

Performance for the basic traversal algorithm, ignoring the processing of a vertex, is $O(\max(N, M))$ or $O(N^2)$, depending on the representation, as illustrated in the following algorithm. You assume that inserting and deleting from the collection are $O(1)$, which they can be with stacks and queues.

```
traverseFromVertex(graph, startVertex, process):
    mark all vertices in the graph as unvisited          O(N)
    add the startVertex to an empty collection           O(1)
    while the collection is not empty:              loop O(N) times
        pop a vertex from the collection                 O(1)
        if the vertex has not been visited:              O(1)
            mark the vertex as visited                   O(1)
            process(vertex)                              O(?)
            add all adjacent unvisited vertices to the
            collection                                   O(deg(v))
```

Note that the value of the expression $O(\deg(v))$ depends on the graph representation.

Graph Components

You can use the traversal algorithms that have been discussed to partition the vertices of a graph into disjointed components. Here, by way of example, each component is stored in a set, and the sets are stored in a list:

```
partitionIntoComponents(graph):
    components = list()
    mark all vertices in the graph as unvisited
    for each vertex, v, in the graph:
        if v is unvisited:
            s = set()
            components.append(s)
            dfs(graph, v, s)
    return components

dfs(graph, v, s):
    mark v as visited
    s.add(v)
    for each vertex, w, adjacent to v:
        if w is unvisited:
            dfs(graph, w, s)
```

Exercises 12.3

1. Assume that the following graph is traversed in depth-first fashion, beginning with the vertex labeled A. Write a list of the labels in the order in which they might be visited.

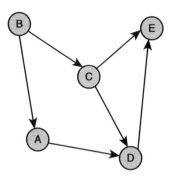

2. Assume that the graph in the preceding exercise is traversed in breadth-first fashion, beginning with the vertex labeled A. Write a list of the labels in the order in which they are visited.

3. Describe, informally without pseudocode, a strategy for performing a breadth-first traversal of a graph.

TREES WITHIN GRAPHS

The function `traverseFromVertex` implicitly yields a tree rooted at the vertex from which the traversal starts and includes all the vertices reached during the traversal. This tree is just a subgraph of the graph being traversed. Consider, for instance, the depth-first search variant of the method. Suppose `dfs` has just been called using vertex `v`. If a recursive call using vertex `w` now occurs, you can consider `w` to be a child of `v`. The edge `(v, w)` corresponds to the parent-child relationship, or edge, between `v` and `w`. The starting vertex is the root of this tree. The tree is called a *depth-first search tree*.

It is also possible to build a breadth-first search tree. Figure 12.13 showed these two kinds of trees within a graph that was traversed from a given vertex.

Spanning Trees and Forests

A *spanning tree* is of interest because it has the fewest number of edges possible while still retaining a connection between all the vertices in the component. If the component contains n vertices, the spanning tree contains $n - 1$ edges. When you traverse all the vertices of an undirected graph, not just those in a single component, you generate a *spanning forest*.

Minimum Spanning Tree

When the edges in a graph are weighted, you can sum the weights for all edges in a spanning tree and attempt to find a spanning tree that minimizes this sum. There are several algorithms for finding a *minimum spanning tree* for a component. Repeated application to all the components in a graph yields a *minimum spanning forest* for a graph. For example, consider the map of air miles between cities. This map is useful to determine how an airline can service all cities, while minimizing the total length of the routes it needs to support. To accomplish this, you could treat the map as a weighted graph and generate its minimum spanning forest.

Algorithms for Minimum Spanning Trees

There are two well-known algorithms for finding a minimum spanning tree: one developed by Robert C. Prim in 1957 and the other by Joseph Kruskal in 1956. Here is Prim's algorithm. Without loss of generality, you assume the graph is connected.

```
minimumSpanningTree(graph):
    mark all vertices and edges as unvisited
    mark some vertex, say v, as visited
    for all the vertices:
        find the least weight edge from a visited vertex to an
        unvisited vertex, say w
        mark the edge and w as visited
```

At the end of this process, the marked edges are the branches in a minimum spanning tree. Here is a proof by contradiction.

Suppose G is a graph for which Prim's algorithm yields a spanning tree that is not minimum.

Number the vertices in the order in which they are added to the spanning tree by Prim's algorithm, giving $v_1, v_2,..., v_n$. In this numbering scheme, v_1 represents the arbitrary vertex at which the algorithm starts.

Number each edge in the spanning tree according to the vertex into which it leads; for instance, e_i leads into vertex i.

Because you are assuming that Prim's algorithm does not yield a minimum spanning tree for G, there is a first edge, call it e_i, such that the set of edges $E_i = \{e_2, e_3,..., e_i\}$ cannot be extended into a minimum spanning tree, whereas the set of edges $E_{i-1} = \{e_2, e_3,..., e_{i-1}\}$ *can* be extended. The set E_{i-1} could even be empty, meaning that Prim's algorithm could go wrong with the first edge added.

Let $V_i = \{v_1, v_2,..., v_{i-1}\}$. This set contains at least v_1.

Let T be any spanning tree that extends E_{i-1}. T does not include e_i.

Adding any more edges to T creates a cycle, so create a cycle by adding edge e_i.

This cycle includes two edges that cross the boundary between V_i and the rest of the vertices in the graph. One of these edges is e_i. Call the other e. Because of the manner in which e_i was chosen, $e_i <= e$.

Remove e from T. Again, you have a spanning tree, and because $e_i <= e$, it too is minimum. But this contradicts the earlier assumption that E_i could not be extended into a minimum spanning tree. So if you have reasoned correctly, the only way to escape this apparent contradiction is to suppose that Prim's algorithm applies to every graph.

Maximum running time is $O(m * n)$. Solution:

Suppose n = number of vertices and m = number of edges, then

step 2. $O(n + m)$ time

step 3. $O(1)$ time

step 4. the loop executes $O(n)$ times

step 5. if this is done in a straightforward manner, then

       look at m edges—$O(m)$ time

       for each edge determine if the end points are visited or unvisited—$O(1)$ time

step 6. $O(1)$ time

       Max Time = $O(n + m + n * m)$

              but $n + m + n * m < 1 + n + m + n * m = (n + 1) * (m + 1)$

              implies $O(m * n)$

You can obtain a better result by modifying the algorithm slightly. Central to the modified algorithm is a heap of edges. Thus, the edge with the smallest weight is on top. Because the graph is connected, $n - 1 <= m$.

```
1    minimumSpanningTree(graph):
2        mark all edges as unvisited
3        mark all vertices as unvisited
4        mark some vertex, say v, as visited
5        for each edge leading from v:
6            add the edge to the heap
7        k = 1
8        while k < number of vertices:
9            pop an edge from the heap
```

```
10              if one end of this edge, say vertex w, is not
                visited:
11                  mark the edge and w as visited
12                  for each edge leading from w:
13                      add the edge to the heap
14                  k += 1
```

The maximum running time is $O(m \log n)$ for the adjacency list representation. Solution:

Suppose n = number of vertices and m = number of edges, then, ignoring lines that are $O(1)$, you get the following:

step 2 — $O(m)$

step 3 — $O(n)$

step 5 — $O(n)$ loops

step 6 — $O(\log m)$

step 5 and 6 — $O(n \log m)$

step 8 — $O(n)$

step 9 — $O(\log m)$ and can happen at most m times; therefore, $O(m \log m)$

step 12 — all executions of this inner loop are bounded by m

step 13 — $O(\log m)$

steps 12 and 13 — $O(m \log m)$

Total

$= O(m + n + \log m + n \log m + m \log m)$

$= O(m \log m)$

$= O(m \log n)$, because $m <= n * n$ and $\log n * n = 2 \log n$

TOPOLOGICAL SORT

A DAG has an order among the vertices. For example, in a graph of courses for an academic major, such as computer science, some courses are prerequisites for others. A natural question to ask in these cases is, to take a given course, in what order should I take all its prerequisites? The answer lies in a *topological order* of vertices in this graph. A topological order assigns a rank to each vertex such that the edges go from lower- to higher-ranked vertices. Figure 12.14 shows a graph of courses P, Q, R, S, and T. Figures 12.15 and 12.16 show two possible topological orderings of the courses in this graph.

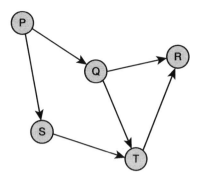

Figure 12.14

A graph of courses.

© 2014 Cengage Learning®

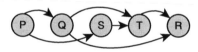

Figure 12.15

The first topological ordering of the graph.

© 2014 Cengage Learning®

Figure 12.16

The second topological ordering of the graph.

© 2014 Cengage Learning®

The process of finding and returning a topological order of vertices in a graph is called a *topological sort*. One topological sort algorithm is based on a graph traversal. You can use either a depth-first traversal or a breadth-first traversal. A depth-first traversal is used here. The vertices are returned in a stack in ascending order (topologically speaking):

```
topologicalSort(graph g):
    stack = LinkedStack()
    mark all vertices in the graph as unvisited
    for each vertex, v, in the graph:
        if v is unvisited:
            dfs(g, v, stack)
    return stack

dfs(graph, v, stack):
    mark v as visited
```

```
    for each vertex, w, adjacent to v:
        if w is unvisited:
            dfs(graph, w, stack)
    stack.push(v)
```

The performance of this algorithm is O(m) when stack insertions are O(1).

THE SHORTEST-PATH PROBLEM

It is often useful to determine the shortest path between two vertices in a graph. Consider an airline map, represented as a weighted directed graph whose weights represent miles between airports. The shortest path between two airports is the path that has the smallest sum of edge weights.

The *single-source shortest path problem* asks for a solution that contains the shortest paths from a given vertex to all the other vertices. This problem has a widely used solution by Dijkstra. His solution is O(n^2) and assumes that all weights must be positive.

Another problem, known as the *all-pairs shortest path problem*, asks for the set of all the shortest paths in a graph. A widely used solution by Floyd is O(n^3).

Dijkstra's Algorithm

You'll now develop Dijkstra's algorithm for computing the single-source shortest path. The inputs to this algorithm are a directed acyclic graph with edge weights greater than 0 and a single vertex that represents the source vertex. The algorithm computes the distances of the shortest paths from the source vertex to all the other vertices in the graph. The output of the algorithm is a two-dimensional grid: results. This grid has N rows, where N is the number of vertices in the graph. The first column in each row contains a vertex. The second column contains the distance from the source vertex to this vertex. The third column contains the immediate parent vertex on this path. (Recall that vertices within a graph can have parent/child relationships when implicit trees are traversed within that graph.)

In addition to this grid, the algorithm uses a temporary list, included, of N Booleans to track whether or not a given vertex has been included in the set of vertices for which you already have determined the shortest path. The algorithm consists of two major steps: an initialization step and a computation step.

The Initialization Step

In this step, you initialize all the columns in the results grid and all the cells in the included list according to the following algorithm:

```
for each vertex in the graph
    Store vertex in the current row of the results grid
```

```
If vertex = source vertex
    Set the row's distance cell to 0
    Set the row's parent cell to undefined
    Set included[row] to True
Else if there is an edge from source vertex to vertex
    Set the row's distance cell to the edge's weight
    Set the row's parent cell to source vertex
    Set included[row] to False
Else
    Set the row's distance cell to infinity
    Set the row's parent cell to undefined
    Set included[row] to False
Go to the next row in the results grid
```

At the end of this process, the following things are true:

- The cells in the `included` list are all `False`, except for the cell that corresponds to the row of the source vertex in the `results` grid.

- The distance in a row's distance cell is either 0 (for the source vertex), infinity (for a vertex without a direct edge from the source), or a positive number (for a vertex without a direct edge from the source). You learn how to represent infinity so that you can use it in arithmetic and comparison operations shortly.

- The vertex in a row's parent cell is either the source vertex or undefined. You represent undefined in the implementation with `None`.

Figure 12.17 shows the state of the two data structures after the initialization step has been run with a given graph.

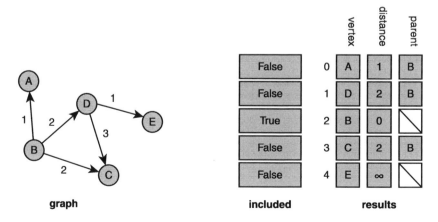

graph   included   results

Figure 12.17

A graph and the initial state of the data structures used to compute the shortest paths from a given vertex.
© 2014 Cengage Learning®

The Computation Step

In the computation step, Dijkstra's algorithm finds the shortest path from the source to a vertex, marks this vertex's cell in the included list, and continues this process until all these cells are marked. Here is the algorithm for this step:

```
Do
    Find the vertex F that is not yet included and has the minimal
    distance in the results grid
    Mark F as included
    For each other vertex T not included
        If there is an edge from F to T
            Set new distance to F's distance + edge's weight
            If new distance < T's distance in the results grid
                Set T's distance to new distance
                Set T's parent in the results grid to F
While at least one vertex is not included
```

As you can see, the algorithm repeatedly selects the vertex with the shortest-path distance that has not yet been included and marks it as included before entering the nested for loop. In the body of this loop, the process runs through any edges from the included vertex to unincluded vertices and determines the smallest possible distance from the source vertex to any of these other vertices. The critical step in this process is the nested if statement, which resets the distance and parent cells for an unincluded vertex if a new minimal distance has been found to the unincluded vertex through the included vertex. Figure 12.18 shows the graph and the state of the data structures after you have run the algorithm.

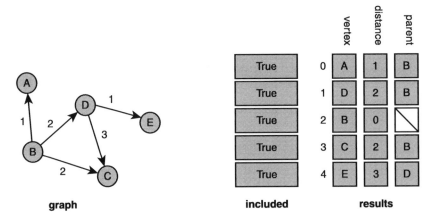

Figure 12.18

A graph and the final state of the data structures used to compute the shortest paths from a given vertex.

Representing and Working with Infinity

Many textbooks represent the value of infinity as a very large integer, or the maximum integer value supported by the language. This strategy is not only inaccurate, but also unnecessary in Python. As long as the operations on numbers are restricted to addition and comparisons, you can represent infinity as a nonnumeric value. In this implementation, you define a constant, INFINITY, to be the string value "-", which prints nicely, and define the arithmetic and comparison operations as specialized functions. For example, here are the definitions of the infinity constant and a function to add two possibly infinite numbers:

```
INFINITY = "-"

def addWithInfinity(a, b):
    """If a == INFINITY or b == INFINITY, returns INFINITY.
    Otherwise, returns a + b."""
    if a == INFINITY or b == INFINITY: return INFINITY
    else: return a + b
```

Note that Python's == and != operators already work correctly for any two operands. The implementation of specialized functions such as isLessWithInfinity and minWithInfinity are left as exercises for you.

Analysis

The initialization step must process every vertex, so it is $O(n)$. The outer loop of the computation step also iterates through every vertex. The inner loop of this step iterates through every vertex not included thus far. Hence, the overall behavior of the computation step resembles that of other $O(n^2)$ algorithms, so Dijkstra's algorithm is $O(n^2)$.

Exercises 12.4

1. Dijkstra's single-source shortest path algorithm returns a results grid that contains the lengths of the shortest paths from a given vertex to the other vertices reachable from it. Develop a pseudocode algorithm that uses the results grid to build and return the actual path, as a list of vertices, from the source vertex to a given vertex. (*Hint*: This algorithm starts with a given vertex in the grid's first column and gathers ancestor vertices, until the source vertex is reached.)

2. Define the functions isLessWithInfinity and minWithInfinity.

Floyd's Algorithm

Floyd's algorithm solves the all-pairs shortest paths problem. That is, for each vertex v in a graph, the algorithm finds the shortest path from vertex v to any other vertex w that is reachable from v. Consider the weighted graph in Figure 12.19.

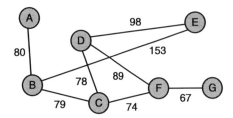

Figure 12.19

A weighted graph.

© 2014 Cengage Learning®

In a preprocessing step, you build an initial *distance matrix* whose cells contain the weights on the edges that connect each vertex to its neighbors. When no edge directly connects two vertices, a value representing infinity is placed in the matrix cell. Figure 12.20 shows the distance matrix for the graph depicted in Figure 12.19.

	0 A	1 B	2 C	3 D	4 E	5 F	6 G
0 A	0	80	∞	∞	∞	∞	∞
1 B	80	0	79	∞	153	∞	∞
2 C	∞	79	0	78	∞	74	∞
3 D	∞	∞	78	0	98	89	∞
4 E	∞	153	∞	98	0	∞	∞
5 F	∞	∞	74	89	∞	0	67
6 G	∞	∞	∞	∞	∞	67	0

Figure 12.20

The initial distance matrix for the graph in Figure 12.19.

© 2014 Cengage Learning®

Floyd's algorithm then traverses this matrix, replacing the value in each cell with the minimum-distance path that connects the two associated vertices, if a path exists. If no path exists, the value of the cell remains at infinity. Figure 12.21 shows the modified distance matrix that results from a run of Floyd's algorithm. As you can see, some of the infinite values have been replaced by the weights of minimum-distance paths.

	0 A	1 B	2 C	3 D	4 E	5 F	6 G
0 A	0	80	159	237	233	233	300
1 B	80	0	79	157	153	153	220
2 C	159	79	0	78	176	74	141
3 D	237	157	78	0	98	89	156
4 E	233	153	176	98	0	187	254
5 F	233	153	74	89	187	0	67
6 G	300	220	141	156	254	67	0

Figure 12.21

The modified distance matrix for the graph in Figure 12.19.

© 2014 Cengage Learning®

Here is the pseudocode for Floyd's algorithm:

```
for i from 0 to n - 1
    for r from 0 to n - 1
        for c from 0 to n - 1
            matrix[r][c] = min(matrix[r][c],
                               matrix[r][i] + matrix[i][c])
```

Note that the `min` and `+` operations must be capable of working with operands that might be infinite. The previous section discussed a strategy for implementing this.

Analysis

The initialization step to create the distance matrix from the graph is $O(n^2)$. This matrix is actually the same as an adjacency matrix representation of the given graph. Because Floyd's algorithm includes three nested loops over N vertices, the algorithm itself is obviously $O(n^3)$. Thus, the overall running time of the process is bounded by $O(n^3)$.

DEVELOPING A GRAPH COLLECTION

To develop a graph collection, you need to consider various factors:

- The requirements of users
- The mathematical nature of graphs
- The commonly used representations, adjacency matrix, and adjacency list

All graphs, whether they are directed, undirected, weighted, or unweighted, are collections of vertices connected by edges. A quite general graph allows the labels of vertices and edges to be any kind of object, although they typically are strings or numbers. Users should be able to insert and remove vertices, insert or remove an edge, and retrieve all the vertices and edges. It is also useful to obtain the neighboring vertices and the incident edges of a given vertex in a graph and to set and clear marks on the vertices and edges. Finally, users should be able to choose, as their needs dictate, between directed and undirected graphs and between an adjacency matrix representation and an adjacency list representation.

The graph collection developed in this section creates weighted directed graphs with an adjacency list representation. In the examples, the vertices are labeled with strings and the edges are weighted with numbers. The implementation of the graph collection shown here consists of the classes LinkedDirectedGraph, LinkedVertex, and LinkedEdge.

Example Use of the Graph Collection

Assume that you want to create the weighted directed graph in Figure 12.22.

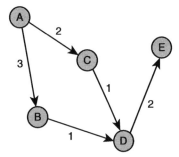

Figure 12.22
A weighted directed graph.
© 2014 Cengage Learning®

The following code segment does this and displays the graph's string representation in the terminal window:

```
from graph import LinkedDirectedGraph

g = LinkedDirectedGraph()

# Insert vertices
g.addVertex("A")
g.addVertex("B")
g.addVertex("C")
g.addVertex("D")
g.addVertex("E")

# Insert weighted edges
g.addEdge("A", "B", 3)
g.addEdge("A", "C", 2)
g.addEdge("B", "D", 1)
```

```
g.addEdge("C", "D", 1)
g.addEdge("D", "E", 2)

print(g)
```

Output:

```
5 Vertices:   A C B E D
5 Edges:    A>B:3 A>C:2 B>D:1 C>D:1 D>E:2
```

The next code segment displays the neighboring vertices and the incident edges of the vertex labeled A in this example graph:

```
print("Neighboring vertices of A:")
for vertex in g.neighboringVertices("A"):
    print(vertex)

print("Incident edges of A:")
for edge in g.incidentEdges("A"):
    print(edge)
```

Output:

```
Neighboring vertices of   A:
B
C
Incident edges of A:
A >:3
A >:2
```

The next subsections present the interfaces and partial implementations for each of the classes in this version of the graph ADT. The completed implementation is left as an exercise for you.

The Class LinkedDirectedGraph

Graphs are rather unlike the collections you have seen thus far in this book, in that they have vertices and edges in quite definite arrangements. For example, although it makes sense to say that a graph can be empty (no vertices), a graph does not have a single length attribute, but has instead a number of vertices and a number of edges. Should the iterator on a graph then visit its vertices, or its edges? It makes sense to compare two graphs for equality and to clone a graph, but what is the result of combining two graphs into a third graph, or of creating a new graph with the contents of another collection?

You'll examine the consequences of taking the following paths of least resistance in the graph implementation:

- You make a graph class a subclass of AbstractCollection.
- You make a graph's size equal to its number of vertices.

- The add method adds a vertex with the given label to a graph.

- You allow a graph's iterator to visit its vertices.

Then the following consequences ensue:

- The len function returns the number of the graph's vertices.

- The graph constructor's source collection contains the labels of the new graph's vertices.

- The for loop visits the graph's vertices.

- The in operator returns True if the graph contains a given vertex.

- The = operator compares vertices in the two graph operands.

- The + operator creates a new graph that contains the vertices of its two operands.

The first three consequences seem unproblematic, but the last three may require some refinement in the implementation. For now, you'll proceed as before and incorporate the graph collections into the collection hierarchy. As other types of graphs, such as undirected graphs or graphs that use an adjacency matrix, are added to your framework, you may also want to refactor some generic code into an AbstractGraph class.

Table 12.1 lists the methods in the class LinkedDirectedGraph. Note that the methods are categorized by their relationships to edges, vertices, and other roles. You have not included preconditions on the methods, but clearly some are called for. For example, the methods addVertex and addEdge should not allow the user to insert a vertex or an edge that is already in the graph. The development of a complete set of preconditions is left as an exercise for you.

Table 12.1   The Methods in the Class LinkedDirectedGraph

LinkedDirectedGraph Method	What It Does
g = LinkedDirectedGraph(sourceCollection = None)	Creates a new directed graph using an adjacency list representation. Accepts an optional collection of labels as an argument and adds vertices with these labels.
Clearing Marks, Sizes, String Representation	
g.clear()	Removes all the vertices from the graph.
g.clearEdgeMarks()	Clears all edge marks.
g.clearVertexMarks()	Clears all vertex marks.

`g.isEmpty()`	Returns `True` if the graph contains no vertices, or `False` otherwise.
`g.sizeEdges()`	Returns the number of edges in the graph.
`g.sizeVertices()`	Same as `len(g)`. Returns the number of vertices in the graph.
`g.__str__()`	Same as `str(g)`. Returns the string representation of the graph.

Vertex-Related Methods

`g.containsVertex(label)`	Returns `True` if the graph contains a vertex with the specified label, or `False` otherwise.
`g.addVertex(label)`	Same as `add(label)`. Adds a vertex with the specified label.
`g.getVertex(label)`	Returns the vertex with the specified label, or `None` if there is no such vertex.
`g.removeVertex(label)`	Removes the vertex with the specified label and returns the vertex, or returns `None` if there is no such vertex.

Edge-Related Methods

`g.containsEdge(fromLabel, toLabel)`	Returns `True` if the graph contains an edge from a vertex with `fromLabel` to a vertex with `toLabel`, or `False` otherwise.
`g.addEdge(fromLabel, toLabel, weight = None)`	Adds an edge with the specified weight between the specified vertices.
`g.getEdge(fromLabel, toLabel)`	Returns the edge connecting vertices with the specified labels, or returns `None` if there is no such edge.
`g.removeEdge(fromLabel, toLabel)`	Removes the edge connecting vertices with the specified labels and returns `True`, or returns `False` if there is no such edge.

Iterators

`g.edges()`	Returns an iterator over the edges in the graph.
`g.vertices()`	Same as `iter(g)` or `for vertex in g:`. Returns an iterator over the vertices in the graph.
`g.incidentEdges(label)`	Returns an iterator over the incident edges of the vertex with `label`.
`g.neighboringVertices(label)`	Returns an iterator over the neighboring vertices of the vertex with `label`.

The implementation of LinkedDirectedGraph maintains a dictionary whose keys are labels and whose values are the corresponding vertices. Here is the code for the class header and constructor:

```
class LinkedDirectedGraph(AbstractCollection):
    def __init__(self, sourceCollection = None):
        """Adds a vertex with the given label to the graph."""
        self._edgeCount = 0
        self._vertices = dict()      # Dictionary of vertices
        AbstractCollection.__init__(self, sourceCollection)
```

Adding, accessing, and testing for the presence of a vertex all use direct operations on the dictionary. For example, here is the code for the method addVertex:

```
def addVertex(self, label):
    self._vertices[label] = LinkedVertex(label)
    self._size += 1
```

Removing a vertex, however, also entails removing any edges connecting it to other vertices. The method removeVertex visits each remaining vertex in the graph to cut any connections to the deleted vertex. It does this by calling the LinkedVertex method removeEdgeTo, as follows:

```
def removeVertex(self,  label):
    """Returns True if the vertex was removed, or False otherwise."""
    removedVertex = self._vertices.pop(label, None)
    if removedVertex is None:
        return False

    # Examine all other vertices to remove edges
    # directed at the removed vertex
    for vertex in self.vertices():
        if vertex.removeEdgeTo(removedVertex):
            self._edgeCount -= 1
    # Examine all edges from the removed vertex to others
    for edge in removedVertex.incidentEdges():
        self._edgeCount -= 1

    self._size -= 1
    return True
```

The methods related to edges first get the vertices corresponding to the labels and then use corresponding methods in the LinkedEdge class to complete the operations. Here is the code for adding, accessing, and removing an edge:

```
def addEdge(self, fromLabel, toLabel, weight):
    """Connects the vertices with an edge with the given weight."""
```

```
    fromVertex = self.getVertex(fromLabel)
    toVertex   = self.getVertex(toLabel)
    fromVertex.addEdgeTo(toVertex, weight)
    self._edgeCount += 1

def getEdge(self, fromLabel, toLabel):
    """Returns the edge connecting the two vertices, or None if
    no edge exists."""
    fromVertex = self.getVertex(fromLabel)
    toVertex   = self.getVertex(toLabel)
    return fromVertex.getEdgeTo(toVertex)

def removeEdge(self, fromLabel, toLabel):
    """Returns True if the edge was removed, or False otherwise."""
    fromVertex = self.getVertex(fromLabel)
    toVertex   = self.getVertex(toLabel)
    edgeRemovedFlg = fromVertex.removeEdgeTo(toVertex)
    if edgeRemovedFlg:
        self._edgeCount -= 1
    return edgeRemovedFlg
```

The graph's iterators access or build the appropriate internal collections and return iterators on these. The method vertices, which returns an iterator on the dictionary's values, is the simplest. The methods incidentEdges and neighboringVertices each call a corresponding method in the LinkedVertex class. The method edges, however, requires that you build a collection of the set of all the incident edges from the set of all their vertices. This result is essentially the union of all the sets of incident edges, which is expressed in the following method definition:

```
def edges(self):
    """Supports iteration over the edges in the graph."""
    result = set()
    for vertex in self.vertices():
        edges = vertex.incidentEdges()
        result = result.union(set(edges))
    return iter(result)
```

The Class LinkedVertex

Table 12.2 lists the methods in the class LinkedVertex.

Table 12.2   The Methods in the Class LinkedVertex

LinkedVertex Method	What It Does
v = LinkedVertex(label)	Creates a vertex with the specified label. The vertex is initially unmarked.
v.clearMark()	Unmarks the vertex.
v.setMark()	Marks the vertex.
v.isMarked()	Returns True if the vertex is marked, or False otherwise.
v.getLabel()	Returns the label of the vertex.
v.setLabel(label, g)	Changes the label of the vertex in graph g to label.
v.addEdgeTo(toVertex, weight)	Adds an edge with the given weight from v to toVertex.
v.getEdgeTo(toVertex)	Returns the edge from v to toVertex, or returns None if the edge does not exist.
v.incidentEdges()	Returns an iterator over the incident edges of the vertex.
v.neighboringVertices()	Returns an iterator over the neighboring vertices of the vertex.
v.__str__()	Same as str(v). Returns a string representation of the vertex.
v.__eq__(anyObject)	Same as v == anyObject. Returns True if anyObject is a vertex and the two labels are the same.

The adjacency list implementation is expressed as a list of edges belonging to each vertex. The next code segment shows the constructor and the method setLabel. Note that setLabel includes the graph as an argument. Resetting a vertex label is tricky, because you actually just want to change the key of this vertex in the graph's dictionary without disturbing the other objects, such as incident edges, that might be related to this vertex. So you first pop the vertex from the dictionary, reinsert that same vertex object with the new label as its key into the dictionary, and then reset this vertex's label to the new label. Here is the code:

```
class LinkedVertex(object):

    def __init__(self, label):
        self._label = label
```

```
    self._edgeList = list()
    self._mark = False

def setLabel(self, label, g):
    """Sets the vertex's label to label."""
    g._vertices.pop(self._label, None)
    g._vertices[label] = self
    self._label = label
```

The LinkedVertex class defines several other methods used by LinkedGraph to access the edges of a vertex. Adding and accessing an edge involve direct calls to the corresponding list methods, as does the iterator method incidentEdges. The method getNeighboringVertices builds a list of the other vertices from the list of edges, using the LinkedEdge method getOtherVertex. The method removeEdgeTo creates a dummy edge with the current vertex and the argument vertex and removes the corresponding edge from the list if it is in the list. Here is the code for two of these methods:

```
def neighboringVertices(self):
    """Returns the neighboring vertices of this vertex."""
    vertices = list()
    for edge in self._edgeList:
        vertices.append(edge.getOtherVertex(self))
    return iter(vertices)
```

```
def removeEdgeTo(self, toVertex):
    """Returns True if the edge exists and is removed,
    or False otherwise."""
    edge = LinkedEdge(self, toVertex)
    if edge in self._edgeList:
        self._edgeList.remove(edge)
        return True
    else:
        return False
```

The Class LinkedEdge

Table 12.3 lists the methods in the class LinkedEdge.

Table 12.3 The Methods in the Class LinkedEdge

LinkedEdge Method	What It Does
e = LinkedEdge(fromVertex, toVertex, weight = None)	Creates an edge with the specified vertices and weight. It is initially unmarked.
e.clearMark()	Unmarks the edge.
e.setMark()	Marks the edge.
e.isMarked()	Returns True if the edge is marked, or False otherwise.
e.getWeight()	Returns the weight of the edge.
e.setWeight(weight)	Sets the edge's weight to the specified weight.
e.getOtherVertex(vertex)	Returns the edge's other vertex.
e.getToVertex()	Returns the edge's destination vertex.
e.__str__()	Same as str(e). Returns the string representation of the edge.
e.__eq__(anyObject)	Same as e == anyObject. Returns True if anyObject is an edge and the two edges are connected to the same vertices and have the same weight.

An edge maintains references to its two vertices, its weight, and a mark. Although the weight can be any object labeling the edge, the weight is often a number or some other comparable value. Two edges are considered equal if they have the same vertices and weight. Here is the code for the constructor and the __eq__ method:

```
class LinkedEdge(object):

    def __init__(self, fromVertex, toVertex,
                 weight = None):
        self._vertex1 = fromVertex
        self._vertex2 = toVertex
        self._weight = weight
        self._mark = False

    def __eq__(self, other):
        """Two edges are equal if they connect
        the same vertices."""
        if self is other: return True
```

```
    if type(self) != type(other): return False
    return self._vertex1 == other._vertex1 and \
           self._vertex2 == other._vertex2 and \
           self._weight == other._weight
```

CASE STUDY: TESTING GRAPH ALGORITHMS

Although this graph ADT is easy to use, building a complex graph for real applications can be complicated and tedious. This case study develops a data model and user interface that allow the programmer to create graphs and use them to test graph algorithms.

Request

Write a program that allows the user to test some graph-processing algorithms.

Analysis

The program allows the user to enter a description of the graph's vertices and edges. The program also allows the user to enter the label of a starting vertex for certain tests. Menu options make it easy for the user to perform several tasks, including running the following graph algorithms:

- Find the minimum spanning tree from the start vertex.

- Determine the single-source shortest paths.

- Perform a topological sort.

When the user selects the option to build a graph, the program attempts to build a graph with some inputs. These inputs can come from the keyboard or from a text file. If the inputs generate a valid graph, the program notifies the user. Otherwise, the program displays an error message. The other options display the graph or run algorithms on the graph and display the results. Following is a short session with the program:

```
Main Menu
    1   Input a graph from the keyboard
    2   Input a graph from a file
    3   View the current graph
    4   Single-source shortest paths
    5   Topological sort
    6   Minimum spanning tree
    7   Exit the program

Enter a number [1-7]: 1
Enter an edge or return to quit: p>s:0
```

```
Enter an edge or return to quit: p>q:0
Enter an edge or return to quit: s>t:0
Enter an edge or return to quit: q>t:0
Enter an edge or return to quit: q>r:0
Enter an edge or return to quit: t>r:0
Enter an edge or return to quit:
Enter the start label: p
Graph created successfully
Main Menu
    1   Input a graph from the keyboard
    2   Input a graph from a file
    3   View the current graph
    4   Single-source shortest paths
    5   Topological sort
    6   Minimum spanning tree
    7   Exit the program
Enter a number [1-7]: 6
Sort: r t q s p
```

The string "p>q:0" means that there is an edge with weight 0 from vertex p to vertex q. The string for a disconnected vertex is simply the vertex label.

The program consists of two main classes: GraphDemoView and GraphDemoModel. As usual, the view class handles interaction with the user. The model class builds the graph and runs the graph algorithms on it. These algorithms are defined as functions in a separate module named algorithms. Portions of these classes are developed, but their completion is left as an exercise for you.

The Classes GraphDemoView and GraphDemoModel

The setup of the command menu resembles command menus in previous case studies. When the user selects one of the two commands to input a graph, the method create-Graph is run on the model with the text from the input source. This method returns a string that indicates either a legitimate graph or a poorly formed graph.

When the user selects a command to run a graph algorithm, the appropriate graph-processing function is passed to the model to be executed. If the model returns None, the model did not have a graph available for processing. Otherwise, the model performs the given task and returns a data structure of results for display. Table 12.4 presents the methods that the model provides to the view.

Table 12.4   The Methods in the GraphDemoModel Class

GraphDemoModel Method	What It Does
createGraph(rep, startLabel)	Attempts to create a graph with string representation rep and the starting label startLabel. Returns a string indicating either success or failure.
getGraph()	If the graph is not available, returns None; otherwise, returns a string representation of the graph.
run(aGraphFunction)	If the graph is not available, returns None; otherwise, runs aGraphFunction on the graph and returns its results.

© 2014 Cengage Learning®

The three graph-processing functions are defined in the algorithms module and are listed in Table 12.5.

Table 12.5   The Graph-Processing Functions in the algorithms Module

Graph-Processing Function	What It Does
spanTree(graph, startVertex)	Returns a list containing the edges in the minimum spanning tree of the graph.
topoSort(graph, startVertex)	Returns a stack of vertices representing a topological order of vertices in the graph.
shortestPaths(graph, startVertex)	Returns a two-dimensional grid of N rows and three columns, where N is the number of vertices. The first column contains the vertices. The second column contains the distance from the start vertex to this vertex. The third column contains the immediate parent vertex of this vertex, if there is one, or None otherwise.

© 2014 Cengage Learning®

Implementation (Coding)

The view class includes methods for displaying the menu and getting a command that are similar to methods in other case studies. The other two methods get the inputs from the keyboard or a file. Here is the code for a partial implementation:

```python
"""
File: view.py
The view for testing graph-processing algorithms.
"""

from model import GraphDemoModel

from algorithms import shortestPaths, spanTree, topoSort

class GraphDemoView(object):
    """The view class for the application."""

    def __init__(self):
        self._model = GraphDemoModel()

    def run(self):
        """Menu-driven command loop for the app."""
        menu = "Main menu\n" + \
               "  1  Input a graph from the keyboard\n" + \
               "  2  Input a graph from a file\n" + \
               "  3  View the current graph\n" \
               "  4  Single-source shortest paths\n" \
               "  5  Minimum spanning tree\n" \
               "  6  Topological sort\n" \
               "  7  Exit the program\n"
        while True:
            command = self._getCommand(7, menu)
            if    command == 1: self._getFromKeyboard()
            elif command == 2: self._getFromFile()
            elif command == 3:
                print(self._model.getGraph())
            elif command == 4:
                print("Paths:\n",
                      self._model.run(shortestPaths))
            elif command == 5:
                print("Tree:",
                      " ".join(map(str,
                                   self._model.run(spanTree))))
            elif command == 6:
                print("Sort:",
                      " ".join(map(str,
                                   self._model.run(topoSort))))
            else: break

    def _getCommand(self, high, menu):
        """Obtains and returns a command number."""
        # Same as in earlier case studies
```

```
    def _getFromKeyboard(self):
        """Inputs a description of the graph from the
        keyboard and creates the graph."""
        rep = ""
        while True:
            edge = input("Enter an edge or return to quit: ")
            if edge == "": break
            rep += edge + " "
        startLabel = input("Enter the start label: ")
        print(self._model.createGraph(rep, startLabel))

    def _getFromFile(self):
        """Inputs a description of the graph from a file
        and creates the graph."""
        # Exercise

# Start up the application

GraphDemoView().run()
```

The model class includes methods to create a graph and run a graph-processing algorithm. Here is the code:

```
"""
File: model.py
The model for testing graph-processing algorithms.
"""

from graph import LinkedDirectedGraph

class GraphDemoModel(object):
    """The model class for the application."""

    def __init__(self):
        self._graph = None
        self._startLabel = None

    def createGraph(self, rep, startLabel):
        """Creates a graph from rep and startLabel.
        Returns a message if the graph was successfully
        created or an error message otherwise."""
        self._graph = LinkedDirectedGraph()
        self._startLabel = startLabel
        edgeList = rep.split()
        for edge in edgeList:
            if not '>' in edge:
                # A disconnected vertex
                if not self._graph.containsVertex(edge):
```

```
                    self._graph.addVertex(edge)
                else:
                    self._graph = None
                    return "Duplicate vertex"
            else:
                # Two vertices and an edge
                bracketPos = edge.find('>')
                colonPos = edge.find(':')
                if bracketPos == -1 or colonPos == -1 or \
                    bracketPos > colonPos:
                    self._graph = None
                    return "Problem with > or :"
                fromLabel = edge[:bracketPos]
                toLabel = edge[bracketPos + 1:colonPos]
                weight = edge[colonPos + 1:]
                if weight.isdigit():
                    weight = int(weight)
                if not self._graph.containsVertex(fromLabel):
                    self._graph.addVertex(fromLabel)
                if not self._graph.containsVertex(toLabel):
                    self._graph.addVertex(toLabel)
                if self._graph.containsEdge(fromLabel,
                                                  toLabel):
                    self._graph = None
                    return "Duplicate edge"
                self._graph.addEdge(fromLabel, toLabel,
                                        weight)
        vertex = self._graph.getVertex(startLabel)
        if vertex is None:
            self._graph = None
            return "Start label not in graph"
        else:
            vertex.setMark()
            return "Graph created successfully"

def getGraph(self):
    """Returns the string rep of the graph or None if
    it is unavailable"""
    if not self._graph:
        return None
    else:
        return str(self._graph)

def run(self, algorithm):
    """Runs the given algorithm on the graph and
    returns its result, or None if the graph is
```

```
        unavailable."""
        if self._graph is None:
            return None
        else:
            return algorithm(self._graph, self._startLabel)
```

The functions defined in the `algorithms` module must accept two arguments: a graph and a start label. When the start label is not used, it can be defined as an optional argument. The following code completes the topological sort and leaves the other two functions as exercises for you:

```
"""
File: algorithms.py
Graph-processing algorithms
"""

from linkedstack import LinkedStack

def topoSort(g, startLabel = None):
    stack = LinkedStack()
    g.clearVertexMarks()
    for v in g.vertices():
        if not v.isMarked():
            dfs(g, v, stack)
    return stack

def dfs(g, v, stack):
    v.setMark()
    for w in g.neighboringVertices(v.getLabel()):
        if not w.isMarked():
            dfs(g, w, stack)
    stack.push(v)


def spanTree(g, startLabel):
    # Exercise

def shortestPaths(g, startLabel):
    # Exercise
```

SUMMARY

- Graphs have many applications. They are often used to represent networks of items that can be connected by various paths.

- A graph consists of one or more vertices (items) connected by one or more edges. One vertex is adjacent to another vertex if there is an edge connecting the two vertices. These two vertices are also called neighbors. A path is a sequence of edges that allows one vertex to be reached from another vertex in the graph. A vertex is reachable from another vertex if and only if there is a path between the two. The length of a path is the number of edges in the path. A graph is connected if there is a path from each vertex to every other vertex. A graph is complete if there is an edge from each vertex to every other vertex.

▪ A subgraph consists of a subset of a graph's vertices and a subset of its edges. A connected component is a subgraph consisting of the set of vertices that are reachable from a given vertex.

▪ Directed graphs allow travel along an edge in just one direction, whereas undirected graphs allow two-way travel. Edges can be labeled with weights, which indicate the cost of traveling along them.

▪ Graphs have two common implementations. An adjacency matrix implementation of a graph with N vertices uses a two-dimensional grid G with N rows and N columns. The cell $G[i][j]$ contains 1 if there is an edge from vertex i to vertex j in the graph. Otherwise, there is no edge, and that cell contains 0. This implementation wastes memory if not all the vertices are connected.

▪ An adjacency list implementation of a graph with N vertices uses an array of N linked lists. The ith linked list contains a node for vertex j if and only if there is an edge from vertex i to vertex j.

▪ Graph traversals explore tree-like structures within a graph, starting with a distinguished start vertex. A depth-first traversal visits all the descendants on a given path first, whereas a breadth-first traversal visits all the children of each vertex first.

▪ A spanning tree has the fewest number of edges possible and still retains a connection between all the vertices in a graph. A minimum spanning tree is a spanning tree whose edges contain the minimum weights possible.

▪ A topological sort generates a sequence of vertices in a directed acyclic graph.

▪ The single-source shortest path problem asks for a solution that contains the shortest paths from a given vertex to all the other vertices.

REVIEW QUESTIONS

1. A graph is an appropriate collection to use to represent a

   a. File directory structure

   b. Map of airline flights between cities

2. Unlike a tree, a graph

    a. Is an unordered collection

    b. Can contain nodes with more than one predecessor

3. In a connected undirected graph, each vertex has

    a. An edge to every other vertex

    b. A path to every other vertex

4. The indexes I and J in an adjacency matrix representation of a graph locate

    a. A vertex with an edge I connecting to a vertex J

    b. An edge between vertices I and J

5. In a complete, undirected graph with N vertices, there are approximately

    a. N^2 edges

    b. N edges

6. A depth-first search of a directed acyclic graph

    a. Visits the children of each node on a given path before advancing farther along that path

    b. Advances as far as possible on a path from a given node before traveling on the next path from a given node

7. The memory in an adjacency matrix implementation of a graph is fully utilized by a

    a. Complete graph

    b. Directed graph

    c. Undirected graph

8. Determining whether or not there is an edge between two vertices in an adjacency matrix representation of a graph requires

    a. Logarithmic time

    b. Constant time

    c. Linear time

    d. Quadratic time

9. Determining whether or not there is an edge between two vertices in an adjacency list representation of a graph requires

    a. Logarithmic time

    b. Constant time

    c. Linear time

    d. Quadratic time

10. The shortest path between two vertices in a weighted directed graph is the path with the

    a. Fewest edges

    b. Smallest sum of the weights on the edges

PROJECTS

1. Complete the adjacency list implementation of the directed graph collection, including the specification and enforcement of preconditions on any methods that should have them.

2. Complete the classes in the case study and test the operations to input a graph and display it.

3. Complete the function spanTree in the case study and test it thoroughly.

4. Complete the function shortestPaths in the case study and test it thoroughly.

5. Define a function breadthFirst, which performs a breadth-first traversal on a graph, given a start vertex. This function should return a list of the labels of the vertices in the order in which they are visited. Test the function thoroughly with the case study program.

6. Define a function hasPath, which expects a directed graph and the labels of two vertices as arguments. This function returns True if there is a path between the two vertices, or returns False otherwise. Test this function thoroughly with the case study program.

7. Add the method makeLabelTable to the LinkedDirectedGraph class. This method builds and returns a dictionary whose keys are the labels of the vertices and whose values are consecutive integers, starting with 0. Include a tester program to build and view a table.

8. Add the method makeDistanceMatrix to the LinkedDirectedGraph class. This method calls the makeLabelTable method (see Project 7) to build a table and then uses the table to build and return a distance matrix. You should define INFINITY as

a class variable with the value "-". Include a tester program to build and view a matrix, along with a function that prints a distance matrix with the rows and columns labeled as in Figure 12.20.

9. Define and test a function named allPairsShortestPaths. This function expects a distance matrix for a graph as an argument. The function uses Floyd's algorithm to modify this matrix to contain the shortest paths between any vertices that are connected by paths. Include a tester program to view the matrix before and after running the function. Test the function with the graph shown in Figure 12.19.

10. The default in, ==, and + operations are based on a collection's iterator. In the case of graphs, the iterator visits the vertices, so these operations need further refinement. The in operator should return True if its left operand is a label of a vertex in the graph, or False otherwise. The == operator should return True if the two graph operands are identical, or they contain the same number of vertices and those vertices have the same labels and are connected by edges in the same manner (including the weights on the edges). The + operator should create and build a new graph with the contents of the two operands, such that each operand produces a separate component in the new graph. Add these methods to the LinkedDirected-Graph class, as well as a clone method, which returns an exact copy of the original graph.

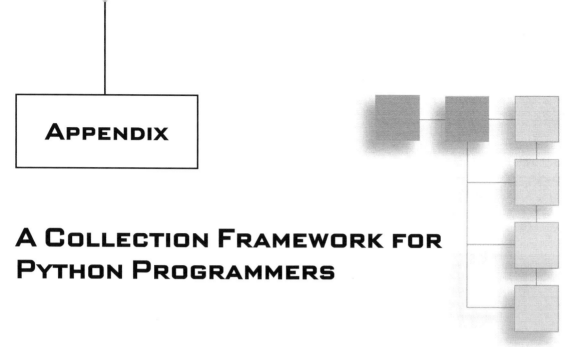

APPENDIX

A COLLECTION FRAMEWORK FOR PYTHON PROGRAMMERS

The diagram in Figure A.1 shows the hierarchy of collection classes discussed in this book. The types of collections include bags, binary search trees, dictionaries, heaps, lists, queues, sets, stacks, and various types of sorted collections, such as sorted bags, sorted dictionaries, sorted lists, sorted sets, and priority queues. The different implementations of each collection type are shown, as well as the abstract classes used to organize the code. Other supporting classes, such as `Array`, `Grid`, `Node`, `TwoWayNode`, `BSTNode`, `AbstractSet` and the list iterator classes are not shown but are discussed in the text. Although Python does not support an explicit interface construct, the code provided on the publisher's companion website for this book (www.cengageptr.com/downloads) includes pseudo-interfaces for all the collection types discussed in the text.

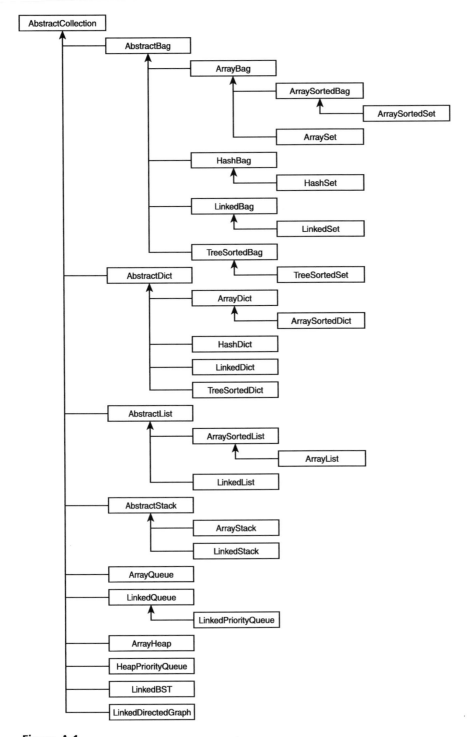

Figure A.1

The collection classes used in this text.

© 2014 Cengage Learning®

INDEX